SPEECH, PLACE, AND ACTION

SPEECH, PLACE, AND ACTION

Studies in Deixis and Related Topics

Edited by
Robert J. Jarvella
and
Wolfgang Klein

JOHN WILEY & SONS LTD
Chichester · New York · Brisbane · Toronto · Singapore

Library of Congress Cataloging in Publication Data:

Speech, place, and action.

  Includes indexes.
  1. Grammar, Comparative and general—Deixis.
2. Gesture. 3. Anaphora (Linguistics) I. Jarvella,
R. J. II. Klein, Wolfgang, 1946–   .
P299.D44S64   415   81–14659

ISBN 0 471 10045 5   AACR2

British Library Cataloguing in Publication Data:

Speech, place, and action
  1. Psycholinguistics
  I. Jarvella, Robert J.
  II. Klein, Wolfgang
  401'.9   BF455

  ISBN 0 471 10045 5

Typeset by Preface Ltd, Salisbury, Wilts.
and printed by Page Bros. (Norwich) Ltd.

the proper study of mankind is man

Alexander Pope, *Essay on Man*

Preface

Language is perhaps our greatest natural achievement, the most unique of those capacities which make us human. It is worth trying to understand. The present book is about how man uses his language, specifically how he uses it to point to people, places, and events in his world and in his speech. Technically speaking, it is largely about those phenomena collectively known in language as 'deixis and anaphora'.

Our reasons for editing this book arise first out of a shared basic interest in how language functions in context, and secondly from a common concern that scientific work on natural language must better recognize its context-dependency. In the field of psychology and language, it is no longer sufficient to treat one's subject matter as an autonomously functioning system or set of forms. Linguistic mechanisms involved in language use are rather co-represented with other information processing systems, which work with and alongside them. The complication this introduces, however, at the same time goes a long way towards aiding our study. Contextual constraints place limits on what can happen when people communicate with language, and we are led by them to look more at what does happen.

The kind of co-operation attempted here has been aimed at producing a coherent set of original papers around the theme of the 'language of context' itself. To the authors who helped complete this task, we owe a special debt of thanks. If this book has any merit as an integrated study, it is largely the result of many people being willing to work in harmony with us. Some authors, we might add, have been more than indulgent in permitting us to mould their presentations to fit the demands of a uniform and readable text.

The development of this book was supported in part by a grant to the Max Planck Gesellschaft from the Stiftung Volkswagenwerk, Hannover, and was further helped into being by a preliminary workshop-conference held on the subject. Fortunately, since it helped give everyone a better idea of what such a volume should contain, most of the contributing authors were able to attend this meeting. Several others working in the field also made needed contributions in that original forum, and therefore we would like to re-extend our thanks on this occasion to Thomas Ballmer, Janellen Huttenlocher, David Leiser, Max Miller and Jürgen Weissenborn, Manny Schegloff, Michael Silverstein, and Bernard Tervoort.

Once the foundation for the book was laid, the writing begun, and the editing proceeding, we were further aided by two people whose technical co-operation we sincerely appreciate: Marlene Arns, who carried through to typescript the many revisions that were made, and sometimes remade, in drafts of the chapters received; and Celia Bird, our editor from John Wiley & Sons, Chichester, who gracefully smoothed out the process leading to final publication.

R.J.J.
W.K.
Nijmegen
March 1981

Contents

Part 3 GESTURE, DEIXIS, AND ANAPHORA

Speech, Place, and Action
Edited by R. J. Jarvella and W. Klein
© 1982 John Wiley & Sons Ltd.

A Brief Introduction

ROBERT J. JARVELLA and WOLFGANG KLEIN

It is not difficult to understand, and quite natural, that language in its ordinary use is dependent on context. There are several senses, however, in which this statement is more or less true. Language being used in particular circumstances, at particular times and places, by particular speakers and listeners to send and receive particular messages of interest, the claim obviously will hold for intentions and their perception, the content of utterances, and the references made in them. The statement also holds, however, and quite literally, for the words that we use to express or refer to such content, above all when they refer *into* the context. For part of every natural language seems to be devoted primarily to the expression of information which a speaker can safely assume is accessible to his or her addressee from the context of speaking. The present book is a series of explorations into this 'language of context', and its actual uses.

Consider just one example. The same sentence may be used by many different speakers of a language, each with a different sense, but still be understood by their respective listeners, to bear just the meaning that was intended. This is not even unusual. To understand properly an utterance of the English sentence 'I told you that yesterday, while she was here', one needs, among other things, to be able to identify who the speaker and the intended hearer were, what were the time and place of utterance, who else was being talked about in it, and part of what was already said. Information of these kinds is, in fact, typically not stated in an utterance itself, but provided only in a form which can be used in co-ordination with knowledge of the linguistic and non-linguistic surround.

The central issue is thus not whether meaning is left to context, but how it is, and how it is re-integrated from what is said and what is only signalled. By what linguistic means can a speaker refer to information his addressee should know, how does he use these means, and how does his message's intended recipient use them? The example sentence which we have given above helps provide some idea of the types of linguistic expression which can be, and conventionally are, used to support the communication process in this general way. Among these are a number which serve to relate what is said in an

1

utterance to its social, spatial, and temporal context of occurrence. The most basic linguistic devices having this character, and probably the most widespread, are those of *deixis*. These will be of central interest, especially in the beginning and middle of the book. Our example sentence, however, also displays an obvious dependence on speaker and listener sharing some reference frame for (and representation of) linguistic context. To a large extent, issues of *anaphora*, or the intratextual uses of such devices, will also arise and be treated.

The importance in language of deixis, and its origin within the speaking situation, was recognized and put forward by Karl Bühler in his classic work *Sprachtheorie* (1934). Led by the insight that the meaning of deictical expressions depends crucially on when, where, and by whom they are used, Bühler systematically formulated the generalization of utterances being rooted in this threefold way in their context of use, and placed the convergence of the 'I', the 'here', and the 'now' at its centre. Corresponding to the more fully defined socio-spatio-temporal axes of the ordinary speech situation, three kinds of such expressions can be distinguished: (a) personal deixis, such as (in English) 'I' and 'you'; (b) spatial deixis, such as 'here' and 'there'; and (c) temporal deixis, such as 'now', 'today', and tense markings. As English and other familiar languages attest, however, there are many transferred uses.

The present book is a collection of modern viewpoints on deixis and related topics taken by a group of prominent linguists and psychologists at the turn of the decade, nearly 50 years after the first publication of Bühler's *Sprachtheorie*. It is intended to represent a wide variety of contemporary thought on the subject, and includes papers in the areas of time, person, and space. Issues of spatial representation and description are given greatest attention, however, since we feel that this domain, having been somewhat neglected in the past, is in greater need of development.

All but one of the papers printed here—an English translation of Bühler's major ideas on deixis—were written specially for this volume, and are published here for the first time. The book is divided into three sections. To help further orient the reader, we will comment briefly on these in turn

Part 1 is headed by the Bühler translation and is primarily theoretical in nature. There are five additional chapters. In the first of these, Charles Fillmore sketches the outlines of a theory of semantic prototypes, and within this framework explores the system of spatial deixis in various languages. Then, George Miller delves into the principal issues of demonstrative reference which should be of natural concern to cognitive psychologists. These include topics in the selection, representation, recall, acquisition, and innovative use of demonstratives. In the next chapter, Arnim von Stechow presents some informal considerations on and a formal analysis of local deictic expressions in German, especially the adverbs *hier*, *da*, and *dort*. This paper is written largely in the framework of a Montague-type grammar and possible worlds semantics. In the final two chapters in Part 1, emphasis then shifts to issues of modality, mood, tense, and aspect. First, John Lyons addresses the question of subjectivity in language, concentrating on the quite subtle means a speaker may employ to convey his subjective view on events or states of affairs on which he may report. And finally, Mark Steedman describes how a language understander in whose memory various partly simultaneous experiences have been recorded might go about answering questions about how they were temporally integrated.

In Part 2, the papers brought together are concerned largely with the dynamics of spoken discourse about space. It is perhaps worth remarking that Karl Bühler himself, in his reflections on deixis and the imagination, found it meaningful to consider man's orientation in space in some detail. Rather than adopting a classically held view of a static head/body position as being basic, however, the cases Bühler chose to analyse all involved changes or transpositions through space, as experienced (or imagined) by a human observer. Besides being of theoretical interest, the problems he seized on were also practical ones. Thus, for example, he wonders how a traveller who begins a walk at a city's train station and wanders into its commercial centre would maintain his bearings, and how he would retrace or describe the path along which he had come. On several other occasions, Bühler considers how one speaker can take over another's orientation, and direct his movements, even though the two are facing in opposite directions. And in a third case, Bühler reflects on how changes in the location of a piece of furniture in a room might be imagined.

Bühler's remarks on these matters are, except in the last instance, quite brief and merely intended to be illustrative. But adventitiously, and rather strikingly, they come close to presaging the situations and kinds of spatial language issues taken up in the empirical studies of spatial description reported on here. The first three chapters in Part 2 all take up route directions which speakers gave when asked how to reach certain destinations in city environments. Wolfgang Klein begins this series with a paper in which he first analyses the problems basic to using local deixis in general, and then goes on to describe the case of route directions in particular. In the following paper, Dieter Wunderlich and Rudolf Reinelt take a largely complementary approach. They present an interactive model of route direction encounters, and within the most purely descriptive phase of such exchanges, an outline of the verbal expressions used to describe the initial, intermediate, and final stages of the route to be followed. The final study investigating this particular genre of language use presents a comparative analysis of route descriptions provided by blind and sighted informants. In this chapter, Michael Brambring is concerned with how spatial mobility is restricted in blindness, and offers some pertinent suggestions, based on the roles visual and non-visual perception seem to play in the construction of discourse about large spaces, for helping the blind increase their radius of locomotion.

The final pair of chapters in Part 2 are concerned with description in situations which less matter of factly influence the spatial perspective a speaker will adopt and the order in which he chooses to mention events. The first, by Veronika Ullmer-Ehrich, is a text-linguistic analysis of single room descriptions, based on data gathered from German university students about their one-room apartments. The second, by Willem Levelt, is primarily a psychological inquiry into orientation and order of mention used by speakers in describing visual patterns. In their separate ways, these two authors identify some of the options which speakers have in mapping a multi-dimensional cognitive representation onto a linguistic sequence, and show how they are used in practice.

The words *deixis* and *deictic*, in their simple, non-specialized use, mean to show or point out directly. Perhaps partly for this reason, in *Sprachtheorie* Karl Bühler himself began his discussion of deixis and the deictic field of language by drawing an explicit analogy between gestural and linguistic means for showing direction or place. The present book is also partly devoted to exploring such relationships. Part 3 in particular takes up some of the referential and formal correspondences between gesture (including linguistic signing), deixis and anaphora.

This third and final section of the book consists of four chapters. The first, by David McNeill and Elena Levy, is mainly concerned with gesture which accompanies speech in general, rather than deixis *per se*. Three principal kinds of gesture, called *iconix*, *beats*, and *metaphorix* are distinguished, and it is argued from videotape analyses that these, together with the generation of speech, form a single, co-ordinated system for expressing speaker meaning. In the paper which follows, Ursula Bellugi and Edward Klima then describe deixis and anaphora in American Sign Language, a fully visual-manual linguistic system. Both the derived use of conventional, non-linguistic pointing, and the amount of abstraction reached in indexing the speech situation and linguistic context in ASL, will be of obvious interest here.

In the last two papers of the book, the main focus of attention shifts to the manner in which reference to persons is initially made, and then subsequently maintained, in extended narrative discourse. The question of whether deixis and anaphora may really be the same is posed in a paper by Konrad Ehlich. After considering various pieces of evidence from partly orally transferred texts, this author concludes that both the communicative functions and instrumental means of the two must be considered to be distinct. Finally, William Marslen-Wilson, Elena Levy, and Lorraine Tyler mount an ambitious attempt to account for the system of third-person reference in English. Working on the basis of a fine-grained analysis of a single videotaped narration, and aided by relevant theorizing about the listening process, Marslen-Wilson, Levy, and

Tyler reach the conclusion that the establishment of linkages between a current utterance and a hearer's representation of what has already been said is the function most basic to the use of referential devices.

REFERENCE

Bühler, K. *Sprachtheorie: Die Darstellungsfunktion der Sprache*. Jena: Fischer, 1934. Reprinted by Gustav Fischer Verlag, Stuttgart, 1965.

Part 1

BASIC CONSIDERATIONS

Speech, Place, and Action
Edited by R. J. Jarvella and W. Klein
© 1982 John Wiley & Sons Ltd.

The Deictic Field of Language and Deictic Words

KARL BÜHLER

[Editors' note: Karl Bühler was born in 1879 in Meckesheim near Heidelberg. From 1922 to 1938, he held a chair in psychology at the University of Vienna. Bühler emigrated to the United States in 1938. He died in Los Angeles in 1963.

Although he is not one of its most typical representatives, Bühler's views are close to those of Würzburg Gestalt psychology. His published work covers a wide range, including the psychology of language. Within the German tradition of language psychology in this century, Bühler is, along with Wilhelm Wundt, the most outstanding figure. His work is closely connected to the development of structural linguistics, especially to the Prague school. His theory of language functions deeply influenced Jakobson, and his 'principle of abstractive relevance' is one of the early formulations of the difference between phonemic and merely phonetic features of speech sounds.

Bühler's linguistic research culminated in his major work *Sprachtheorie: Die Darstellungsfunktion der Sprache*, first published in 1934. This book, whose title is translatable as 'Language Theory: The Representational Function of Language', has since been reprinted in German (Stuttgart: Fischer, 1965), but remains largely inaccessible, though known, to the English-speaking world. It consists of four major sections. In Part 1, 'Die Prinzipien der Sprachforschung' (the principles of linguistic research), Bühler presents and discusses various basic features of language and concepts which are relevant to its investigation. Among these is the distinction between expressions which are linked immediately to the speech act (Sprechakt) itself (deictic words and the deictic field of language), and expressions which are less context dependent, and more abstractly reflect symbolic representation of objects, properties, and events (the symbolic field of language and naming words). The second and third parts of the book are devoted to these two types of expressions respectively. Part 4, 'Aufbau der menschlichen Rede: Elemente und Kompositionen' (the structure of human speech: elements and composition) deals with selected aspects of phonology and syntax.

9

Bühler's *Sprachtheorie* abounds with fascinating observations and original insights. Its empirical content, however, is primarily illustrative in nature, and leads to some vagueness and oversimplification in the statement of generalizations. The style of writing is also unusual for scientific work, enthusiastic and elegant in some passages but stilted in others. These facts, together with the general decline of German psychology in the 1930s, may explain the relatively weak resonance of the work, in both disciplines to which Bühler wanted to address it.

In the present chapter, we present an abridged English version of Part 2 of *Sprachtheorie*, 'Das Zeigfeld der Sprache und die Zeigwörter', especially Chapters 7 and 8. In these sections, Bühler presents his main thesis: that deictic expressions refer to a deictic field of language whose zero point—the *Origo*—is fixed by the person who is speaking (the 'I'), the place of utterance (the 'here'), and the time of utterance (the 'now'). He then tries to explain other deictic phenomena as derivative, and deals to some extent both with anaphora and what he calls *Deixis am Phantasma* (deixis at phantasma or in the imagination). It is our belief that, despite occasional unclarities and the fact that some of Bühler's ideas have since become almost commonplace, these passages form a stimulating text and make rewarding reading, as well as being of historical interest. In our editing, we have omitted some material which we considered tangential to our (and to Bühler's) purpose. Generally, we provide short summaries of what has not been translated in these cases in brackets.

Because of Bühler's peculiarities of style, the translation printed here proved to be anything but easy to extract from the German. However, our major strategy has been to try to keep as close to the original text as possible, even to the point of capturing the nuances and plays on words within it. There were some instances, on the other hand, where rendering a maximally accurate translation would have led to very strange and perhaps even un-intelligible English; in these cases, we have retreated somewhat and sacrificed this principle for the sake of a more understandable result. Given the intricacy of this enterprise, we have few illusions about its complete success, and any suggestions on how to improve the English text would be welcome.

Two final comments may be helpful to the reader. Freyer and Klages, who are mentioned right at the beginning, are now almost forgotten, but at the time of writing were well known German philosophers. Brugmann, Delbrück, Wackernagel, and Wegener were major figures in Indoeuropean linguistics from the late nineteenth century. The remaining persons mentioned in the text were experimental psychologists. Second, on several occasions Bühler briefly alludes to his treatment of anaphora elsewhere. The passages indicated in these references are mainly from Part 4 of *Sprachtheorie*, and are not included in the present translation.]

The arm and finger gesture in man, to which our pointing finger owes its name, has its further replica in the extended 'arm' of the signpost, and is alongside the image of the arrow a widespread sign for pathway or direction. Modern thinkers such as Freyer or Klages have accorded this gesture the recognition it deserves, and characterized it as being specifically human. To be sure, there is more than one way to indicate by gesture, but let us stick to the case of the signpost. At crossroads, or in foreign terrain, an 'arm' or 'arrow' visible at a considerable distance is sometimes erected, an arm or arrow which normally bears a place name. It will do the traveller good service, if all goes well, for which it is first necessary that the signpost stand correctly in its *deictic field*. Let us take just this trivial insight and raise the question whether there are also, among spoken signs, some which function as way-indicators. The answer resounds 'yes'. Deictic words like *here* or *there* function in a very similar way.

Now, the concrete speech event differs from the wooden arm standing motionless in the countryside in one important respect, namely that it is an event. But still further, it is a complex human action. And in this action, the sender has not only, like the signpost, a fixed position in the terrain, but also plays a *role*: the role of the sender as opposed to the role of the receiver. For it is not only for a wedding that two are needed, but in every social happening, and the concrete speech event must be described first on the full model of verbal exchange. When a speaker 'wants to refer' to the sender of the talk just then occurring, he will say 'I', and when he wants to refer to the receiver he will say 'you'. 'I' and 'you' are deictic words as well, and primarily nothing else. This thesis sounds somewhat less surprising if we take the usual name which these words carry—'personal pronoun'—and translate back to the Latin *persona* or Greek *prosopon*, 'face, mask or role'. It is primarily nothing but being in the role of the sender at some point in a signal exchange which characterizes the current *I*, nor anything but being in the role of the receiver which characterizes the *you*. The first Greek grammarians saw this very clearly and placed the personal pronouns among the deictic signs in language.

The oldest documents in the history of Indoeuropean languages no less than the facts themselves demand that, under the name of 'deictic language sign', we first think of such words, words which resist classification under the inflectional (e.g. declinable) naming words and which were therefore more deprecated than labelled with the term 'deictic particles' by language scholars. What one cannot decline, one takes to be a particle. Sematological analysis is in no way blind to the function of these ultimately still declinable items, standing in the symbolic field of language *pro nominibus*, and thus achieving the rank of pronouns. The language theoretician's proposal for a *distinctio rationis*, and for first taking into account the deictical aspect which these words exhibit even when declined, is unquestionably justified. This by the fact that all phenomena of verbal deixis belong together, because they receive their fullness and precision of meaning not in the symbolic field of language, but in the deictic field, from case to case, *and can do so there alone*. What 'here' and 'there' is varies with the speaker's position precisely as the 'I' and 'you' switches back and forth between speech partners with the exchange of roles as sender and receiver. The concept of 'deictic field' enables us to take this both familiar and strange matter of fact as a point of departure in our considerations.

That there is only one deictic field in language, and that the filling out of the meaning of deictic words is tied to, and remains dependent upon, perceptible deictic aids and their equivalents, is the fundamental assertion to be laid out and substantiated here. There are distinct modes of pointing. I can demonstrate *ad oculos* and, in less situationally bound discourse, use the same deictic words *anaphorically*. There is still a third mode, which we shall characterize as *deixis at phantasma*. In these phenomena the index finger as the natural tool of *demonstratio ad oculos* is replaced by other deictic aids. It is already replaced in the case of discourse about currently present objects. But the help which it or its equivalent provides never disappears entirely or is completely lacking, not even in anaphora, the strangest and most language-specific way of pointing. This insight is the central point around which our theory of the deictic field in language will revolve.

Everything original I can offer in these matters should be seen as a further accomplishment beyond what Wegener and Brugmann began. Even before them, and dealing with the most diverse phenomena, modern linguists came across the fact that an adequate analysis of the concrete speech event jointly requires a far-reaching grasp of given situational features. But only Wegener and Brugmann appropriately described the function of deictic words under the most perceptive viewpoint of their being *signals*. These scholars did not dispose of this term, but of the right designative perspective. But it is the case for their novel description what is also true of everything to which some conceptual order is applied, namely that the value of an approach can be known only by testing its limits. Just as the deictic words demand that they be characterized as signals, naming words require a designation which would be inadequate for signals; the conventional one. The naming words function as *symbols*, and receive their specific complete and precise meaning within the synsemantic field; I suggest the term *'symbolic field'* for this other kind of structure, which should not be confused with situational features. Thus, from a purely formal viewpoint, the theory advanced in this book is a two-fields theory.

[In the following paragraphs, Bühler extensively discusses Brugmann's theory of the Indoeuropean deictic system. Brugmann distinguishes a number of types of deixis in Indoeuropean languages:

(1) 'Dér-deixis' or '*to-deixis', which led to, among other things, English 'the' and 'that'.

(2) 'Ich-deixis', which corresponds to 'I', 'here', and other close-to-the-speaker terms (Wackernagel replaced this by 'hic-deixis').

(3) 'Du-deixis', corresponding to 'you', 'these', and other close-to-the-listener terms (Wackernagel's 'istic-deixis').

(4) 'Jener-deixis', which is maintained in English by 'yon', 'yonder', etc. (Wackernagel's 'ille-deixis').

Bühler basically follows Brugmann, relating his conceptions to the idea of 'Zeigfeld'. The deictic word 'here' gets its full meaning as a position signal from the 'origin quality' of voice sound, and 'I' gets its full meaning as an 'individual signal' from the personal characteristics of the voice sound. He then turns to a more systematic account in Chapter 7.]

§7 THE ORIGO OF THE DEICTIC FIELD AND ITS MARKING

Two intersecting perpendicular strokes on the page can serve as a coordinate system for us with O as the origo, the point of origin for the coordinates:

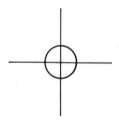

I maintain that three deictic words must be put at the place of O, if this scheme is to represent the deictic field of human language, namely the deictic words *here*, *now*, and *I*. These lexical items, so simple in their sound structure, might induce the language theorist into esoteric philosophical abysses or to respectful silence, when challenged to determine their function. Rather, he should simply acknowledge that it is certainly very peculiar, but nevertheless precisely statable, how they function in a concrete utterance. When I, as the official starter of a race, give the signal to begin, I first prepare the competitors by saying 'get ready', or 'on your marks', and then say 'go' or 'now'. The signal giving the time on the radio is, after an appropriate verbal introduction, a short stroke of a bell. The small word *now* in place of the command *go* or of the stroke of the bell functions like any other *moment marker*; it is *the* verbal *moment marker*. Normally, words do not speak to us in this way, in fact quite the opposite: they turn us away from the sound material out of which they are built, and from the accidental features of their occurrence; their occurrence is neither used as a time marker nor as a place marker in verbal exchange. Let us stay for a moment with the opposition of form and substance which has made itself apparent here. In the sound form, in the phonetic pattern of the words *now*, *here*, *I*, there is nothing conspicuous; it is only peculiar that they ask, each in turn: look at me as a sound phenomenon, take me as a moment marker, as a place marker, as a sender marker (sender characteristic).

And this the naive speech partner has learned, and does take them in this way. Without difficulty—what is there special about it, anyway? Only the logician is baffled, because such a manner of use disrupts his manner of theorizing, or appears to. It is an occupational hazard that this or that in the world can cross him up. But it is hoped that we can ease his deliberations via our coordinate concept; because the 'setting up' of a coordinate system always has a specific function, as the logician knows. In our case, it is just the coordinate system of 'subjective orientation', to which all parties in verbal exchange are and remain attached. Everybody behaves in a well oriented way in his own, and understands others' behaviour. If I stand as a leader facing an aligned formation of gymnasts, I would conventionally choose commands such as 'forward, backward, to the left, to the right' not in my own system of orientation, but in theirs, and the translation is psychologically so straightforward that every group leader learns to master it. That it works well, and that it can be done without mental gymnastics is a fact, and one which no logic can change; if it knows what it's about it will not even try. Let us first take what good logicians have said about the deictic words, and then turn to the linguistic findings.

(1) How remarkable it is that what the logic of the ancient grammarians and modern formal logic say about the deictic words fits, in crucial respects, so neatly together. The former stated that deictic words, *unlike* naming words, provide no 'what-determination' ($\pi o\iota \acute{o} \tau \eta s$), and the latter denies that as conceptual signs they are as simple to define objectively as other words. This is quite right, and the two claims belong intimately together. To be suitable for intersubjective exchange, a 'conceptual sign' must have the property of being used by anyone and everyone as a symbol for the *same* object, and that is (neglecting proper names for the moment) only the case if the word meets a what-determination of the object; that is, if it is applied to the object, used for it, such that it has this and that fundamental property which across its circumstances of use is upheld. This holds for no deictic word, and cannot hold. For anyone can say *I*, and anyone who does say it refers to a different object than any other; we need as many proper names as there are speakers,

if the many intersubjective values of that one word *I* are to be transferred, by the mode of naming, into unambiguous linguistic symbols, as the logician demands. And, in principle, this holds for all other deictic words as well.

Where this seems not to be the case, as with the word *here*, with which the Viennese refer to Vienna and Berliners to Berlin, that is due to a quite transparent and logically unsatisfactory laxity or indeterminateness in the extended meaning of this positional deictic word. Strictly speaking, *here* indicates the instantaneous position of the speaker, and this position may change with every speaker and every act of speaking (*Sprechakt*). And similarly, it is strictly a matter of chance if *you*, when used on two occasions, refers twice to the bearer of the same proper name or not; the rules for using *you*, in any case, make no such guarantee. And it is precisely this that the one-to-one correspondence between language symbols and objects demanded by the logician comes to. Where it exists, we have naming words; where it doesn't, we don't. This is indeed a clear separation, and an unappealable logical distinction concerning the question of whether *I* and *you* and all other deictic words should be counted as language symbols in the logician's sense or not. Formal logic is correct in initially excluding deictic words from the list of conceptual signs (and thus from the list of language 'symbols') usable in intersubjective exchange.

[In the following paragraphs, Bühler discusses the mode-evaluation of deictic words by some logicians; he stresses the functional flexibility of these words and the difference between symbols and signals; that both are important in language. He then turns again to the coordinate system.]

(2) It is from the origo of the perceptible 'Here' that all other positions are verbally identified, as from the origo 'Now' that all others time points are. What we are saying for the moment refers only to *pointing*; obviously, positions, like everything else in the world, can also be indicated by conceptual signs. An utterance like 'the church beside the parsonage' establishes the position of one thing relative to another, and for this uses a good clear conceptual word, the preposition 'beside'. The Indoeuropean prepositions as such are not deictic words, but are often coupled with deictic words. So exist compounds of the kind 'thereafter, hereby', and unbound groups like 'from there on, up to now'. In these constructions, deixis at phantasma is often involved or they function pointing by anaphora. It is better to postpone their treatment until, after a psychological analysis of the deictic modes, we can give a sufficiently general answer to the question of in what form pointing and naming are realized at the same time, be it in a simple word or a compound.

After this important exclusion, let us think of the basic deictic words *here*, *now*, *I* in their, so to speak, absolute function as verbal markers of place, time, and individual. Experts in Indoeuropean languages teach us that the person suffixes on verbs and isolated pronouns like *I* and *you* are generally differentiated from deictic words of position or location. But there are sufficient facts, both regarding form and meaning, where common origin and repeated cross-breeding of the two classes come to the fore. Still more obvious as such a coming and going is the appearance of the characteristic 'third' person in Indoeuropean; I quote from the standard work, Brugmann and Delbrück's comparative grammar:

> 'Between these two groups there are clear interconnections and cross-overs. First, the third person pronouns are not clearly separable from the demonstratives, and *conceptually often coincide with them* [italics Bühler's]. They are, one could say, demonstrative pronouns with substantive function, which refer to what is being talked about, what has been said or will immediately be said in discourse (hence deictic words in anaphoric use). For example, French *il* from Latin *ille*, or Gothic *is* (Modern German *er*) is identical to Latin *is*. But the "I" and "you" pronouns also seem at least partially to have once been demonstratives, since, for example, Greek ἐμοῦ, etc., and Old Indian *áma-h*, "this one here", or Old Indian *te*, Greek τοι, Latin *tibi* and Old Indian *tá-m*, Greek τόν (reference to something spoken about which does not belong to the sphere of "I", but which happens to be close to the speaker) probably belong together' (second edition, vol. 2, part 2, p. 306).

[Bühler then discusses two other cases of close relationship between 'here' and 'I', namely the Armenian suffix *-s*, as in *tér-s* 'the lord here' or 'I, the lord', and a possible common source of Latin *ego* and *hic* in proto-Indoeuropean *ĝho, mentioned by Brugmann; he then continues.]

The point I want to make here does not hinge on whether this hypothesis cast into an example is correct or not. Comparative linguistics in any event demonstrates a kinship between the Indoeuropean words which serve to define Brugmann's 'here-deixis' and the first person pronouns.

Whereupon the psychologist seizes the word to say that this is so very sensible phenomenologically that one could nearly have foretold it. For two moments of relevance are to be found in the use of any signal of acoustical exchange, namely first its (spatial) nature of origin, and second its acoustical overall character. And the sound signs of language belong psychologically after all to those of acoustical exchange. For a sensitive signal receiver, there is nothing more natural than to turn towards the sound source. In the case of verbal exchange signs, this is the speaker and is located at the speaker. Both 'here' and 'I' require this reaction, or at least come close to it. To this extent their function as deictic words is the same. But, then, the intention (or interest) which they stipulate is partitioned, in the first case focusing upon the position and situation in the environment of the speaker, and, in the second case, upon the speaker himself with a physiognomic or pathognomic eye. At this divide, a 'Here' includes a call to take up the first direction of interest, and an 'I' the second. This is the least assumption laden and most general analysis which one can offer. It is, by the way, a maximally 'objective' analysis, which still neglects the speaker's subjective experience.

Hence, nothing is more natural than the fact that there are periods in the development of language, where the separation at this divide did not yet occur. Perhaps those expert in the matter know of entire language families where this is the case. In any case, we have in the domain of Indoeuropean the evidence of Armenian *ēr-s* and the putative proto-Indoeuropean *ǧho. I know of a German child who was at a stage where it was trying to understand and to learn the correct use of 'I' and in a particular situation, having once again confused *ich* with *hier* and been laughingly corrected by the adult speech partner, angrily rejected this fancy of the adults. If one can analogously apply the developmental rule of progress going from less differentiated to richer inventories of form, the historical finding of an Indoeuropean main stem *ko – *ki – (*kio), from which according to the authorities most deictic words of here-deixis (and doubtlessly of I-deixis, too) come, can be interpreted as parallel to the observation in that child. The *ko-stem 'appears in all language branches except the Aryan', states Brugmann.

(3) If the constantly evoked mutual assistance of psychology and linguistics is to bear fruit, specialists on both sides must dare to intervene in the others' conception. We are all subject to the law restricting human capacities. Here, one psychologist has set forth how he thinks certain linguistic facts should be interpreted. If this or that has been taken over by him from linguistics in a distorted or incomplete way, then a professional correction from that side will be necessary to advance the discussion. It would be best if that answer spoke the other way around, directly to the psychologist's conception, as was the case with the example of Brugmann. Brugmann's phenomenological analysis of the human speech situation in general, and of the factors in it which take up individual language signs or full complexes of language signs and determine their full meaning is excellent. Nothing is lacking in it but the final consequence to be drawn for linguistic theory. I quote:

> 'They (the positional words) are not only, like any other element of discourse, a general request to the addressee to turn his attention to the concept in question, but *simultaneously* (italics mine) acoustical handsigns, audible beckoning, they always contain (as Wegener, *Grundfragen des Sprachlebens*, p. 100, states it) a *look here* or a *here there is something going on*' ('Die Demonstrativpronomina der indogermanischen Sprachen', 1904).

What is striking and deserving of further thought in this characterization is above all the word 'simultaneously', which I myself emphasized, and let me add that Brugmann gives exactly the same characterization with this strange 'simultaneously' for the personal pronouns, for the role-deictic words. We claim that, in their original form, both are nothing but deictic words; this is enough to begin with. They are not just naming words incidentally. That they cannot be incidentally and on the side. A few sentences earlier in Brugmann's text he writes: 'They have in common with the other pronouns that they do not denote an object according to its specific quality'. This is the old feature, that they are lacking the determination of Poiotes. Take this seriously and everything will be all right. Brugmann says further:

'The question of whether from the beginning the demonstratives were always and by necessity tied to pointing gestures when referring to what was currently perceivable cannot be decided by means of historical research' (p. 7).

It cannot be decided by means of psychological research either, if by 'gesture' is meant only finger gesture. But if one takes it to mean more than that, as is required by the facts, then psychologically even more can be decided than this point at issue, of how things originally may have been. It can be shown namely how they still are today and could never have been and can never be any different. Instead of the finger gesture, other optical or acoustical cues can be used, and instead of all of them together, situational indices or conventional aids of interpretation can enter in. But of what has been listed here, nothing can be omitted.

Not simply because of that, but because any deictic word without such guidelines is running blind to its meaning. It would only give us a sphere, an environment which is not sufficient to find what is referred to there. Think of that use of deictic words from which an initial refutation of our thesis can be expected, namely their anaphoric use. Where should such a perceptible guideline be, when I refer in German with *this* and *that* to something mentioned in the just preceding discourse? Answer: Well, admittedly a sensible guideline does not exist in this case. But in its place a convention takes effect that the listener look back and take up in his mind what has last been mentioned in the case of *this*, as nearby and what has first been mentioned as more distant in the case of *that*. This convention could as easily be reversed. Then, one would run in natural order through what was already present in a discourse, and *this* would refer to what came first and *that* to what came last. A priori, it does not seem unlikely that here and there in language communities this reversed convention is the normal case.

In any case, it becomes clear what the substitutes for sensible guidelines of deixis can be. Where phonemic hints such as grammatical agreement and the like are lacking, it is an *ordering schema* within the domain of the deictic field. This notion has to be explicated in detail later. When I say to a stranger on the street: 'Go straight ahead, the second cross-road on the left is what you are looking for', I am operating in principle exactly as by the use of such an ordering schema in place of a sensible guideline in verbal deixis. For I am using the road before us as an ordering schema, and within that, accidentally or deliberately, the spatial orientation of the questioner; it is within this coordinate system that I talk to him. The words 'straight ahead' and 'right' in my discourse are unambiguous only by virtue of the fact that the stranger's nose already points in the direction in which he needs to go.

(4) Then to *I* and *you*. It is a sound and fruitful principle of lexicology to look for original meaning in sense perception. Anyone can address me and say *I*. I shall glance at him or, where this is impossible, only listen to the speaker. That this should occur with physiognomic or pathognomic eye, this and nothing else is the first beginning of the meaning of *I*, its archifunction. Briefly speaking, the words *I* and *you* refer to the role holders in the on-going speech drama, in the speech action. In *prosopon*, the Greeks had an excellent name for it, and the Romans meant nothing by *persona* but the role in the speech act. It is this antique meaning of the name *persona* that language theory has to recapture with the fullest clarity and consequence. Brugmann and Delbrück are not to be blamed in this respect, but we should be conse-quent. The main and original function of personal pronouns like *I* and *you* is not to *denote* sender and receiver, just as names *denote*, but only to refer to these role holders in the sense already correctly pointed out by Apollonius.

Certainly, more is evoked if it is an acquaintance who says *I* to me, and someone standing at the door who answers my question 'Who's there?' by saying '*I*' is relying on my ability to identify him from among the host of my friends by the sound of his voice. Phonologically determined and sufficiently distinct from all other words of the German language, the created form '*ich*' sounds similar out of millions of mouths. It is individuated only by the voice matter, by the sound image, and this is the function of the answer of my caller beyond the door, that the phonemic shape, the verbal fabric of his '*ich*' may draw my, the questioner's attention to his voice character. Admittedly, this is a very peculiar relation; the form of something serves the function of drawing attention to the specificity of the matter in which the form is realized. This relation, however, is not quite as idiosyncratic as one might think. But for brevity's sake, we shall not discuss illustrative parallels here.

[In the following two paragraphs, Bühler rephrases this characterization of *I* and opposes it to the function of proper names.]

Suffice it to illustrate conceptually the primary meaning function of *I* by a single example. In the case of *you*, the situation is similar. Except that right from the beginning we have to bring those cases of *you* into our theoretical account where it has almost purely an appeal function: *du* (*paß mal auf*), *ich will dir was sagen* ('You (listen), I want to tell you something'). This is a preliminary to communicating with someone nearby which starts with an appeal word and then distributes the roles of the speech act announced. It is easy enough to select an expressive or request register, too, with the tone of such an appeal *du*, as may be done in principle with the tonal and other modifications of any word. This belongs to a different chapter of language theory and need not concern us here. The sort of pure deictic function of *du* shows up in those turns of a conversation, where the sender feels tempted to disambiguate the word with a finger gesture or other perceivable aids. A *du da, du dort* ('you there'), and the like differ from *dér da, dér dort* ('that one over there') in these cases only by the *prosopon* in the Greek grammarians' sense. That there is a third *prosopon* at all and that it is diacritically marked for grammatical gender both in pure personal deictics such as *er, sie, es*—i.e. those personal deictic words not showing position—and in positional signs like *dér, díe, dás* ('this one'), this is a matter of Indo-european languages and goes beyond the topic of deictics proper, as we have delimited it here. *I* and *you* could be treated equally so, and the third proposon be missing altogether. Then, the positional deictics of Brugmann's dér-deixis would—both in the *demonstratio ad oculos* and the anaphoric use—be purely 'impersonal' deictics, as they perhaps once were in the Indo-european languages, when they still had the character of indeclinable 'particles'.

[In the following subsection, Bühler discusses and criticizes Brugmann–Delbrück's and Steinthal's theories of the origin of deictics and demonstratives.]

§8 DEIXIS AT PHANTASMA AND THE ANAPHORIC USE OF DEICTIC WORDS

With *dieser* ('this') and *jener* ('that') (or *hier* ('here') and *dort* ('there') and the like) we refer back to things just treated in discourse; with *dér* (*derjenige*) ('this') and other deictics, we refer forward to things immediately to be treated. This is traditionally called anaphora. To explore its full domain, it is indispensable that one look for the deictic moment in those words, too, where it is intimately bound up with more specific grammatical functions. Thus, not only the relative pronouns in the narrower sense of the word, but also the Indo-european conjunctions involve a deictic moment, and, to be sure, a pointing to something which is not to be sought for and encountered at places in the space of perception but at places in the whole of discourse. As an illustration, I point to German *da* ('there') in its various functions, which it fulfils in isolation or together with other particles. In the perceptual field, it is a positional deictic; it becomes anaphoric in *darum* = *deshalb* ('therefore') and (both in its real-time use and its anaphoric use) in *danach* ('thereafter'); and, finally, it again shows up in isolation as a conjunction in causal clauses (= because), without having lost in any way (backwards or forwards) its anaphoric moment.

This far, I think, one's notion of what is anaphoric has in the first instance to extend, if we don't want to let what historically belongs together be pulled asunder, and to do justice to the whole matter of deixis. Simple enough: there is also some pointing to places in the organization of discourse, and for this kind of pointing, the Indoeuropean languages use largely the same words as for *demonstratio ad oculos*. Simple (as we called it) at least, if no more, is the description of the facts: on the one hand, an ordering in space with places in it; on the other, an ordering in the flow of discourse with places in it, or discourse parts, to which reference is made to find what was meant; and the reference is performed by and large by the same apparatus of deictic words.

From a psychological viewpoint, any anaphoric use of deictic words presupposes that both sender and receiver *have access to the flow of discourse as a whole*, where parts may be re-taken up and anticipated.[1] This whole must be accessible to sender and receiver, so that a wandering is possible, comparable to the passing of one's gaze over an optically present object. None of this surprises the psychologist, for he knows that not only the flow of discourse, but also other acoustical chains formed require and admit such a wandering, repeated taking up, and building in advance. The adequate production and reception of any piece of music, for example, requires not exactly this, but something similar. Assuming then that operations of this kind are known in the domain of so-called immediate memory or, to be more accurate, of immediate retention, the philological base of anaphoric pointing is indicated; about it nothing specific has to be explored.

[Bühler then points out that the comparison made with music is partly misleading and that he will take it up later.]

Faced with some ability in the domain of so-called *immediate* retention, the psychologist will look for similar abilities in the domain of no longer immediate, but *mediate* retention, that is in the domain of grown-up *memories* and of the constructive *imagination*. His expectation to encounter deictic words there as well will not be disappointed, but confirmed to an extent not even suspected. And what is confirmed, too, is our premonition, taken from Brugmann's sketchy remarks, that a dramatic moment inherent to verbal representation shows up here in a particularly clear and scientifically well capturable way. Let us call this third mode of pointing deixis at phantasma. Thus, we distinguish *demonstratio ad oculos*, anaphora, and deixis at phantasma.

It is sensible to begin the psychological analysis by opposing the first and third mode, keeping anaphora apart. As we shall see, it differs from the two other modes of pointing in several crucial respects, and it would be incomprehensible without a second symbolic field in language, apart from deixis, that is, a syntax. To put it differently, to an eminent degree, anaphora seems to receive its vocation just for linking pointing with representing proper. It seems more reasonable to treat it systematically only after the theory of the symbolic field (that is, in Part 4). It will become clear there that the growing context of a discourse itself is raised to the status of a deictic field when we point anaphorically; a highly peculiar phenomenon, and one also unusually characteristic of verbal representation. The two fields, the (objective) deictic field and symbolic field of language, are (if you prefer) linked together by a third one, namely by the contextual deictic field. Logically, however, it seems to me more correct to characterize this third one not as a *new* field but as a subspecies of the one and only deictic field; since what is rare and peculiar is only the moment of reflection by which it is obtained. The developing discourse, so to speak, turns to itself, either backwards or forwards, in the phenomenon of anaphora; but apart from that (and neglecting some specific reflexive words), the same deictic words are used here as there.

(1) To answer the psychological questions about deixis at phantasma clearly, we need to go back a little farther. If someone wants to show something to someone else, then both of them, the one who is doing the leading and the one who is being led, must have a sufficient degree of harmonious orientation; orientation within an order schema in which the reference object has its place. Roughly speaking, a city guide must be oriented in the city, and a museum guide in the museum where he wants to indicate this or that. And the one who is being guided, or listener? It can be proven that also in the case of verbal demonstrations, and especially for those of the second and third mode, he too has to bring with him a good deal of activity of his own and a certain degree of orientation in the order schema of what is to be referred to. As long as it only comes down to making contact with what is detectable by the bare eye and ear and by using words like 'here' and 'there', 'I' and 'you'. Because this is present in the shared perceptual field, one need not bother to present in detail a refined analysis of the harmonious orientation of the partners within this field. Our common sense seems enough to apprehend the conditions given; we think we understand how and why the receiver can locate what the sender means. The natural (preverbal) aids which are at their disposal have been indicated and analysed, as far as we know them. Here, there is nothing to add.

The situation changes abruptly, however, it appears, where the narrator takes the listener into the realm of the memorable absent, or fully into the realm of constructive imagination, treating him there to the same deictic words that he may see and hear what is there to be seen and heard (and to be touched or perhaps even to be smelled or tasted). Not with the outward eye, ear, etc., but with what, in contrast, is conventionally called the 'inner' or the 'mind's' eye or ear in everyday language and, for the sake of convenience, in psychology, too. The situation *must* become a different one there, evidently, because the preverbal deictic aids which are indispensable for *demonstratio ad oculos* are absent in deixis at phantasma. He who is led by phantasma cannot follow the arrow of the speaker's outstretched arm and pointed finger with his gaze to find the something out *there*; he cannot use the spatial origin quality of the voice's sound, to find the place of a speaker who says *here*; the voice character of an absent speaker saying *I* also does not belong to written language. And still, a rich variety of these and other deictic words are offered to one in vivid accounts of absent objects and by absent narrators. A look at any travel report or novel will essentially confirm this on the first page. Indeed, for a theoretical understanding to be reached, what is psychologically more refined about this requires some additional thought.

The central psychological question, then, is how such a leading and being led in this absence is possible. But as often occurs in science, the researcher on his quest for what is more distant is led back by the facts themselves to something which he thought he understood through and through, namely to pointing at that which is present. Here, he must look at the situation with a fresh perspective in order to be equipped for that further research. Up to now, we have talked completely naively about a shared perceptual space as an order schema in which everything falls together: objects to be pointed at, sender and receiver of the pointing instructions, and where the two persons in contact display a harmony-suitable behaviour. The interplay, the harmony of this behaviour, is not quite so obvious as one who is psychologically naive might think. Yet we will not deal here with the ultimate epistemological problems raised by the facts, but rather be content with a maximally straight-forward description of the orientation of A and B, the conversation partners in their perceptual space.

This is, moreover, necessary because it turns out that this orientation *in toto* intervenes and is transposed into the 'imagination space', to the somewhere-realm of pure imagination and of the there-and-there in memory. The pre-supposition out of which astonishment over the possibility of deixis at phantasma arises is largely false. It is not the case at all that the natural deictic aids, upon which the *demonstratio ad oculos* is based, are *completely* missing in deixis at phantasma. Rather, it is such that speaker and listener in a vivid description of something absent dispose of the devices and means which permit an *actor* on stage to make the absent present, and which permit the *spectator* of the play to interpret that which is present on stage, as a mimesis of the absent (see my book *Ausdruckstheorie*). 'Imaginative' or vivid language is thoroughly adapted to this fictional playing, and only to the extent to which language uses this possibility should it be called such. Not that it need be identical to what the actor does *in all respects*; rather, there is alongside this a second possibility, cultivated by the epic writers. *Quod erit demonstrandum*.

(2) Anyone in a waking state and 'in his right senses' is oriented within the perceptual situation given; this means primarily that the flow of sense data to him is registered in an order schema, a system of coordinates, whose origin

is given by the reference of *here*, *now*, *I*. These three words have to be placed at the fixed point of the order schema we wish to describe.

[The following short passage omitted concerns differences in orientation between 'normal' and other states, including the states of mind of the sick and injured.]

(3) Now something more subtle about the *spatial component* within this total orientation of the waking person who is in his right senses. We are 'visual animals', that is, visual space is not everything, but it dominates the spatial orientation of sighted beings like ourselves. This also holds for the deictic device of verbal exchange, as we have 'seen' in connection with Brugmann. How do psychologists proceed, to describe the visual space experienced? The older phenomenologists of visual space such as Hering and Hillebrandt, Helmholtz, Bourdon, Witasek and others knew in this only one approach and direction for advancing scientific analysis. Suppose everything is stable, the things around us as well as we ourselves (the whole body, head and eyes), and that we don't look with two, but first with a single motionless eye; this does not 'gaze', but only receives whatever spatial data is offered to it from a so-and-so defined visual field. To the older researchers, this seemed to be the only adequate research approach. Binocular vision and movements of all kinds were introduced in the second instance and stepwise as complicating conditions of spatial perception. Now, we truthfully owe enough to those pioneers to acknowledge that this approach was not wrong.

But we know equally well that the analysis is methodologically just as unobjectionable if it starts the other way around, and perhaps it has to start there to validate and fill out the findings. Suppose then, someone, who is to fill in the particulars, is strolling, free and unhindered, from the train station in a strange city into the hustle and bustle of its shopping streets. After some time, he also will be able to give us information which can serve as a point of departure for our chapter on 'spatial orientation'. Perhaps our wanderer will begin reflecting because he now has to go back, and has lost his orientation with respect to the station; or he may in fact be able to give the direction and distance to the station with sufficient precision for practical use. Both cases, if well received and thought through, are of scientific interest. If he has kept his orientation, he has documented an ability which, in an enormously elaborated form, we find in reports about human scouts, or, still more impressive and perhaps theoretically more transparent, too, which we recognize in other well oriented animals; horses find their way back and birds, and so do ants, bees and wasps.

I compile this colourful list of experts here to indicate that the linguist who wants to be seriously informed should not plunge into and get lost in the physiological detail which differs again and again, if every species and human ability of visual orientation is inspected. For however many ways it is done, there is one central fact in all these cases—that a registration mechanism functions and provides the form of life which has it with an *orientation table* for its practical behaviour. Any one of them may move in its own way, according to its *action system*, so we confirm by straightforward observation the fact that in their actions, all of the animals named remain more or less correctly oriented with respect to certain objective spatial data or spatial directions which are crucial for the animals' survival.

And if one of the animals oriented this way, namely the human being, opens his mouth and begins to speak deictically, for example saying '*the station must be* **there**', in doing so he assumes the posture of a transistory signpost. The word lexicon taking its field values from the same orientation is by no means exhausted by *there*. If the same person uses words like *before*, *behind*, *left*, *right*, *above*, *below*, a new fact becomes apparent, namely the fact that he also *feels his body in relation* to his visual orientation, and uses it deictically. His (conscious, experienced) *body feeling representation* (Körpertastbild) stands in relation to the visual space. Spatial orientation can never, either in man or animal, be simply a matter of conceptually isolated vision. In that case, a mass of well known facts would not be understandable to us. We know about humans that data from vision, audition, and feeling are perceived and processed *together* by that already mentioned registration device and that another group of contributions is registered there too, contributions of so-called kinesthesis derived from specific intrinsic movements of head and body. Among other things, it is the important regulator of the 'static' apparatus of the semicircular canals that must not be forgotten in this enumeration. And concerning the connection between directions of gaze and body feeling representation we have run, in particular, into some well known facts must be reported which are of great importance to an analytic understanding of verbal deixis. I shall present them as succinctly as possible in the next section.

(4) It is known above all that the origin—the starting point of the coordinates of the directions of gaze—*wanders* within the body feeling representation. Roughly speaking, the perceptual *Here*, even when essentially visually understood, is not always at the same place in the body feeling representation. There is already a fundamental shift if we go from the monocular to the uniform binocular visual field. This is a fact which was already known to the older spatial phenomenologists; to account for it, Hering suggested the theoretical concept of a Cyclopean eye at the bridge of the nose. In fact, it is 'from there' that we see binocularly uniform directions of gaze, just as if each of us were a Polyphemus with a single Cyclopean eye. A scholastic worshipper of the Greeks might use this to demonstrate how humanly meaningful the creations of their imaginations have been, while a modern physician might come to no less important insights in a different direction.

The fact has a much greater relevance than might be supposed on first hearing.

The main point is, to say it in the fewest possible words, that with this first step, the very close *organ linkage* of the 'perceptual image' in Brugmann's sense, that final ordering to be accounted for in linguistic theory is *loosened*. And this liberation goes on and may be pursued step by step. Only someone who has thought through all of these freeing steps systematically will be capable of an authentic understanding of this apparently arbitrary and colourful variety of deictic words and deictic features, about which researchers in languages exotic and strange to us have so much to relate. The speakers of those languages are not that different from us as it appears. The relatively little I was able to learn from surveying the literature, for example, about the peculiar deictic means in many American Indian languages can be brought under one psychological edifice, and, more importantly, in a *systematic* way which we can all observe here and there and follow up in our own behaviour. Psychologists have found and described it without having an idea that there are some languages which have raised one deictic procedure to generality, and others another. I shall restrict myself to sketch schematically the mentioned steps of liberation of the spatial conscience from its more narrow organ linkages, and I shall report only what reliable psychologists in their various investigations have discovered and documented.

There are some phenomena almost completely within the domain of so-called pure perception, which are most easily accounted for by going on and concluding our theoretical construction of wandering of the visual *Here* in the body feeling representation. There are cases in which *before* and *behind*, rather than directly from the eye, are determined and 'perceived' in relation to the globe which is our head. In our own body feeling representation the head also has its *before* and *behind*, *left* and *right*, and it is this system that is crucial for what is seen. G. E. Müller simply calls it the system of *head coordinates*. A further change occurs when the head is so to speak set free and the *chest coordinates* become relevant, and finally, when head and upper body are set free and the leg and pelvis part of the body feeling representation takes over the role of defining the coordinates. Then, 'front' is where the pelvis, the knee, and step 'sense', and it is irrelevant where the eyes, head, and chest are turned. This is the most important system of *positional coordinates*.

We need not concern ourselves further with the details of the pertinent psychological observations; it is clear enough, that, step by step, this after that in the body feeling representation becomes dominant, and that the visual data are arrayed correspondingly. Actually, this is all we need. Except we point out right away a still farther-reaching jump in perceptual spatial orientation, the jump from *egocentric* to *topomnestic* orientation, as it has been called. As a kind of transition to that, we may view the important case, for example, of a vehicle (carriage, ship, locomotive, car) where one's orientation immediately and not only conceptually, but of necessity perceptually, follows the conventional direction of movement of the object. Just as naturally as with animals and other humans. When a teacher of gymnastics facing a dressed line of gymnasts gives commands, the orders *left* and *right* are conventionally given and understood according to the gymnasts' orientation. That is a paradigmatic case for whose explanation one must note the astonishingly easy translatability of all field values of the visual system and the verbal deictic system from someone in another plane of orientation.

This very translatability already contains the preconditions of a transition to so-called 'topomnestic' spatial orientation. And this flourishes whenever anything is registered according to the four directions of the compass. An accurate pursuit of topomnestic orientation beyond these most easily understandable (from the egocentric perspective) cases would need to rely on speculation, given the present state of our knowledge, and this should be avoided. Let us then conclude with the report on the psychological analysis of the normal spatial orientation of the waking human being in his given perceptual situation.

[(5) In this brief section, Bühler draws some further comparisons between *now* and *here*.]

(6) After that indispensable first step, let us again raise the question of the psychological basis of deixis at phantasma.

[Bühler then briefly points out that not in all cases of imagination is a whole situation evoked.]

We deal here only with situation-phantasmas, with the aid of which 'pointing' is done. To come quickly to the point, I just want to answer the question of what happens when a person who is awake and remains conscious (and thus is not dreaming), while talking or describing himself, or as a listener (reader), becomes 'lost' in memories, undertakes imaginary travels, or constructs imaginary inventions. What about the verbal pointing he himself performs or which he follows in his 'phantasma'? As we agreed, in doing so he should not become removed, in the literal sense of the word, from his perceptual situation. And a normal person usually will not; and so, the return back to present day affairs and the needs of the moment is not experienced as a real waking out of a dream, if one has taken up a travel description or a novel scene at some point that day. This and some other criteria allow for a sufficiently sharp distinction between real delirium and a 'transposition' done without losing control, vivid as this transposition may be.

I say *transposition* (Versetzung) and thus anticipate the second major case which may come up. Metaphorically speaking, either Mohammed goes to the mountain or the mountain moves to Mohammed. Where, incidentally, in real life the mountain is often much more cooperative than in the fable. What is being imagined, in particular if it is something movable like human beings, often comes to us, that is, into the indicated perceptual order schema, and there, it may be, if not actually 'seen', then still localized. Results on eidetic imagery have taught us that there are multifarious nuances between the normal perception with the body's eye and the normal appearance of the object of imagination before the so-called mind's eye. But these nuances are programmatically less interesting here than the simple fact that the imagined object appearing in the normal (non-eidetic) way before the mind's eye also may have a place before, beside, or behind me and directly among the objects in the room in which I find myself, the objects which I partly perceive, partly imagine. Whoever wants to try this out should attempt, for example, to localize in his imagination a familiar piece of furniture at an empty spot in the perceptual space where it has never before stood, and see whether he can decide by looking there how far it would reach in height and breadth and how it would look in the environment as a whole.

According to the results of a study by L. Martin, many people are able to do this. And if they did not succeed in visually placing an imaginary flower pot on the perceived table before them in the experiment, still most of them could report clear localization in other cases, where the mountain, in one of its possible manifestations, had come to them. Even those who have no visual impression at all in these cases still know, for example, that the internally heard voice of a friend who is the subject of a current memory, seemed to come from the right or from the left side. One tries to imagine a piece of conversation, hearing it in the voice characteristic of the friend, and suddenly realizes that it sounded as if he, the speaker of this utterance, were standing here at the desk and had directed it to us from over there. Enough said. This *first major case* occurs in many variations and should be seen as typical.

Exactly the opposite is what happens in the *second major case*, where Mohammed goes to the mountain. After a characteristic foregoing event or immediately and suddenly, one is transported in the imagination to the geographical place of what is being imagined, one has this present before the mind's eye from a determinate point of view, which may be given and at which is found the self's own position in the imagined scene. Imaginarily turning to face what was behind and walking on, one again sees, figuratively, what one has seen before in real wandering. But it is far more comfortable and goes faster, this being transposed in fairy tale-like bounds to new places, to where-ever one's thought is hurrying ahead. A narrative technique which is fitted to a child's abilities, and sometimes used in modern films to support the imagination as such. In the *Arabian Nights*, a magic bird lifts you into the air, the film rushing via a few overlapping pictures from one spatial position over to the next. An analysis by J. Segal, whose careful work I am relying on here, among others, revealed analogues to all this in the experience of his adult and trained observers.

One more point, which sounds strange at first, but which is completely sound and can be derived from our theory. There is an intermediate case between staying here and going there; both mountain and Mohammed remain where they are, but Mohammed perceives the mountain from his current location. This *third major case* is usually a labile and transitory experience. Its characteristic feature lies in the fact that the experiencer is in a position to indicate with his finger the direction in which something which is absent is seen from the mental eye. Approximately as our city wanderer can indicate the direction of the train station. If I ask, for example, the 500 students in my lecture 'Where is Saint Steven's Cathedral?' about 300 index fingers will be raised and point (with all kinds of interesting deviations) somewhere within the lecture hall. As I mentioned, this third major case is not very frequent in fantasy descriptions of some complexity and compactness. Psychologically speaking, a dreamland is to be found in the Somewhere, with which a linkage to the Here cannot be given. But it may also be somehow different, and the third major case can be considered established.

All in all, this makes understandable many of the features of imaginary wandering so carefully described by Segal. And I mean, to recapitulate, that a great deal in the technique of narration and the functional pleasure of the imagination to be found in fairy tales can only become understandable by a deeper study of what was briefly sketched here. Going from Grimm's fairy tales and their simple, psychologically transparent technique of leading the reader along, to many what must be more subtle narrative techniques whose details are still unknown to our discipline. But however differently these subtle verbal artists may proceed, I dare to claim until the contrary is proven that everything which they bring about in guiding the imagination or by deixis at phantasma can be brought under the scheme of the three major cases described above.

[Bühler then begins subsection (7) by rephrasing the idea developed in the preceding section: the body feeling representation is transposed, either completely or in part, into the realm of the imagination.]

It now becomes clear why we stated that it would be an error to assume that deixis at phantasma lacks natural deictic aids. It does not lack them to that extent that transpositions occur and anyone who is transposed 'takes along' his present body feeling representation, figuratively speaking. This is taken along in the second major case (transposition); in the first major case, the present body feeling representation together with his visual perceptual orientation are maintained from the very beginning, and integrated into what is imagined. The third major case proves to be an additive whole or, to put it differently, a superposition of two localizations, one of them corresponding conceptually to the first and the other to the second major case. To what extent such a superposition or some other combination is possible remains in the purely psychological sense an open question. Enlightenment will have to be forthcoming here from experts on languages and in central language disturbances.

[In subsection (8), Bühler stresses the role of transposition (Versetzung) and gives some further examples, especially in connection with drama and scenic narratives. Finally, in Chapter 9 and the concluding pages of Part 2 of *Sprachtheorie*, 'Egocentric and topomnestic deixis in languages', Bühler deals not so much with this distinction itself, but with remnants such as inclusive versus exclusive 'we', Latin *hic*, *hinc*, *huc*, and others.]

NOTE

1. 'Anticipation' of something not yet said is psychologically fully understandable, since we know how regularly a more or less 'empty' sentence scheme mentally precedes the thought needed to fill it. It is to places in this scheme that prior reference is made. Brugmann once calls this forward reference 'preparatory' use of demonstratives, as opposed to backward referring anaphora. The new term 'preparatory' is not very precise, and whenever the two need to be distinguished, we shall say reference backwards and reference forwards (or looking back and looking ahead). Otherwise, a second Greek word needs to be sought out, and this would be *cataphora*. Just as we do, the Greeks said 'above' and 'below' in the text ($\alpha\nu\omega$ and $\chi\alpha\tau\omega$); they were entirely correct in doing so, given their text roles. Let us make a note of this origin for an exact theoretical treatment of anaphora and cataphora. In Brugmann's time, this insight into the true character of both has been lost, and needs to be restored . . . .

Speech, Place, and Action
Edited by R. J. Jarvella and W. Klein
© 1982 John Wiley & Sons Ltd.

Towards a Descriptive Framework for Spatial Deixis[1]

CHARLES J. FILLMORE

1 INTRODUCTION

In this paper I propose a set of discriminations for describing and contrasting the systems of grammar and vocabulary for spatial deixis in natural languages. My account locates the topic in the intersection of spatial semantics and deixis, the theoretical point of view being that of prototype semantics. My goal is to present an 'etic' descriptive framework within which systems of deictic locating expressions in different languages may be compared with each other with respect to their pragmatic, semantic, syntactic, and morphological characteristics.

In Section 1 I offer introductory comments on the notion of the semantic prototype, on deixis as a semantic domain, on the semantics of spatial notions, and on the special character of spatial deixis. In Section 2 I discuss three kinds of departure from prototype meanings in this domain: (a) one which introduces a point of view by using a basically deictic expression in such a way that somebody other than the participants in the discourse counts as the 'centre' of the deictic field; (b) one which finds in the deictic field set up by the communication situation reference objects needed for the interpretation of linguistic material which is itself not primarily deictic; and (c) one which combines the two processes. In Section 3 I introduce the basic descriptive vocabulary for spatial deixis, including the terms needed for describing the structure and function of locating expressions and the 'anchoring role' played by the speaker's location and activities in certain classes of locating expressions. In Section 4 I examine the character and the range of variation of systems of demonstratives; and in Section 5 I offer some initial suggestions on a notation for the description of selected sets of demonstrative forms.

1.1 A general statement on prototype semantics

The theoretical position I take in this study is one which favours a 'prototype' rather than a 'checklist' representation of lexical meaning.[2] It is an approach

31

which seeks to represent the meaning of a linguistic expression, not through a statement of the necessary and sufficient conditions for membership in a category—the category which the expression 'connotes'—but rather through the presentation of a prototype, or paradigm case, supplemented with an analysis of instances (or near instances) of the category in terms of approximations to the prototype. The notion is similar to, and obviously based on, the concept of the prototype in studies of natural human category formation, especially in the work of Eleanor Rosch (e.g. Rosch, 1977), but it is here taken merely as providing a means for describing the senses and uses of specific lexical and grammatical forms and categories.

The notion of prototype in linguistic semantics has both a sychronic and a diachronic aspect. In a synchronic statement, the semantic prototype is taken as representing the current meaning of an expression. In a diachronic statement, a 'reconstructed' prototype is seen as providing an historical basis for a current state of polysemy. It is characteristic of the prototype notion in semantics that in the analysis of departures from and approximations to given semantic prototypes it is not always important to decide whether an acount is to be taken as synchronic or diachronic in effect.

Semantic prototypes can be realized in at least six ways, named here by typical English words which exemplify them: CLIMB, LONG, BIRD, RED, BACHELOR, and DECEDENT.

Case 1: Type CLIMB   The category is identified in terms of a disjunction of mutually compatible conditions, and the best examples are those in which all members of the disjunction are present.

The English verb *climb* can be taken in illustration of Case 1. Its two critical conditions may be named Clambering and Ascending. A monkey climbing up a flagpole satisfies both of these and thus exemplifies the prototype well. A monkey clambering down a flagpole, or clambering horizontally in the rafters of a warehouse, can also be said to be climbing, even though in that case only the Clambering component is present. A snail ascending a wall, in the way a snail usually moves, can be said to be climbing (up) the wall, even though in that case only the Ascending component is present. (Snails, lacking limbs, cannot clamber.) But the snail when returning to the bottom of the wall cannot be described as climbing, since it is neither ascending nor clambering. Either of the two critical conditions may be absent; but they may not both be absent.[3]

Case 2: Type LONG   The category is identified in terms of a disjunction of conditions, but one condition has a privileged status, and the best examples of the category are those in which the privileged condition is present. Other instances are seen as derivative of this primary use.

The adjective *long*, by virtue of its possibility of use in both spatial and temporal extent measurement, can be taken as an example of this second version of the prototype notion. Native speakers are generally in agreement that the spatial extent is basic ('six metres long', 'a long stick'), and the temporal use derivative ('six months long', 'a long vacation').

In this case little would be lost in describing the situation as one of polysemy, the connection between the two senses being merely the metaphor which provided the motivational basis for the diachronic development of the more derivative sense. What characterizes a commitment to prototype semantics in a case like this is negative: a prototype semanticist would explicitly *not* choose to construct a single general formulation of the meaning of the word that would simultaneously cover both its spatial and its temporal uses.

Case 3: Type BIRD The category is identified in terms of a fixed set of conditions, but the best examples are those which are close to an idealization of the category, this idealization being a conjunction of the features which provide 'cue validity' for the category.[4]

Any technical definition of, say, *bird*, will be equally well satisfied by a robin, a penguin, or an ostrich, but speakers are in general agreement that of the three, the robin most closely fits the idealization, is somehow 'birdier' than the other two. What this means in practice is that, although in the performance of classifying acts ('A penguin is a bird') the unadorned word *bird* is perfectly suitable, in general descriptions of scenes that use the word *bird* with no further explanation that word is regularly taken as designating a prototypic bird. You do not expect 'a cookie in the shape of a bird' to have the outline of an ostrich, and you would feel cheated if, on wishing that you were a bird you suddenly turned into a turkey.

Case 4: Type RED The category is one of a set of categories in which each is defined as a range around a 'target' area, the best examples being those that are 'on target'.

The theory of 'focal hues' in the semantics of colour terms (Berlin & Kay, 1969; Rosch, 1975) provides the clearest illustration of this version of the semantic prototype. Within such a domain it makes sense to say that while two elements are both undeniably acceptable instances of a category (as of two hues being each undeniably red), one can nevertheless be 'better' than the other. In such a domain it makes sense to say that an entity is 'sort of' or 'more or less' a member of a given category. (On the notion of approximations to full membership in a category, see Lakoff, 1973.)

Case 5: Type BACHELOR   The category is defined in terms of a set of conditions, but the best examples are those which are situated in a standard or prototypic background setting.

The noun *bachelor* can be defined as an unmarried adult man, but the noun clearly exists as a motivated device for categorizing people only in the context of a human society in which certain expectations about marriage and marriageable age obtain. Male participants in modern long-term unmarried couplings would not ordinarily be described as bachelors; a boy abandoned in the jungle and grown to maturity away from contact with human society would not be called a bachelor; John Paul II is not properly thought of as a bachelor.

It is characteristic of the prototype view of semantics that it is not important to decide whether in each of the above cases the men involved are or are not bachelors (whether, in other words, 'bachelor' can be 'truthfully' predicated of any of them), because prototype semantics is not concerned with the 'boundaries' of concepts. The assumption that a word is being properly used brings with it the assumption that the conditions obtain within which the existence of the category is motivated.

Case 6: Type DECEDENT   The category is defined in terms of a set of conditions, but the best example of a *use* of the category is one in which the speaker is appropriately engaged in the sort of activity in connection with which the category has been given a special name.

Not much is at stake on the issue of whether this last case really deserves inclusion in this survey. It is not a prototypic instance of a semantic prototype. The exemplary word *decedent*, as I understand it, can be used to refer to a deceased person when the discourse is about the question of the inheritance of that person's property and the participants in that discourse are operating in a 'legal' context.

Here the point is that many expressions have conventional settings for their most natural use, and that when they are used under conditions that are markedly different from those settings there is a departure from the prototype. Obviously the whole topic of 'registral' information could be fitted into this last category.

Applications   Of the several demonstrated versions of the prototype notion, the first and the second will be most relevant to the discussions of demonstratives and spatial deixis given below. We shall see that certain interpretations of distance categories in demonstrative systems by which, for example, a particular category can be presented as either 'a short distance from the Speaker' or 'relatively closer to the Hearer', show similarities to the 'free disjunction' situation seen in *Case 1: Type CLIMB*. An important distinction between basically deictic words which can be used non-deictically and basically non-deictic words which have some deictic uses will require the analysis of the 'privileged disjunct' of the sort we saw in *Case 2: Type LONG.*

1.2 A general statement on deixis

Deixis is the name given to uses of items and categories of lexicon and grammar that are controlled by certain details of the interactional situation in which the utterances are produced. These details include especially the identity of the participants in the communicating situation, their locations and orientations in space, whatever on-going indexing acts the participants may be performing, and the time at which the utterance containing the items is produced.

There are two general ways in which one speaks of deixis in natural language: first, in terms of the manner in which the socio-spatio-temporal anchoring of a communication act motivates the form, or provides material for the interpretation, of the utterance that manifests that act; and second, in terms of the grammatical and lexical systems in the language which serve to signal or reflect such anchoring. That is to say, we can either ask how speakers succeed in using their current situation for anchoring referential acts in space and time, or we can ask what grammatical or lexical materials a given language has dedicated to such purposes.

It is the former sense that Lyons has in mind when he defines deixis as:

'the location and identification of persons, objects, events, processes and activities being talked about, or referred to, in relation to the spatiotemporal context created and sustained by the act of utterance and the participation in it, typically, of a single speaker and at least one addressee' (Lyons, 1977, p. 637).

This is the sense in which we can speak of the Sender in an act of communication as constituting the centre of a system of coordinates, the orientation of the Sender's body as determining a relevant set of axes, and the moment of the performance of the communication act as establishing a zero point on a scale of temporal reference. In the second sense of deixis, by contrast, we are interested in the classes of words and grammatical categories whose primary function in a linguistic system is that of indexing specific aspects of the communication act setting. The most common types of structural subsystems which serve this function are pronouns, tenses, and demonstratives.

The present study is concerned with the classification and description of the kinds of linguistic material that prototypically have, or that can be given, deictic function. A reason for needing to be clear about the distinction between the forms and the uses to which they can be put is the need to recognize cases in which elements which are prototypically deictic may also have non-deictic uses as well as cases in which basically non-deictically functioning elements can be used deictically. The two kinds of transfer of use, as we shall see below, seem to have importantly different functions. In particular, when primarily deictic elements are used non-deictically (more correctly stated, when their interpretation does not depend on the actual speech context in which they are produced), the semantic effect is that of presenting a 'point of view' which is independent of that of the speaker of the utterance. In the opposite case, when basically non-deictic elements are used in such a way that they require for the interpretation reference to the speech context, they are what I shall refer to as 'deictic by default'. By this expression I mean that, under the circumstances of their use, it is only the communication act setting which can provide the grounding or the 'reference points' that are needed for their interpretation. The expressions themselves, however, freely take other reference points in other contexts.

Were we to be insensitive to these distinctions, we might just see a large set of linguistic devices, all of which have the potential for either deictic or non-deictic uses, and we might then be inclined to conclude that deixis is to be viewed exclusively as a matter of language use, not at all as a matter of linguistic system. A theory of prototype semantics allows us—indeed requires us—to separate primary and derived senses of linguistic expressions.

1.3   A general statement on spatial semantics

Space as a general category figures in the semantic description of lexical and grammatical material in connection with each of the following: (a) the ways in which physical objects are said to be located—or in which events are said to occur—in particular places in the physical world, in particular the ways in which the assumed locations of certain objects allow them to be used as landmarks for establishing the locations of other objects; (b) the spatial properties of physical objects, such as their size, their dimensionality, and their contours; (c) the position of objects in space with respect to established directions (from some reference point) provided by the environment (as in the case of 'south of', 'uphill from', etc.); (d) orientations in space defined in terms of a given reference object's asymmetries of form; and (e) the path taken by a moving object, expressed in terms of both its contours and its contained and terminating points.[5]

In the treatment of spatial notions in natural language semantics (as opposed to the geometer's space with its arbitrary zero points and vectors) it is common to speak of a system of coordinates having three axes, which we might refer to as *up/down*, *front/back*, and *left/right*. These three axes are cognitively available to us in different ways. The up/down axis is determined by our recognizing the direction of the pull of gravity, and is therefore not to be explained in terms of egocentric or anthropocentric predispositions of language users.[6] The front/back axis is determined by certain inherent asymmetries of a reference object, that object's front side determined with reference to its ability to move with a fixed orientation, to a canonical means of human access to the object, or to the object's similarities with the human body. The left/right axis is cognitively available, it seems, through unanalysed personal experiences with the basic bilateral asymmetries in the workings of our own bodies. I think it would not be misleading to suggest that left/right is essentially egocentric (in that we recognize the distinction in the first instance in our own bodies), that front/back is essentially anthropocentric (in that we first learn to deal with it in terms of the bodies of the humans in our environment), while the up/down axis is founded on relations existing in the environment independently of ourselves.

The spatial concepts that are built on such a three-dimensional coordinate system, it should be pointed out, are not primarily deictic. Expressions which represent these categories can become deictic just in case the speaker of the utterance containing them implicitly takes his or her own body, or that of his interlocutor, as a 'deictic centre'.

1.4 Spatial deixis

The subject of this paper is spatial deixis. Spatial deixis is that aspect of deixis which involves referring to the locations in space of the communication act participants; it is that part of spatial semantics which takes the bodies of the communication act participants as significant reference objects for spatial specification.

The subject of spatial deixis has three natural subtopics: systems of demonstratives inasmuch as these are structured with reference to the locations and gestures of the communicating participants; prepositional and other devices for constructing locating expressions in which the current location of a communicating participant can become an implicit landmark; and systems of motion verbs for whose interpretation reference must be made to the current or expected location of a communicating participant. This paper is limited to the first two, confining itself thus to the language of 'locating expressions'.

2   THE TWO TRANSFERS

I suggested above that it has proven necessary to distinguish elements of language which are primarily deictic, independently of whether they also have non-deictic uses, from elements which are primarily non-deictic, independently of whether they also have deictic uses. Some prototypically deictic elements can be used with their deictic centre 'transferred' to something other than the speaker of the current utterance, and some deictically usable expressions are best described as being basically non-deictic in character. The distinction is crucial to an explanatory account of the transferred uses, since on the one hand we want to say that it is by virtue of an element's participation in a deictic system that its transfer brings about a particular 'dramatizing' effect, and on the other hand it is by virtue of the deictic space/time moment that we have with us always that it is possible to find the intended reference object in spatial and temporal locating expressions in which the identity of the reference object is not made textually explicit.

2.1 Point of view

As an easy illustration of an extended use of an element of a deictic system we can consider the time-deictic word *ago*. The word fits most properly in constructions containing a time-measurement phrase in combination with the simple preterit, where the indicated time point is at a distance in the past measured backward from the moment of speech. What defines the word as deictic is the interpreter's need to use the moment of utterance as the zero-point for the temporal distance measurement.

A pure deictic interpretation is clearly required in sentence (1):

(1)   Several years ago he lived near the beach.

Important for evaluating these observations is the fact that non-deictic counterparts of *ago*, such as *before* or *earlier*, do not freely occur in that context with that interpretation, as is seen in the unacceptability of sentence (2):

(2)   *Several years before, he lived near the beach.

In combination with the pluperfect tense, however, where a temporal reference point has been created in the discourse flow, the word *before* (or *earlier*) is perfectly at home, but this time *ago* is out of place. Compare the acceptability judgements for sentences (3) and (4):

(3)   Several years earlier, he had lived near the beach.
(4)   *Several years ago, he had lived near the beach.

In recording the unacceptability of sentence (4), with the prefixed asterisk, what I have in mind is its unacceptability in ordinary discourse. The sentence is, in fact, acceptable in a passage taken from a narrative in which at this point what is being presented is the inner experience of a central character, the 'he' of the passage. That is the kind of transfer I have in mind when I speak of a basically deictic word being used 'non-deictically'. The characterization is potentially misleading, since it is precisely the deictic effect associated with the word which is responsble for the communicated 'point of view'. What justifies me in describing it as non-deictic is its not being anchored in the current speech event, the event in which the utterance is produced.

If, through this example, I have succeeded in establishing the phenomenon of 'taking a point of view' by means of transferring a temporal deictic element to 'another centre', we can then see that spatial deictic expressions are usable in the same way and with the same effect. By substituting *here* for *near the beach* in our examples we create in (5) a sentence in which both *here* and *ago* have to be interpreted with reference to the acutal event of an utterance of the sentence, and in (6) a sentence in which both of these elements are to be interpreted as somehow present in the thoughts of the central character at the narrative time.

(5)   He lived here several years ago.
(6)   He had lived here several years ago.[7]

2.2   Deixis by default

As suggested above, the vocabulary appropriate to the spatial coordinate systems up/down, front/back and left/right is basically non-deictic, even though we find many deictic uses of the words and categories that make up this system. The point is an important one to make, I think, since some of the most important work on deixis in recent years focuses attention on precisely this domain.[8]

The anchoring of the front/back axis for a locating expression is established in the first instance with reference to the intrinsic orientation of an assumed reference object. Expressions like (7) and (8) assume, in their prototypic use, that buildings and horses have designated fronts and backs and that it is in terms of these designations that the locational information is being presented:

(7)   The children are in front of the building.
(8)   It's not safe to stand behind the horse.

In general, to be *in front of* a thing is to be closer to its front than to any of its other sides, and to be *behind* or *at the back of* a thing is to be closer to its back than any of its other sides. In the usual case, of course, the sentence also communicates the understanding that the object being located is in a relevant way close to the reference object.

The building and the horse were used as explicit reference objects in (7) and (8). In the uses I refer to as 'deictic by default' the reference object is the speaker's body, and it is left implicit. Thus a sentence like (9) can be said to mean something like (10):

(9)   They're up front.
(10)   They're ahead of where we are now.

Sentence (11), with speaker and hearer assumed to be facing the same direction, invites the hearer to use his own left/right axis (the one which is in effect while he is facing the building) to find the indicated room:

(11)   His room is up there, to the left of that open window.

And the *below* in sentence (12), if said by an airplane pilot flying over Paris, communicates the same thing that *below us now* could communicate in that context:

(12) The Eiffel Tower is just below.

It would appear that expressions linked with all three axes have both non-deictic and default-deictic uses. In addition, there is a privileged set of possibilities open to expressions of the front/back axis, in English and some other languages, and that is the topic of the next section.

2.3 A more complicated case

With expressions appropriate to the front/back axis we find, in many languages, a more conventionalized kind of transfer, one which allows, so to speak, a double transfer: first, a transfer from a non-deictic use to a use which recognizes a deictic centre; and then a transfer from having the speaker as deictic centre to having another person (or an observation conceptually taken as the point of view of another potential person) as its centre.

In the class of uses I have in mind, the historical prototype is a situation in which things are located with reference to objects which bear inherent front/back orientations. Examples of the prototype use are sentences (7) and (8) above, sentences whose interpretations are independent of any facts about the settings in which they are spoken.

The first transfer I have in mind, then, is that by which the orientation of the reference object is determined, not by any of *its* inherent asymmetries, but rather by its relation in space to the speaker. The situation can be set up most clearly by taking as such a reference object an entity which lacks an intrinsic front/back axis, such as a tree or a rock. Expressions of the sort seen in (13) and (14) treat the tree or rock as having been given, for the occasion, a front or a back side as determined by the location and orientation of the speaker at the time of the utterance:

(13) The child is in front of the tree.
(14) There's a rabbit behind that rock.

Sentence (13) is understood as saying what (15) says, as (14) is understood as saying what (16) says:

(15) The child is near the tree, on the side of the tree closest to me.
(16) The rabbit is near the rock, on the opposite side of the rock from where I am now.

The reason it is important to regard this situation as exemplifying a transfer from a prototype, rather than being merely a further instance of a single general interpretation of the category of the front/back axis, is, as Hill (1975) has convincingly shown, that languages differ in how and whether this transfer is achieved. Hill has compared Hausa with English, finding that Hausa uses what he calls an 'ego-aligned' strategy for making the transfer, while most Western languages use what he calls an 'ego-opposed' strategy. In the ego-opposed strategy, the tree is, so to speak, facing me, so that something that is between me and it is *in front of* the tree; in the ego-aligned strategy, on the other hand, the tree and I are facing in the same direction, and what is between me and it is *behind* the tree. A way of making this distinction clear is to realize that by taking the ego-opposed strategy (i.e. *our* strategy) it is natural to say things like (17); but if we were users of the ego-aligned strategy we would instead find it most natural to say (18):

(17)   I can't see the baby; she must be behind the tree.
(18)   I can't see the baby; she must be in front of the tree.

Hill has shown that different languages transfer the front/back axis to independent non-self-oriented objects in different ways. It also appears to be the case that some languages do not make such a transfer at all. Japanese appears to be such a language. The words for 'front' (*mae*) and 'back' (*usiro, ura*) are not normally used for locating things with respect to the locations of non-self-orientated objects. Special forms exist for such identifications: *mukoogawa* for 'on the other side', *kotiragawa* for 'on this side'.

Now it happens that, in English at least, the language of the front/back axis can be transferred away from the assumed deictic use to a use in which the point of view of somebody else is taken. Such a transfer is possible, not only in a third-person narrative which assumes a point of view (as illustrated in sentence (19)), but also in sentences which, by means of an explicit embedding verb, represent somebody's cognitive experiences (as in sentence (20)).

(19)   He stepped into the garden; there it was, in front of the tree.
(20)   He sensed that somebody was standing behind the curtain.

The functional difference between the two kinds of transfer—the transfer from deictic to non-deictic with its literary effect and the transfer from non-deictic to deictic with its mere 'time-saving' function—can be seen in the fact that the two transfers are not inverses of each other. Constructions in which both transfers have occurred have both effects.

One might wish to say that in the case of the deictic use of terminology related to the front/back axis the prototype explanation has a diachronic value only, since the transfer has been thoroughly conventionalized. This appears not to be true. Hill's research has shown that the derived orientations are better expressed as tendencies than as rules: not every speaker of Hausa or English automatically knows which orientation to use, and situations can be manipulated in which either choice can be induced (Hill, 1975).

3.   A DESCRIPTIVE VOCABULARY FOR SPATIAL DEIXIS

In this section I introduce the categories and distinctions which I believe will prove necessary for describing spatial deictic semantic systems in natural languages. Emphasizing systems of demonstratives, I examine here the functions, semantic contrasts, and lexicalization patterns that can be observed in these lexicogrammatical systems in various languages. My personal interest in developing this catalogue is that of eventually devising a procedure and a checklist for investigating deictic systems in a field situation. I have found it difficult, in my own work, to set up the right elicitation contexts for exploring the uses of deictic elements in field investigations, and, from the often unsatisfactory descriptions of deictic systems in published grammars, I am convinced that other investigators have experienced similar difficulties.

In choosing the vocabulary needed for describing the basic context of the communication act, I shall take advantage of the fact that I am working within the framework of a prototype semantics and can thus allow myself to use words which, while appropriate to the prototype situation, do not cover all the situations for which the category needs to be used. Giving myself this freedom, then, I shall identify the source of a linguistic message as the Speaker, acknowledging, without here worrying about, the fact that this term, strictly speaking, is not general enough to cover communication by means other than speech. (The words 'sender' or 'message source' would be more appropriate if my audience were to require me to abstract away from the prototype situation.) And while I recognize the important difference between the 'addressee', the intended hearer of an utterance,[9] and the 'hearer' (a term that could fit a mere overhearer), I shall allow myself to use the more common term Hearer as the second participant in the prototype speech communication setting.

By allowing myself these terminological simplifications, my locutions can be shorter and easier to understand than would be possible were I to adhere to more careful standards. Where I need to be more careful I will find a way.

3.1   The structure of Locating Expressions

I shall use the term Locating Expression to include any linguistic expression which has the function of associating an object with a location. A Locating Expression will make explicit or implicit reference to a Place, that being identifiable as a neighbourhood, surface, or interior of an entity near, on, or in which things can be situated, or as a set of coordinate values capable of specifying an object's location. Following Talmy (1980), I shall refer to the thing being located as the Figure. Thus, in the terminology used here, a Locating Expression associates a Figure with a Place.

Whenever through language a Speaker successfully locates a Figure in a

Place, this is accomplished through reference to something else whose location can be taken for granted. We can refer to such a reference object, again following Talmy (1980), as the Ground. The Ground in a Place phrase is either an entity which itself possesses surfaces or parts capable of serving as Places, or an entity with reference to which a Figure can be located using either coordinates given by the environment, as illustrated in sentence (21), or coordinates generated by the Ground entity's own shape asymmetries, as seen in sentence (22):

(21)   Our village is seven miles downriver from Candlebury.
(22)   It's about seven metres in front of Harry.

A direction *downriver* from the Ground element Candlebury is determined by the environment; a position *in front of* Harry taken as Ground is determined by the direction Harry is currently facing.

A Locating Expression, then, is an expression by which a Figure is said to be at a Place identified with reference to a Ground. In the particular case of *deictic* Locating Expressions, the Ground is the Speaker's (or in some cases the Hearer's) body.

3.2   The functions of Locating Expressions

For various reasons it is necessary to distinguish three functions of Locating Expressions: (a) Informing; (b) Identifying; (c) Acknowledging.

In the Informing function, the Speaker is letting the Hearer know that a particular Figure is to be found in a particular Place. A sentence illustrating this function is (23).

(23)   The umbrella is on the kitchen floor.

The Informing function can be achieved deictically either by means of a reference to the Speaker's current location, as seen in sentence (24), interpreted as sentence (25), or by means of reference to the Speaker's current gesturing act, as exemplified in sentence (26), interpreted as sentence (27):

(24)   She lives here.
(25)   She lives in the place where I am now.
(26)   Your hat is over there.
(27)   Your hat is in the place at which I am now pointing.

Distinct from an Informing or 'predicating' function in Locating Expressions is an Identifying or 'referring' function. In this case, the Speaker is letting the Hearer know which of several possible objects is being mentioned and is accomplishing this by appealing to the Hearer's ability to associate the intended Figure with the given Place. Non-deictically the Identifying function can be illustrated with an utterance like that in (28):

(28)   Bring me the chair that's in the kitchen.

Deictically it can be achieved with the use of a demonstrative adjective, as in (29), or a demonstrative pronoun, as in (30):

(29)   Sit in this chair, not that one.
(30)   What do you suppose this is?

A third use of Locating Expressions, importantly different from the other two but seldom discussed in writings on demonstrative systems, is that of Acknowledging or 'presupposing' the Place with which the Figure is associated. In this case the Speaker assumes that the Hearer knows, independently of any information provided by the expression, both which Figure the Speaker has in mind and the Place in which that Figure is located.

For English certain kinds of 'angry speech' provide the most ready examples of what I have in mind. Consider a sentence like (31) spoken in anger by a father to his daughter in the presence of only one snake:

(31)   Susan, get that snake out of this house!

Here both the *that* and the *this* are used in what I am calling the Acknowledging function. Here the locations and identities of both the snake and the house can be taken as known to the Hearer independently of the spatial meanings of the demonstratives, and independently of any indexing act being performed by the Speaker. The choice of a demonstrative determiner in these cases serves neither an Informing nor an Identifying function, yet the contrast between them—i.e. the reason for choosing *that* in one case and *this* in the other—is based on the same spatial relations to the Speaker that determine their choice in the more characteristic Identifying uses.

Another example of the Acknowledging use in English, this time one in which the rhetorical effect is not easy to articulate, comes from the discourse of a man who was remarking on his own ugliness. He said (32):

(32)   You can look at this face and not laugh?

Here the phrase *this face* is a substitute for *my face*, but in the context it was clear that the Speaker was in no way choosing the deictic expression to help the Hearer figure out which face was under discussion.

To look farther from home for more examples, we find in Dyirbal, an Australian aboriginal language described by Dixon (1972), an obligatory class of noun-marking morphemes, one of which must be chosen with each noun. The system of categories provided for this morpheme class requires the Speaker to indicate whether the entity designated by the noun is being presented ostensively, or, if not, whether it is far from or near to the Speaker, and, if far from the Speaker, whether or not it is visible to both Speaker and Hearer. (One of the categories in this system is unmarked and is used for discourse reference, in which case the deictic distinctions just enumerated are irrelevant.) Since this system of contrasts is obligatory, they most frequently occur in an Acknowledging use rather than in either an Informing or an Identifying use.

Elements of demonstrative systems that have primarily the Informing function are the demonstrative adverbs, the *here* and *there* (or, in directional expressions, the *hence* and *thence*, *hither* and *thither*) of English; those that have mainly the Identifying function are the demonstrative determiners and the demonstrative pronouns, the *this* and *that* (serving both functions) of English. The Informing and Identifying functions may be thought of as the prototypic uses of demonstratives, the Acknowledging use being derivative and secondary. With the deictic motions verbs (*come* and *go*, etc.), however, the Acknowledging function is primary.

3.3   The role of the Speaker as Ground

There are various ways in which the Speaker can serve as the Ground element in a Locating Expression. In the simplest case, the Place being indicated is merely, in a general way, the current location of the Speaker. For (33), for example, the interpretation is that John is in the Place where the Speaker is located at the time the sentence is spoken, while for (34) the room being designated is the room currently containing the Speaker:

(33)   John is here.
(34)   John's in this room somewhere.

In such cases the Hearer is able to identify the indicated Place simply by knowing where the Speaker currently is.

Extensions of this simplest case are found (a) when the Hearer accepts the location of the Speaker as the zero point for a system of coordinates whose orientation is provided by the environment, and (b) when the orientation of the Speaker's body is seen as generating a system of coordinates which moves and rotates as the Speaker's body moves. In English these ways of anchoring Locating Expressions in the deictic centre figure in the interpretation of elements accompanying demonstratives rather than in the interpretation of the demonstratives themselves. Examples are (35) and (36), in which the orientations are provided by the environment (the direction of the pull of gravity in once case, the points of the compass in the other), and (37), in which the Speaker's body provides both the zero point and the directional base:

(35)   He's right upstairs.
(36)   We should probably be a little further south.
(37)   It's up ahead, over there to the left.

A second major role of the Speaker in a deictic locating act is that of presenting a stance, gesture, or non-incidental bodily orientation that can direct the Hearer's gaze to the indicated Place or the indicated Figure. We can refer to such movements and stances as Indexing Acts. Examples of Indexing Acts include the pointed index finger in our culture, the lifted chin or puckered lips in other cultures. When indexing acts are accompanied by deictic expressions (in any of the three functions discussed in Section 3.2, the combination has the effect of telling the Hearer, 'Notice what I'm pointing at!'.

We can refer to the basic function of an Indexing Act as that of Indicating, by which I have in mind the performing of an act which allows the Hearer to trace, by symbolic extrapolation, a path from the gesture to the thing. Important subtypes of indexing acts, slightly different from what I have arbitrarily named 'Indicating', are acts of Touching and Presenting. Pounding on a table and saying *this table* or holding a wine bottle in someone's view and saying *this bottle* are examples of what I have in mind. The reasons such acts need to be separated from the usual sorts of indexing are that in these cases especially the Hearer has no need to project from the Indexing Act to find the indicated Place. This being so, no distinguishing function can be served by the choice among contrastive demonstrative forms that are distinguished according to relative distance from the Speaker. As we said in the discussion of angry speech earlier, linguistic forms which are used in contexts in which they cannot in principle serve their prototypic function tend to acquire new functions. In English the choice of *this* versus *that* in acts of the Touching and Presenting kind appears, in some cases, to reflect the assumption of a point of view. Thus if while touching the indicated object I were to say (38) rather than (39), you might assume I was taking my own point of view, whereas if I were to say (39) you might feel I was taking your point of view:

    (38)   Would you like this one?
    (39)   Would you like that one?

I am not sure what kind of evidence it would take to back up my judgements on shifting point of view in these examples; the point is merely that with those involvements of the Speaker's body of the Touching and Presenting types, the distance categories cannot have their primary contrastive functions and have apparently been given something else to do in this context. A similar phenomenon will be shown below with Bakwiri, in Section 4.5, where the distance categories in a context in which their basic contrast can be expected to be otiose are used to signal the distinction between the first thing indexed and the second thing indexed.

A third and final way in which we can speak of the Speaker's role (and in this case also the Hearer's) in the use and interpretation of an expression of spatial deixis is that in which the Speaker's and Hearer's position in the physical world defines a field of shared visual experiences. In a number of languages, as will be illustrated below, a difference between being In-Field and Out-of-Field is reflected in contrasts operating within the demonstrative system.

4   THE ORGANIZATION OF DEMONSTRATIVE SYSTEMS

In this section, after presenting a survey of the possible syntactic functions of demonstrative words or morphemes, I shall show some of the ways in which demonstrative systems of natural languages can differ from each other with respect to (a) the elaboration of distance features, most typically involving relative remoteness from the Speaker of the indicated Place or Figure; (b) the patterns by which deictic and non-deictic features are jointly or separately lexicalized; (c) degrees of morphological motivation, i.e. the degrees to which the separate semantic features of a complex demonstrative expression are separately manifested in word-shapes; and (d) patterns of usage.

4.1   The possible syntactic functions of demonstratives

Demonstratives in a language can function as sentences, adverbs, pronouns, or determiners. A linguistic form can be described as a Demonstrative assigned to one or another of these syntactic functions if it is the case that the form exists independently for serving just that function. Thus *here* in English is a demonstrative adverb, where its paraphrase *in this place* is not: the latter is better described as an adverbial phrase which contains a demonstrative determiner.

A Sentential Demonstrative, which we can represent as

D/Se[__(NP)]

is a demonstrative that can stand alone as a sentence, having what can be called a Presentative function. These are sentences whose meanings are something like 'Behold!' or maybe 'Look at this!'. Latin *ecce*, French *voilà*, Serbo-Croatian *evo*, are examples of Sentential Demonstratives. Often a noun or pronoun indicating the object being presented occurs in construction with a Sentential Demonstrative, as in French *Le voilà*, Serbo-Croatian *Evo ga*, both meaning 'Here he is'.

A Demonstrative Adverb can have any of several adverbial functions: Locative, symbolizable as

D/Lo[__],

as with English *here* and *there*; Directional, indicating either Source, as with the obsolescent forms *hence* and *thence*, representable as

D/So[__]

or Goal, as with *hither* and *thither*, symbolizable as

   D/Go[__];

or Manner, as with Japanese *koo* 'in this way' or *soo* 'in that way', representable as

   D/Ma[__].

A Demonstrative Pronoun, symbolizable as

   D/NP[__]

is capable of functioning as a noun phrase in its own right, in contrast to a Demonstrative Determiner, representable as

   D/NP[__N]

which can appear in a noun phrase only in construction with a noun. In English the words *this* and *that* and their corresponding plural forms serve each of these functions, but in other languages the two are often kept distinct. In Japanese, for example, the forms *kore* : *sore* : *are* are Demonstrative Pronouns (D/NP[__]), while the forms *kono* : *sono* : *ano* are Demonstrative Determiners (D/NP[__N]).

4.2   The distance categories and their extensions

Characteristically, though not exceptionlessly, Demonstrative Adverbs, Demonstrative Determiners, and Demonstrative Pronouns come in paradigmatic sets that contrast with respect to degrees of distance from the speaker's body. Languages differ from each other with respect to (a) the number of distance contrasts they recognize; (b) the particular syntactic or semantic subsystems in which given contrasts hold, and (c) the Pivot (whether Speaker or Hearer) around which the distance categories are anchored.

English has a two-way contrast, symbolizable as

   D/[+Proximal]

for 'relatively close to the Speaker' and

   D/[−Proximal]

for 'relatively remote from the Speaker'. Many languages, including Latin, Greek, Japanese, and Spanish, have a three-way contrast, representable as

   D/[Proximal],   D/[Medial],   D/[Distal].

(The presence or absence of '+' with 'Proximal' indicates whether it is to be seen as the proximal term of a two-way or a three-way system.)

Sometimes a language is described as having more than three distance categories, but it is my opinion that there are never really more than three. In most of the descriptions I have seen, some contrast other than distance from the Speaker always appears to be involved, either a Pivot contrast (taking Speaker or Hearer as Pivot) or a contrast between being or not being in the shared visual field. In Section 4.2.1 I suggest that a Hearer-Pivot category is an evolutionary development out of the distance category D/[Medial]; and in Section 4.2.2 I argue that the visual field categories emerge out of the distance category D/[Distal]. In both cases the development involves the separation of elements of a CLIMB-type semantic prototype.

4.2.1 Extensions from a proposed semantic prototype for D/[Medial]

Since the deictic categories develop out of reference points that can be assumed in a typical language communication situation, it would make sense (in the manner of sketching out the background for a prototype of the BATCHELOR type) to characterize that situation as one in which the Speaker and Hearer are fairly close to each other, engaged in a face-to-face interaction, and in which there is a general coincidence between being 'a small distance from the Speaker' and being 'close to the Hearer'. The category D/[Medial] might be usefully described, in its historical origin at least, as representing in its prototype the two features (a) being a small distance from the Speaker, and (b) being near the Hearer. This proposed state of affairs could make intelligible the apparent reality that in some languages the conditions for using the D/[Medial] category are satisfied if *either* condition (a) or condition (b) is present, while other languages seem to have made one or another of them criterial, and still others have seen fit to introduce separate lexical realizations of the two features.

In a field situation demonstratives should be first elicited in a prototypic setting, with features (a) and (b) coinciding. Let us assume that under such conditions we have found a three-step demonstrative system for some language, the terms of which can be labelled D/[Proximal], D/[Medial], and D/[Distal]. The category D/[Medial] was identified in the prototypic setting; but it is now an empirical question whether this form can be used when *only* condition (a) *or* condition (b) is present. To check this out we need to devise situations in which one is clearly present and the other is clearly absent.

One situation in which the Hearer-Pivot condition (b) is satisfied independently of the Speaker-Pivot middle-distance condition (a) has the Speaker and the Hearer at a relatively great distance from each other, as when shouting across a valley. If the D/[Medial] form is appropriate in such a case, then we know that proximity to the Hearer is at least one possible condition for the form. Using this test we find that D/[Medial] is the appropriate form for Japanese and for Bakwiri (a Bantu language spoken in the Cameroons). A situation in which the Speaker-Pivot middle-distance condition is independently present is one in which the object to be identified is a short distance from the Speaker but farther from the Hearer than from the Speaker, as, for example, when the Speaker and the Hearer are face to face and the object to be indicated is behind the Speaker. Bakwiri, according to my informants, does not use D/[Medial] in this situation. Japanese has dialect variation on just this point: in the standard dialect the middle category is not appropriate, but in some of the western dialects it is.[10]

If we find that the category D/[Medial] is used in one of these contexts and not the other, then the prototype explanation can be seen as having a diachronic force; if, however, we find it used in each of these contexts, even when they are independently established, then the prototype has a synchronic explanatory value.

I believe that for each three-step demonstrative system that we examine we need to ask what choice the language has made with its middle term (or whether it has made one) with respect to conditions in which the two aspects of the prototype occur independently of each other. We may then find languages whose demonstrative systems have developed separate forms for a Hearer-Pivot category.

In our notation the middle category, either before it has been further analysed or when it has the prototype usage, will be labelled D/[Medial]. In cases where the two components of the prototype figure separately in the description, we can represent middle-distance from the Speaker as

   D/[SMedial]

and close-distance to the Hearer as

   D/[HProximal].

For languages which have separated pivot categories from distance categories, the features of Speaker-Pivot and Hearer-Pivot can be symbolized as

   D/[SPivot],   D/[HPivot]

and can appear in combination with the familiar distance categories.

4.2.2   Extensions from a proposed semantic prototype for D/[Distal]

We sometimes find three-step systems in which the third category, D/[Distal], appears to alternate between two conditions: (a) being at a great distance from both Speaker and Hearer's visual field, or (b) being outside the Speaker's and Hearer's visual field. A prototype-semantic explanation for the concomitance of these two features would be that things which are far away are relatively hard to see. Again we have a development which is similar with what we saw with D/[Medial], in the sense that for some languages the use description of the category is truly a disjunction of the two conditions, for some languages one of the two conditions has become criterial, and for still others the two conditions have become separately lexicalized.

Yidiny, an Australian aboriginal language, is described by Dixon (1977, p. 180 ff.) as having a three-step system for which the D/[Distal] term means 'remote from Speaker' in some dialects but 'not visible to Speaker' in others. In the history of English *yon* and *yonder* there appears to have been variation in respect to distance versus visibility considerations. The *Oxford English Dictionary* tells us, with *yon* and *yonder*, that the Figure is 'at some distance but within sight' and that this interpretation is what is 'usually, and in the later literary language, always' intended. In a field methods class using Bakwiri, in 1978, the investigators were surprised to learn that a category that until then had always been associated with extreme, but gesturally indicatable, remoteness, could also be used to refer to something very close by but obstructed from view. One of the uses of a distance category had lost all association with distance.

Of the two features characterizing the D/[Distal] prototype, remoteness and reduced visibility, some languages settle on one, some on the other, some accept both, and still others develop an additional category. We may add to our notation the opposed pair of features

D/[+ Visible],   D/[− Visible].

4.2.3 *Association of distance categories with non-deictic features*

In some languages the distance categories of the demonstrative system take part in semantic systems involving other features as well. For example, in Lahu (Matisoff, 1973, p. 51) the D/[Medial] and D/[Distal] features exist only for indicating horizontal distances, there being separate demonstrative adverbs for indicating places above and below the location of the Speaker. In Dyirbal a three-step distance system is provided for locations that can be seen as uphill or downhill from the Speaker; a two-step system exists for locations that are upriver or downriver from the Speaker; and a single distance category exists for locations whose distance from the Speaker is expressible independently of rivers and hillsides (Dixon, 1972, p. 48).

Sometimes the distance categories can vary in the number of effective contrasts that operate across grammatical systems. In Brazilian Portuguese (Margarida Salomão, personal communication) the D/[Proximal]: D/[Medial] contrast has been neutralized among the Demonstrative Determiners and the Demonstrative Pronouns, but still operates among the Demonstrative Adverbs. For this we would need to use D/[+Proximal] versus D/[−Proximal] for the former, D/[Proximal], D/[Medial], and D/[Distal] for the latter.

4.3   Lexicalization pattern differences

Space-deictic semantic features can be co-encoded (i.e. instantiated in the same lexical item) with other sorts of information, both grammatical and semantic, in a wide variety of ways. To begin close to home, we have already seen that English encodes the distinction between Singular and Plural with its Demonstrative Determiners and Demonstrative Pronouns. To essentially the same configuration, French adds gender agreement markings, and on top of that many other languages add case agreement information.

The syntactic functions are lexically separated or united with demonstrative categories in different ways in different languages. Japanese lexically separates Demonstrative Determiners, Demonstrative Pronouns and Demonstrative Adverbs from each other with the morphemes *-no* (Determiner), *-re* (Pronoun), and *-ko* (Locative) and *-tira* (Goal Directional). English unites the Pronouns and the Determiners in identical forms; and Quechua reportedly unites them all in a single lexical category.

A number of systems have been described which are of considerable complexity. Asiatic Eskimo, according to Haarmann, quoting Menovščikov (Haarmann, 1975, p. 7), distinguishes horizontal and vertical distances from the speaker, visibility and non-visibility, and definiteness versus indefiniteness, in its system of demonstratives. Aleut, according to Swadesh (1971, p. 196) adds information about the Figure's position, distinguishing sitting from standing, and includes several categories of Figure-positioning based on the Speaker's location among a group of people inside a dwelling. Dyirbal has morphemes combinable in the same word with demonstratives having such meanings as 'out in front of Speaker and Hearer' (Dixon, 1972, p. 48). The Eskimo dialect described by Denny (Denny, 1980; Denny & Issaluk, 1971) indicates distance and pivot information separately: it encodes with the absence or presence of a prefix *ta-* the difference between Speaker-Pivot and Hearer-Pivot, and with other means the distinction between D/[+ Proximal] and D/[− Proximal]. In this language the D/[− Proximal] is obligatory combined with other distinctions, such as whether the Figure is inside or outside of an enclosure, above or below the Pivot, visible or non-visible, or whether it can be regarded as 'extended' or 'non-extended'.

4.4   Differences of morphological patterning

In Section 4.2.3 I was concerned with the dependence of systems of distance contrasts on other syntactic or semantic categories, as with languages that use a two-step system in some context and a three-step system in others. In Section 4.3 my concern was with the grammatical or semantic information that could appear in the same words with information from the system of demonstrative categories. In this section my concern is slightly different: here

I am concerned with mappings between semantic features and elements of the morphological segmentation, that is, with the extent to which the various segments of grammatical and semantic content are represented with separate linguistic material in words expressing demonstrative categories.

English *this* and *here* share the deictic feature D/[+ Proximal], but there is no recurring morphological segment corresponding to this semantic feature. In Dyirbal the distance categories are parasitic on other semantic categories (uphill versus downhill, upriver versus downriver), having no separable morphological realization. At the analytical extreme we find in Japanese that the three-step distance categories are consistently signalled by prefixed forms *ko-*, D/[Proximal], *so-* D/[Medial], and *a-*, D/[Distal], throughout the whole system of demonstrative words.

The study of morphological patterning and paradigms will in some cases show demonstrative systems figuring as part of more inclusive paradigms. The relevant system in Japanese, in fact, includes the interrogative words: alongside of *kore* ('this'), *sore* ('that'-Medial) and *are* ('that'-Distal), there is *dore* ('which?'), and alongside of *koo* ('in this way'), *soo* ('in that (M) way'), and *aa* ('in that (D) way'), we find *doo* ('how?'). An analogous but more limited (and obsolescent) system is found in English with the demonstrative and interrogative locative and directional adverbs: *here* : *there* : *where*; *hence* : *thence* : *whence*; *hither* : *thither* : *whither*.

4.5 The various uses of demonstrative categories

Since different uses of a single demonstrative category in one language can correspond to different morpholexical categories in another language, it will be necessary, in a contrastive study of demonstrative systems, to inquire into the various uses to which the words and categories of the systems can be put. Such a description will take the Informing and Identifying functions as basic, these being by definition essential functions for any system of spatial deixis, and will go on to describe the language-specific exceptions, extensions, and qualifications.

A careful examination of extended uses of demonstrative categories even in English could easily be of monograph length. Here I shall merely identify a small number of such uses and warn the reader that there are many more.

Text reference One extremely common extension of demonstrative categories is from spatial to textual identifications. Most commonly, perhaps, the Proximal category is used for text-referring cataphora, a non-Proximal category for text-referring anaphora. Examples in English can be seen in (40)–(42):

(40) Here's what I propose: let's move in from the west.

(41)   This is his message: let's move in from the west.

(42)   We've got to move in from the west. That's what I've been trying to tell you.

Shared and unshared knowledge   Demonstratives used to identify individuals introduced in a discourse, rather than individuals pointed out in the communicators' deictic space, sometimes distinguish between shared-knowledge and unshared-knowledge identifications. In English this function is given to the Demonstrative Determiners, D/[+Proximal] signalling unshared knowledge, D/[−Proximal] signalling shared knowledge. Thus if I were to say (43) to you, I would give you the impression that I do not intend to let you know right away who my friend is; with (44), however, I would have to assume that you already knew who I was talking about:

(43)   I was visiting this friend of mine last night.

(44)   That man is an absolute idiot.

In Japanese, with its three-step system, essentially the same contrast is handled with the categories D/[Medial] and D/[Distal] respectively (Kuno, 1973, p. 283). In (45), Medial *sore* refers to an experience of the Speaker's which the Hearer did not share; in (46) the Distal form *are* refers to an experience which the Speaker and the Hearer had in common.

(45)   Sore wa yokatta yo. 'That was really nice'.
       'that' (M) + Topic + 'was good' + 'I say'

(46)   Are wa yokatta ne. 'That was nice, wasn't it?'
       'that' (D) + Topic + 'was good' + n'est-ce-pas?'

Serial order   In some languages the preferred rhetoric for indicating two close-by objects is to alternate the distance categories in a particular way. In English we are perfectly happy saying a sentence like (47) while pointing, one after the other, to two different objects:

(47)   Do you want this one or this one?

In Bakwiri, on the other hand, if a speaker identifies two things, each at a distance which would normally call for a D/[Medial] identification, it is most natural to use D/[Distal] for the second object. This usage is so common that informants are likely to translate the D/[Distal] Demonstrative Determiner as 'the other' even when no contrasting situation has been set up.

Others   Many other uses of demonstratives could be isolated, such as those I illustrate without comment with sentences (49)–(51):

(49)   He spoke about this loud.

(50) I never thought I'd be this poor.
(51) I can never expect to be that rich.

Many language-specific restrictions on the use of demonstratives could be listed as well, such as the difference in function between Demonstrative Determiners and Demonstrative Pronouns we find in English. The Pronouns appear to be restricted to inanimate objects (or animate objects that can be treated as inanimate objects), except as the subject of a copulative sentence. The phenomenon is illustrated in sentences (52)–(57) below:

(52) That man is my brother-in-law.
(53) This acorn fell in my soup.
(54) That man married my sister.
(55) That is my brother-in-law.
(56) This fell in my soup.
(57) *That married my sister.

5 SUMMARY AND SAMPLE DESCRIPTIONS

Syntactic functions Demonstratives occur as Sentential Demonstratives, or Presentatives; Demonstrative Pronouns; Demonstrative Determiners; and Demonstrative Adverbs of types Locative, Goal, Source, and Manner. We have symbolized these as D (for Demonstrative) marked with

Se[__(NP)],   NP[__],   NP[__N],
Lo[__],   Go[__],   So[__],   Ma[__].

Distance contrasts and their extensions Demonstratives may have no distance contrasts, or may have a two-step or a three-step distance contrast. The two contrasting systems were represented as

[+ Proximal] : [− Proximal],
[Proximal] : [Medial] : [Distal].

The Medial category in a three-step system has 'short distance from Speaker' and 'close to Hearer' as the two elements of its semantic prototype. Where these, by historical development or specialization, require special mention in the description of the semantics of a Medial form, the notation we have suggested is

[SMedial] : [HProximal].

In those cases where Speaker-as-Pivot and Hearer-as-Pivot have been separated within the demonstrative paradigm, we have suggested using the following features in combination with the usual distance categories:

[SPivot] : [HPivot].

The Distal category in a three-step system has 'far from the Speaker' and 'invisible to Speaker' as the two elements of its semantic prototype. Where visibility has entered into the semantic or morphological structure independently we can use the features:

[+ Visible] : [− Visible].

Other features that combine with demonstrative categories can be taken from the standard terminology of other grammatical and semantic domains, such as

[Plural],   [Accusative],   [Uphill].

Secondary uses can be described informally.

Here are some sample descriptions of demonstrative forms, using the symbols and categories introduced above. The elements of the description include the following: Morphology (the analysis, where appropriate, of the morphological composition of the form), Syntax (the syntactic character of the demonstrative form), Distance Feature, Combining Features, and Usage Notes.

HERE (English)
    Morphology: NA
    Syntax: Lo[__]
    Distance [+ Proximal]
    Combining Features: NA
    Usage Notes: has cataphoric textual use
THOSE (English)
    Morphology: (th- common in expressions of definite reference)
    Syntax: NP[__N]
    Distance: [− Proximal]
    Combining Features: [Plural]
    Usage Notes: anaphoric in discourse; shared knowledge
HITHER (English)
    Morphology: (h- common in Proximal forms; -ither common in Goal forms)
    Syntax: Go[__]
    Distance: [+ Proximal]
    Combining Features: NA
    Usage Notes: obsolescent
ECCE (Latin)
    Morphology: NA
    Syntax: Se[__(NP)]
    Distance: NA
    Combining Features: NA

Usage Notes: introduced NP is either nominative or accusative

EVO (Serbo-Croatian)

  Morphology: (similar pattern, *eCo*, found in other presentatives: *eno* and *eto*)

  Syntax: Se[__NP]

  Distance: [Proximal]?

  Combining Features: NA

  Usage Notes: introduced NP is either nominative or genitive

ATIRA (Japanese)

  Morphology: *a*- is [Distal], *-tira* is Go[__]

  Syntax: Go[__]

  Distance: [Distal]

  Combining Features: NA

  Usage Notes: usable as Lo[__] in polite speech

ènèέ (Bakwiri)

  Morphology: (similar pattern, as in ɔnɔɔ́, with other gender classes)

  Syntax: NP[__N]

  Distance: [Distal]

  Combining Features: here, selection for nouns of a particular gender class

  Usage Notes: usable in indicating 'second object' in a series, even when at a distance ordinarily calling for [Medial]

KIUNGA (Inuktitut Eskimo)

  Morphology: *ki*-, external to a bounded area; *-unga*, Go[__]

  Syntax: Go[__]

  Distance: [−Proximal]

  Combining Features: [Exterior], taken from a five-way contrast for [−Proximal] forms, translated as 'up there', 'down there', 'in there', 'out there', and 'over there'

  Usage Notes: Speaker must be inside the bounded area which the Figure comes to be outside

NOTES

1. I am indebted to the Max Planck Institute for Psycholinguistics, Nijmegen, The Netherlands, for giving me, on two occasions, opportunities for discussing the subject of this paper with the Institute's staff and facilities for working on the various revisions it has passed through in the past two years.

2. For a statement of the contrast I have in mind, see Fillmore (1975).

3. A feature of Locomotion, also required, does not take part in the prototype character of the concept.

   There are alternative interpretations of the observations just outlined. One is that precisely because of the acceptability and interpretation judgements that have just been reviewed, each of the proposed semantic features of the verb has been shown to be inessential and therefore not part of the meaning of the word. The fact that the descending monkey can be described as climbing shows that the Ascending condition is not criterial; and the fact that the ascending snail can be said to be climbing shows that the Clambering condition is not criterial. The essential semantic character of our verb, according to such an argument, would have to be some property or properties distinct from each of these. If such a core feature for *climb* could be discovered, then, of course, this verb would cease to serve as an example for prototype semantic descriptions of this first type. But I insist that it will not do for the theoretician to posit an unanalysed feature that, by fiat, will stand for whatever it is that characterizes *climb* in all of its instances. That would amount to no more than disguising, by finding a name for, the problem we have been facing.

A second interpretation that would allow us to do without a prototype account of *climb* is that, whatever the word's original meaning might have been, it is now polysemous, so that in any given occurrence of it, it will have either its Ascending or its Clambering sense. If we were to take such a view, then we would expect that whenever we hear a report that a monkey has climbed up a tree, we would be inclined to ask—and we would find it sensible to ask—'In which sense of *climb* did you mean that?'. But such a question would clearly be inappropriate.

4. On the notion 'cue validity' see Rosch (1977).

5. The importance of all of these factors in a semantic description has been demonstrated with particular force and clarity in David Bennett's stratificationalist treatment of the semantics of English locative prepositions (see Bennett, 1975; see also Talmy, 1980; Leech, 1969).

6. Clark (1973) argues, however, that properties of human beings might be relevant to explaining the 'markedness' relations of the oppositions in the up/down axis.

7. For a discussion of the linguistic reflexes of point of view in literary texts, see especially Banfield (1973) and Fillmore (1976).

8. See, for example, Tanz (1980) and Hill (1974, 1975).

9. In important and common departures from the prototype situation, we find situations in which the 'addressee' cannot be characterized as the 'intended hearer'. One can intend to be overheard.

10. See Hattori (1968). Of special interest is Hattori's report that he lived in Tokyo for decades before discovering this particular discrepancy between his speech and that of the Tokyo standard. Since in the two dialects the D/[Medial] category has the same prototypic use, the situations in which their disagreements could be revealed come up naturally only rarely. One wonders what social mechanisms allow features of this sort to be areally distributed.

REFERENCES

Banfield, A. (1973). Narrative style and the grammar of direct and indirect speech. *Foundations of Language*, **10**, 1–39.
Bennett, D. C. (1975). *Spatial and temporal uses of English prepositions: an essay in stratificational semantics*. London: Longmans.

Berlin, B., & Kay, P. (1969). *Basic color terms: their universality and evolution*. Berkeley: University of California Press.

Clark, H. H. (1973). Space, time, semantics and the child. In T. E. Moore (ed.), *Cognitive development and the acquisition of language*. New York: Academic Press.

Denny, J. P. (1980). Semantics of the Inuktitut (Eskimo) spatial deictics. Research Bulletin No. 503, Department of Psychology, University of Western Ontario (revised version).

Denny, J. P., & Issaluk, L. (1971). Semantically organized tables of Inuktitut locatives. Research Bulletin No. 352, Department of Psychology, University of Western Ontario.

Dixon, R. M. W. (1972). *The Dyirbal language of North Queensland*. London: Cambridge University Press.

Dixon, R. M. W. (1977). *A grammar of Yidiny*. London: Cambridge University Press.

Fillmore, C. J. (1975). An alternative to checklist theories of meaning. In C. Cogen, H. Thompson, & J. Wright (eds), *Papers of the first meeting of the Berkeley Linguistic Society*. Berkeley: University of California.

Fillmore, C. J. (1976). Pragmatics and the description of discourse. In S. Schmidt (ed.), *Pragmatik II*. Munich: Wilhelm Fink Verlag.

Haarman, H. Sprachtypologische Analyse des deiktischen Systems und ihre pragmatische Verwertbarkeit. Linguistic Agency, University of Trier, Germany.

Hattori, S. (1968). Kore, sore, are to this, that. In *Eigo kiso goi no kenkyuu*. Tokyo: English Language Educational Council.

Hill, C. A. (1974). Spatial perception and linguistic encoding: a case study in Hausa and English. *Studies in African Linguistics*, **5**, 135–148.

Hill, C. A. (1975). Variation in the use of 'front' and 'back' by bilingual speakers. In C. Cogen, H. Thompson, & J. Wright (eds), *Proceedings of the first annual meeting of the Berkeley Linguistic Society*. Berkeley: University of California.

Kuno, S. (1973). *The structure of the Japanese language*. Cambridge, Mass.: M.I.T. Press.

Lakoff, G. P. (1973). Hedges: a study in meaning criteria and the logic of fuzzy concepts. In C. Corum, T. C. Smith-Stark, & A. Weiser (eds), *Proceedings of the ninth annual meeting of the Chicago Linguistic Society*. Chicago: Chicago Linguistic Society.

Leech, G. (1969). *Towards a semantic description of English*. London: Longmans.

Lyons, J. (1977). *Semantics*, Vol. 2. London: Cambridge University Press.

Matisoff, J. A. (1973). *The grammar of Lahu* (Publications in Linguistics No. 75). Berkeley: University of California Press.

Rosch, E. (1975). Universals and cultural specifics in human categorization. In R. Brislin (ed.), *Cross-cultural perspectives on learning*. New York: Halstead Press.

Rosch, E. (1977). Human categorization. In N. Warren (ed.), *Advances in cross-cultural psychology*, Vol. 1. London: Academic Press.

Rosch, E., & Mervis, C. B. (1975). Family resemblance: studies in the internal structure of categories. *Cognitive Psychology*, **7**, 573–605.

Swadesh, M. (1971). *The origin and diversification of language*. London: Aldine Atherton Press.

Talmy, L. (1980). The representation of space by language. Manuscript, Cognitive Science Program, University of California at San Diego.

Tanz, C. (1980). *Studies in the acquisition of deictic terms*. London: Cambridge University Press.

Speech, Place, and Action
Edited by R. J. Jarvella and W. Klein
© 1982 John Wiley & Sons Ltd.

Some Problems in the Theory of Demonstrative Reference[1]

GEORGE A. MILLER

The same thought, when entertained by different people or by the same person at different times, can evoke different actions. I may remember, for example, that I need to buy a present for a friend. If I am busy when this thought occurs to me, it may evoke no action, but if I have the same thought near a shopping district, it may lead to obtaining a present. And if you had the same thought—that George Miller needs to buy a present for a friend—you would act still differently.

Two senses of 'thought' are involved here, corresponding to the distinction between types and tokens. Tokens occur in different contexts; types are abstracted away from contextual particularities. A psychological theory of thinking must presuppose some way to individuate tokens of the same type of thought; the only apparent way to do so is in terms of the contexts in which thought-tokens occur. Two different thought-tokens of the same thought-type can evoke different actions; it is the thought-token in-a-context that determines action.

To utter a sentence is to take a kind of action, so it is not surprising that the same thought, when entertained by different people or by the same person at different times, can evoke different utterances. In the example above, I would express the thought by uttering 'I need to buy a present for my friend', whereas you would express the same thought by uttering 'You need to buy a present for your friend'. If you were to say 'I need to buy a present for my friend', you would express a different thought. This situation is usually described by saying that different sentences can express the same proposition, or the same sentence can express different propositions, depending on the occasion of use.

In order to determine what thought a person expresses by the utterance of a particular sentence, therefore, it may be necessary to take account of the context in which the sentence is uttered. Perhaps it is always necessary, even for eternal sentences like 'Snow is white' or 'The moon is a sphere', if the speaker's intentions are taken as part of the thought. But it is certainly necessary whenever a sentence contains deictic words or phrases, which are defined as expressions having the property that the manner of determining their reference in various circumstances depends crucially on the context in which they are used.

There are, therefore, obvious similarities between the psychological problem of relating thoughts to actions and the linguistic problem of relating sentences to thoughts. The linguistic problem has been analysed in great detail; a psychologist might profit from considering that analysis as a model. Fortunately, some reasonably definite proposals have been advanced by David Kaplan (1977), which can be taken as a starting point.

KAPLAN ON DEMONSTRATIVES

Kaplan divides the indexical words that he is concerned with into demonstrative indexicals ('that', 'there', 'he') and pure indexicals ('I', 'here', 'now'). These words may be used for other purposes, but Kaplan is interested in their use to establish a referent in some given context of use.

Demonstratives (pronouns or adjectives) preserve a gestural component in spoken language; they are incomplete without an associated *demonstration*—an ostensive gesture (or even a definite description) that demonstrates a particular individual (person, thing, event), the *demonstratum*. When a demonstration is set in a particular context, it must select an individual 'that has the appearance A from here now', if there is one; otherwise it demonstrates nothing. Thus, the demonstration determines the relevant perspective from which the demonstratum is presented—the *manner of presentation* of the demonstratum.

Pure indexicals need not be accompanied by a demonstration, although they may be. If we think of the indexical system Kaplan is concerned with as being 'speaker oriented', then pure indexicals are the unmarked cases: 'I' is the speaker, 'here' is the speaker's location, 'now' is the time of the speaker's utterance. The pure indexicals define a point of origin for a spatio-temporal manifold in which demonstrative indexicals (marked by demonstrations) can be produced and interpreted.

All indexicals are, in Kaplan's terminology, 'directly referential'. That is to say, in order to evaluate the truth of any proposition expressed by a sentence using one of these words in a particular context, it is always the referent of the word in that context that is relevant. In order to evaluate the truth of 'He (accompanied by the demonstration of a particular person) is a thief', it is only the person demonstrated who is relevant; the fact that other persons could have been demonstrated does not affect the truth value of what was said. By contrast, the truth value of 'The butler is a thief' will depend on who the butler is; it may be true of some butlers and false of others.

To define 'he' as, say, 'the male person that the speaker is demonstrating', is not completely correct, therefore, since 'he' is directly referential, whereas the definite description, 'the male person that the speaker is demonstrating', is not directly referential. Kaplan introduces a one-place functor 'dthat' to represent the general case; it has the effect of converting any description a into a directly referential expression: dthat $[a]$, where a is any singular term that functions as the associated demonstration. For example, the pure indexical 'I' means the same as 'dthat [the individual who utters this token]'; the demonstrative indexical 'that', when completed by a demonstration involving the special appearance A, means the same as 'dthat [the individual having the appearance A from here now]'.

It would seem, therefore, that there is one sense in which a deictic word has variable meaning, since it can refer to different individuals in different contexts of use, and another sense in which it has constant meaning, since all speakers of English use it in the same way. Kaplan introduces a valuable terminological distinction between these two kinds of meaning, which he calls *content* and *character*.

The content of a sentence is what it says, the proposition it expresses (roughly the same as a Fregean Sinn or an intension); content is represented by replacing all deictic terms by the demonstrata they determine. 'The chair is over there', for example, when accompanied by an appropriate demonstration, means that the chair at time t (the time of utterance) is located at the spatial coordinates (x, y, z) (the place indicated by the speaker's demonstration). Content is sensitive to context; the same sentence used in a different context (a different chair, a different room, a different time) could have a different content. The truth value of the sentence is evaluated by considering its content in a variety of factual or counterfactual circumstances (possible worlds).

On the other hand, the character of a sentence is not sensitive to context. It is part of our linguistic knowledge of English that 'there' always refers directly to a demonstrated location whenever it is used in a demonstrative sense, and that it may refer to different locations on different occasions. Thus, a character is a semantic rule that we can use to determine the content in different contexts. In short, character maps contexts into contents, and content maps circumstances into extensions (into truth value, in the case of propositional contents). The distinction between *contexts* in which sentences are uttered and *circumstances* in which their contents are evaluated as true or false is basic in Kaplan's theory.

The character of a demonstrative can be taken either broadly or narrowly. That is to say, the character of a demonstrative can be thought of simply as the semantic rule, in which case two uses of a demonstrative with different demonstrations would be taken as having the same character. Or the demonstrative can be thought of as assuming a character only when completed by a particular demonstration, in which case two uses of a demonstrative with different demonstrations would be taken as having different characters. Kaplan seems to favour the narrow, more discriminating version, so that two demonstrations of the same individual will have different characters if the appearance A of that individual in one demonstration is different from its appearance A' in the second. In that case, the identification of the character of an indexical with the semantic rule that every speaker of English knows would be legitimate only for the pure indexicals, which need not be accompanied by demonstrations.

The difference between content and character has been generally overlooked because character is fixed in non-deictic language. That is to say, in non-deictic language the same content is invoked in all contexts, and it is natural to identify character with the content it determines. In deictic language, however, the situation is different. Deictic terms refer directly. (The semantic rules do not provide a complex which together with a circumstance of evaluation yields an object; they simply provide an object.) Although the demonstrative 'there' *refers* to the place at which the speaker is pointing, 'there' and 'the place at which the speaker is pointing' are not synonyms. If they were truly synonyms, it should follow that, if the speaker was not pointing to a place, it would not be there. Indexicals do not have synonyms.

Kaplan notes that 'I'm here' (when 'here' is used as a pure indexical) will be true in every context in which it is uttered.[2] By the logic of demonstratives, 'I'm here' is logically true. Note, however, that 'It is necessary that I am here' is false, since the speaker might well have been somewhere else. He offers 'I am here' as an example of an expression that is both analytic and contingent. It is analytic by virtue of the character of 'I', 'am', and 'here', but it is contingent because the content it expresses on any given occasion of use will be true under some circumstances and false under others.

EPISTEMOLOGICAL REMARKS

If we accept Kaplan's distinction between content and character, we can ask about their epistemological status. We have seen that it is necessary to distinguish between a thought and the cognitive significance of a thought—between, say, 'I need to buy a present for a friend' and the significance of this thought for my actions in different contexts. Kaplan associates the epistemological notion of a thought with the semantic notion of a content, and the epistemological notion of the cognitive significance of a thought with the semantic notion of character.

Imagine that a chair you want to sit in is across the room. You look at the chair and say to yourself, 'The chair is over there'. Then you walk across the room, after which you say, 'The chair is here', and sit down. The thought (content) expressed in both sentences is the same, namely, that the chair is located at the spatial coordinates (x, y, z). The cognitive significance of the thought differs, however, on its two occurrences: in the first context it evokes walking, in the later context it evokes sitting. This difference in cognitive significance is correlated with different characters—'over there' versus 'here'—and Kaplan accordingly proposes that cognitive significance is identified with character.

Appreciating the character of an expression entails being able to handle the logic of indexical terms. No special or direct knowledge of the things involved is required. Kaplan considers a kidnapped heiress, locked in the trunk of a car, knowing neither the time nor where she is, who thinks, 'It's quiet here now'. 'Here' still refers directly to her spatial location and 'now' to the time of the thought, even though, by the definition of content, the kidnapped heiress would be unable to determine the content of her own thought. 'It is quiet here' is meaningful—there is some sense in which the heiress knows what she is thinking—even when she cannot use the semantic rules to determine the place in any other way and could not tell whether a later occurrence of 'It is quiet here' was the same or a different thought.

The assumption that character is the semantic counterpart of cognitive significance enables Kaplan to propose an explanation for how the sentence 'This is identical to that', if true, could convey new information. If the sentence is true, the content of 'this' and the content of 'that' (and also, of course, their demonstrata) must be identical in the context of utterance. Therefore, the cognitive difference between 'this' and 'that' cannot be explained as a difference of content (as it can be in Frege's example, 'The Morning Star is identical to the Evening Star'). It can be explained, however, as a difference of character if we assume that the character of an expression includes, in addition to the general semantic rule, the appearance of the demonstratum: the manner of presentation accompanying 'this' could be sufficiently different from the manner of presentation accompanying 'that' that the identity would be nonobvious. (Imagine an object passing behind a screen.)

In proposing this explanation Kaplan assumes that, since a demonstration in context determines a content, a character may be likened to a manner of presentation of a content. If different apprehensions of the same thought are to be individuated by their differences in manner of presentation, then characters must be similarly individuated. If the character of an expression were nothing more than the general semantic rule for determining the content of a type of word or phrase, no informative uses of 'that = that' could occur.

The need to complete the character of an expression by including the appearance of the demonstratum can be illustrated by the example of crossing the room to a chair. Suppose that, instead of saying to yourself 'The chair is over there' and 'The chair is here', you had said, 'I'm here', and again, after crossing, 'I'm here'. In this case, the content of the two sentences is different, since the speaker is in different places. The character of the two sentences, however, involves the same semantic rule and so, if that rule were all there was to character, the character would be the same. By the same argument as before, we should conclude that the cognitive significance of a thought is associated with the content of the sentence: different contents evoke different actions, while character remains unchanged. In order to save Kaplan's identification of cognitive significance with character, it is necessary to include the appearance of the demonstratum as part of the completed character, since then 'I'm here' will also have a different character in its two uses. Then both the content and the character are different before and after, and we have no basis for deciding which relates to the different cognitive significance of the two thoughts.

The use of 'I'm here' to individuate places is puzzling, however, if only for the reason that this sentence involves pure indexicals which generally require no associated demonstration. Without a demonstration of an individual having the appearance A from here now, there can be no difference in character. In this example (it is not Kaplan's), the association of character with cognitive significance seems to be persuasive only under a particular choice of the deictic expressions you happen to use.

Perhaps there is no semantic correlate for the epistemological notion of the cognitive significance of a thought.

MEMORY REPRESENTATIONS

Kaplan also raises the problem of cognitive dynamics. How are beliefs that are originally formulated with deictic expressions retained in memory? Is it the content or the character that is remembered? How, for example, do you remember where you were before you crossed the room to sit in the chair? Obviously, you cannot remember it as 'I'm here'. Is there some standard adjustment that you make in the character of what you retain, similar to the adjustments required when deictic expressions are reported in indirect quotation? Or must all deictic expressions be replaced in memory by non-deictic expressions, and the content remembered with fixed character?

If only content were remembered, then a person like the kidnapped heiress who has lost track of space and time would not be able to remember what had happened. Or she might not be able to make the appropriate adjustments in character: to switch correctly, say, from 'It was quiet here today' to 'It was quiet here yesterday'. In particular, what happens when you change your mind? Consider another of Kaplan's examples: If, on glancing in a mirror, I first believe that his pants are on fire and then discover that my pants are on fire, I will still believe that the pants of the man seen in the mirror are on fire (the content is the same), but the character ('my pants' versus 'his pants') has changed. If only content is retained, how do I remember this incident?

A cognitive psychologist might take these puzzles as arguments for the view that what is retained in memory is not retained either in linguistic form (with an appropriately adjusted character) or in propositional form (with all references determined and explicit). Perhaps what is retained is a mental representation of the episode itself—a representation that is non-linguistic, yet adequate to support linguistic descriptions, with or without deictic terms, at a later time. The nature of that representation is psychologically mysterious, but it seems closer to the manner of presentation of the entire episode than to either the content or character of sentences used to describe it.

The claim that memory representations are not stored in linguistic or propositional form need not imply that what is retained is indifferent either to habitual modes or thought or to obligatory forms of linguistic expression. Memory is selective. The grounds for selection are various: a person's interests, intentions, and expectations can be shown to affect what is recalled, as can the language that the person speaks. If, for example, a language requires a speaker to know ages in speaking of kinfolk, it will be habitual for users of that language to take special note of people's ages in what they remember, but that information need not be stored in linguistic or propositional form.

If, in what I take to be the spirit of Kaplan's epistemological remarks, we take the manner of presentation as what is retained in memory, then what is retained must be the appearance A of some individual as determined from the perspective given by a particular demonstration. But this, as many cognitive psychologists would prefer, is not a linguistic or propositional object of thought. It is a (selectively incomplete) mental representation of the demonstratum itself.

OSTENSIVE DEFINITION

Parents and teachers often explain the meaning of a word to children by demonstrating one or more instances. This method of instruction can be highly effective for proper nouns and for many common nouns denoting concrete objects. Its effectiveness poses a puzzle, however, because there is usually an indefinite variety of hypotheses that a child could entertain as to what has been demonstrated. If, for example, an adult points to a cat and says 'That is a cat', how does a child know that 'cat' refers to the whole animal, and not to some property of the cat (colour, size, weight, odour, warmth), or to some part of the cat (head, body, tail, hair), or to some posture, developmental stage, or orientation of the cat, or to some combination of these, or even to some aspect of the act of demonstration itself? Coupling 'cat' with a variety of instances differing in non-criterial attributes is supposed to eliminate some hypotheses (assuming that children are capable of abstracting common features and discarding others), but it also opens up the possibility that 'cat' refers to the sequence, number, or timing of the instances.

In order to understand how children grasp so quickly the demonstrata that adults have in mind, we must assume that their perceptual experiences are

organized by the same principles as are adults'. In particular, their perceptions are organized into figure and ground, by familiar laws of gestalt. Then
we can assume the priority of the figure: in any stable perceptual field the
most salient figure experienced from the perspective determined by the
demonstration will be taken as the demonstratum, and the ground will be
taken as its context.

The problem with this assumption, of course, is that we often do define
properties, parts, relations, or other features ostensively. If the salient figure
is always the demonstratum, how can we refer ostensively to anything else?

DEFERRED OSTENSION

Quine (1971) has noted that the referent of a deictic expression is not always
the demonstratum of the associated demonstration. We point to a gas gauge,
for example, in order to show that there is gasoline in the tank. Quine calls
this *deferred ostension* and notes that it occurs very naturally when we have a
correspondence in mind between the demonstratum and the referent.

The nature of the correspondence that we have in mind must be rather
special, however. Surely there is a correspondence (in some sense) between a
son and his father, yet it would seldom be possible to point at a son in order to
refer to his father. Why does the correspondence between gas gauge and
gasoline support deferred ostension, whereas the correspondence between
son and father does not?

An obvious answer is that the correspondence between gas gauge and
gasoline derives from a particular social convention about gauges, and no
corresponding convention exists with respect to sons and fathers. But this
merely rephrases the question. Under what conditions is it possible to establish a convention that one thing can point to another?

Our ability to understand deferred ostension does not always depend on a
referential convention. It can occur spontaneously in novel situations. Nunberg (1977) gives the example of a waitress saying 'He's sitting at table 20'
while pointing to a ham sandwich.[3] Someone unfamiliar with any referential
conventions of restaurant personnel can understand that 'he', accompanied
by a gesture to an inanimate object, is intended to refer to a person somehow
associated with that object—in this case, associated by virtue of the relation
'the x who ordered y', where x is the referent and y the demonstratum. This
relation, which is part of our general knowledge of what goes on in restaur-
ants, will support deferred ostension. It is a relation that selects a unique
referent associated with the demonstratum.

Nunberg uses such examples to argue that a complete account of demonstrative reference will require (at least) two theories. One, like Kaplan's, will
explain how a deictic term enables a hearer to identify a physically present
demonstratum. The other will explain how the hearer's knowledge of the

demonstratum enables him to identify the referent of the deictic term; it will provide a function that takes the demonstratum as its argument and provides a referent as its value. He calls this function the *referring function* of a given use of a term. (It should be noted, however, that deferred ostension is possible only with demonstrative indexicals, not with pure indexicals.)

Nunberg argues that deferred ostension will work when the speaker chooses as the referring function that function relating the demonstratum to the referent that has the greatest cue validity. A property has high cue validity for an individual b in a set B if it is likely that people will believe that b has that property and nothing else in B does. (If there is only one red book on a shelf, then 'red' has high cue validity for that book.) Thus, given a range of alternative referents appropriate to the discourse, the cue validity of a function f for a referent b depends on the degree to which people are likely to believe that, for a given demonstratum a, b has the property of being the value of $f(a)$, and nothing else in the range of appropriate alternatives has that property. Thus, the choice of the best function (the function with highest cue validity) for referring to b must be made in the light of what the speaker believes that other people are likely to believe.

According to Nunberg, the reason that 'father of' will not usually serve as a referring function is that the demonstratum himself is usually in the range of possible referents. Otherwise said, when 'he' is used with a male person as the demonstratum to refer to a male person, the function with the highest cue validity for selecting an individual from the set of male persons is the identity function, $f(a) = a$. When the context is such that the identity function is applicable, it will always be chosen because it has the highest cue validity. In order that the identity function be rejected, the context must allow that the demonstratum not be in the range of possible referents.

An instance of deferred ostension occurs when we demonstrate an individual in order to refer to one of its properties—when, to use one of Quine's examples, we point to grass in order to refer to green—in which case the referring function is 'is the colour of'.

Or, again, we demonstrate an individual in order to refer to all individuals of that type. Nunberg gives the example, 'The chair you're sitting in is commonly seen in eighteenth century interiors', where the definite description, 'the chair your're sitting in', demonstrates a particular individual, but the predicate phrase is understood as applying to individuals of that type. Even clearer: 'That (pointing to the chair) is commonly seen in eighteenth century interiors'. One might ask why, since the identity function seems to be available, this sentence is not understood unequivocally as meaning that the particular token demonstrated is moved through many different interiors. (Imagine many different stage settings.) Such an interpretation is available; the ground for rejecting it is its implausibility (outside theatrical contexts), given our general (non-linguistic) knowledge of eighteenth century interiors and the conventions of chair ownership. From the context we assume that the range of possible referents is types of furniture, not particular articles of furniture.

Nunberg assumes that there are certain prime functions available to use as referring functions (or to combine into compound referring functions), one of which must be 'is a type of'. This 'hypostatic function', like the identity function, has high cue validity. A substitution of the hypostatic for the identity function in the case of the chair that is commonly seen in eighteenth century interiors leads to a more plausible interpretation, and goes so smoothly that we scarcely notice that the demonstratum of the subject phrase is not the referent.

A kind of ostensive metonymy occurs when we demonstrate part of an object with the intention of referring to the whole. When we point to the nearest side of an object without intending to exclude its unseen parts, no deferred ostension need be intended; the salient figure from the perspective determined by the demonstration can be the whole object. But often there will be a salient part of the larger whole, in which case the referent may be mistaken unless the context excludes either the part or the whole from the range of possible referents.

Nunberg's analysis raises important questions for psychologists. What prime functions are available for use as referring functions? Does deferred ostension occur in all languages and, if so, are the same prime functions universally available? Are some prime functions innate and, if not, how are they learned by children? How, in detail, are the values of such functions computed, and how is the cue validity of a function for a particular hearer computed? How are prime functions combined to yield compound referring functions? Are referring functions involved, as Nunberg believes, in semantic extensions? In metaphor and metonymy? It should be apparent that this is a picture, not a theory, of deferred ostension, and that much remains to be done. The virtue of the picture, however, is that it shows what a theory relating demonstrata to referents would have to do, and suggests the range of phenomena to which it is related.

One product of such a theory should be an explanation of the effectiveness of ostensive definitions for teaching children the meanings of words. It is apparently a fact (Nelson, 1973) that the first words children learn for concrete objects are names of things easily seen as integral, manipulable figures against a ground: 'doll', 'cookie', 'doggie', 'ball'. Such observations argue for the priority of the figure as the demonstratum that a child will initially assume an adult is naming. Words for properties, parts, stages, and the like are learned later. For example, if a white cup is used as a demonstratum to teach the word 'white', a child who has not already learned that cups are called 'cup' should mistake 'white' for the name of the cup. Presumably, a child who does already know 'cup' will recognize that something else is being demonstrated and will induce the colour after seeing a sufficient variety of instances. The relation, '*ref* = colour (*dem*)', however, is not easy for young children to grasp. The difference between the identity and the hypostatic relations ('Mary' versus 'a doll', for example) seems to be learned much earlier (Katz, Baker & Macnamara, 1974), perhaps because common nouns are marked in English by determiners.

EXTENDED DIRECT REFERENCE

What are the implications of deferred ostension for Kaplan's claim that indexicals are directly referential? A singular term is directly referential if it determines an individual that *is* the propositional content corresponding to that term; a singular term is not directly referential if it determines a propositional content that, together with a set of circumstances, determines an individual. The manner of presentation is more complicated in the case of deferred ostension, but it is still only the referent of the demonstrative that is relevant for evaluating the truth of what was said. Referring functions are not propositional contents associated uniformly with particular demonstratives; different referring functions can be used with the same demonstrative, or the same referring function can be used with different demonstratives. The insertion of a referring function between the demonstratum and the referent of a demonstrative term does not affect the claim that the demonstrative is directly referential. We can regard it as an extended form of direct reference.

The part of Kaplan's argument that requires modification is the formulation of character. In the case of demonstrative indexicals, character can involve a combination of two mappings: (a) one that maps contexts into demonstrata, and (b) another that maps demonstrata into contents. Nunberg has suggested that the functions required for (b) should be called referring functions. It would be misleading to use character to refer to the functions involved in (a), since Kaplan has dedicated that term to the composite mapping. Therefore, let us use *demonstrative functions* to refer to the functions in (a), which depend on an accompanying demonstration. For extended direct reference, therefore, we need three levels of functions: (i) demonstrative functions map contexts into demonstrata; (ii) referring functions map demonstrata into contents; (iii) content maps circumstances into extensions.

With extended direct reference, the sentence 'I am here now' is not analytic—true in all contexts by virtue of the logic of indexicals—because 'here' can be used as a demonstrative, rather than a pure indexical. A person in New York who points to Chicago on a map and says 'I am here now' is using a referring function to go from the demonstratum of 'here' (the point demonstrated on the map) to the referent (Chicago). Obviously, referring functions can be used falsely. Kaplan's logic of indexicals is limited to pure indexicals and to those cases of demonstrative indexicals where the identity function is used to determine the referent.

The critical point for any psychology of demonstrative reference, however, is that referring functions not only presuppose that a speaker is able to select a function with high cue validity on the basis of general knowledge of the relations between the referent and the demonstratum, but that this selection must be conditioned by the speaker's beliefs about the hearer's knowledge of those relations. As Nunberg demonstrates, the pragmatics of demonstrative reference is a rich and interesting topic.

NOTES

1. Preparation of this paper was supported in part by Grant No. BNS77-16612 from the National Science Foundation to The Rockefeller University. I am indebted to Stanley Peters and Nathan U. Salmon for comments on earlier versions of this paper.

2. When someone points to a map and says 'I'm here', 'here' is used as a demonstrative, not a pure indexical.

3. Stenning (1978) notes that such deferrals also occur in anaphora. In 'Fred painted his front door red, whereas Freda painted it white', the anaphoric pronoun 'it' can be understood either as Fred's front door (the salient antecedent) or, by deferral, as Freda's front door. He comments that 'Anaphors can even take their sense from ostensions of non-linguistic context rather than from linguistic antecedents' (Stenning, 1978, p. 184). Perhaps the distinction between anaphoric and demonstrative pronouns is not as sharp as is often assumed.

REFERENCES

Kaplan, D. (1977). Demonstratives: An essay on the semantics, logic, metaphysics, and epistemology of demonstratives and other indexicals. Paper presented for Symposium on Demonstratives at a meeting of the Pacific Division of the American Philosophical Association.

Katz, N., Baker, E., & Macnamara, J. (1974). What's in a name? A study of how children learn common and proper nouns. *Child Development*, **45**, 469–473.

Nelson, K. (1973). Structure and strategy in learning to talk. *Monographs of the Society for Research in Child Development*, No. 149.

Nunberg, G. D. (1977). The pragmatics of reference. Doctoral dissertation, City University of New York. Reproduced by the Indiana University Linguistics Club, Bloomington, Indiana.

Quine, W. V. (1971). The inscrutability of reference. In D. D. Steinberg & L. A. Jakobovits (eds), *Semantics: an interdisciplinary reader in philosophy, linguistics and psychology*. Cambridge: Cambridge University Press.

Stenning, K. (1978). Anaphora as an approach to pragmatics. In Halle, J. Bresnan, & G. A. Miller (eds), *Linguistic theory and psychological reality*. Cambridge, Mass.: MIT Press.

Speech, Place, and Action
Edited by R. J. Jarvella and W. Klein
© 1982 John Wiley & Sons Ltd.

Three Local Deictics

ARNIM VON STECHOW

1 INTRODUCTION

In this paper I will be concerned mainly with the syntax and semantics of the German demonstrative adverbs *hier* ('here'), *da* ('there'), and *dort* ('yon'). In recent years, the semantics of some uses of these words and deictic words in general has become much clearer, especially as a result of papers by Fillmore (1975) and Kaplan (1977). However, Fillmore gives an informal account of some phenomena connected with deixis and Kaplan offers a logical treatment. So neither approach can be adapted in a straightforward way to German grammar. Fillmore offers no grammar at all and Kaplan develops a formal language quite distant from any natural language such as English or German. This situation has been changed by work done by Bennett (1978). Bennett has tried to integrate deictic words into a Montague grammar. His work is in several aspects closely related to Kaplan's, but there are differences. The main difference is, of course, that Bennett offers a syntax which comes close to the actual syntax of English. Other differences concern details. Both agree on the fact that a word like *here* is *directly referential*, i.e. it has no descriptive content but refers directly to some place. The sentence

(1) *It's snowing here.*

may express the proposition that it is snowing on the Axalp or that it is snowing in Brienz, dependending on the circumstances whether (1) is uttered on the Axalp or in Brienz. In the first case, the content of *here* is the Axalp (a place above Brienz) and in the second case, the content of *here* is Brienz (a place, too). Places are not concepts but simply individuals. So deictic words like *here* 'express' individuals in some sense. Brienz or the Axalp may be parts of a proposition expressed by an utterance of (1). This is Kaplan's point. I will accept this view and it has, as we will see, interesting consequences for the semantics of *hier*, *da*, and *dort*.

But there is presumably at least one important difference between Kaplan's and Bennett's approach, namely the way the two authors treat the demonstrative pronoun *this*. Consider the following sentence:

73

(2) *This man drinks Moishe Shicker liquor.*

Although Kaplan doesn't treat the word *this* explicitly, it is in the spirit of his theory that the term *this man* is directly referential. If (2) is uttered in a context where Wolfgang is the only man, then (2) expresses the proposition that Wolfgang drinks Moishe Shicker liquor. If Ede is the only man at the context of utterance, then (2) expresses the proposition that Ede drinks that liquor. Bennett (1978) suggests that such a treatment can't be correct because (2) entails sentence (3).

(3) *Exactly one man is here.*

But the proposition that Wolfgang drinks Moishe Shicker liquor certainly does not entail the proposition that there is exactly one man here. Wolfgang might be a dog or a chamois. For Bennett, this alleged entailment between (2) and (3) is reason enough for claiming that a term like *this man* is a disguised description. It is supposed to mean the same as *the man here*. Similarly, *that man* is, according to Bennett, equivalent with *the man there*. And the latter NP is no longer directly referential. It means something like 'the man there, whoever that may be'. Call this reading of the definite term an attributive reading (following Donnellan, 1972). Such a treatment can explain the entailment between (2) and (3)—in what way will be seen later. Yet it runs into another serious difficulty.

On 22 August of this year I went to the Rothorn Hotel together with my friend Wolfgang. We saw Peter Stähli, the leading Swiss fortune-teller. Since he was very occupied there was not time for consulting him. I said to Wolfgang:

(4) *Next year, I will consult this fortune-teller.*

I think that I thereby expressed the proposition that I will consult Peter Stähli next year. Now, it is known that the Rothorn Hotel is in any year the residence of the leading Swiss fortune-teller *then*. He is elected by the Swiss magicians' association and, up to now, each year a different person has had the honour of taking that position. Next year, the association will probably elect either Urs Rubi or Jacques Appenzeller. However, according to Bennett's claim, (4) is synonymous with the following sentences:

(5) *Next year, I will consult the fortune-teller here.*

Bennett's treatment predicts two readings for this sentence when it is uttered in the situation mentioned above. One is the proposition that I will visit Peter Stähli next year. But the second reading is the proposition that next year I will visit the fortune-teller at the Rothorn Hotel, whoever this may be, e.g. Urs Rubi or Jacques Appenzeller. But, if *this* is used as a demonstrative, then (4) can't have this reading. Bennett is aware of this dilemma. But he can't solve it.

My conclusion from these examples is that the terms *this fortune-teller* and *the fortune-teller here* are not fully synonymous. I shall try to work out a solution in which the former term is directly referential whereas the later is not. Nevertheless, I accept Bennett's point that *this fortune-teller* entails in a certain sense that there is exactly one fortune-teller. In what sense will become clear later.

Bennett has considered only cases where local adverbs are not modified by other expressions. In this article I also try to analyse sentences where *hier, da,* and *dort* co-occur with quantificational adverbs or relatives. Consider the following sentence:

> (6) *Hier überall   finden Sie ein COOP-Restaurant.*
> Here everywhere find   you a   COOP-restaurant.

(6) is written on an advertizing brochure indicating all the towns in Switzerland having COOP-restaurants: Aarau, Adelboden, Allschwill-Betten, Allschwill-Lindenplatz, Arbon, Ascona, Baar, Balsthal, Basel, Bellinzona, Bern, Bern-Bümpliz .... So in this context, the complex adverbial *hier überall* means something like 'at each place listed'. Our aim must be to show that this comes out in the right way.

To consider another example, take the case where a local adverb is modified by a relative:

> (7a) ⎰*Hier* ⎱
> (7b) ⎱*Da* ⎰, *wo   letztes Jahr das Bellevue stand, ist heute ein großes Loch.*
> (7c) ⎰*Dort*⎱ where last year the Bellevue stood, is today a big   hole.

There is an interesting difference between *hier* on the one hand and *da* and *dort* on the other hand. (7a) seems to have only an appositive reading, whereas the most prominent readings of (7b) and (7c) seem to be restrictive interpretations. In other words, these sentences have the following paraphrases:

> (8a) *An dieser Stelle stand letztes Jahr das Bellevue. Heute ist da*
> At this   place stood last   year the Bellevue. Today is there
> *ein großes Loch.*
> a big   hole.

> (8b) *An derjenigen Stelle, wo   letztes Jahr das Bellevue*
> At the   place where (restrictive) last   year the Bellevue
> *stand, ist heute ein großes Loch.*
> stood is today a big   hole.

Notice that I have paraphrased *hier* by *an dieser Stelle* (at this place). Although it will be seen that these two adverbials are not fully synonymous, this paraphrase illustrates in a neat way why the adverb *hier* can't be restricted. It denotes a place completely determined by the context of use. And whenever denoting terms are modified, you always get an appositive reading. On the other hand, in connection with relatives, *da* and *dort* can mean 'at the place'. And this concept clearly can be restricted to the concept 'at the place such and such'. Our treatment will have to account for this difference.

The discussion has been very informal so far. I have spoken of contexts, of propositions expressed, of direct reference, of entailment and the like. I think that almost everyone has his own associations with such locutions. Therefore, it seems to be necessary to say more precisely how I use these terms. Only then shall I say something about other uses of *hier, da*, and *dort*. For instance, in (9) we have an *anaphorical* use of *da*, whereas the *da* in (10) is bound (see Kasher, 1979, for a similar example).

(9) I: *Nächstes Jahr fahre ich auf eine   griechische Insel.*
                   Next   year go   I   to some Greek   island.
     Wolfgang: *Was   machst du   da?*
                   What do   you there?

(10) *Kein Land   ist so schlecht, als daß man da   nicht leben könnte.*
       No   country is so bad   that one there not   live   could.

The semantic notions which I will introduce are much in the spirit of Kaplan. The syntax is more in the spirit of Montague, although nothing I will say is incompatible with other syntactical approaches, for instance, transformational grammar. Although I have tried to avoid any superfluous technicalities, the reader might still find the syntactical Section 3 somewhat tedious to read. I can't help here. Syntax is always difficult. But it is my conviction that we have to take it seriously. One of the deepest questions in linguistics seems to be this: What is the relation between syntax and semantics? I wish to contribute to an answer to this question by investigating some German local deictics. But this means that my syntax must be reasonably realistic. The sentences generated must look like German sentences and not like formulae in some artificial language. And the syntactical analysis must be general enough, i.e. compatible with data not considered here.

This said I now proceed to semantics.

2   SEMANTIC NOTIONS

Consider the following sentence:

(1) *Ich wohne hier*
      I   live   here.

If Angelika utters (1) in Nijmegen she expresses the proposition that she lives in Nijmegen. But if Ede utters (1) in Kreuzlingen he expresses thereby the proposition that he lives in Kreuzlingen. So we can express different propositions by means of the same sentence. And the proposition which is expressed by (1) at a particular context of utterance is determined by the meaning of (1). This observation—not my own, cf. Stalnaker (1972), Cresswell (1973), Kaplan (1977), Lewis (1977)—motivates the following distinction. Call that which is expressed by an expression in a particular context *the content of that expression relative to that context*. And let us call that which determines an expression's content in each context of use the expression's meaning. (This is more or less Kaplan's (1977) terminology.)

Different types of expressions have different types of meanings. For instance, in a given context of use sentences express propositions, verbs and common nouns express properties, and names denote individuals.

For the purposes of this paper, I regard a proposition as something which is true or false in a given world at a given place and at a given time. Hence we can identify propositions with sets of triples $\langle w, t, p \rangle$, where w is a world, t a time (interval), and p is a place. Thus, if W is the set of possible world histories (for short, *worlds*), T is the set of *times* and P is the set of *places*, then any subset of $W \times T \times P$ is a *proposition*.

We say that the proposition Π *is true in the world* w *at time* t *and place* p iff $\langle w, t, p \rangle \in \Pi$. (If Π is not true, then it is false.) The proposition Π *entails* the proposition ρ iff Π is a subset of ρ.

Consider the following example:

(2) *Es schneit*. (It is snowing).

If (2) is uttered at time t_0 it expresses the proposition that it is snowing at t_0. This is the set $\Pi = \{\langle w, t, p \rangle: \text{It is snowing in } w \text{ at } p \text{ and } t_0\}$. So Π is true in our world at Brienz and any time t whatsoever iff it is snowing at Brienz at t_0 in our world. Π doesn't tell us anything about a particular place. It is *neutral as to place*. But it is about a particular time, namely t_0. Therefore, Π is *specific as to time*. In contrast to (2), the following sentence expresses a proposition *specific with respect to place*:

(3) *Es schneit in Brienz*. (It is snowing in Brienz.)

The difference between a proposition that is neutral with respect to place and a proposition that is specific to place is that the former may be true at one place and false at another. This is not possible for place-specific propositions. In ordinary language, it does not make much sense to say 'the proposition that it is snowing in Brienz is true at Bern'. But, in our theoretical framework, we will use this construction. This expression will mean the same as 'the proposition that it is snowing is true in Brienz'. This is so by virtue of the place specificity of the proposition expressed by (3).

From these remarks it should be obvious how the concepts of neutrality or specificity with respect to world (history) or time are to be introduced. Let us call a proposition Π *perfect, eternal*, and *ubiquitous* iff Π is true in every world, at every time, and at every place respectively. If a proposition has all of these features together then it is *necessary*. Obviously, each *necessary* proposition is $W \times T \times P$. If a proposition is false in every world, no matter what the time and the place is, then it is impossible.[1]

The next thing we need is the notion of property. Suppose we are given n different sets $A_1, \ldots, A_n$ of entities, where the entities in each of these A_i ($i = 1, \ldots, n$) are of the same 'logical type' (for instance, individuals, propositions, properties of the same kind, and so on). Then an *n-place property* (of entities in $A_1, \ldots, A_n$) is a function from $A_1 \times \ldots \times A_n$ into the propositions.

Let us consider an example. Take the verb *wohnen*. It expresses the two-place property ω defined for physical things and places such that for any physical thing a and place p^* $\omega (a, p^*)$ is true in a world w at time t and place p if a lives in w at p^* and t. So this property assigns to Frau Stähli and Hofstetten the proposition that Frau Stähli lives at Hofstetten.

We say that the *n*-place property ω is *true of* $(a_1, \ldots, a_n)$ iff the proposition $\omega(a_1, \ldots, a_n)$ is true (both clauses relativized to worlds, times, and places).

This is almost all we need by way of semantic terminology. Let me say a few words about times and places. I take times as primitives. They may be regarded as time intervals. An important feature of interval semantics is that something may be true at an interval without being true at any proper part of the interval.[2]

Places are special individuals. An important feature of places is that they may be located at other places: Brienz is in the canton of Bern, Bern is located in Switzerland, Switzerland is part of Europe, and so on. I am not enquiring into the properties of this 'part of' relation holding between places. I make use of it in a naive way. At a later stage, when we have a clear intuition of what this relation is, someone may come and describe it more accurately.

Let us now say something about context-dependency. I have said that an expression's content usually depends on the context of its utterance. Like Kaplan (1977), I regard the notion of context as a primitive. Let us denote the *set of all contexts* by C. Think of contexts as situations. A context always determines a particular place c_p, the *place of the context*. If c is a context in which something is uttered, then c_p is the place where the utterance takes place. A context c determines a time, too. Let us denote this time by c_t. And of course, each context c belongs to some world which is denoted by c_w. The notion of context is a fairly general one. There are contexts in which nothing happens and there are contexts where, among other things, something is uttered. Let us call contexts of the latter kind *contexts of utterance*. Kaplan (1977) assumes that each context of utterance determines an agent (a speaker, a writer, a thinker, or the like). I think Kratzer (1978) and Bennett (1978) are right in assuming that such an assumption is not profitable. Consider the following sentence.

(4)   *Hier essen Sie gut   und preiswert.*
      Here eat   you good and   at a reasonable price.

Whenever you read this inscription on the COOP restaurant, then the *hier* refers to that COOP. The place of the context is simply the location where this inscription is. There is no speaker at all. Nevertheless, an utterance of (4) takes place when you read it. Sometimes expressions are uttered even in cases when there is neither a speaker nor a receiver. On 11 August 1979 there was an announcement at the 'Hotel Axalp' saying this:

(5) *Heute Berner Platte*! (Today Bernian perversities!)

Since the weather was horrible all day nobody went there. Even the hotel manager did not read the inscription. He had had it fixed on the wall the day before. Nevertheless, I think of (5) being uttered at any time of that day and, in that context, (5) expressed that there were Bernian perversities available that day.

On the next day, the announcement was still there. Wolfgang and I asked for Bernian perversities. But the hotel manager said: 'Oh, you could have received them yesterday. I forgot about the announcement'. You can eat Bernian perversities only on the day the pig is slaughtered. What is not consumed on that very day is eaten by the dog and the cat. I am inclined to say that (5) was not uttered on 12 August 1979. You might say it was and that it said something wrong. But I think the case is similar to when we read an old newspaper containing the announcement '*Today dance at the Golden Spider*'. I believe this announcement cannot have the content that there is a dance at the *Golden Spider* on the day we read the newspaper. The utterance of the sentence quoted took place on the day when the newspaper appeared. And the adverb 'today' refers to that day.

As far as I am concerned, this story supports my opinion that a sentence containing deictic words can have a content only if it is uttered. We cannot simply say that a sentence together with a context determines a content. It must be uttered in that context. In the example with the newspaper, a particular sentence is present in a context without being uttered there.[3]

This said, I can say what the *meaning of a sentence* is: it is a partial function from the set C of all contexts into the set of propositions, i.e. into $\mathscr{P}(W \times T \times P)$.

Meanings must be partial functions because a context c must fulfil certain preconditions before a sentence-meaning can be applied to it: the sentence must be uttered there, the reference of the deictic words must be clear, and so on. Let us call these preconditions 'contextual presuppositions'. More accurately:

The *sentence-meaning m contextually presupposes* the proposition Π iff, for any $c \in C$, $m(c)$ is a proposition only if Π is true in c_w at c_t and c_p.

(For a discussion of this treatment see von Stechow (1980) and Cresswell

(1973).) Let me illustrate this definition by means of a very rough meaning rule for sentence (1).

2.1   The meaning of *Ich wohne hier* (1) is the following partial function m from C into the set of propositions:

- (a) For any $c \in C$, m is defined for c only in the case in which (1) is uttered in c by exactly one speaker.[4]
- (b) Let c be any context satisfying condition (a) and let u be the speaker of (1) in c. Then $m(c)$ is the following proposition:
  For any $\langle w, t, p \rangle$, Π is true in w at t and p iff u lives at c_p in w at c_t.

Remember that c_p is the place and c_t is the time of utterance.

Condition (a) of this meaning rule concerns the contextual presuppositions. Thus the meaning of (1) contextually presupposes the proposition that *Ich wohne hier* is uttered by exactly one speaker. Condition (b) fixes the content of sentence (1) for appropriate contexts. Suppose that Angelika uttered (1) on 8 August 1979 in Salzburg. Then Angelika expressed the proposition that Angelika lived at Salzburg on 8 August 1979. This is a proposition specific as to place and time.[5]

2.1 gives a description of the meaning of sentence (1) taking that sentence as an unanalysed expression. But (1) has an internal structure, of course. Its meaning is a function of the meanings of its parts. In order to describe this aspect of (1) we have to do some syntax. This remark leads us to the next section.

3   SYNTACTIC RULES AND THEIR INTERPRETATION

I will construct sentence (1) in the manner indicated by the derivation (2).

(1)   *Ede wohnt hier*

(2)   1. $[[wohnen]_V]_{VP}$ $_{\langle[+\text{ nomi}],\,[+\text{ loc}]\rangle}$,   (L1)

     2. $[hier]_{Adv}$ $_{[+\text{ loc}]}$

     3. $[[hier]_{Adv}\,[wohnen]_V]_{VP}$ $_{\langle[+\text{ nomi}]\rangle}$,   (S1)

     4. $[Ede]_N$ $_{3\text{rd pers. sing. nomi}}$,   (L3)

     5. $[[Ede]_N\,[hier]_{Adv}\,[wohnt]_V]_S$, $_{[+\text{ fin}]}$ (S2)

     6. $[[wohnt]_{Fin}\,[Ede]_N\,[hier]_{Adv}]_S$,   (S3)

     7. $[[Ede]_N\,[wohnt]_{Fin}\,[hier]_{Adv}]_S$,   (S4)

We see from this derivation that each of the syntactic rules (S1)–(S4) takes one or more (in our case, at most two) structures as input and yields a new labelled structure as output. Thus each syntactic rule is a transformation assigning an output structure (conclusion) to one or more input structures (premises).

Before explaining the rules, let me say something about the notation. Most of the labels I use are self-explanatory. The angle brackets '⟨ ⟩' used in connection with Vs (verbs) or VPs (verb phrases) indicate the complements required.

$$[[wohnen]_V]_{VP}$$
$$\langle[+\text{ nomi}]\,,[\text{loc}]\rangle$$

means that *wohnen* is a verb phrase that requires a local adverb or prepositional phrase (PP) as complement. The subject is a nominative N or NP. The notation $[hier]_{[\text{Adv}, +\text{loc}]}$ means of course that *hier* is an adverb having the feature $[+\text{loc}]$. If a feature $[f]$ is excluded I will use the notation $[-f]$. All this is standard. $[wohnt]_{[V, +\text{fin}]}$ means that *wohnt* is an (intransitive) finite verb. Instead of $[V, +\text{fin}]$ I use the abbreviation Fin. This said, let us consider the syntactic rules (S1)–(S4).

S1 *Verb phrases*

$$\frac{[\alpha]_{VP} \qquad\qquad, [\beta]_{[+\,f_n]}}{[[\beta]_{[+\,f_n]}\alpha]_{VP}} \,, \qquad n > 1.$$

with $\langle[+f_1],\ldots,[+f_n]\rangle$ above and $\langle[+f_1],\ldots,[+f_{n-1}]\rangle$ below.

This rule combines an *n*-place verb with an appropriate complement, thus making an $(n-1)$-place verb.

Notice that the Greek letters are variables running over words or expressions provided with labelled bracketings (labelled trees). These variables must not be confused with the syntactic variables in transformational grammar.

S2 *Sentence formation (present)*

$$\frac{[\alpha_1\,[\alpha_2]_V]_{VP}\,, [\beta]_{[N, f, \text{per(a), num(b)}]}}{[[\beta]_N\,\alpha_1[\alpha_2']_{Fin}]_S}\,,$$

with $\langle[f]\rangle$ under the VP term.

where α_2' is the per(a) num(b) present form of the verb α_2.

In most cases f = nominative. Impersonal verbs are subcategorized by [es]. [per(a)] refers to a person and [num(b)] to a number. The rule is very informal, of course. It is not an easy matter to describe in an explicit way the third person singular present for each verb. For *wohn-en* it is *wohn-t* (regular). For *lauf-en* it is *läuf-t* (Umlaut) and for *sein* it is *ist* (irregular). Let us assume here that this part of morphology is described by means of a finite list.

In the conclusion of (S2), I have not repeated the subcategorization for N. Henceforth I will specify only those features in a conclusion which are new or are changed. What remains unchanged is not explicitly mentioned.

Notice that I consider the final position of the finite verb as basic for German (for arguments, see Bierwisch, 1966). The first and second positions of the *finitum* are derived via the movement rules (S3) and (S4). Notice further that I combine verbs only with names and not with quantifying phrases like *niemand* ('no one') or *kein Schwein* ('no pig'). NPs of the latter kind come in via a quantifying-in-rule. The reason for this move is only that I do not want to complicate the semantic treatment. The semantics for verbs taking quantifiers as complements is much more complicated.

Finally, notice that I introduce tenses syncategorematically. The verb is specified as to present, past, or future when it takes a subject. Three different sentence rules will be needed, one for each of the three tenses mentioned. This treatment is as in Montague (1974b). I won't justify it here, but see Bäuerle & von Stechow (1979).

The movement rules (S3) and (S4) are organized according to an idea of Thiersch (1978). First, the finite verb is moved to the initial position. Then any constituent can be moved before the verb. (The reality of German is much more complicated. But these rules are at least a bit realistic.)

S3   *Fronting of the finite verb*

$$[\alpha[\beta]_{\text{Fin}}]_S \Rightarrow [[\beta]_{\text{Fin}} \alpha]_s$$

S4   *Topicalization*

$$\frac{[[\alpha]_{\text{Fin}} \beta_1 [\gamma]_A \beta_2]_S}{[[\gamma]_A [\alpha]_{\text{Fin}} \beta_1 \beta_2]_S}, \qquad A = \text{N, NP, Adv, PP}$$

These rules justify the derivation (2). Sentence (1) is obtained from (2) 7. by deleting the brackets.

It is obvious that the syntax sketched so far is a Montague syntax. In order to obtain a fully specified grammar, we have to interpret the syntactic rules. This works in the following way.

3.1   Suppose R is an n-place syntactic rule, i.e. R makes a new labelled expression out of n labelled expressions. Then *the interpretation of R, f_R*, is an n-place function that creates a new meaning out of n given meanings.

This is a very sloppy formulation. The details of the interpretation of such rules are found in Montague (1974a). The idea behind 3.1 is this. If the syntactic rule R combines the expressions $[\alpha_1]_{A_1}, \ldots, [\alpha_n]_{A_n}$ into the new expression $[\beta]_B$, then the meaning of $[\beta]_B$ is $f_R(m_1, \ldots, m_n)$, provided that $m_1, \ldots, m_n$ are the meanings of $[\alpha_1]_{A_1}, \ldots, [\alpha_n]_{A_n}$ respectively.

Let us reconstruct the lexicon of our language as syntactic rules without premises. Then, for each lexical rule L, the interpretation of L, F_L, is a zero-place function, i.e. F_L is a meaning.

It is now an easy matter to give a recursive definition of the meaning of any expression generated by our syntax. The only thing we have to consider is the fact that one and the same expression may be ambiguous and thus be generated in more than one way. For instance, the sentence *everyone loves someone* would have the surface structure $[[\text{everyone}]_{NP} [\text{loves}]_{Fin} [\text{someone}]_{NP}]$.

This structure can be derived in two ways, corresponding to different readings. But it is easily shown that we have enough information if at each step we interpret a pair consisting of a structure (an expression with labelled brackets) and a syntactic rule. Montague (1974a) calls derivations like (2), where at each step we have an expression and the rule generating it from the premises, an *analysis*. Let us now interpret analyses.

3.2 A. Suppose we are given the pair $\langle \alpha, R \rangle$, where α is an expression obtained by means of the syntactic rule R from $\beta_1, \ldots, \beta_n$. Suppose further that $\beta_1, \ldots, \beta_n$ are obtained by means of the rules $R_1, \ldots, R_n$ from appropriate premises. Then *the meaning of* $\langle \alpha, R \rangle$, $V(\alpha, R)$, is $F_R(V(\beta_1, R_1), \ldots, V(\beta_n, R_n))$.

B. If $\langle \alpha, R \rangle$ is obtained from no premises by means of the lexical rule R, then $V(\alpha, R) = F_R$.

What this definition says is very simple indeed: take the meanings of a rule's input structures, apply the meaning of the rule to them, and you get the meaning of the output structure. Let us now interpret our rules. We begin with the lexicon.

L1 (a) *Syntax*

$\Rightarrow [wohnen \ _V]_{VP}$
$\langle [+ \text{nomi}], [+ \text{loc}] \rangle$

(b) *Semantics*

For any context c, $F_{L1}(c)$ is the two-place property ω. ω is true of $\langle a, b \rangle$ in a world w at a place p and a time t iff the following conditions hold:

(i) a is a physical object.

(ii) b is a place.

(iii) a lives at b in the world w at time t.

It can be seen from this entry that each syntactic rule has two parts, a syntactic one and a semantic one. (L1) is a lexical rule. This rule states that the verb *wohnen* is a [VP, + loc]. No premise is needed. And the semantics says that this VP expresses in any context the property true of a thing and a place if the thing lives at that place. So the meaning of *wohnen* F_{L1} expresses the same content in any context. Such meanings are called *stable*.

Henceforth I will use a more sloppy but self-expanatory notation for the lexical rules.

L2 $[hier]_{[\text{Adv} + \text{loc}]}$
$F_{L2}(c)$ is defined only if *hier* is uttered at c.
For any such c, $F_{L2}(c) = c_p$.

Remember that c_p is the place of the utterance. It is seen from this rule that I treat *hier semantically* as a name. I don't claim that it is a name syntactically. Together with a verb like *wohnen* the adverb *hier* behaves, semantically, like a name. In connection with other verbs, for instance *arbeiten* (to work), it has a different function. This difference is explained via syntax. But the lexical meaning of *hier is always* F_{L2}. So I am making a distinction between the syntactic and semantic functions of a word. These two aspects may go together but they need not.

It is clear that *hier* denotes in general a different place in a different context of utterance. Words which change their content with their utterance-context are called *context-dependent*. There is another peculiarity connected with *hier*. The content of this word is a place, hence an individual. The content of *wohnen* was a property, i.e. a concept. Words whose contents are plain individuals are called *directly referential*. Notice a further fact. Whenever *hier* is uttered or muttered its reference is clear: it's the place of the utterance. Context-dependent words which refer without any need for a demonstration are called *pure indexicals*. Other pure indexicals are *ich* (I) and *jetzt* (now). (Most of this terminology is due to Kaplan (1977).)

If *ich* is uttered by Ede, then its content is Ede. Hence the meaning of *ich* should be that function f such that $f(c)$ is the utterer of *ich* for any utterance context c. Thus, the meaning of *ich* should be a function from contexts into individuals. However, I will not describe it in this way. Rather I will say that the meaning of *ich* assigns to each utterance context of *ich* the constant function f such that for any $\langle w, t, p \rangle$, $f(w, t, p)$ is the person who utters *ich* in c. I will treat the other directly referential words in the same way. The reason is a purely technical one: I want to treat all definite terms as Ns. But a term like *the President of the USA* is not necessarily directly referential. Its content may be Jimmy Carter, but it may be also the President of the USA, whosoever this may be. Hence our terminology needs to be modified a little bit: A word is directly referential if its content is always a constant function assigning the same individual to any $\langle w, t, p \rangle$. Direct referential words in *this* sense are what Kripke (1972) calls rigid designators. If a directly referential word is uttered and expresses the constant function f whose value is always the individual a, then we say that the word *denotes a in this context*.

It should be clear from these remarks that the semantics for $[hier]_{Adv}$ need a slight modification:

L2   *Semantics revised*
F_{L2} (2) is defined only if *hier* is uttered in c. For any such c, F_{L2} (c) is that function ζ such that for any $\langle w, t, p \rangle$, $\zeta(w, t, p) = c_p$.

Let us continue now to interpret the words occurring in derivation (2).

L3 $[Ede]_{[N, \text{3rd pers. sing., nomi}]}$
F_{L3} (c) is that function ζ such that for any $\langle w, t, p \rangle$, $\zeta(w, t, p) = $ Ede.

Obviously, *Ede* is a directly referential word. After the description of the words occurring in (1), let us interpret the rules.

S1   *Semantics*
Suppose χ^n is the meaning of an n-place VP (hence assigning n-place properties to contexts). Suppose further that ζ is the meaning of the nth complement of this verb (in this paper $\zeta(c)$ (w, t, p) will always be an individual or place). Let c be any context such that both χ^n and ζ are defined for c. Then F_{R1} (χ^n, ζ) (c) is that $(n - 1)$-place property ω^{n-1} such that for any $a_1, \ldots, a_{n-1}$ and $\langle w, t, p \rangle : \langle w, t, p \rangle \in \omega^{n-1}$ $(a_1, \ldots, a_{n-1})$ iff $\langle w, t, p \rangle \in \chi_n$ (c) $(a_1, \ldots, a_{n-1}, \zeta(c)$ $(w, t, p))$.

This interpretation looks horrible but it mercifully is the most complicated of this paper. Let us apply the definition at once.

Take a context c such that the expression *hier wohnen* is uttered at c. Suppose further that the analysis which underlies this utterance is the tree (2) from the beginning down to (2.3), i.e. the following structure:

(2)   1. $[wohnen]_V]_{VP}$,   (L1)
          $\langle[+ \text{nomi}] [+ \text{loc}]\rangle$
                    2. $[hier]_{Adv}$,   (L2)
                         $[+ \text{loc}]$
     3. $[[hier]_{Adv}[wohnen]_V]_{VP}$,   (S1)

Then the content of *hier wohnen* with respect to c is $V((2.3), (S1))(c)$
$= F_{R1}(V([[wohnen]_V]_{VP}$, (L1)), $V((2.2), (L2)))(c)$, by definition
                $\langle[+ \text{nomi}] [+ \text{loc}]\rangle$

3.2(A). = that property ω such that for any $\mathbf{a}$ and $\langle w, t, p \rangle$: ω is true of $\mathbf{a}$ in w at t and p iff $\langle w, t, p \rangle \in$ V((2.1), (L1))(c) $(\mathbf{a}$, V((2.2), (L2))(c) $(w, t, p))$, by definition of F_{R1}.

Now by definition 3.2 (B) and F_{L2}, V((2.2), (L2)) (c) $(w, t, p) = c_p$, i.e., the place of the utterance. And by 3.2(b) and F_{L1}, V((2.1), (L1)) (c) is the property ω^* true of $\langle \mathbf{a}, c_p \rangle$ in w, t, p iff a lives at c_p in w at t (and $\mathbf{a}$ is a physical object and c_p is a place). Therefore the property ω mentioned above is true of $\mathbf{a}$ in w at t and p iff a lives in w at t and c_p. Thus, with respect to the context c, our VP *hier wohnen* expresses the property of living at c_p. This is what we want, of course. The interpretation of the rest of our rules is easy enough.

S2. *Semantics*

Suppose we are given the meaning χ of an intransitive VP, the meaning ζ of an N and a $\langle w, t, p \rangle$. Then $\langle w, t, p \rangle \in F_{S2}(\chi, \zeta)$ (c) iff $\langle w, c_t, p \rangle \in \chi$ (c) $(\zeta(c)$ $(w, t, p))$.

It is easily checked that, by this rule, the pair (2.5)

$$[[Ede]_N \ [hier]_{Adv} \ [wohnt]_{Fin}]_S, \tag{S2}$$

denotes the proposition that Ede lives at c_p during c_t. Thus, the present tense is interpreted as 'It is the case in the time of the context'. (This is grossly simplified. For a more thorough account, see Bäuerle & v. Stechow (1979).) The interpretation of (S3) and S4) is identity:

S3 *and* S4 *Semantics*

$F_{S3}(\chi) = F_{S4}(\chi) = \chi$, for any sentence meaning χ. So the movement rules don't change the meaning of our construction (2). Hence the meaning of $\langle (2.7),$ (S4)$\rangle$ is the same as the one of $\langle (2.5), (S2) \rangle$. This conclusion completes this section.

4   THE DEMONSTRATIVE USE

In the preceding section I was concerned only with the purely indexical use of *hier*. *Hier* always referred to the place of utterance. But suppose I utter (1) while pointing to the Rothorn:

(1)   *Dort   schneit* es.
       There snows it.

Then I express the proposition that it is now snowing on the Rothorn. Such a use, where an indexical is accompanied by a demonstration, is called *demonstrative use*. *Hier* can have a demonstrative use as well. I may say

(2)   *Ede schläft hier, Cordula hier und Wolfgang hier.*
       Ede sleeps here, Cordula here and *Wolfgang* here.

and I may point at different beds during the respective utterance of *hier*. In the following I will symbolize the demonstrative use of deictic words by superscripts. So, $hier^n$, da^n, and $dort^n$ are demonstratives.[6] *Hier* without any superscript still symbolizes the purely indexical use.

In this paper, I will assume that demonstratives are always directly referential.[7] Therefore $hier^n$, da^n, and $dort^n$ always refer to places, namely to the places indicated by the demonstrations associated with utterances of these words. But this is not all that can be said. There are different appropriateness conditions for the use of $hier^n$, da^n, and $dort^n$. In other words, these adverbs have different contextual presuppositions (cf. for the following, Klein, 1978): the place indicated together with an utterance of $hier^n$ must be relatively near to the *origo* of the utterance. (This term is due to Bühler (1934).) On the other hand, when $dort^n$ is uttered, the associated demonstration can't point to a place which includes the *origo*. There seem to exist almost no special requirements for demonstrations accompanying da^n. Hence da^n is the most neutral demonstrative adverb in German.

What is meant by *origo*? I have spoken so far only of the place where the utterance takes place. But where is this? Is it in my room, in the chalet Ahorn, on the Axalp, in Brienz, in Canton Bern, in western Switzerland, in Middle Europe, etc? Each of these places is in some sense correct.[8] Nevertheless, all these places seem to be centred around some point, which is something like 'the smallest place occupied by the utterance' (if there is such a thing). And this ideal centre is *the origo*.

This said, we can formulate the meaning rules for $hier^n$, da^n, and $dort^n$.

$L4^n$ $[hier^n]_{[Adv+loc]}$.
$F_{L4^n}(c)$ is defined only in the case in which $hier^n$ is uttered in c and there is a demonstration associated with that utterance which points to a place c_{hier^n} relatively near to the origo of the utterance in c. For any such c and any $\langle w, t, p \rangle$, $F_{L4^n}(c) (w, t, p) = c_{hier^n}$.

According to what has been said so far, the rules for da^n and $dort^n$ are obvious. $dort^n$ must always refer to a place c_{dort^n} which excludes the origo and da^n may be used in order to refer to any place whatsoever, provided that this place can be demonstrated. Let us call the meaning rules for da^n and $dort^n$ $(L5^n)$ and $(L6^n)$ respectively.

Let us now analyse the verb phrase da^{17} *pennen* (to sleep there). Its derivation is this.

(3) 1. $[[pennen]_V]_{VP}$, $\qquad\qquad\qquad\qquad\qquad$ (L4)
$\qquad\qquad$ $[\langle[+nomi]\rangle]$
$\qquad\qquad$ 2. $[da^2]_{[Adv,+loc]}$, $\qquad\qquad\qquad\qquad\qquad$ (L5)
$\qquad$ 3. $[[da^2]_{Adv} [pennen]_V]_{VP}$, $\qquad\qquad\qquad$ (S5)

Starting from this intrasitive VP, we could derive sentence (1) of this section in the same way as we have done with sentence (1) in the preceding section. For the interpretation of (3), we need two further rules.

L4 $[[pennen]_V]_{VP[([+\text{ nomi}])]} F_{L4}$ (c) is true of an individual a in a world w at time t and place p *iff* **a** is a physical object and **a** sleeps in w at t and p.

S5 *Syntax*

$$[\alpha]_{VP}, [\beta]_{[Adv, +loc]} \Rightarrow [[\beta]_{Adv} \alpha]_{VP}$$

Semantics
Suppose $[\alpha]_{VP}$ is obtained by means of the rule R and $V([\alpha]_{VP}, R) = \chi$. Suppose further that $[\beta]_{Adv}$ is obtained by means of R' and $V([\beta]_{Adv}, R') = \Psi$. Then $\langle w, t, p \rangle \in F_{S5}$ (χ, Ψ) (c) (a) *iff* $\langle w, t, \Psi$ (c) (w, t, p)$\rangle \in \chi$ (c) (a), provided that β is [-Q] and $\langle w, t, p \rangle \in \Psi$ (c) ($\chi(c)$), if β is [+Q], for any individual **a** and any $\langle w, t, p \rangle$. The distinction of cases in this rule refers to quantificational local adverbs like *überall* (everywhere) or *nirgends* (nowhere). I shall come to this in a moment. [+Q] means 'quantificational'.

It is obvious from our rules that da^2 *pennen* expresses the property of sleeping at c_{da^2}, provided this expression is uttered at c and the demonstration associated with da^2 refers to the place c_{da^2}.

Next, consider the sentence (4):

(4) *Ede Schläft irgendwo   da²*
     Ede sleeps   somewhere there

The key for the analysis of this sentence is the following structure:

(5) 1. $[[da^2]_{Adv} [pennen]_V]_{VP}$,   (S5), (3.3)
        $\langle[\text{nomi}]\rangle$

     2. $[irgendwo]_{[Adv,+loc,+Q]}$,   (L5)

     3. $[[irgendwo]_{Adv} [da^2]_{Adv} [pennen]_V]_{VP}$,   (S5)
        $\langle[\text{nomi}]\rangle$

We need a rule for the quantificational adverb *irgendwo*.

L5 $[irgendwo]_{[Adv, +loc, +Q]}$.
Suppose we are given a one-place property of individuals ω and an individual **a**. Then $\langle w, t, p \rangle \in F_{L5}$ (c) (ω) (a) *iff* there is a place p^* : p^* is a part of p and $\langle w, t, p^* \rangle \in \omega$ (a), for any context c and any $\langle w, t, p \rangle$.

It should be obvious from this definition that, in an appropriate context c, (5.3) expresses the property of sleeping somewhere at c_{da^2}, if c_{da^2} is the place referred to by da^2 in c. So we are able to analyse (4) in the right way. The next thing we do is to consider the semantical relations between demonstrative adverbs and the demonstrative pronouns *dieser*[n]. We will analyse the following sentences:

(6a) *Diese*[7] *Frau   pennt*
      This   woman sleeps
(6b) *Jene*[7]   *Frau   pennt*
      Yonder   woman   sleeps

(7a)
(7b) *Die Frau* $\begin{Bmatrix} hier^7 \\ da^7 \\ dort^7 \end{Bmatrix}$ *pennt*
(7c)
      The woman here (there, yon) sleeps

(8a)
(8b) *Diese*[6] *Frau* $\begin{Bmatrix} hier^7 \\ da^7 \\ dort^7 \end{Bmatrix}$ *pennt*
(8c)
      This woman here (there, yon) sleeps

(9a)
(9b) *Jene*[6] *Frau* $\begin{Bmatrix} {}^*hier^7 \\ da^7 \\ dort^7 \end{Bmatrix}$ *pennt*
(9c)
      Yonder woman (*here, there, yon) sleeps.

Sentence (6) is derived in the following way.

(10)

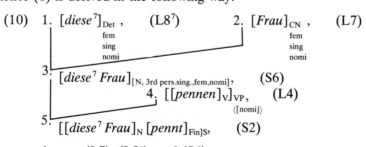

The new rules are (L7), (L8″), and (S6).

S6   *Definite terms*.

$[\alpha]_{[\text{Det},\text{num(a) gen(b) cas(c)}]}$
$[\beta]_{[\text{CN, num(a) gen(b) cas(c)}]}$
$[\alpha\beta]_{[\text{N,num(a) gen(b) cas(c) 3rd pers.}]}$

Suppose ζ is a Det-meaning and χ is a CN-meaning. Then $F_{S6}(\zeta, \chi)(c) = \zeta(c)(\chi)$, for any context c in the domain of ζ and χ. Thus the content of this rule is just functional application of the Det-content to the CN-meaning.

L7 $[Frau]_{\text{[CN, fem, sing, nomi]}}$.
F_{L4} (c) (a) is true in a world w at time t and place p iff **a** is a woman in w at t and p.

L8^n $[diese^n]_{\text{[Det, fem, sing, nomi]}}$
Suppose c is a context and χ is a CN-meaning. Then $F_{\text{L8}^n}(c)$ (χ) is defined only if (1) holds.

1. $diese^n$ is uttered in c with a demonstration leading to exactly one individual u such that χ (c) is true of u in c_w at c_t and c_p.
2. For any such c and any $\langle w, t, p \rangle$,

$$F_{\text{L8}}n \ (c) \ (\chi) \ (w, \ t, \ p) = u.$$

We are now able to interpret the construction

(10.5) $[[diese^2 \ Frau]_{\text{N}} \ [pennt]_{\text{Fin}}]_{\text{S}},$ (S2).

Suppose I utter (10.5) in a context c where $diese^7$ refers exactly to one woman, say Senta. Then, with respect to c, (10.5) expresses the proposition that Senta sleeps at c_t and c_p. Thus $diese^7$ $Frau$ is a directly referential term. Therefore this treatment seems to be open to the objection of Bennett which I mentioned in section 1. Bennett thinks that the content of (10.5) with respect to c should *entail* the proposition that exactly one woman is at c_p. And this is certainly not so, according to our rules. But, by (L8^n.1), the meaning of (10.5) *contextually presupposes* the proposition that $diese^n$ refers to exactly one woman. So the meaning of (10.5) tells us that this sentence speaks, in a certain sense, about exactly one woman. Yet this information is not treated on the propositional level but on the presuppositional level. So Bennett's intuition is accounted for by this analysis. On the other hand, my treatment does avoid the difficulties of Bennett's: there is no attributive reading of the definite term in (10.5). I find this result very satisfying.

For the analysis of (6b), we need a meaning rule for $jene^n$. This rule is like (L8^n), the only difference being that $jene^n$ can't refer to an individual located at the origo. Call this rule L9^n.

Next, consider the sentences (7). The key to their analyses are the terms *die Frau hier^7 (da^7, $dort^7$)*. The last N has the following structure.

(11)   1. $[Frau]_{\text{CN}},$ (L7)   2. $[dort^7]_{\text{[Adv,+loc]}}$

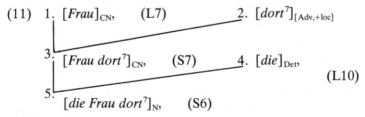

3. $[Frau \ dort^7]_{\text{CN}},$ (S7)   4. $[die]_{\text{Det}},$ (L10)

5. $[die \ Frau \ dort^7]_{\text{N}},$ (S6)

The new rules are (S7) and (L10).

S7 *Local adverbs as attributes*

$$[\alpha]_{\text{CN}}, [\beta]_{[\text{Adv}, +\text{loc}, -\text{Q}]} \Rightarrow [\alpha\beta]_{\text{CN}}$$

Suppose χ is a CN-meaning and ψ is an $[\text{Adv}, +\text{loc}, -\text{Q}]$-meaning. Then F_{R7} (χ, ψ) (c) is that property ω which is true of an **a** in w at t and p *iff* $\langle w, t, p \rangle \in \chi$ (c) (**a**) and **a** is located at ψ (c) (w, t, p) in w at t.

Suppose I utter *Frau dort*[7] in a context where *dort*[7] refers to the place c_{dort}[7]. Then this common noun phrase expresses at c the property of being a woman located at c_{dort}[7]. Next, let us treat the definite article.

L10 $[die]_{[\text{Det, fem, sing, nomi}]}$.
For any CN-meaning χ, any context c and any $\langle w, t, p \rangle$: F_{L10} (c) (χ) $(w, t, p) = u$, provided that there is exactly one individual v such that χ (c) is true of v in w at t and p and u is that v. Otherwise F_{L10} (c) (χ) $(w, t, p) = \dagger$. ($\dagger$ is a special object falsifying any property whatsoever.)

According to these rules, sentence

(7c)   *Die Frau dort*[7] *pennt*

expresses the proposition that the woman at place c_{dort}[7] sleeps at c_t, whoever this woman is, provided c is a context of utterance of (7c) such that *dort*[7] refers to c_{dort}[7].

There is a neat difference between (7c) and

(8c)   *Diese*[6] *Frau dort*[7] *pennt.*

The meaning of (8c) contextually presupposes that *diese*[6] *Frau* refers to exactly one woman. But (8c) never expresses a proposition that entails the existence of some woman or her being located some where. On the other hand (7c) entails the existence of some woman at the place of utterance. But it doesn't presuppose so. This difference is due to the fact that *die Frau* is an attributive term, while *diese*[6] *Frau* is a referential one. The definite article *die* may be used as a demonstrative as well. This use is symbolized as *die*[n] and analysed exactly in the same way as *diese*[n]. *Diese*[n] seems to have only the referential use, provided it is not used anaphorically. I will say a few words about anaphors in the last section.

Before leaving this section, let us treat modified local adverbs as they occur in 12(a) and (b).

(12)   (a) *Da* ⎱
       (b) *Dort* ⎰ wo   Ede pennt schneit es.
          There where Ede sleeps snows it.

The adverbial in (12a) has the following structure.

(13)   1. $[da]_{[\text{Adv},+\text{loc}]}$

2. $[wo\ Ede\ pennt]_{[\text{S},+\text{rel},\,+\text{loc}]}$,   (S8)

3. $[da\ wo\ Ede\ pennt]_{[\text{Adv},+\text{loc}]}$,   (S9)

The derivation of (12a) would then be the following one:

(14)   1. $[[Es]_\text{N}\ [da\ wo\ Ede\ pennt]_\text{Adv}\ [schneit]_\text{Fin}]_\text{S}$,   (S2),
                 es   (Compare (2.5) in section 1)
        2. $[[schneit]_\text{Fin}\ [es]_\text{N}\ [da\ wo\ Ede\ pennt]_\text{Adv}]_\text{S}$,   (S3)
        3. $[[da\ wo\ Ede\ pennt]_\text{Adv}\ [schneit]_\text{Fin}\ [es]_\text{N}]_\text{S}$,   (S4)

Since I am not analysing relatives in this paper (but see v. Stechow (1979b)), I introduce *wo Ede pennt* by the syntactic rule (S8).

S8 $[wo\ Ede\ pennt]_{[\text{S},\,+\text{rel},\,+\text{loc}]}$.
    $F_{\text{S8}}(c)$ is the property ω true of a place iff Ede sleeps at p and c_r.
    We have to formulate rule (S9) in a way such that *da wo Ede pennt* gets an attributive reading. This adverbial expresses the place where Ede sleeps, wherever this may be. The local adverb *da* is completely redundant for the semantics of this adverbial. Therefore I didn't care which rule *da* was introduced by into the derivation (13).

S9

$$\frac{[\alpha]_{[\text{Adv},\,+\text{loc}]},\ \alpha = da, dort \qquad [\beta]_{[\text{S},\,+\text{rel},\,+\text{loc}]}}{[\alpha\beta]_{[\text{Adv},\,+\text{loc}]}}$$

Suppose, ζ is any N-Meaning and χ is any [S,+rel,+loc]-meaning. Then

$$F_{\text{S9}}(\zeta, \chi)(c)(w, t, p) = \begin{cases} \text{the unique place } p^* \text{ such that } \langle w,t,p\rangle \in \chi(c)(p^*), \\ \text{if there is such a place and } \dagger, \text{ otherwise} \end{cases}$$

Thus, if *da wo Ede pennt* is uttered in c, its content is for any $\langle w,\ t,\ p\rangle$ the unique place such that Ede sleeps there at the utterance time.
    Notice that, for a full interpretation of (14.3), we still need a rule for the verb *schneien* (to snow). It is this.

L11 $[[schneien]_\text{V}]_\text{VP}$
                   $\langle[es]\rangle$

$F_{\text{L11}}(c)$ is the property ω true of an **a** in w at t and p iff it is snowing in w at t and p.

The subcategorization of *schneien* by [es] means that the subject must be the N *es*. Whatever we chose as meaning for this pronoun, in virtue of (L11), the content of *Es schneit* will always be that it is snowing at the utterance time. This is so because the property expressed by *schneien* does not depend on the subject. Thus we can express the idea that *schneien* is syntactically an intransitive verb. Semantically it expresses a proposition.

(L11) completes the treatment of the sentences discussed in this section. Let us finish this article by saying a few words about boundness and anaphoricity.

5 BINDING AND ANAPHORA

I have not made up my mind whether binding and anaphora should be regarded as special cases of the same general phenomenon or not. Take the examples I have mentioned in the first section.

(1)   *Kein Land   ist so schlecht als daß man da   nicht leben könnte.*
      No   country is so bad   that one there not   live   could.

I will call this an occurrence of *da bound*. The main characteristic of a bound symbol is that it has no meaning in isolation. The *da* in (1) does not refer to something nor does it express something. (It certainly does not express the same as *kein Land*!) It can only be interpreted within the syntactic structure where it occurs. It is a syncategorematic symbol.

(2)   A: *Was   macht Ede in London?*
         What does   Ede in London?
      B: *Der macht da   Ferien.*
         He makes there vacations.

In this context, *da* is coreferential with the adverb *in London* which refers to some place. So, if a deictic word is used as an anaphor it certainly has a content. Yet this content changes with the linguistic context. So the anaphora relation seems to play here the same role as the demonstration does in the case of demonstratives.[9] So there seems to be a close analogy between anaphors and demonstratives. Nevertheless, there is at least one important difference: demonstratives are always directly referential. Anaphors are not necessarily so. This is seen by this example.

(3)   A: *Dagobert reist   jedes Jahr in   das reichste Land   der*
         Dagobert travels each year into the richest country of the
         Welt.
         world.
      B: *Was   macht er da?*
         What does   he there?

The *da* in B clearly has the same content as *im reichsten Land der Welt* (in the richest country of the world). And this content need not to be directly referential. The term may pick out each year a different country. Cases of anaphors like the ones in (2) and (3) were still simple ones. We can think of the linguistic mechanisms necessary for the interpretation of anaphors in the following way: There is an anaphoric relation between an anaphoric word and some other construction. Take the content of the latter construction. This is the content of the anaphoric word. But the facts are more complicated, if we consider a case like the following one.

(4)　　A: *Nächstes Jahr fahre ich auf eine   griechische Insel.*
　　　　　Next　　year go　　I　　to　some Greek　　Island.
　　　　B: *Was   machst du   da?*[10]
　　　　　What do　　you there?

A need not yet have made up his mind when uttering his sentence. Thus, in this context, the *da* in B's question presumably means 'the Greek island where you are going next year, whichever this may be'. It is a difficult matter to recover this reading just by means of an anaphorical relation going from *da* to the term *eine griechische Insel*. The only approach where anaphors of this sort are treated at least in a tentative way is due to Evans (1977). The content of *da* in (4B) is still an N-content. But what happens in the following case?

(5)　I:　　　　　*Nächstes Jahr steige ich auf alle Schweizer Vulkane.*
　　　　　　　　　Next　　year climb I　on　all　Swiss　　volcanoes.
　　Wolfgang: *Was   machst du   da   jeweils?*
　　　　　　　　What do　　you there in any case?

Jeweils is almost not translatable into English. What is the *da* in (5. Wolfgang)? Is it an anaphor or is it a bound adverb? It seems to me that the *jeweils* indicates that *da* is bound somehow.

(5. Wolfgang) means something like

(6)　(For all Swiss volcanoes that you will climb next year, x) (What are you going to do at x?)

This paraphrase doesn't explain much, of course. One would have to say first what it means to quantify in an interrogative. Secondly, one has to explain how the representation (6) is recovered by (5) together with some information which indicates by what the *da* in (5. Wolfgang) is bound.

Notice that, among the demonstrative adverbs *hier, da* and *dort*, only *da* and *dort* can have a bound use.

(7)　*Wir gingen in   kein Wirtshaus, von dem   bekannt   war, daß es*
　　　We went into no   resthouse of　which known　was that
　　　*da (dort, *hier)   keine Rösti gab.*
　　　there (yon, *here)no   Rösti were.

On the other hand, all of our demonstrative adverbs can have an anaphorical use. The following example showing this is discussed in Klein (1978).

(8) *Endlich erreichten wir El Dorado. Hier (da, dort)   blühten*
     Finally   reached   we El Dorado. Here (there, yon) bloomed
     schon   die Geldbäume.
     already the money-trees.

All of these adverbs are coreferential with *El Dorado*. Nevertheless, they have different connotations. Klein says that in the case of *hier*, the origo necessary for interpreting this this word *is shifted* while in the case of *da* and *dort* this is not so. I am not sure whether this is a happy terminology. The origo should always be the ideal center of the place of utterance. Hence it can't be shifted.[11] What seems going on in the case of (8) is a change of *point de vue*. If (8) occurs within some story and the story-teller uses *hier*, he thereby indicates that he is looking onto the event reported in the second sentence from El Dorado. He places himself so to speak mentally at that place. In case he uses *da* or *dort*, his *point de vue* coincides with his actual place. So, normally the origo and the point of view coincide, but this is not necessarily so. However, since I have no idea in which way this idea of *point de vue* should be integrated into semantics, I will drop it here.

What can we say then about anaphorical symbols? Let us symbolize anaphors by right-hand subscripts:

$hier_n$, da_n, $dort_n$, er_n, sie_n, es_n, $dieser_n$, ...

There is one rule for the interpretation of these symbols. It is, I admit, a very vague one.

$L12_n$ $[hier_n]_{[\text{Adv}, +\text{loc}]}$.
$F_{L12_n}(c)$ is defined only if there is some anaphorical relation in c yielding the $[\text{Adv}, +\text{loc}]$-meaning ζ. For any such c, $F_{L12_n}(c) = \zeta(c)$.

It should be clear from this definition that an anaphorical *hier* is not necessary directly referential. So *this* intuition about anaphors is captured. But the main problem concerning anaphors lies in the locution 'anaphorical relation yielding an $[\text{Adv}, +\text{loc}]$-meaning'. I have said nothing about it. It is obvious from $(L12_n)$ how the meaning rules for other anaphorical symbols are to be defined.

In this paper I have not gone into the problems of quantification in natural language. Introducing the syntax and semantics of quantifying in rules would require some more pages. But the paper is too long anyway. Let me therefore sketch only how I would derive example (6) of Section 1:

(9) *Hier überall   finden Sie ein COOP-Restaurant.*
     Here everywhere find   you a   COOP-Restaurant.

This sentence is derived on the basis of the following structure.

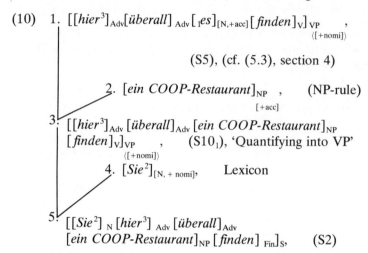

(10)   1. $[[hier^3]_{Adv}[\ddot{u}berall]_{Adv}[_1es]_{[N,+acc]}[finden]_V]_{VP}$,
$\langle[+nomi]\rangle$

(S5), (cf. (5.3), section 4)

2. $[ein\ COOP\text{-}Restaurant]_{NP}$,   (NP-rule)
$[+acc]$

3. $[[hier^3]_{Adv}[\ddot{u}berall]_{Adv}[ein\ COOP\text{-}Restaurant]_{NP}$
$[finden]_V]_{VP}$,   (S10$_1$), 'Quantifying into VP'
$\langle[+nomi]\rangle$

4. $[Sie^2]_{[N,+nomi]}$,   Lexicon

5. $[[Sie^2]_N[hier^3]_{Adv}[\ddot{u}berall]_{Adv}$
$[ein\ COOP\text{-}Restaurant]_{NP}[finden]_{Fin}]_S$,   (S2)

From (10.5), we can derive (9) by means of (S3) and (S4). (S4) needs to be modified a little bit: we must be able to move several adverbs of the same kind to the beginning of the sentence.

It can be seen from (10.1) that I have symbolized the bound pronoun *es* by $_1es$. (S10$_n$) is a rule for quantifying into verb phrases. There is another rule for quantifying into sentences. I did use (S10$_n$) in order to have the NP *ein COOP-Restaurant* in the scope of tense. The techniques for the formulation of such rules are found in Montague (1974b) or Cresswell (1973). You need variable assignments for the interpretation of such syncategorematic symbols as $_nes$ ($_nit$).

Semantically, the rule (S10$_1$) roughly does the following. (10.1) expresses the property ω^2 true of $\langle a, b \rangle$ if **a** finds **b** everywhere at the place denoted by *hier*^{3}. The NP *ein COOP-Restaurant* expresses the second-order property ζ true of a first-order property ω if there is an x such that x is a COOP-Restaurant and x is an ω. Let us denote the property which is true of a b iff ω^2 (a, b) is true by $\lambda^* b\ [\omega^2(a, b)]$. Then, the content of (S10$_n$) combines ζ and ω^2 into the one-place property ω^1 which is true of an **a** if ζ is true of $\lambda^* b[\omega^2$ (**a**, **b**)]. This is the property of finding a COOP-Restaurant everywhere at the place indicated by *here*^{3}. And this is the correct content of (10.3).

6 CONCLUDING REMARKS

Almost nothing I have said in the preceding sections is new when taken in isolation. What is new is the integration of particular facts and considerations into a systematic description covering syntax and semantics of German. I think that the rules presented here work quite nicely for most of the examples considered. It remains to see how general they are, when we consider further data.

Several questions remain open. How can one deal with binding and anaphora? Furthermore, is the thesis that the pronoun *dieser* is directly referential correct? The above sentences suggest so. But Angelika Kratzer has brought the following sentence to my attention.

(1) *Wenn diese Frau   nicht Züs Stähli ist, muß sie die Schwester von*
    If   this woman not   Züs Stähli is, must she the sister   of
    Züs Stähli sein.
    Züs Stähli be.

The pronoun *diese* can't refer to Züs Stähli because sentence (2) expresses an absurdity, provided the two occurrences of Züs Stähli refer to the same person.

(2) *Wenn Züs Stähli nicht Züs Stähli ist, muß Züs Stähli die Schwester*
    If   Züs Stähli not   Züs Stähli is must Züs Stähli the sister
    von Züs Stähli sein.
    of   Züs Stähli be.

This is an example supporting Bennett's view that *diese Frau* means the same as *die Frau da* (the woman there). But sentence (4) in Section 1 was an example against this paraphrase. Perhaps one needs to offer a more general treatment, mediating Kaplan's and Bennett's view. It could be something like this: a demonstrative always signals the presence of *some* deictic (i,e, directly referential) element. In (4) of Section 1 *this* referred to a person. In the case of (1) in the present section, *diese* does not refer to a person. We have to form a Bennett-paraphrase, which contains a deictic word referring to a place.

It should be obvious from these remarks that the semantics (and the syntax) of demonstratives are still far from being clear. And it is a fine old custom to say that one expects more clarity from future research.

NOTES

1. This definition has a curious consequence. It can be shown easily that a proposition specific as to world, time, and place is either necessary or impossible. Suppose that *It is raining in this world here and now* expresses the proposition $\{\langle w, t, p\rangle$: It is raining in w_0 at t_0 and $p_0\}$) This set is either $W \times T \times P$ or $\emptyset$ depending on whether it is raining or not at w_0 at t_0 and p_0. This seems to be highly counterintuitive. I don't know exactly what the appropriate reaction should be with respect to such a case.

2. Cresswell (1976) discusses the example *John polishes every boot*. More about the nature of time intervals is said in Manor (1979).

3. This view is in contrast to Bennett's (1978) opinion. For him, a context and a sentence determine a content. He thinks that the study of utterances belongs to speech act theory and not to semantics. I have more to say on the particular arguments which he gives, but lack of space precludes my doing this in the present article.

4. The notion of speaker is very problematic. There are buttons with the inscription 'Ich bin gegen Atomenergie' (I am against nuclear energy). If you carry such a button you count as the speaker of this sentence. Problems connected with *ich* are discussed in detail in Kratzer (1978).

5. From the above meaning rule, it is clear that I am using the so-called method of *double indexing*. For each meaning rule there are two relevant sequences of indices: $\langle c_w, c_t, c_p \rangle$ and $\langle w, t, p \rangle$. The first sequence refers to the context of utterance and the second utterance is needed for the description of the content. This method is amply justified in Kaplan (1977). A particularly clear explanation is found in Lewis (1977).

6. There are complications, however. I may point to a car and say *Dies Auto taugt nichts* (This car is no good) and I may thereby refer to the model. See the paper by G. Miller in this volume and Nunberg (1978).

7. More accurately, one should interpret different *occurrences* of one symbol together with a particular demonstration. But this would be technically complicated. See von Stechow (1979*a*).

8. The two last sentences are plagiarized from Schegloff (1972), where this point is made.

9. Bühler speaks of 'sachlich zeigen' in the case of demonstratives and of 'syntaktisch zeigen' in the case of anaphors.

10. This example is inspired by Kasher's (1979) following example. A: 'I am going to travel to a certain Greek island to rest a while'. B: 'Will you read a lot of books there?' Kasher's example is somewhat less problematic if his claim that 'a certain Greek island' is a referring term is correct.

11. No feature of the context can be *shifted*. The context is what it is. Cf. Lewis (1977) concerning the point.

REFERENCES

Bäuerle, R., & von Stechow, A. K. D. W. (1979). Finite and non-finite temporal constructions in German. In C. Rohrer (ed.), *Tense and quantifiers*. Tübingen: Niemeyer.

Bennett, M. (1978). Demonstratives and indexicals in Montague grammars. *Synthese*, **39**, 1–80.

Bierwisch, M. (1966). *Grammatik des deutschen Verbs*. Studia Grammatika II. Berlin: Akademie.

Bühler, K. (1934). *Sprachtheorie*. Jena: Fischer.

Cresswell, M. J. (1973). *Logic and languages*. London: Methuen.

Cresswell, M. J. (1976). Interval semantics (mimeo).

Cresswell, M. J. (1978). Presuppositions and points of view. *Linguistics and Philosophy*, **2**, 1–41.

Donnellan, K. S. (1972). Proper names and identifying descriptions. In D. Davidson & G. Harman (eds), *Semantics of natural language*. Dordrecht: Reidel.

Evans, G. (1977). Pronouns, quantifiers and relative clauses. *Canadian Journal of Philosophy*, **7**, 467–536.

Fillmore, C. J. (1975). Santa Cruz lectures on deixis, 1971. Bloomington, Ind.: Indiana University Linguistics Club.

Kaplan, D. (1977). Demonstratives. An essay on the semantics, logic, metaphysics of demonstratives and other indexicals (mimeo).

Kasher, A. (1979). Three kinds of linguistic commitment (mimeo).

Klein, W. (1978). Wo ist hier? Präliminarien zu einer Untersuchung der lokalen Deixis. *Linguistische Berichte*, **58**, 18–40.

Kratzer, A. (1978). *Semantik der Rede*. Kronberg: Scriptor.

Kratzer, A., & von Stechow, A. (1977). Äußerungssituation und Bedeutung. *Zeitschrift für Literaturwissenschaft und Linguistik*, **22/23**, 98–130.

Kripke, S. (1972). Naming and necessity. In D. Davidson & G. Harman (eds), *Semantics of natural languages*. Dordrecht: Reidel.

Lewis, D. (1977). Index, context and content. Paper presented at the Anniversary Symposium on Philosophy and Grammar, Uppsala University, June 1977.

Lutzeier, P. (1974). *Der 'Aspekt' Welt als Einstieg zu einem nützlichen Kontext-begriff für eine natürliche Sprache*. Doctoral dissertation, University of Stuttgart.

Manor, R. (1979). Intervals with underdetermined edges (mimeo).

Montague, R. (1974a). English as a formal language. In R. Montague, *Formal philosophy*. New Haven: Yale University Press.

Montague, R. (1974b). The proper treatment of quantification in ordinary English. In R. Montague, *Formal philosophy*. New Haven: Yale University Press.

Nunberg, G. D. (1978). *The pragmatics of reference*. Doctoral dissertation, University of California, Berkeley.

Pietsch, R. (1976). Syntax und Semantik von Lokaladverbien in einer λ-Kategorialsprache. Staatsarbeit, University of Freiburg.

Schegloff, E. A. (1972). Notes on a conversational practice: formulating place. In D. Sudnow (ed.), *Studies in social interaction*. New York: Free Press.

Stalnaker, R. (1972). Pragmatics. In D. Davidson & G. Harman (eds), *Semantics of natural languages*. Dordrecht: Reidel.

von Stechow, A. (1979a). Occurrence-interpretation and context-theory. In D. Gambara, F. lo Piparo, & G. Ruggero (eds), *linguaggi e formalizzazioni*. Rome: Bulzoni.

von Stechow, A. (1979b). Visiting German relatives. In R. Bäuerle, U. Egli, & A. von Stechow (eds), *Semantics from different points of view*. Heidelberg: Springer.

von Stechow, A. (1980). Presupposition and context. In U. Mönnich (ed.), *Aspects of philosophical logic*. Dordrecht: Reidel, to appear.

Thiersch, C. L. (1978). *Topics in German syntax*. Doctoral dissertation, M.I.T., Cambridge, Mass.

Wunderlich, D. (1971). Pragmatik, Sprechsituation und Deixis. *Zeitschrift für Literaturwissenschaft und Linguistik*, **1/2**, 153–190.

Speech, Place, and Action
Edited by R. J. Jarvella and W. Klein
© 1982 John Wiley & Sons Ltd.

Deixis and Subjectivity: *Loquor, ergo sum?*

JOHN LYONS

The title of this article, by making use of the term 'subjectivity' and coupling it with 'deixis', recalls both the title and part of the content of a famous paper by Benveniste (1958). More generally it relates what I have to say in the article to a point of view that is characteristic, not only of Benveniste himself, but of many French linguists who have been influenced by him (cf. Kristeva *et al.*, 1975)—a point of view that is perhaps aptly referred to as post-Saussurean phenomenological structuralism. As to my subtitle: I will explain what I mean by this presently. But for the moment, it too may be thought of as being no more than a deliberately Cartesian (or anti-Cartesian) reformulation of one of Benveniste's points: 'C'est dans et par le langage que l'homme se constitue comme *sujet*; parce que le langage seul fonde en réalité, dans *sa* réalité qui est celle de l'être, le concept d' "ego" ' (Benveniste, 1966, p. 259). Or again: 'l'homme ne naît pas dans la nature, mais dans la culture' (Benveniste, 1974, p. 24). Taken together, these two quotations express an attitude towards man and towards language which is strongly opposed to the attitude most commonly adopted these days by English-speaking linguists, logicians, and philosophers of language.

It is worth observing at this point that the notion of subjectivity with which Benveniste operates—as does Bühler (1934), incidentally, in his seminal work on deixis—is one that plays a key role in traditional French and German philosophy. The French 'subjectivité' and the German 'Subjektivität' do not necessarily carry the pejorative connotations that the English 'subjectivity' has recently acquired, in popular usage at least, by virtue of its opposition with a positivistic interpretation of 'objectivity' (cf. Williams, 1976, pp. 259–263). When 'subjectivity' is contrasted with 'objectivity' in this article, it is not intended to have the pejorative implication of unreliability and failure to correspond with the facts that it commonly bears in everyday English: it is to be understood as having the same meaning as 'subjectivité', and 'Subjektivität'.

A metalinguistic comment should also be made about the term 'subject',

101

which is less closely related to 'subjectivity', in the relevant sense, than the French term 'sujet' is to 'subjectivité'. Philosophical usage has preserved such collocations in English as 'the subject of consciousness' and, in more specialized works at least, 'the knowing subject' (cf. Popper, 1972). But the English-speaking linguist does not have as part of his stock of ready-made terms the expression 'the speaking subject', as the French-speaking linguist has, and constantly employs, 'le sujet parlant'. Furthermore, whereas the French-speaking linguist can draw simultaneously upon the two traditional senses of 'sujet' when he distinguishes 'le sujet de l'énonciation' ('the subject of the act of utterance') from 'le sujet de l'énoncé' ('the subject of what is uttered'), the English-speaking linguist cannot, without at least the appearance of deliberate equivocation, use the phrase 'the subject of the utterance' to refer to the speaker, or more generally to the locutionary agent. Great play is made with the distinction between the two senses of 'sujet', and with their ultimate interdependence, by French linguists who belong to the movement that I described earlier as post-Saussurean phenomenological structuralism (cf. Todorov, 1970; Kristeva, 1971); and Culioli and his followers are currently attempting to formalize both the distinction and the interdependence within their own terminological and notational framework (cf. Culioli et al., 1970; Desclés, 1976). It is arguable that there is a genuine equivocation between the two senses of 'sujet' in much of this work and that the equivocation is facilitated by the acceptability in more or less everyday French of 'sujet de l'énonciation', on the one hand, and of 's'énoncer', on the other. Granted that this is, or may be, so (and I believe that the theories of linguists are to a considerable degree influenced by their everyday metalanguage: cf. Rey-Debove, 1978), I would not wish to deny the importance of the phenomenon of subjectivity, and intersubjectivity, upon which these linguists have concentrated or the truth of a good deal of what they have said about it. Indeed, the whole of this article is very much in the spirit of the work to which I have just referred.

What then is meant by 'subjectivity' in the present context? In so far as we are concerned with language, the term 'subjectivity' refers to the way in which natural languages, in their structure and their normal manner of operation, provide for the locutionary agent's expression of himself and of his own attitudes and beliefs. Thus characterized, the property of subjectivity looks innocent enough. After all, no one would wish to deny that human languages, as we know them, enable their users to refer to themselves and to deliver themselves of their own opinions. There is a sense, then, in which no one would deny that natural languages have the property of subjectivity. For subjectivity, characterized as it has been so far, is nothing other than indexicality (cf. Bar-Hillel, 1954); and it is universally accepted that few, if any, of the utterances of everyday language-behaviour are free of the property of

indexicality. It can be maintained, however, that standard treatments of indexicality in mainstream Anglo-American linguistics, logic, and philosophy of
language fail to do justice to the property of subjectivity. Let me explain what
I mean by this assertion.

One can use the English verb 'express', in the relevant contexts, either
reflexively or non-reflexively (in the traditional grammarian's sense of 'reflexive'). The same is true of the more or less equivalent verbs, in their metalinguistic employment, in several European languages: French 'exprimer', German 'ausdrücken', Russian 'vyskazatj', etc. Furthermore, in English (though,
for reasons having to do with differences of grammatical structure, not in all
European languages) it is possible to co-ordinate, without producing zeugma,
a reflexive and non-reflexive direct object after the verb 'express': cf. 'the
locutionary agent's expression of himself and of his own attitudes and beliefs'
in the preceding paragraph. The fact that the resultant co-ordinate noun-
phrase is not felt to be zeugmatic is an indication that the reflexive and the
non-reflexive use (in the relevant metalinguistic contexts) involve the same
sense of the verb. In this respect, 'express' is like hundreds of other transitive
verbs in English: cf. 'shave' in *Bertrand Russell's barber shaved himself and
everyone in the village at least once a week*. But there is a very important difference, from the point of view of semantics, between 'express' and most other
verbs in English that have the syntactic property in question. Although the
proposition 'X expresses himself and his beliefs, attitudes, etc.' is not zeugmatic, it would generally be held to be pleonastic: self-expression is nothing
other than the expression, or externalization, of one's beliefs, attitudes, etc. In
other words, and to make the point more formally: the syntactically reflexive
'X expresses himself' is equivalent to the conjunction or disjunction of a
perhaps open set of syntactically non-reflexive propositions, comprising 'X
expresses his beliefs', 'X expresses his attitudes', 'X expresses his feelings',
'X expresses his personality', 'X expresses his emotions', and so on.

I do not wish to get into the difficult and philosophically controversial
question of what constitutes a person and of the relation that holds ontologi-
cally between the subjective self of first-person reference and the objective
individual that is referred to by means of a third-person pronoun, a proper
name, or a definite description. The point I want to make is simply that there
is a problem here, which linguists may not be able to resolve, but which they
must recognize as being of relevance to their concerns. Modern Anglo-
American linguistics, logic, and philosophy of language has been dominated
by the intellectualist prejudice that language is, essentially, if not solely, an
instrument for the expression of propositional thought. This prejudice is
made manifest in Katz's (1972, pp. 18 ff.) defence of the principle of effabil-
ity; in Lewis's (1972, pp. 205 ff.) treatment of non-declaratives; in Dummett's (1973) sustained argument to the effect that, whereas languages

might exist in which it is impossible to ask questions or issue commands, a language in which one cannot make assertions is inconceivable; in Chomsky's (1966, 1968, 1975) version of Cartesian, or neo-Cartesian, rationalism; in Fodor's (1978) formulation of the thesis that there is a universal language of thought, whose structure is more or less isomorphic with that of natural languages; and in many other influential works which, though they might differ considerably on a wide variety of issues, either pay no attention at all to the non-propositional and non-assertive components of language or play down their importance. In doing so, they fail to do justice to the phenomenon of subjectivity. One cannot reduce the speaker's expression of himself in his utterance to the assertion of a set of propositions. Still less can one reformulate all of these propositions, without loss or distortion in terms of a neutral metalanguage with an objective, or transcendent, point of reference.

My subtitle, *Loquor, ergo sum?*, is intended to suggest another way of looking at the phenomenon of subjectivity. I have inserted the question-mark in order to indicate that I am not fully committed to the thesis that it encapsulates. What I have to say about the linguistic effects of the locutionary agent's expression of himself in his utterance is not crucially dependent upon the validity of the particular version of subjectivism which results from the substitution of *Loquor* for *Cogito* in the Cartesian original. It is worth noting at this point that the original, *Cogito, ergo sum*, is customarily mistranslated into English: it should be translated, not as *I think, therefore I am*, but as *I am thinking, therefore I am*. However we judge the success or failure of Descartes' attempt to found all knowledge on the indubitability of self-consciousness, we must realize that his application of the *Cogito* rests upon the thinking subject's awareness of himself in the act of thinking. Neither Latin nor French (*Je pense, donc je suis*) grammaticalizes the distinction between a progressive and a non-progressive, or between an imperfect and a non-imperfect, in the present tense. But English does; and, as we shall see presently, at least some instances of the choice between a progressive and a non-progressive depend upon the degree, or manner, of the speaker's subjective involvement in his utterance. It would be a gross misrepresentation of the Cartesian position to assign either a generic or a habitual interpretation to Descartes' *Cogito*. Similarly, with my *Loquor, ergo sum?*: whatever its validity, it is to be translated, not as *I speak, therefore I am?*, but as *I am speaking, therefore I am?*

There are several ways in which one might interpret, and seek to defend, the thesis of what I might refer to, only half seriously, as locutionary subjectivism. Most obviously, one might, following either Plato, on the one hand, or the behaviourists, on the other, say that, in so far as thought is internal speech, Cartesian subjectivism turns out to be nothing other than locutionary subjectivism. Furthermore, as Hintikka (1962) points out, Descartes' *Cogito* has something of the quality of a performative utterance about it, so that an appreciation of the force of Descartes' argument not only depends upon the introspective awareness of oneself as thinking, but also presupposes an ability to appreciate the logic of the first-person pronoun 'I': and one derives one's understanding of performative utterances and, more generally, of the logic of the first-person pronoun from one's experience of alternating between the roles of *ego* and *tu*, of speaker and addressee, in everyday conversation.

One might also seek to defend the thesis of locutionary subjectivism from the viewpoint of existentialism or phenomenological structuralism (which have much in common), arguing that the individual is in a variable and dialectical relationship with the world he inhabits; that the thinking and perceiving self, or subject, becomes such—becomes a self and the self that he is—as a consequence of his being, potentially by genetic endowment and actually by enculturation, a speaking self (i.e. a locutionary agent); and that one's personal identity is not fixed and immutable, but is created and continually restructured by one's use of language. Benveniste himself appears to have subscribed to this view:

'Or nous tenons que cette "subjectivité", qu'on la pose en phénoménologie ou en psychologie, comme on voudra, n'est que l'émergence dans l'être d'une propriété fondamentale du langage, Est "ego" qui *dit* "ego". Nous trouvons là le fondement de la "subjectivité", qui se détermine par le statut linquistique de la "personne" ' (Benveniste, 1966, pp. 260).

But this is, of course, a philosophically controversial view; and, as I said earlier, I do not wish to get embroiled in the deep and troublesome philosophical issues connected with the notion of personal identity.

Nor am I concerned in this article, with the epistemological questions that have worried Descartes and his successors. Although the slogan *Loquor, ergo sum*? is perhaps defensible on philosophical grounds, I have used it primarily for its rhetorical effect: as a deliberate antithesis to Cartesian and neo-Cartesian intellectualism in linguistics. The notion of locutionary subjectivism with which I am operating presupposes no more than the following: (i) that the term 'self-expression' is to be taken literally and cannot be reduced, theoretically, to the assertion of a set of propositions; (ii) that there is a distinction to be drawn, in the structure and use of language, between a subjective component in which the speaker (or, more generally, the locutionary agent) expresses himself and an objective component comprising a set of communicable propositions. As far as (ii) is concerned, it can be plausibly argued, first, that the distinction between the subjective and the objective is gradual, rather than absolute, and, second, that what is here described as objective is, in origin, intersubjective, so that language is even more deeply imbued with subjectivity than I am supposing. This may be so. But I am not here defending a more radical version of locutionary subjectivism than (i) and (ii), taken together, imply. A further question that I explicitly raise, in connection with (ii), is whether different natural languages differ in respect of the degree of subjectivity that they impose upon their users. Everyday experience of familiar languages, on the one hand, and the descriptions published by linguists of certain less familiar languages, on the other, would suggest that the answer to this question is in the affirmative.

So far I have mentioned indexicality, but not deixis. The two are of course very closely connected. Peirce's term 'index' is but one of a set of grammatical and philosophical terms, traditional and modern, all of which are based, in one way or another, upon the notion of pointing: 'deixis', 'demonstrative', 'ostension', etc. Bühler (1934), to whom we are indebted for the modern employment of the term 'deixis', draws a general distinction between pointing words (Zeigwörter) and naming words (Nennwörter), calling the former signals and the latter symbols. He talks about pointing words in much the same way that Peirce talks about indexicality; and, despite the fact that he associates the expressive function (Ausdruck) with symptoms, rather than signals, he not only draws throughout on the notion of subjectivity (cf. especially, Bühler, 1934, pp. 299 ff.), but insists explicitly on the expressive and subjective nature of deixis (Bühler, 1934, pp. 102 ff.). Bühler's position is in fact very similar to the one that I am adopting here, not only with respect to the interdependence of subjectivity and deixis, but also in general: 'Das sprachtheoretische Axiom, dass alle Sprachzeichen *Symbole* derselben Art sein müssen, ist zu eng' (Bühler, 1934, p. 107).

Of course, Bühler is not the only one to have protested against the attempt made by some philosophers of language to handle the whole of linguistic meaning in terms of symbolic representation (Darstellung). As Black (1968, p. 127) puts it: 'A striking feature of twentieth-century studies of language has been an increasing realization of the central and crucial role of "non-cognitive" aspects of language, in fields as diverse as aesthetics, ethics philosophy, education and politics'. He refers, in this connection, to several of the distinctions that philosophers and psychologists have made, including Bühler's threefold distinction between what Black (1968, p. 150) calls 'the expressive, the presentative and the dynamic aspects or dimensions of an utterance' (Ausdruck, Darstellung, Appell). It is worth noting, although Black himself does not make this point, that Bühler's scheme is strikingly similar to that put forward by Russell (1940), who recognized as distinguishable functions of language: (i) that of indicating facts (cf. Bühler's Darstellung), (ii) that of expressing the (psychological) state of the speaker (cf. Ausdruck); (iii) that of modifying the (psychological) state of the addressee (cf. Appell).

Russell drew upon this tripartite scheme when he was discussing amongst other things the logical character of first-person utterances containing a predicate of sensation, e.g. *I am hot*. Such utterances, he said, simultaneously indicate a fact (Darstellung) and express the speaker's feelings (Ausdruck). In so far as they serve to express the speaker's feelings, they have the property that I am calling subjectivity; in so far as they present, or convey, the proposition that a particular person is hot, they purport to be objectively true or false. Although there is no obvious grammaticalization of the subjectivity of such utterances in English, there appears to be in Japanese. Kuroda (1973), who makes explicit reference to the epistemological problem discussed by Russell, tells us that the normal Japanese translation of *I am hot* would make use of an adjectival form, whereas the translation of *You are hot* or of *John is hot* would employ a verbal form, of the word meaning 'hot'. On the other hand, if *I am hot* is translated by means of a verbal form (in what is roughly the equivalent of the English progressive aspect), the effect is that of an utterance which refers simultaneously to two kinds of ego, or self: to the subjective, experiencing, internal self and to the objective, observing, external self. This is but one of the structural facts of Japanese that Kuroda cites in a series of recent papers devoted to the interconnection of grammar, epistemology, and narration (cf. Kuroda, 1973, 1974, 1975).

I would draw attention, at this point, to the distinction between the subjective experiencing self and the objective observing self, and to the possibility of combining both kinds of self-reference in particular styles, notably in what is called free indirect speech (cf. Banfield, 1973). Although English may not grammaticalize the distinction between the subjective and the objective point of view in the case of *I am hot, You are hot*, etc., it does so elsewhere. For example, there is a clear semantic contrast in this respect between

(1) I remember switching off the light

and

(2) I remember myself switching off the light.

Of these, (1) exemplifies the normal subjective mode of reference to what is necessarily a personal and incommunicable experience, whereas (2) is not only closer in grammatical structure to

(3) I remember you switching off the light,

but can also be interpreted, like (3), as reporting the memory of something observed, rather than experienced. That the truth-conditions of (1) and (2) are not identical is more evident if we consider events that a speaker might have observed in a film, but of which he is unlikely to have any subjective experiential memory: e.g. *I remember myself being born* is more likely to be a true report than *I remember being born*. Now, just as, according to Kuroda (1973), the use of a verbal, rather than an adjectival, form in the Japanese translation of *I am hot* produces the effect of combining a reference to the subjective, experiencing, internal self with a reference to the objective, observing, external self, so may the use of the experiential participial construction in English with a third-person, rather than a first-person, subject in what purports to be narrative. Thus

(4)   He remembered switching off the light

might be appropriately used, in free indirect speech, to report a mental state or event from two points of view: from that of the objectively reporting self (the speaker or narrator), which accounts for the past tense and the third-person pronoun, and from that of the truth, at the time referred to by the past tense, of *I remember switching off the light*. What I have to say below, on the basis of assymetries within the categories of tense and aspect in English and other languages, rests upon the distinction between the experiential and the non-experiential point of view. It is remarkably close to what Kuroda says in his account of what are, at first sight, quite different phenomena in Japanese. I find this encouraging.

I have illustrated the distinction between the experiential and the non-experiential by means of (1) and (2). Let me now illustrate the distinction between the propositional and the non-propositional by contrasting both of them with

(5)   I remember that I switched off the light.

The difference between (5), on the one hand, and (1) and (2), on the other, is that (5) could be used, in principle, when the speaker has neither experienced nor observed the event described by the propositional content of the complement clause: for example, he might have switched off the light whilst sleep-walking and, having been reliably informed of this fact later, come to believe it and store it in memory as he might believe and remember any other fact that is communicated to him in propositional form.

The distinction between the experiential and the non-experiential is not to be identified with the distinction between the non-propositional and the propositional. It is important to make this point, since I shall be operating with both distinctions in this article. At the same time, I want to emphasize that, as the experiential is more subjective a mode of description than the non-experiential, so the propositional mode of description, or report, is more objective than the non-propositional. It is my contention that languages may vary in terms of the degree of objectification that they impose or permit, and that propositionalization is one kind of objectification. I am not concerned with the syntax and semantics of the complements of different classes of verbs in English. It so happens that 'remember' exemplifies clearly, in the constructions that it takes and the entailments that hold between them, what is meant by 'experiential' versus 'non-experiential' and by 'propositional' versus 'non-propositional'. It will be noted that, although (5) does not entail either (2) or (1), and (2) does not entail (1), (1) entails (2) and (2) entails (5). Because this is so, it is tempting to treat 'remember' always as a verb of propositional attitude, comparable with 'know', 'think', etc. We must guard against this temptation if we wish to do justice to the semantic structure of English.

It is now widely accepted that much of the information that is transmitted, or conveyed, in everyday language-behaviour is implied rather than asserted, and that what is implied (in the broadest sense of 'imply') often depends crucially upon the deictic features of the utterance. All sorts of more or less familiar examples could be given of the subjective value of what are generally regarded as deictic phenomena. Bühler himself, taking up a point made by Brugmann, refers to the dramatic, secondary use of *ich*-deixis in the narration of past events (cf. Bühler, 1934, p. 85). Benveniste (1958), in his more wide-ranging treatment of subjectivity, also discusses uses of the tenses and of the first and second person, as well as noting the subjective component in the employment of explicit performatives and parenthetical verbs of propositional attitude. One could refer to the selection of 'come' rather than 'go' in particular circumstances in English (cf. Clark, 1974); to the choice between *hin-* and *her-* in German (cf. Berthoud, 1979, pp. 90 ff.); to the empathetic incorporation of a first-person reference in what would otherwise be a second-person pronoun or pronominal adjective of address (cf. *Why are you crying? Have we lost our dolly then?*); to a variety of phenomena which serve to distinguish free indirect speech from straightforward narrative, on the one hand, and from indirect, discourse, on the other (cf. Banfield, 1973). It would be impossible to exemplify, let alone discuss, everything that falls within the scope of subjective deixis in the space available. I will take just two, rather different, sets of phenomena, the first having to do with modality, and the second with tense and aspect.

As far as modality is concerned, the distinction between the subjective and the objective has long been recognized, though it has often been confused by linguists with the equally well established, but independent, distinction between epistemic and deontic (or root) modality. Even though it may not be clear from the verbal part of an utterance, and sometimes not even from its prosodic and paralinguistic features, whether it is subjectively or objectively modalized, on the one hand, and whether it is epistemically or deontically modalized, on the other, it is quite easy to demonstrate, for certain languages at least, both the validity of the two distinctions and their independence (cf. Lyons, 1977, pp. 787–849). For example,

(6)   You must be very careful

is ambiguous between a deontic and an epistemic interpretation, on the one hand, and between a subjective and an objective interpretation, on the other. Out of context it may well be that the objective deontic interpretation is more probable (cf. Halliday, 1970, p. 326); but, provided the context is appropriate, it will sustain all four interpretations. Construed objectively, (6) would be held to be making a factual assertion: its modality, whether deontic or epistemic, is part of the true or false proposition that is being asserted. Under the subjective deontic interpretation, (6) is a directive; under the subjective epistemic interpretation, it is a more or less qualified statement of opinion or inference. Using the traditional terms 'will' and 'judgement', we can say that in the one case the locutionary (and illocutionary) agent expresses his will and in the other his judgement. This formulation makes it clear that the subjectivity of utterances like (6), in the appropriate interpretation, is indeed subjectivity of the kind that concerns us in this article.

It is an established fact that there are languages in which it is not possible for a speaker to make a simple categorical assertion by uttering a subjectively unmodalized declarative sentence. One such language is Hidatsa (a language of the Siouan family), in which statements necessarily include one of a set of five modal particles, the function of which is to express the speaker's attitude or degree of commitment or to give some indication of the evidential basis for the proposition that is being conveyed (cf. Sadock & Zwicky, forthcoming; Matthews, 1965). Other languages, which do possess a modally unmarked declarative, have a set of optional, but frequently employed, particles enabling their users to express the same kind of subjective information that Hidatsa, apparently, obliges its users to express: German is a familiar example of such a language. It is notoriously difficult, if not impossible, to translate the modal particles of German satisfactorily into English. Up to a point, what German expresses by means of modal particles, especially in the more colloquial registers, English expresses by means of intonation (cf. Schubiger, 1965). But German makes use of modal particles in addition to, rather than instead of, intonation (cf. Bublitz, 1978, p. 39). In fact, subjective epistemic modality is probably marked prosodically in all spoken languages regardless of whether it is also marked grammatically or not.

The general point I now want to make is that subjectively modalized utterances cannot be translated or paraphrased by means of unmodalized declaratives and that any attempt to do so (without making use of intonation or optional modal particles which carry over the subjectivity, more or less satisfactorily) has the effect of adding to, or subtracting from, what is said. Let us consider the contrast that holds in certain styles of French (notably in newspaper articles) between declarative sentences in the indicative, which may be regarded as modally unmarked, and declarative sentences in the so-called quotative conditional (conditionnel de citation). Though it is not usually referred to in this connection—possibly because it is stylistically restricted and is thought of as being a particular use of the conditional mood—the quotative conditional of French is very similar in meaning to the evidential, or inferential, mood of, say, Turkish or Bulgarian. The advantage of taking a French construction, rather than one in some less familiar language, is that what I have to say about it will be the more widely understood and, if falsifiable, will be the more readily falsified. It is important to realize that the construction in question is typical of a whole class of phenomena found in many languages.

The following sentence, appropriately interpreted, exemplifies the quotative conditional:

(7)   Le premier ministre serait malade.

It is my contention that this cannot be satisfactorily translated into English or paraphrased in French by means of a declarative sentence in which *serait* is replaced with *est*. But surely, it might be insisted, (7) must have a literal meaning, which, as Tarski's (1956) principle of universality tells us, is translatable (though perhaps unidiomatically and with a good deal of circumlocution), not only into English, but into any natural language. What then is the literal meaning of (7)? Indeed, what does the term 'literal meaning' mean in respect of expressions that are not clearly ambiguous between a metaphorical and a non-metaphorical interpretation? One can invent all sorts of more or less plausible derivations of the so-called quotative interpretation of (7) from what is then regarded as its basic, conditional, meaning ('The prime minister would be ill') and justify them by postulating an underlying apodosis of one kind or another. But how would that advance the task of translation? Setting aside the question of literal meaning as irrelevant, one might propose any one of the following as a translation of (7) into English, in the appropriate interpretation: *The prime minister is reported to be ill, The prime minister is thought/believed to be ill, We (are given to) understand that the prime minister is ill*. One could go on almost indefinitely supplying more or less approximate translations. I submit that they all import into the English version something which the French does not actually say, though it may be held, in context, to imply it.

Furthermore, if we make truth-conditional identity our criterion for full semantic equivalence, within one language and across languages, we have two problems to face: first, that (7) is not obviously different, truth-conditionally, from

(8)   Le premier ministre est malade;

and, second, that all the English versions proposed at the end of the previous paragraph differ truth-conditionally from one another and from both (7) and (8). The second of these problems is perhaps eliminated if we adopt as our translation of (7), though not of (8): *The prime minister is reportedly ill* or even *The prime minister is, reportedly, ill*. But, once again, these sentences are more explicit than (7) in that they say (albeit parenthetically), and do not merely imply, that the proposition 'The prime minister is ill' is a matter of second-hand report. Despite the label by which it is commonly known, the quotative conditional (le conditionel de citation) can be used when there is no question of any prior assertion of the propositional content of the utterance in which it is employed. What it does is to express the illocutionary agent's restricted commitment, on evidential grounds, to the truth of the proposition that is conveyed. It expresses a particular kind of subjective epistemic modality, as does the Turkish inferential (cf. Lewis, 1967, p. 122) or, in appropriate contexts, the German 'sollen' (*Der Premierminister soll krank sein*).

This kind of evidential epistemic modality is not grammaticalized as a difference of mood in English. However, in so far as the inferential uses of 'must' and 'will' overlap with those of the French quotative conditional (and the Turkish inferential) and the oppositions within the set of modal verbs are grammatical, rather than lexical, evidential epistemic modality can be said to be grammaticalized in English, as it is so much more obviously grammaticalized in many other languages. It is only in certain contexts that *The prime minister must be ill* would translate (7) at all satisfactorily. And *The prime minister must be ill*, as we have seen, has both a subjective and an objective interpretation. Objectively interpreted, it can be used as the complement of a verb of saying or of propositional attitude (in particular, 'know'); it can even be used in the protasis of a conditional assertion. Subjective epistemic modality, of whatever kind, is not carried over into genuine indirect discourse constructions (cf. Banfield, 1973, p. 7). Such constructions presuppose the objectification of everything that is within the scope of the verb of communication or propositional attitude; and the objectification of either epistemic or deontic modality makes it part of the propositional content of an utterance (i.e. something which affects the truth-conditions of the sentence that is uttered).

Our discussion of (7) has brought out the general point that one language may permit, or indeed oblige, its users to say what another language permits or obliges them merely to imply, or indicate (cf. also Récanati, 1979, pp. 131 ff.). Furthermore, languages appear to differ, not only in detail, but globally, with respect to the objectification and propositionalization of modality. Indeed, it may very well be the case that in the vast majority of the world's languages it is impossible for a speaker to assert the objective existence of either epistemic or deontic possibilities (cf. Lyons, 1977, pp. 841–849). It is difficult to be sure of this, since very few languages have been described in sufficient depth and with due appreciation of the subtleties of meaning that their lexical and grammatical resources permit. We can be fairly certain, however, that grammarians have more often unconsciously assimilated the structures of less familiar languages to the structure of their own native languages, or of well studied literary languages, than they have either unconsciously or deliberately exaggerated the structural differences between familiar and less familiar languages. (In saying this, I am not blind to the undoubted excesses of what might be referred to loosely as Whorfianism: most of the descriptive grammars to which linguists appeal have been little affected by the Whorfian point of view.) This being so, since grammars frequently invoke the notion of subjective modality, but only rarely that of objective modality, the balance of evidence would seem to be in favour of the thesis that, whereas subjective modality, both epistemic and deontic, is universal in natural languages, objective modality is not.

Even in languages which allow for the objectification of modality in the verbal component of declarative sentences, as English undoubtedly does over a wide range of constructions, the objectification of epistemic modality by an illocutionary agent is far less common in everyday life than is the objectification of deontic modality. (This may account for the tendency to confuse the subjective/objective distinction with the epistemic/deontic distinction.) For example, not only *It may rain*, but also *It is possible that it will rain* (which would seem to be especially well adapted, as far as the lexical and grammatical structure of its verbal component is concerned, for the expression of objective epistemic modality), might be used to express the speaker's subjective evaluation of the truth of the unmodalized proposition 'It will rain'. And yet linguists who are currently engaged in the attempt to formalize the whole of the meaning of sentences in terms of their truth-conditions would probably be inclined to treat the objectively modalized interpretation of *It may rain*, and even more so of *It is possible that it will rain*, as being more basic than their subjectively modalized interpretation. What is at issue here is not a matter of empirically ascertainable fact, but of more or less justifiable metatheoretical decision. The fact that *It may rain* can be given an objective epistemic interpretation brings its meaning, under this interpretation, within the scope of formal, truth-conditional, semantics.

Granted that the formalization of semantics from this point of view 'is already well advanced within philosophy and logic' and that, 'if linguists could take over this well-established theory, a large amount of their work in semantics would have been done for them' (Smith & Wilson, 1979, p. 151), it must be remembered that philosophers and logicians who have made these technical advances in formal semantics have been concerned, for the most part, not with the full range of uses to which languages are put, but with the way they are used in the careful discussion of matters of philosophical import: the validity of reasoning, the foundations of ethics and aesthetics, the ontological status of entities to which reference is, or appears to be, made by means of language, and so on. In so far as the linguist's or the logician's objectification of subjective modality rests upon the view that the basic function of sentences is that of making true or false statements, it can be attributed to what Austin (1946) identified as the descriptive fallacy. It is comparable, in this respect, with the formal semanticist's treatment of performatives and other token-reflexive utterances (cf. Lyons, 1977, p. 744).

But what has all this to do, it may now be asked, with deixis? The answer is that, when it comes to the more subjective dimensions of deixis, it is very difficult to draw a sharp distinction between modality and deixis. At first sight, it might appear that the deictic category of tense is clearly distinguish-able, at least conceptually, from epistemic modality: tense is a matter of temporal reference and epistemic modality is not. If we read Whorf's (1938) classic description of what he calls the reportive, the expective, and the nomic forms of the Hopi verb, we cannot but be struck, as he is, with the fact that, although they must be translated into English in terms of differences of tense, they do not fall within the traditional definition of this category: they take no account of the difference between past, present, and future, but refer instead to different 'realms of validity'. In so far as the term 'mood' is traditionally reserved for the grammaticalization of modality and the Hopi verb-forms express what appear to be differences of epistemic modality, the reportive, the expective, and the nomic are moods, not tenses. However, it is easy to exaggerate the difference between mood and tense. All the so-called tenses of English, and indeed of all the Indo-European languages, have functions which correspond closely with what Whorf identifies as the definitive functions of the Hopi moods. Furthermore, even if we treat these more obviously modal functions of the Indo-European languages, whether legitimately or not, as non-basic, it is not always possible to draw a sharp formal or functional difference between the Indo-European moods and tenses (cf. Lyons, 1968, pp. 309–310).

The traditional view that tense has to do with time has been challenged, notably by Joos (1964) for English and by Weinrich (1964) for a wider range of languages. Two points may be made in this connection. The first is that, if one is looking for a set of general meanings (Gesamtbedeutungen) for each of the tenses of English and other European languages, there is little hope of finding these in the traditional notions of past, present, and future. On the other hand, a case can be made for subsuming even the temporal uses of the tenses under the category of epistemic modality (cf. Lyons, 1977, pp. 810–820). It is only within a theory of semantics that recognizes the validity of the distinction between basic meanings (Grundbedeutungen) and non-basic meanings (Nebenbedeutungen), deriving the latter from the former, that the traditional definition of tense in terms of temporal reference can be maintained. The alternative to adopting one or other of these two positions, as far as tense is concerned, is to leave the intuitively obvious connections between the temporal and the non-temporal uses of the tenses unaccounted for. The same point can be made in respect of other deictic categories that are defined in terms of spatial or temporal notions, but are acknowledged to have additional, more subjective, uses. Personally, I find the notion of basic mean-ing (Grundbedeutung) more attractive than that of general meaning (Gesamtbedeutung); and I am prepared to accept the traditional view that tense is, by definition, the category which grammaticalizes deictic temporal reference.

The second point is that (whether tense is held to be essentially or only contingently associated with temporal deixis) the temporal functions of tenses are more objective than are their non-temporal functions having to do with epistemic validity. But there are differences in respect of the objectification of tense among languages that are otherwise very similar in their use of tense for deictic temporal reference. For example, tense can be made part of the propositional content of an embedded complement of a verb of saying in English, though not in Latin. If tense, in the traditional sense, results from the objectification in certain languages of what other languages fail to objectify—the degree of objectification varying from one language to another—Hopi, as described by Whorf (1938), is more deeply imbued with subjectivity in this respect than English is. But the difference between them is not adequately characterized by saying that one has tense and the other does not.

We turn now to tense and aspect in relation to the notion of subjectivity. At first sight, aspect, like mood and modality, might appear to be irrelevant to the topic being dealt with in this article. True, the notion of subjectivity is frequently invoked in theoretical discussions of aspect (especially by those who distinguish aspect from Aktionsart). But aspect, in contrast to tense, is non-deictic; and, unlike subjective modality, it is part of the propositional content of the utterance. However, as mood intersects and merges with the deictic category of tense in many languages, so too does aspect—especially with so-called secondary tense, the subjective basis of which is obvious (cf. Lyons, 1977, pp. 689–690). What I am concerned with here is not the relation between tense and aspect as such, but the fact that in languages in which both tense and aspect combine it is commonly the case that there are restrictions upon their combination: restrictions in the language-system itself and restrictions, statistical if not absolute, upon the use that is made of the system by speakers. It is my contention that these restrictions are far from random or accidental: they can be explained by invoking the distinction between a more and a less subjective mode of description, or point of view, and associating the choice of one or the other with what is normal for different kinds of discourse.

The connection traditionally assumed to hold between aspect and what has been aptly described as temporal contour (Hockett, 1958, p. 237) is, if anything, more controversial than the connection between tense and temporal reference. Once again, the view that one takes of this issue will be partly determined by one's metatheoretical decisions about general meanings and basic meanings. The view taken here is that aspects, like tenses, have basic meanings, from which various non-basic meanings can be derived; and that the basic meanings of the aspects in the languages to which reference is made below are determined by differences of temporal contour.

Even since Jakobson (1932) put forward his analysis of the verbal categories of Russian, it has been common to apply the Prague School notion of markedness to the analysis of aspect, not only in Russian and the other Slavonic languages, but more widely (cf. Comrie, 1976; Friedrich, 1974). It has been less commonly noted that markedness, in the sense of semantic specificity and statistical infrequency, is relative to tense and mode of description. For example, the perfective is generally taken to be the marked member of the perfective/imperfective opposition in Russian and in other Slavonic languages (cf. Ridjanović, 1976, p. 75). In past-tense narrative, however, there can be little doubt that it is the imperfective that is marked in relation to the perfective, as the imperfect (imparfait) is marked in relation to the simple past (passé simple) in literary French, the imperfect in relation to the historic perfect (i.e. the perfect with non-primary sequence of tense) in Latin, and the past progressive in relation to the simple preterite in English. As far as the analysis of English is concerned, it is of course conventional enough to treat the progressive as being marked in relation to the non-progressive, if only on morphological grounds. What must be pointed out here, however, is that in utterances with true present-time reference, the progressive is the unmarked choice in English for all but stative verbs. We cannot say without further qualification that the progressive is the semantically marked member of the progressive/non-progressive opposition in English.

Just what the basic meaning of the English progressive is has been much discussed. I will here assume that the English progressive resembles the Slavonic imperfective and the imperfect of the Romance languages and of Latin (or Ancient Greek) in that it expresses durativity, but that it differs from them in that it also expresses dynamism, or non-homogeneity of temporal contour. It is this latter component of its meaning which accounts for the normally operative restriction on the occurrence of stative verbs in the progressive aspect and for some of the non-basic meanings that many scholars have associated with its several less normal, though of course perfectly acceptable, uses: cf. 'concomitant meanings or overtones that go with progressive aspect, such as limited duration, incompletion, . . . , vividness of description, emotional colouring, and emphasis' (Quirk *et al.*, 1972, p. 93). It is important to realize that 'normal' does not here mean 'grammatical' or 'acceptable'; and 'non-normal', in this sense, does not mean 'unacceptable', or even 'unusual'. Norms are not rules constitutive of the language-system. Although they are generally respected, they can be broken; and, unless the violation of what was once recognized as the norm becomes itself normal, deviations from the norm produce special effects.

Representatives of the school of phenomenological structuralism, to which reference was made at the beginning of this article, and more particularly Culioli and those influenced by him, have drawn attention to those uses of aspectual distinctions that can be seen as leaving in the surface structure of utterances a trace of the speaker's involvement in the act of utterance (une trace d'une opération due sujet parlant: cf. Culioli *et al.*, 1970; Fuchs & Rouault, 1975; Desclés, 1976). Adamczewski (1974) has provided an interesting analysis of the function of the English progressive from this point of view. What he says about certain uses of the progressive that I would identify as special, or non-normal, corresponds closely with what I will say here. However, he operates with a notion of general meaning which denies that there is any temporal basis to the category of aspect; and he does not draw upon the distinction between what I have called the experiential and the historic mode of description (Lyons, 1977, p. 688). To my mind, it is this distinction that provides an explanation for the otherwise puzzling gaps and asymmetries in the aspectual systems of various languages and for the relativity of aspectual markedness to differences of tense.

There is nothing particularly original about the recognition of some such distinction as the one that I am making. It is similar to the distinction drawn by Benveniste (1959) between narration (histoire) and discourse (discours), on the one hand, and to that drawn by Hamburger (1968; cf. Kuroda, 1974, 1975) between narration (Erzählen) and statement (Aussage) or by Weinrich (1964) between narration (Erzählen) and commentary (Besprechen), on the other. The scholars just mentioned are far from being in complete agreement as to the use that they make of their dichotomies; and the differences of terminology reflect genuine differences of viewpoint. It is noticeable, however, that they all have a category of narration to which another category is opposed; and they all agree that the non-narrative category is more subjective in various respects than the category of narration. It is my view that none of the three dichotomies just mentioned can be accepted as it stands: discourse can contain both narrative and commentary, or statement; and if Benveniste's notion of discourse is too strongly determined by his belief in the priority of spoken language, it can be argued that the formulation of the narrative/commentary or narrative/statement distinction by Weinrich and Hamburger is heavily influenced by their concern with literature. My own dichotomy of 'historical' and 'experiential' emphasizes the distinction between the relative objectivity of straightforward narration and the greater subjectivity that is associated with the description of personal experience.

Let us now apply this dichotomy of the historical and the experiential to the problem in hand, keeping in mind that, unlike some of the authors mentioned above, we have no wish to deny that both tense and aspect, in their basic uses, have to do with time. The several elements of what has just been described as a problem can be recapitulated briefly as follows:

(i) In many languages (French, Russian, Turkish, Ancient Greek, Latin, etc.), there is an aspectual opposition involving what is commonly identified as durativity which operates in the past, but not the present, tense (cf. Lyons, 1977, p. 688). Although the progressive/non-progressive opposition exists in both the present and the past tenses in English, the progressive does not contrast semantically with the non-progressive in the same way in the two tenses (in normal uses): in describing a present situation the speaker does not have a choice between *It rains today* and *It is raining today*, as he has a choice between *It rained yesterday* and *It was raining yesterday* when he describes a past situation.

(ii) The notion of markedness must be relativized to the aspectual character (Aktionsart) of different classes of predicates and to tense. For example, *It rains today* is marked in relation to *It is raining today*, whereas *John is being British* is marked in relation to *John is British*. But *It rained yesterday* is certainly not marked (in straightforward narrative at least) in relation to *It was raining yesterday*. As for *John was being British*, this is no less marked, or non-normal, than *John is being British*. The important point here is that, in so far as markedness is a semantic notion, it implies choice. It does not make sense to say that the simple present of French or the imperfective present of Russian is either marked or unmarked (within the category of aspect). Nor do we need to look for any of the 'concomitant meanings or overtones that go with progressive aspect' (Quirk *et al.*, 1972) in the semantic analysis of *It is raining today*, though we might well wish to do so in respect of *John is/was being British*, and perhaps also of *It was raining yesterday*.

(iii) Mode of description is also relevant to the markedness of particular aspects. In straightforward narration (histoire, Erzählen), it is the aspect that is employed for the chronological sequencing of events and for the advancement of the narrative that is the stylistically unmarked member of the opposition: the simple preterite in English, the perfective in Russian, the simple past in literary French. The marked member of the opposition serves in contrast, in so far as its function is temporal, to present enduring states and processes as the background against which the foregrounded, narrative-advancing, serially ordered events stand out. The historical mode of description makes use, then, of both marked and unmarked forms in their normal function of assigning a temporal contour to the narrative; and in this function the marked forms do not necessarily indicate any switch to the experiential mode or introduce any 'concomitant . . . overtones' (cf. *It was raining when I got up this morning*). In everyday, non-literary, usage the historical mode of description (or narration) is employed predominantly in the recounting of events that have taken place in the past. It is possible that the use of the English simple present in explicit performatives (cf. Reid, 1970, p. 157), sports commentaries, etc., can be explained, diachronically if not synchronically, in terms of its having, in these uses, a historical rather than an experiential function. However that may be, there is no doubt but that it is the experiential mode that is used, most characteristically, for the description of currently occurring events and processes.

(iv) The experiential mode is more subjective in that it describes what the speaker is, or could be, currently perceiving or feeling. Situations are presented not in their successivity in relation to one another; nor are they temporally contoured in terms of the foregrounding of one against the background of another. They are presented by the speaker as having just occurred, if they are momentary events (cf. *It's fallen down*), or as extending on either side of the moment of utterance if, as is usually the case, they are not momentary events (cf. *It is raining*). This being so, it is not surprising that there should be no need for a contrast between a durative and a non-durative aspect in the experiential mode and that, in view of the characteristic association between the use of the historical mode of description and the narration of past events, many languages have developed a durative/non-durative opposition in the past, but not the present, tense.

These then are the elements of the problem, as also of its solution. We have seen that the gaps and asymmetries that we find in the aspectual systems of various languages can be accounted for, as Benveniste (1959), Weinrich (1964), and others have suggested, by invoking the differences between two modes of description, of which the one is, in the nature of things, more subjective and the other more objective. It now remains only to make the further point, with particular reference to deixis and subjectivity, that the speaker can project himself, in memory or imagination, to a point of reference different from that of the situation of utterance and, from that point of reference, describe situations in the experiential mode as if they were currently taking place. He can, in fact, simultaneously adopt a double point of reference and mix the two modes of description. As we saw earlier, *John remembered switching off the light* embeds an experiential complement in what we may now identify as a historical structure; and there is implicit in this construction a second point of reference from which the event of switching off the light is described experientially. It means, as it were: 'At t_1 John recalled an event which, if he had described it at t_2 (when it occurred), he would have described by saying *I am switching off the light*'. There are more obvious examples, in English and other languages, in the style known as free indirect speech (discours indirect libre, erlebte Rede). It has been conclusively demonstrated that this style has features that distinguish it from both direct and indirect speech, but relate it to both (cf. Weinrich, 1964; Hamburger, 1968; Banfield, 1973; Kuroda, 1973, 1974, 1975). Notably, 'the free indirect style retains the immediate and present versions of adverbs of time and place like *now* and *here, today, yesterday*, etc., as they occur in direct speech: . . . It does not change them into the "distanced" forms of indirect speech (e.g. *then* and *there*)' (Banfield, 1973). On the other hand, the reference of the tenses and of the personal pronouns is generally governed by the same principles in free indirect speech as it is in normal indirect speech. It follows that a sentence like

(8)   John was coming tomorrow

can have two quite different interpretations with respect to the reference of *tomorrow*. One of them does not necessarily involve the experiential mode of description (though it may be held to do so in particular contexts of utterance); the other does. In both interpretations the form *was coming* manifests what Palmer (1974, p. 38) calls epistemic tense. This restricts the validity of the proposition that is expressed to some time prior to t_0 (the time of utterance). But epistemic tense, like epistemic modality, can be either objective or subjective. If *tomorrow* is interpreted as referring to the day following the day of utterance, as perhaps it must be in (cf. Palmer, 1974, p. 38).

(9)   Yesterday John was coming tomorrow,

we do not need to invoke any notion of experientiality or of subjective projection into the consciousness of another (though there might be other reasons, in context, for so doing). However, if (8) is interpreted, as far as the reference of *tomorrow* is concerned, in the same way as either

(10)   John said/thought 'I am coming tomorrow'

or

(11)   He/she said/thought 'John is coming tomorrow',

the whole utterance is clearly in the free indirect speech construction. In any analysis of its meaning, we need to invoke, in addition to two objectively different and chronologically ordered points of reference, two different subjects of consciousness, the speaker and some other person (why may be, exceptionally, the speaker's alter ego). Furthermore, we have to posit the speaker's projection of himself into the consciousness of the other. The truth-conditions of (8)—whatever they are—in this more subjective interpretation are different from those of (10) and (11): (8) does not assert that the proposition 'John is coming tomorrow' or 'I am coming tomorrow', as such, was ever explicitly entertained, let alone asserted, by the other subject of consciousness with which the speaker associates himself. Indeed, no linguistically encoded proposition at all need have been entertained at the time referred to by the tense of *was coming* for (8) to be appropriately and truly uttered. For this and other reasons (many of them having to do with deixis: there are further complications not mentioned here), it seems to be impossible to treat free indirect speech as being no more than a stylistic variation upon normal direct speech. Even more obviously, it cannot be treated as a variation upon normal indirect speech (cf. Banfield, 1973).

Once the syntactic and semantic distinctiveness of what is clearly free indirect speech in terms of its mixed characteristics is conceded, the way is open for the recognition of the fact that there are many sentences which, though they do not bear the marks of free indirect speech, must often be interpreted as such in the context in which they are uttered. This is true of *John was coming*, which is just as ambiguous in respect of temporal reference, despite the absence of any non-past deictic adverbial, as (8) is and would be given two different translations in certain languages.

The final stage in the argument depends upon the recognition of the further fact that tense itself, even in its basic function of establishing temporal reference, is ultimately subjective (though it can be objectified and made part of the propositional content in certain languages). What I have referred to elsewhere as the Augustinian theory of tense—the theory 'that past, present and future are all located (in memory, observation or anticipation) in the experiential present' (Lyons, 1977, p. 821)—rests upon this view. As the speaker can project himself subjectively, with shifted deixis, into the consciousness of another, so he can project himself, in imagination or memory, into another state of his own consciousness: i.e. into a shifted experiential present. When this happens, he will use the aspect that is appropriate for experiential description, but combine it with the tense that indicates that a shift has been made into the past or, in certain cases, the future; and the utterance will have, implicitly or explicitly, two deictic points of reference. This possibility of transferring the experiential present—or of embedding one experiential present within another—accounts for some of the marked uses of the durative aspects in many languages: uses that have often been described in terms of their greater vividness. The so-called picturesque imperfect (imparfait pittoresque) of French has been much discussed in this connection: several reasons have been advanced for its systematic use by Flaubert and nineteenth century writers of the naturalist school, on the one hand, and for its encroachment upon the ordinary narrative imperfect (imparfait narratif)—with a consequent loss of semantic markedness—in more recent writing (cf. Weinrich, 1964, pp. 166–167; Reid, 1970, pp. 162–165).

I will not go further into this question. Nor will I discuss any of the other areas apart from modality, tense, and aspect in which deixis is, at least in part, subjectivized. It remains, however, to make explicit the possibility of adopting a much more radical view than I have done here—one which might commend itself to some of the phenomenological structuralists to whom I referred at the very beginning of this paper.

I have taken the view that, whereas modality is basically subjective and may be objectivized differently and to a greater or less extent in different languages, the basic function of deixis is to relate the entities and situations to which reference is made in language to the spatio-temporal zero-point—the here-and-now—of the context of utterance. Admittedly, this zero-point is egocentric, as everyone who ever talks about deixis would agree. But its egocentricity is not necessarily subjective in the sense of this paper: space and time can be treated as objective dimensions of the external world, in which speaker and addressee are located and interrelated as might be any other middle-sized physical objects. From this point of view, it is simply a matter of convenience that speakers should use the place and time of utterance as part of the point of reference: they might, in principle, use the spatiotemporal location of something else, fixed or variable, in the physical environment.

(This does of course happen, to a limited extent, in certain languages, in which the demonstrative pronouns incorporate a reference to a river, a mountain range, the position of the sun, etc. But as far as I know these languages all have egocentric deixis as well.)

In the last resort, I have perhaps no valid reason for treating the spatiotemporal co-ordinates of deixis as being basically objective—no reason, that is to say, other than adherence to the same ontological prejudice as leads me to treat what I call first-order nominals as being more basic than either second-order or third-order nominals (cf. Lyons, 1977, p. 446; 1979). This prejudice may be no more than the residue of a fairly traditional Anglo-Saxon empiricism! A thoroughly subjectivist theory of deixis would clearly be more comprehensive than the one to which, so far, I continue to subscribe and which necessarily rests, as I pointed out earlier, upon the distinction between basic and derived functions.

REFERENCES

Adamczewski, H. (1974). BE + ING revisited. In S. P. Corder & E. Roulet (eds), *Linguistic insights in applied linguistics*. Paris: Didier.

Austin, J. L. (1946). Other minds. *Proceedings of the Aristotelian Society*, Suppl. Vol. 20. Reprinted in J. L. Austin, *Philosophical papers*. London: Oxford University Press, 1961.

Banfield, A. (1973). Narrative style and the grammar of direct and indirect speech. *Foundations of Language*, **10**, 1–39.

Bar-Hillel, Y. (1954). Indexical expressions. *Mind*, **63**, 359–379. Reprinted in Y. Bar-Hillel, *Aspects of language*. Jerusalem: Magnes, 1970.

Benveniste, E. (1958). De la subjectivité dans le langage. *Journal de Psychologie*, **51**, 257–265. Reprinted in E. Benveniste (1966), *q.v.*

Benveniste, E. (1959). Les relations de temps dans le verbe francais. *Bulletin de la Société de Linguistique*, **54**, 69–82. Reprinted in E. Benveniste (1966), *q.v.*

Benveniste, E. (1966). *Problèmes de linguistique générale*. Paris: Gallimard.

Benveniste, E. (1974). *Problèmes de linguistique générale*, Vol. 2. Paris: Gallimard.

Berthoud, A.-C. (1979). Projet d'étude 'La déixis en tant que problème d'apprentissage': Etude de quelques verbes de mouvement. *Travaux du Centre de Recherches Sémiologiques, University of Neuchâtel*, **33**, 77–99.

Black, M. (1968). *The labyrinth of language*. New York: Praeger. British editions: London: Pall Mall, 1970; Harmondsworth: Penguin Books, 1972. (Quotations and page references in the text are from the Penguin edition.)

Bühler, K. (1934). *Sprachtheorie*. Jena: Fischer.

Bublitz, W. (1978). *Ausdrucksweisen der Sprechereinstellung im Deutschen und Englischen*. Tübingen: Niemeyer.

Chomsky, N. (1966). *Cartesian linguistics*. New York: Harper & Row.

Chomsky, N. (1968). *Language and mind*. New York: Harcourt, Brace & World.

Chomsky, N. (1975). *Reflections on language*. New York: Random House.

Clark, E. V. (1974). Normal states and evaluative viewpoints. *Language*, **50**, 316–332.

Comrie, B. (1976). *Aspect*. London: Cambridge University Press.

Culioli, A., Fuchs, C., & Pêcheux, M. (1970). Considérations théoriques à propos du traitement formel du langage. Centre de Linguistique Quantitative, University of Paris VII.

Desclés, J.-P. (1976). Description de quelques opérations énonciatives. In J. David & R. Martin (eds), *Modèles logiques et niveaux d'analyse linguistique*. Paris: Klincksieck.

Dummett, M. (1973). *Frege: philosophy of language*. London: Duckworth.

Fodor, J. A. (1978). *The language of thought*. New York: Crowell & Hassocks.

Friedrich, P. (1974). *On aspect theory and Homeric aspects* (Indiana University Publications in Anthropology and Linguistics; Memoir 28 of *International Journal of American Linguistics*). Bloomington, Ind.: Indiana University Press.

Fuchs, C., & Rouault, J. (1975). Towards a formal treatment of the phenomenon of aspect. In E. L. Keenan (ed.), *Formal semantics of natural language*. Cambridge: Cambridge University Press.

Halliday, M. A. K. (1970). Functional diversity in language as seen from a consideration of modality and mood in English. *Foundations of Language*, **6**, 322–365.

Hamburger, K. (1968). *Die Logik der Dichtung*. Stuttgart: Klett.

Hare, R. M. (1971). *Practical inferences*. London: Macmillan.

Hintikka, J. (1962). Cogito, ergo sum: inference or performance? *Philosophical Review*, **71**, 3–32. Reprinted in J. Hintikka, *Knowledge and the known*. Dordrecht: Reidel, 1974.

Hockett, C. F. (1958). *A course in modern linguistics*. New York: Macmillan.

Hopper, P. J. (1979). Some observations on the typology of focus and aspect in narrative language. *Studies in Language*, **3**, 37–64.

Jakobson, R. (1932). Zur Struktur des russischen Verbums. In *Charisteria Guilelmo Mathesio Quinquagenario*, Prague. Reprinted in J. Vachek (ed.), *A Prague school reader in linguistics*. Bloomington, Ind.: Indiana University Press, 1964; also reprinted in E. P. Hamp, F. W. Householder & R. Austerlitz (eds), *Readings in linguistics II*. Chicago: Chicago University Press, 1966.

Joos, M. (1964). *The English verb*. Madison, Wisc.: University of Wisconsin Press.

Katz, J. J. (1972). *Semantic theory*. New York: Harper & Row.

Kristeva, J. (1971). Du sujet en linguistique. In J. Kristeva (ed.), *Épistemologie de la linguistique*. Paris: Didier & Larousse. Reprinted in J. Kristeva, *Polylogue*. Paris: Seuil, 1977.

Kristeva, J., Milner, J.-C., & Ruwet, N. (eds) (1975). *Langue, discours, société: pour Emile Benveniste*. Paris: Seuil.

Kuroda, S. Y. (1973). Where epistemology, grammar and style meet—a case study from Japanese. In S. Anderson & P. Kiparsky (eds), *Festschrift for Morris Halle*. New York: Holt, Rinehart & Winston, 1973. French translation in Kuroda (1979), *q.v.*

Kuroda, S. Y. (1974). On grammar and narration. In C. Rohrer & N. Ruwet (eds), *Actes du colloque franco-allemand de grammaire transformationelle*. Tübingen: Niemeyer. French translation in Kuroda (1979), *q.v.*

Kuroda, S. Y. (1975). Réflexions sur les fondements de la théorie de la narration. In J. Kristeva, J. C. Milner, & N. Ruwet (eds), *Langue, discourse, société: pour Emile Benveniste*. Paris: Deuil. English version in T. van Dijk (ed.), *Pragmatics of language and literature*. Amsterdam: North Holland, 1976.

Kuroda, S. Y. (1979). *Aux quatre coins de la linguistique*. Paris: Seuil.

Lewis, D. (1972). General semantics. In D. Davidson, & G. Harman (eds), *Semantics of natural language*. Dordrecht: Reidel.

Lewis, G. L. (1967). *Turkish grammar*. Oxford: Oxford University Press.

Lyons, J. (1968). *Introduction to theoretical linguistics*. London: Cambridge University Press.

Lyons, J. (1977). *Semantics*, Vols 1 and 2. London: Cambridge University Press.

Lyons, J. (1979). Knowledge and truth: a localistic approach. In D. J. Allerton, E. Carney, & D. Holdcroft (eds), *Function and context in linguistic analysis*. London: Cambridge University Press.

Matthews, G. S. (1965). *Hidatsa syntax*. The Hague: Mouton.

Palmer, F. R. (1974). *The English verb*. London: Longman.

Popper, K. (1972). *Objective knowledge*. London: Oxford University Press.

Quirk, R., Greenbaum, S., Leech, G., & Svartvik, J. (1972). *A grammar of contemporary English*. London: Longman.

Récanati, F. (1979). *La transparence et l'énonciation*. Paris: Seuil.

Reid, T. B. W. (1970). Verbal aspect in modern French. In T. G. S. Combe & P. Rickard (eds), *The French language: studies presented to Lewis Charles Harmer*. London: Harrap.

Rey-Debove, J. (1978). *Le métalangage*. Paris: Le Robert.

Ridjanović, M. (1976). *A synchronic study of verbal aspect in English and Serbo-Croatian*. Cambridge, Mass.: Slavica Publishers.

Russell, B. (1940). *An inquiry into meaning and truth*. London: Allen & Unwin.

Sadock, J. M., & Zwicky, A. M. forthcoming. Sentence types. In S. Anderson, T. Givón, E. Kennan, T. Shopen, & S. Thompson (eds), *Language typology and syntactic field work*.

Schubiger, M. (1965). English intonation and German modal particles: a comparative study. *Phonetica*, **12**, 65–84. Reprinted in D. Bolinger (ed.), *Intonation: selected readings*. Harmondsworth: Penguin, 1972.

Smith, N. V., & Wilson, D. (1979). *Modern linguistics: the results of Chomsky's revolution*. Harmondsworth: Penguin.

Tarski, A. (1956). *Logic, semantics, and metamathematics*. London: Oxford University Press.

Todorov, T. (ed.) (1970). *L'Énonciation*. Paris: Didier & Larousse.

Weinrich, H. (1964). *Tempus: Besprochene und erzählte Welt*. Stuttgart: Kohlhammer. French edition, *Le temps*. Paris: Seuil, 1964.

Whorf, B. L. (1938). Some verbal categories in Hopi. *Language*, **14**, 275–286. Reprinted in B. L. Whorf, *Language, thought and reality*. Cambridge, Mass.: MIT Press, 1956.

Williams, R. (1975). *Keywords: a vocabulary of culture and society*. London: Fontana.

Speech, Place, and Action
Edited by R. J. Jarvella and W. Klein
© 1982 John Wiley & Sons Ltd.

Reference to Past Time[1]

MARK J. STEEDMAN

1 PRELIMINARIES

1.1 Introduction

Lyons (1977, p. 637) has defined deixis as 'the location and identification of persons, objects, events, processes and activities being talked about, or referred to, in relation to the spatiotemporal context created and sustained by the act of utterance . . .'. The present paper examines the linguistic apparatus of tense and other related categories which is used to accomplish such deixis to events and states of affairs in the past. In particular, it is concerned with the precise way in which such adjuncts as *when* clauses do sustain, and indeed change, the spatiotemporal context to which these categories refer.

The problem in formulating the semantics of time reference has always been the extraordinary ambiguity or non-specificity apparent in the linguistic categories that are involved. It seems as if a wide variety of different meanings[2] are distributed rather haphazardly among a handful of linguistic devices. For example, a simple English clause in the past tense, such as

(1) John played 'Cherokee'

may refer to a single occasion of playing, either incomplete or completed, or to a period of repeated playing of the tune. It may also refer to a rather more indefinitely extended period of habitual playing of the tune, or even to the instant with which its playing began. These various meanings may be brought out by the inclusion of different time adverbials, such as *for a few minutes, in a few minutes, for ten hours, in those days*, and *at half past nine*, respectively. (Temporal description is of course only one class of meaning carried by past tense. Others are *oratio obliqua* and counterfactuality. Only the purely temporal meanings will be considered here.) The meanings of time adverbials and subordinate clauses such as *when* and *while* clauses, which will be termed 'time adjuncts', are themselves also typically ambiguous. For example, two events related by a complex sentence involving a *when* clause may either be

125

simultaneous, or sequential, as in

(2a) When she took my queen, she gave me check.
(2b) When she took my queen, I took hers.

Of course, such protean shifts of temporal description as those ascribed to (1) may also occur in the complex sentences typified by (2). In the following sentence the main clause tends to undergo a change in character from the basic stative meaning of clauses involving the verb to *know*, to refer to the instantaneous event with which the state of knowing begins.

(3) When he left the party, I knew something was wrong.

Such context-dependent shifts in temporal descriptive meaning occur with great facility, and make the semantics of tense, mood, the auxiliaries, and the time adjuncts particularly hard to capture. They also mean that the literature of this area is unusually fraught with examples of unnoticed ambiguities, and of conflicting and uncertain intuitions. Moreover, while this vast literature describes the varieties of meaning that each category may convey, it has generally proved more difficult to show why just those particular functions, rather than some other arbitrary collection, should have been brought

	When John left, . . .	When the band played, . . .	When the band was playing, . . .	When John had left, . . .
. . . , Fred left	| -------- | →	|/ / / / | -------- | →	|/ / / / | -------- |	|/ / / / / -------- |
. . . , Fred danced with Alice.	| -------- |/ / | →	|/ / / / | -------- |/ / / / | →	|/ / / / | -------- |/ / |	|/ / / / / -------- |/ / |
. . . , Fred was dancing with Alice.	| -------- |/ / / / |	|/ / / / | -------- |/ / / / / / |	? |/ / / / | -------- |/ / / / |	? |/ / / / / -------- |/ / / / |
. . . , Fred had left.	| -------- |/ / / / |	|/ / / / | -------- |/ / / / / / |	|/ / / / | -------- |/ / / / / / |	?? |/ / / / / -------- |/ / / / |

Figure 1   Various temporal relations that can be conveyed by complex sentences including *when* clauses depend upon the verbs and auxiliaries of the two clauses

	While the band played, . . .	While the band was playing, . . .
. . . , Fred left	? | / / / / / | – – – – – – – – – |	| / / / / / / | – – – – – – – – – – |
. . . , Fred danced with Alice.	| / / / / / | – – – – – – – – – | / / / / / |	| / / / / / / | – – – – – – – – | / / / |
. . . , Fred was dancing with Alice.	| / / / / | – – – – – – – – – – | / / / / / / |	| / / / / | – – – – – – – – – | / / / / |
. . . , Fred had left.	? | / / / / | – – – – – – – – – | / / / / / / / |	? | / / / / | – – – – – – – – – | / / / / / / / |

Figure 2   Various temporal relations that can be conveyed by complex sentences including *while* clauses

together under a single linguistic roof. As Bennett (1975) has pointed out, it is essential for a semantic theory to meet this latter criterion.

In this paper, it is proposed that certain apparent ambiguities of tense, the progressive and perfect auxiliaries, and *when* and *while* time adjuncts in English can best be understood as ambiguities of the process of reference, rather than of sense or semantics, and that, given an appropriate account of the mechanism of reference, some apparently diverse meanings conveyed by these categories can be seen to be derived from a single sense.

Some impression of the complexity of the interactions of these categories can be gained from Figures 1 and 2, where tables are presented showing temporal relations typically expressed by *while* and *when* in complex sentences. In each cell of the tables, the temporal extent defined by the subordinate clause appears above a line representing the dimension of time. The temporal extent defined by the main clause appears below. Where the relation is unspecific, an arrow represents the direction of variability. Where the sentences in a cell are odd or anomalous, the anomaly is indicated by one or more question-marks.

1.2   Reference

It has often been pointed out that tense is anaphorically and deictically referential in character (McCawley, 1971; Partee, 1973; Isard, 1974; Lyons, 1977). That is, just as the anaphoric pronoun *he* demands an antecedent in the preceding conversation, so, as McCawley points out, sentences like (1) must have an antecedent past time for their tense to refer to. If no such reference time has been established in the preceding conversation, say by a *when* clause such as *When I was at Jim's last night*, . . . , then (1) will be unacceptable.

It is arguable that the most successful theories of reference to date are those theories which have been expressed as or exemplified by computer programs, of which Winograd's (1972) was an early example. Winograd's program could carry on a 'conversation' with a human operator concerning states of affairs in a simulated universe of discourse representing a table-top upon which a number of child's blocks were to be found. The program's principal capabilities were to obey orders concerning this 'Blocks World', and to answer questions both about its current state, and about past situations that had occurred in the course of the conversation. The orders and questions could involve a wide range of expressions referring to objects in the world, including quantified expressions, such as *the box, a big red pyramid, all blocks, any cube*, and so on. Some of these references could be anaphoric in nature. For example, an expression like *the block*, in the context of a simulated world containing several blocks, achieves its reference by causing the recent conversation to be examined for mention of a suitable object, as do more purely anaphoric expressions such as *it* and *that*.

Winograd's program also allows a simple kind of reference to events that have taken place during the conversation. For example, it can answer questions such as

(4)   Did you pick up anything red while you were building the steeple?

As an account of time reference, it is greatly simplified with respect to the problems outlined in the introduction to this paper, and his way of handling questions like (4) is rather different to the procedures that will be suggested here. However, the present theory shares the feature of being embodied in a computer program, and also exploits the clear relation that such programs express between the semantics of an expression and the context in which it is used, in order to express both the sense and the reference of tense, the progressive and perfect auxiliaries, and the time adjuncts.

1.3   The nature of temporal descriptions in English

It has frequently been noted that many languages embody a parallel between concepts of space and of time. In English, nearly all locative prepositions are also temporal prepositions, and the concept of deixis has been applied to time as well as to space. In particular, tense is a quasi-spatial, deictic category (cf. Lyons, 1977; Miller & Johnson-Laird, 1976).

The classic localist account of the nature of tense and time reference is that of Reichenbach (1947). According to his scheme, the distinctions of tense are distinctions between the relationships of three points along a time-line. These three points are the utterance time, or time of speaking (U), the reference time (R), and the event time (E). For example, the past perfect in sentence (5) is held to describe the event of John's winning as being in the past with respect to a reference time which is itself in the past with respect to the time of utterance:

(5)   John had won.

By contrast, a simple past tense conveys an event time simultaneous with the reference time, both being in the past with respect to the utterance time. Such relationships are conveniently represented pictorially, as in (6):

(6)   E   R   U   E, R   U
     ---|----|----|--   ---|----|---
        past perfect   simple past

Reichenbach's scheme was intended, in part, to explicate the meaning of time connectives, such as *when*. For example, the meaning of

(7)   When Fred arrived, John had won

depends on the identity of the reference points in the two clauses, and may be represented diagrammatically as follows, where E_1 represents Fred's arrival and E_2 John's winning:

(8)   E₁, R   U
        ----|-----|-----|----
          E₂

where E_1, R and U, and E_2.

Reichenbach (1947) embodied this behaviour of *when* clauses in the principle of the 'positional use of the reference point'.

Reichenbach's scheme neatly expresses the quasi-spatial and deictic nature of tense and time reference and many subsequent theories of tense and the auxiliary system have built upon its foundation (e.g. Bull, 1963; Isard & Longuet-Higgins, 1971; Smith, 1975, 1978; Hornstein, 1977). In particular, Isard (1974) considerably extended the idea to encompass the semantics of conditionals and counterfactual conditionals, of modal verbs, and of *when* relative clauses. The current paper stems directly from his work on the last of these categories.

1.4   Tense and time reference

The task for Isard's (1974) program was to answer questions, posed in type-written English, concerning the moves in a game of tic-tac-toe, or noughts-

and-crosses, which it played with its operator. Typical questions were

(9a)   Could you have taken square four when I took square five?
(9b)   If I had taken square four when I took square five, what would you
       have done?

The *when* clause in such questions was evaluated first, to yield a new referent
for the past tense marker—in the above cases, by searching for that situation
in the game's history at which the operator took square five, or for the
situation immediately following. (Counterfactual conditionals and modal
verbs were handled using simulated possible states of play, in addition to the
single Reichenbach line of factual time.) Once this had been done the main
clause could be evaluated solely by examination of the situation that had been
identified by the *when* clause. Where there was no *when* clause in a question,
for example

(10)   Could you have won?

the program would take the reference time to be the one most recently
established.

In expressing the role that *when* clauses play in setting up a temporal
referent, Isard's account goes considerably beyond Reichenbach's. It is not
enough to say, as he did, that the reference times of main and subordinate
clauses must coincide. The *order* in which subordinate and main clause are
evaluated is crucial for the language understander, since natural language
expressions are typically extremely ambiguous with respect to the events to
which they refer. For example, consider the following question, asked about a
party at which the hearer was present:

(11)   When the band played 'Autumn Leaves', did Arthur dance with
       Alison?

There may have been many occasions on which Arthur danced with Alison.
In answering the question, the order in which the two events are considered
makes no difference, *once the particular events in question have been identified*. But in order to identify the particular instance in question of Arthur's
dancing with Alison, it is essential to first identify the period of the band's
playing the tune in question, and only then to search for an instance of the
main clause event in that temporal vicinity. (This will be necessary if further
questions about this *particular* instance are to be answered, for example.) It is
in explicating these pragmatic aspects of *when* clauses that the computational
account can be claimed to add something to the logic-based accounts of
Reichenbach and his direct descendants.[3]

It was a virtue of Isard's program that its extremely circumscribed universe
of discourse allowed him to tackle several difficult problems in the semantics
of tense, mood, and aspect. Nevertheless, it is inevitable that certain idiosyn-

cracies of the world of tic-tac-toe games makes his account less than general. In particular, the fact that the only events that can be discussed are instantaneous moves of the game, and the fact that only one of these events can occur at a time, mean that a great deal of the semantics of connectives like *when* and of sentences in the perfect, and all of the semantics of *while* and of progressive sentences, cannot be illustrated. Moreover, as he pointed out himself, his method of resolving the ambiguity of *when* clauses, as between the 'simultaneous' and 'sequential' meaning, exemplified by sentences (9a) and (9b), was *ad hoc*.

1.5 'Events' and 'situations'

The distinction between instantaneous events and those which occupy a period of time is only the most obvious of those which are made more or less explicit in natural languages. Many linguists and philosophers have been concerned to enumerate the varieties of temporal or 'aspectual' event-descriptions that are distinguished in English, some of which were mentioned in passing in the introduction to this paper. In particular, Vendler (1967), working in a philosophical tradition that includes Ryle (1949) and Kenny (1963), classified English verb-groups into four temporal categories. He derived his classification by observing restrictions upon the co-occurrence of the verb-groups with time-adverbial phrases, such as *in an hour* and *for an hour*. More recently, Verkuyl (1972), Dowty (1972, 1977, 1979), Heinamaki (1974), Bennett (1975), Comrie (1976), Steedman (1977), and Ritchie (1979) have elaborated this basic scheme.

Many of these authors have pointed out that few verbs fit neatly into a single one of these temporal categories. Indeed, most verbs, whatever their 'core' or basic temporal category, can be made to take on *any* temporal category by an appropriate choice of auxiliary or adverbial, as in example (1). Hence, as Verkuyl (1972) argued, these categories should be regarded as classifications of whole propositions, rather than of verbs. It will therefore be important to bear in mind throughout the discussion below that the temporal character of a proposition whose verb we regard as bearing a certain core temporal category may without warning take on a quite different character. While many of the distinctions drawn by Vendler and his followers, such as that between periods with and without conclusions, will not be treated here (but cf. Steedman, 1977), the way that instants can become periods of intermittent repetition of the core instant will be treated. One basic distinction of temporal character will be very frequently drawn upon. A distinction will be drawn between 'events' and 'situations'. The former category includes all definite instants and periods of activity, subsuming in particular Vendler's categories of 'achievements', 'activities', and 'accomplishments'. The latter category includes Vendler's 'states', but also includes sentences bearing progressive and perfect auxiliaries. (McCawley (1971) and Longuet-Higgins

(1973) have pointed out the similarities between such verb groups and statives.) The distinction is related (but not identical) to the durative/non-durative distinction of Heinamaki (1974) and the point/interval distinction of Ritchie (1979).

1.6   Representing episodes and events

A computer program is being developed that is to answer a wide variety of questions involving the categories discussed above. Its universe of discourse is the changing state of affairs on a computer 'operating system'. An operating system is itself a program which has the role of overseeing the simultaneous use of a large computer by a number of human users. The users share certain resources, such as printers and paper-tape readers. Apart from the fact that only one person can use such a resource at a time, the users are free to pursue their activities, such as editing and running their programs, at the same time. It should be stressed, however, that the present program uses a simplified *simulation* of the passage of events in such a system.

The program is to answer questions involving tense, the progressive and perfect auxiliaries, time adverbials and time adjuncts, concerning the course of events on an operating system, much as a witness in a courtroom or in the closing chapter of a detective story might be questioned in detail concerning the precise relation in time of events at the scene of a crime. Such a universe of discourse is considerably more complex than both the Blocks World and the tic-tac-toe world of Winograd and Isard. At the time of writing only the semantic and referential mechanisms have been developed. The syntactic problem of producing the semantic representations from questions posed in English will not be treated here.

The first problem that must be solved in constructing such a program is that of selecting a suitable representation for the history of the universe of discourse. There is no doubt that a simple predicate logic can express the state of each element of the operating system world at each instant of its history, and be used to infer the truth of temporal relations between events in that history. The program employs what amounts to such a logic, embedded in a subset of the POPLER programming language (Davies, 1973) which is itself a descendant of Hewitt's (1969) PLANNER. PLANNER and its descendants can be regarded as theorem provers in which the number of axioms has been reduced at the expense of increasing the number of inference rules (Davies and Isard, 1972).

However, there is still a serious problem with such a representation of episodes in the operating system world—that is, a logic (albeit one of a rather unfamiliar kind) representing the history of the operating system world in a body of formulae and a number of inference rules. The problem arises from the fact that a body of formulae in a logic is essentially *unordered* and *unstruc-*

tured. That is to say that if you are searching for a particular one, you simply have to go through the lot until you find the one you want, or until there are none left. Everything that is known about 'episodic memory', or memory for events, including our intuitions about what happens when we answer questions involving *when* clauses and the like, suggests that our memory of events is very highly structured, and that it is in fact linearly ordered, by analogy with the temporal sequence that it represents. Moreover, it has already been remarked, in considering Isard's model, that it is of the essence of complex sentences involving *when* clauses that the *when* clause be considered *first*, and that the tense of the main clause be interpreted in anaphoric relation to the referent thus established. However, this obvious intuition about the process of answering questions about episodes is not captured by the kind of model that we have considered so far. Consider, for example, the question

(12)   When your son was born, was it snowing?

Having identified the reference time when the child was born, we would still have to examine every formula, including those referring to all occasions on which it was snowing, even though most of these can immediately be rejected as not referring to the reference instant in question. Since we have to examine them, we might as well have found all occasions on which it was snowing *first*, and *then* found the reference time. Simply on grounds of efficiency, it would be sensible to go for a different kind of representation, in which the establishment of the reference time restricts the search to some particular subset of the formulae.

Such a representation can be achieved by structuring the formulae into a linear sequence of bundles, each bundle consisting of just those formulae which define successive situations. Stephen Isard (1974) used a very simple version of such a representation. The successive situations were the successive states of the tic-tac-toe board. The description of any given situation consisted in effect of a set of facts defining the ownership of the squares by the two parties. And since each successive state of the game only differs from its predecessor and successor in respect of the ownership of a single square, all that really needed to be kept was an ordered sequence of *moves* of the game: from these, any given situation could be constructed. Such a representation has an 'analogue' character, directly representing and exploiting a property of the world which goes in the literature by the name of the 'Frame Property'—that is, the fact that there are continuities between successive situations in the real world. This aspect of the representation clearly effects a saving in the number of facts that need to be stored. In such a miniscule world the saving may not be too important, but it will be crucial in representing the more complex episodes of the operating system world. (It was also essential to Isard's program's understanding of conditionals and modals, as called on by questions like the following:

(13) If I had taken square three when I took square four, what would
you have done?

The same expedient was adopted by Winograd.)

The current program exploits the advantages of this kind of representation
in a similar way. As in Isard's program, an ordered list of events that have
affected the state of the world is kept. And again, a representation of the state
of the world at a given time is maintained, as a set of formulae. Also, the
effect of a time adjunct such as a *whole* or *when* clause, is to cause this world
model to be set to a certain situation in the past. The main clause is then
interpreted with respect to that situation. However, apart from this basic
similarity to Isard's program (and to some extent to Winograd's) it turns out
that the problems associated with handling the kinds of event descriptions
that have been described in the introductory sections require a considerable
elaboration of the basic scheme.

1.7   Representing period events

In setting up a representation of the kind described in the last section, the
first problem is to decide how to represent periods, and how to represent their
use as referents, as in

(14) While my program ran, how much CPU time did I use?

Since the representation of the history of the episode is to consist solely of
changes in the state of the world, and changes of state are by definition
instants, the solution to the first part of the problem is simple: we represent
periods in the history by noting the instants with which they begin and end.
For example, a very much simplified 'history' of a session is illustrated in
Figure 3.

The figure represents an ordered sequence of 'bundles' of propositions
each defining a number of simultaneous instantaneous changes to the state of
the universe of discourse. Each proposition is represented as a data structure
enclosed in square brackets, such as

(15a) [[INSTANT START PERIOD] ANN PRINT FILE1],
(15b) [[INSTANT] BETTY LOGIN].

Such data structures correspond to atomic formulae in more traditional logical inference systems. Each begins with a substructure identifying its type
(that is whether it is a simple instant like someone logging into the system or
the start or end of a period). The type is then followed by a string of symbols
which define the particular nature of the event. It will be observed that the
history in question is a somewhat artificial one: there are rather a lot of events
that coincide exactly in time. It has been set up in this way deliberately, to

```
1 – [[INSTANT] ANN LOGIN]
    [[INSTANT] ALF LOGIN]
    [[INSTANT] ARTHUR LOGIN]
    [[INSTANT] ALISON LOGIN]
    [[INSTANT START PERIOD] ARTHUR TALK TO ALISON]
    [[INSTANT START PERIOD] ALF EDIT FILE1]
    [[INSTANT START PERIOD] ANN PRINT FILE2]

2 – [[INSTANT] BETTY LOGIN]
    [[INSTANT] BILL LOGIN]
    [[INSTANT] BERT LOGIN]

3 – [[INSTANT STOP PERIOD] ARTHUR TALK TO ALISON]
    [[INSTANT] CATHY LOGIN]
    [[INSTANT] CHARLES LOGIN]

4 – [[INSTANT] ALF LOGOUT]
    [[INSTANT STOP PERIOD] ANN PRINT FILE2]
    [[INSTANT STOP PERIOD] ALF EDIT FILE1]
    [[INSTANT START PERIOD] ARTHUR TALK TO ALISON]
    [[INSTANT START PERIOD] ANN PRINT FILE3]

5 – [[INSTANT STOP PERIOD] ARTHUR TALK TO ALISON]
    [[INSTANT STOP PERIOD] ANN PRINT FILE3]
    [[INSTANT START PERIOD] CATHY EDIT FILE4]
    [[INSTANT] BILL LOGOUT]

6 – [[INSTANT] BETTY LOGOUT]
```

Figure 3   A simplified history of an episode in the
operating system world

allow full scope for the examples that are to follow without making the history
too complex.

Such a representation of the history is not unlike that used by Isard, apart
from the fact that more than one thing can happen at a time. However, it is
clear that in order to represent the temporal reference *periods* established by
utterances like (14) it is no longer possible to identify the temporal referent
with a single instantaneous situation or state of the world. Instead, the temporal referent must correspond to a whole segment of the time line, from the
start to the end of the reference event, in this case *my running my program*.
Thus the temporal referent itself must be distinguished from the model of the
state of the world at any given instant. For the moment, it will suffice to think
of the temporal referent established by (14) as a pair of numbers defining the
extent of the reference 'windows' on the time line.

It should be noted in passing that although the history includes a repeated
occurrence of Arthur talking to Alison, and in English these events can be
referred to collectively as a repeated event of the kind discussed in the introduction, the fact that instant 1 is the start of such a repetition is *not* marked
explicitly in the history. Such instants must be *inferred* in a way to be discussed below. Thus, although instants are the primitives of the system, not all

instants are primitive. Certain other kinds of event also are not directly represented in the history—for example, the instants at which the system prints messages to a user that have been left for him by the other users: there is a general rule of inference which says that people get their messages when they log in to the system, to be used in answering questions like

(16)   Has Fred received the message that I sent him?

1.8 'Simple' past tense

As long as questions about the operating system world do not involve progressive or perfect auxiliaries, the basic apparatus developed by Stephen Isard is quite adequate, despite the extension to events occupying a period of time. Consider for example

(17a)   When Betty logged in, did Bert log in?
(17b)   When Betty logged in, did she get my message?

As before, the referent-setting *when* clause is evaluated first, and it seems to set the context either to the instant of Betty's logging in, or to the instant just after that. And again, the main clause is evaluated with respect to that reference time.

While clauses involving periods behave in a similar manner, at least when they do not involve the progressive auxiliary, as in

(18)   While Ann edited her file, did she use the printer?

The above *while* clause sets a reference period as the context for the main clause, and behaves in every respect like a *when* clause. For example, the tense of the following supplementary question has the same 'pronominal' reference to the period of Ann's editing.

(19)   How much processor time did she use?

A slight complication is introduced when a *when* clause involves a period. At first glance the following question seems to ask much the same as (18)—that is, whether the two events were coextensive.

(20)   When Ann edited her file, did she use the line printer?

However, this is not generally true of *when* clauses involving periods. Consider

(21a)   When Ann edited her file, did John use the line printer?
(21b)   When Ann ran her program, did John sign off?

In the first of these it is not necessarily the case that editing and printing were co-extensive, and in the second, the two events *cannot* be co-extensive, since one is a period, and the other an instant.

The behaviour of these sentences is due to an aspect of questions with *when* clauses that has not been made explicit up to now. A distinction was drawn using examples such as (2) between a 'simultaneous' and a 'sequential' relationship between events related by a *when* adjunct. However, the latter relationship would be better described as 'con-sequential'. Questions involving the so-called sequential relation invariably implicate or presuppose a consequential effect of the event in the subordinate clause upon that in the main clause, such as *enabling* or *causing* its occurrence. It is this meaning that is understood in all of the above three questions. They take on their particular meanings because one knows, for example, that if someone signs off *because* someone else runs a program then they may do so at some time during the run, but if someone uses a printer as a consequence of running their own program, then they tend to start at the same time and continue until they stop. The same ambiguity between questions about causation and simulaneity arose in Isard's (1974) tic-tac-toe world. The apparent difference in reference between

(22a)   When I took five, did you take seven?

and

(22b)   When I took five, did I win?

was handled by Isard simply on the basis of whether the subjects of the two clauses were the same or different. As he pointed out, this was unsatisfactory. In particular, it would give an inappropriate result for a question like

(23)   When John logged in, did he get a message?

—where the two events are presumably consequent rather than simultaneous, despite having the same subject. The question of causal or consequential interpretations of time adjuncts is a complicated one, and will be discussed later in the context of the perfect auxiliary, whose meaning is intimately bound up with ideas of intention and cause. The question of exactly what it means to describe two events as standing in this 'consequential' relationship will also be deferred until then.[4]

While does not produce any ambiguity between a temporal meaning and a consequential one. Indeed, it seems expressly to *exclude* the idea of a logical connection between the two events: if you have reason to suppose that Ann's editing *caused* John's use of the printer, then you should ask a question like (21a), rather than the corresponding *while* question. The program represents a *while* or *when* question as a sequence of three 'goals' or steps of inference. The first of these goals is to establish a reference interval as the value of a variable *ref*, by searching the entire history of the episode for examples of the event or situation in the subordinate clause. The second stage is to search the history within that interval for any example(s) of the main clause event or situation. The temporal extent thus defined becomes the value of another variable, *anaphor*. The third goal is to check that the two times defined by *ref* and *anaphor* stand in the relation specified by the type of adjunct and main clause. For example, the question

(24)   While Ann edited her program, did anyone use the line printer?

should only be answered affirmatively if the two times are co-extensive—that is, if the main clause event lasts throughout the reference interval defined by the subordinate clause.

The only constraint that has been placed on the search for the main clause events in the above example is that the search be conducted within the bounds of the reference time. Hence it may well happen that more than one instance will be found matching the main clause description. For example, in answering the last question, it may be the case that someone used the printer several times. These states of affairs can be represented graphically by the same kind of extension of Reichenbach's time-line diagram that was used in Figures 1 and 2.

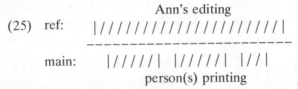

In such a context, the simple procedure outlined above behaves in a manner which is strikingly similar to the way that hearers seem to behave with respect to the systematic ambiguity in English between single and repeated events. That is, the program will find *all* the instances within the reference period, whether there is one or there are many. These are collected into one compound event description. Once the period that has been found has been proved to be co-extensive with the reference time, as the *while* demands, the program can answer the question, either with a list of the people who have used the printer, or with a single name, whether or not this person's action was repeated. (Of course, in the case of a repeated action, a human question answerer might well judge it to be helpful to the questioner to mention this fact, by replying 'Jane did, *several times*'. However, the decision to give such a helpful amplification would depend upon inferences concerning the likely purposes of the questioner in obtaining the information. Such inferences are not the concern of this paper (but cf. Steedman & Johnson-Laird, 1978). The important goal for the program is merely to obtain the factual information from which such replies might be constructed. Presumably, a language which marks iterative aspect would only differ in that the last goal of the sequence, corresponding to the relationship established by the subordinate clause, would explicitly specify either a compound repeated event or a simple event.

Perhaps a more important respect in which the program appears to correspond to the human speaker's treatment of this distinction is in the way it often *does not* consider the ambiguity. If the program is asked the same question in a context in which, although many people used the line printer, only one such occasion occurred within the scope of the reference period, then it will simply never consider the possibility that the iterative meaning of the question is intended, because its search for the main clause event never proceeds beyond those confines. This too seems to be a natural treatment of the distinction. Consider the case where two human conversants are discussing a party which one of them attended and the other asks

(26) While you talked to Mary, was the band playing?

If the band played several tunes in the relevant period, as part of a longer period of intermittent playing, the events can be represented by the familiar sort of diagram, thus:

```
         ref:          | / / / / / / / / / / / / / / / / / |
(27)           _____
         main:         | / / / / / |  | / / / / / |  | / / / / / |
```

In such a context, the non-iterative meaning of the main clause does not seem to arise. By contrast, if the question is

(28) When Jane arrived, was the band playing?

then it is the iterative meaning that does not seem to arise. In particular, if the band wasn't actually engaged in playing at the relevant time, as in the diagram below, it does not seem possible to answer 'Yes' to the question, at least without giving further explanation, even if its silence merely represents a temporary lull in a period of repeated playing.[5]

```
(29)   ref:                                        |
           _____
       main:        | / / / / / |  | / / / / |  | / / / / |  | / / / / |
```

Similar remarks can be made about the 'inchoative' aspectual interpretation of past tense, in which a clause, such as one of the interpretations of sentence (1) in the introduction to this paper, denotes the beginning of the period to which it 'basically' refers. However, further discussion of these questions will be deferred until the discussion of causation, with which they are considerably involved.

To summarize: a simple procedure for answering questions about an episode has been presented. It has been argued that the sense of such time connectives as *while* and *when* can be naturally expressed within such a framework, and that certain ambiguities of tensed sentences, notably so-called iterative aspect, can be regarded as a natural consequence of the process of establishing reference, rather than as ambiguities of sense. In the next sections, this argument is extended to sentences including progressive and perfect auxiliaries.

2 THE PROGRESSIVE

2.1 During, throughout, and the progressive auxiliary

While clauses which include the progressive auxiliary verb *be* also function to set a temporal reference point for succeeding main clauses, like those with simple past tense. Thus the following sequence is directly analogous to the earlier examples:

> (30a) While Anne was editing her program, did Betty log in?
>   YES.
> (30b) Did Alf log in?

As before, the supplementary main clause (b) is understood to refer to the reference time established in the previous question. However, the nature of this reference time is rather different from that of a definite reference instant or period. For, of course, it is not necessarily the case that Betty's and Alf's logging in to the system should have occurred at the *same* instant during Ann's editing—merely that they both did it at *some* such instant.

The notoriously indefinite character of the progressive (Geis, 1970) is not easily captured in the time-line diagrams of Reichenbach's account, and it is not surprising that those whose work stems most directly from Reichenbach's (Smith, 1975, 1978; Hornstein, 1977) have not treated the topic in depth (but cf. Bull, 1963).

In order to capture the semantics of *while* clauses including the progressive auxiliary, two components of Reichenbach's temporal reference point must be distinguished. One is a definite period or instant, corresponding to the reference *event*. The other is a reference *relation*, defining the temporal relationship of the main clause event to the reference event. In the case of a temporal referent established by a progressive time adjunct, as in (30) above, the relation of the main clause event to the reference event is that of being *included* in its scope, and it is this relation which is understood to persist and be available for subsequent simple clauses such as (30b), rather than the time of the main clause event of (30a).

The separation of the step in the computation at which the reference event is found from that at which a particular relation between the two events is tested was made in the earlier account of simple past tense, although it only becomes crucial to make this separation in dealing with the auxiliaries. The separation amounts to a distinction between two components in Reichenbach's reference time R, as between the reference *event* and the reference *relation*. It is not the same as the similarly-named distinction drawn by Smith (1975), which is rather a translation of Reichenbach's scheme into componential semantic terms. It is, however, related to distinctions drawn by Ritchie (1977, 1979). The two temporal relations that are concerned in the contrast between simple past tense and the progressive are those expressed in English using the prepositions *throughout* and *during*, respectively.

The existing apparatus might seem to be adequate to handle progressives as well as simple tensed clauses, simply with the addition of the procedure to test the relation of inclusion as well as that for testing coextension. However, once the effect of progressive main clauses is considered, it becomes clear that some extensions to the theory are necessary. In particular, the program's model of the state of the world needs further elaboration.

Consider the question

(31)   While I printed my files, was Ann editing her program?

—which can be represented by the usual sort of diagram, as follows:

(32)   ref: | / / / / / / / / / / / / / |
        ————————————————————————————————————
        main: | / / / / / / / / / / / / / / / / / / / |

As matters stand so far, the only things that are present in the machine's representation of a state of affairs in the world are the instants which compose the history of the episode, such as the one laid out in Figure 3. Since the basic procedure for answering questions about events is to conduct a search for the main clause event *within* the window defined by the reference event, and the instants with which the main clause event begins and ends do not fall within that window, the existing apparatus will not allow the program to answer such questions.

The solution lies in elaborating the program's representation of the state of the world at a given instant. The program represents data about period events that are in progress in a body of facts, or a 'data-base', that describes the state of the world at any given instant, perhaps using atomic formulae of a form like the following

(33)   [[IN-PROGRESS PERIOD] ANN EDIT **PROGRAM3**]

Of course it would be possible simply to include such facts among the 'bundles' of instants in the history of the episode. However, with the addition of a few simple 'housekeeping' procedures it is easy to make the program add these facts automatically to a representation of the state of the world at any given instant as it searches up and down the history. The apparatus for maintaining such models is well established, and in fact is provided ready-made in

```
[TIME 6]
[[STATE] ANN BE PRESENT]
[[STATE] ARTHUR BE PRESENT]
[[STATE] ALISON BE PRESENT]
[[STATE] BETTY BE PRESENT
[[INSTANT] BETTY LOGOUT]
[[STATE] BERT BE PRESENT]
[[STATE] CATHY BE PRESENT]
[[STATE] CHARLES BE PRESENT]
[[IN-PROGRESS PERIOD] CATHY EDIT FILE4]
```

Figure 4   The state of the world at time 6
of the history shown in Figure 3

POPLER, in the form of its version of PLANNER 'antecedent theorems'. The same device is used for certain other varieties of situation, such as an individual's being present on the system. The data base representing the state of affairs at time 6 in the history represented in Figure 3 is shown in Figure 4.

Using such a representation of states of affairs in the operating system world, questions like (30) can be answered quite simply; once the reference period in that question has been found, the representation of the state of affairs at every instant in it will express directly the fact that the main clause event is in progress.

The above representation of the progressive is quite compatible with the apparatus described earlier for establishing temporal referents. Since the standard procedure of searching through the episode for instances that match the pattern of the subordinate clause collects *every* such instance, the same process applied to a progressive such as the one in (34), below, will simply collect together all instants at which the corresponding progressive is in force in a manner precisely similar to the way in which an iterative or repeated event is found:

(34)   While Ann was running her program, did Fred log in?

And the period that this process delivers will be of exactly the same extent as the corresponding question with a simple past tense subordinate clause. The difference lies in the reference *relation*, rather than the temporal extent of the reference *event*. It is perhaps worth noting in passing that a number of puzzling facts about the relationship between the progressive and simple tenses are explained by such a mechanism. The time adjuncts *while she was playing* and *while she played* only differ in the reference *relationship* that they establish, and this relationship is only investigated as the last step in computing the meaning of sentences that include them. Hence it is only investigated *after* the events in question have been identified. It is therefore not surprising that, while the second of the two following statements is strictly speaking anomalous (since John's leaving cannot have been co-extensive with the playing of the sonata), nevertheless informants are very inconsistent in their judgements.

(35a)   While she was playing the sonata, John left the room.
(35b)   ?While she played the sonata, John left the room.

Secondly, just as the theory of reference explains why languages are free to vary as to whether they explicitly mark iterative aspect, so it explains why they are similarly free with regard to the marking of imperfective aspect. If the reference relation is distinguished in some other way, there is no practical difference between the progressive and simple tense. (French is an obvious example of a language which has in general no explicit mark of imperfective aspect.) The rule that determines the reference relationship used in the third step of the procedure for *while* is as follows:

(36)   When the subordinate clause is of the 'event' variety, the relation is one of co-extension. When the subordinate clause is of the 'situation' type, the relation is one of inclusion.

It will be noted that this procedure allows the context to resolve the ambiguity between simple and iterated events in exactly the same manner as was described before for simple past tense.

To summarize this section: by addition of a data base, (of a kind quite standard in the literature of Computational Inference), which represents the state of the world at any given instant in its history, and by distinguishing two components of Reichenbach's concept of reference time, it is possible to extend the model to cope with certain uses of the English progressive,[6] whilst preserving the efficiency of the earlier representation, and also preserving its natural handling of the disambiguation of iterative and simple meanings of event descriptions. In the next section a further extension to deal with the perfect is considered.

3   THE PERFECT

3.1   Causation and consequence

Of all the categories under discussion here, the perfect is the most complex. Any attempt to characterize the perfect and past perfect in purely temporal terms, as 'past in present' and 'past in past' does not do it justice, whatever the virtues of Reichenbach's original scheme and Smith's (1975) translation of it into componential semantic terms. Unlike the uses of the progressive discussed above (but cf. note 6), the relations that it denotes are not purely temporal. It is not the case that *He had arrived at noon* means no more than *He arrived before noon*. The most basic meaning of the perfect appears to be to do with the idea that the *consequences* of the event in question are in force at the (past or present) reference time. Thus, to felicitously say (37) below, it is not enough that John's arrival be in the past with respect to the reference time (which is in this case the time of utterance). The consequences of John's arrival, in particular his *being present*, must *also* hold at that time.

(37)   John has arrived.

All of the many uses that have been distinguished for the English perfect (discussed by Comrie, 1976) appear to partake of this basic idea. Indeed, it seems likely that its temporal meaning may be merely secondary to the 'consequent state of affairs' meaning, and stems from the fact that it is in the nature of consequences to succeed their causes in time. (Such a proposal also has the merit of making auxiliary *have* seem closer to other causative uses of the verb, in sentences like *She had it stuffed, I have a bone to pick,* and *He had to put a finger in the dyke*.)

Much of the complex behaviour of the perfect can be explained in terms of this analysis. Sentences with auxiliary *have*, unlike progressive and simple tensed sentences, do not at first glance appear to behave in at all the same manner in time adjuncts as in main clauses. So, whereas (37) refers to the state of affairs consequent upon John's arrival, the perfect in (38a) seems at first glance to have much the same effect as the simple past tense of (38b):

(38a)   When the guest of honour had arrived, the speeches began.
(38b)   When the guest of honour arrived, the speeches began.

However, *two* meanings of *when* clauses have to be distinguished, one in which *when* can very roughly be paraphrased by *just as*, and another which has been rather vaguely related to the idea of causation and consequence, and in temporal terms seems to mean *just after*. It is only with respect to the *second* meaning of *when* that the above sentences are approximate paraphrases. In fact, *when* with the perfect can *never* mean the same as *just as*. Thus, the following sentences are not paraphrases, and the second is anomalous, because the situation of *being* speaking can hardly be caused by an arrival that occurs after it has begun. Such an arrival could only plausibly cause something like the *beginning* of speaking.

(39a)   When the guest of honour arrived, the chairman was speaking.
(39b)   ?When the guest of honour had arrived, the chairman was speaking.

On such an account, the reference time set up by both past tensed *and* perfect *when* clauses will be something like the 'consequent state' of the event in question. And the reference relation will similarly not be purely temporal, but will have to do with the main clause's being a consequence of the event in the subordinate clause. Very often, of course, an event which is a consequence of another event occurs *just after* that event. But such is by no means always the case, either for perfect or for simple *when* clauses, as the following examples will show:

(40)   When Fred $\left\{ \begin{array}{c} \text{had finished} \\ \text{finished} \end{array} \right\}$ the course, did he $\left\{ \begin{array}{c} \text{take the exam?} \\ \text{get the degree?} \\ \text{get a job?} \end{array} \right\}$

It appears to make very little difference here whether the subordinate clause is in the perfect or not. (There is nevertheless one crucial difference, which will be discussed below.) And since all of the alternative main clauses are plausible consequences of the reference event, the fact that they would normally occur at very different intervals of time after it (and in the last case, after quite a long interval) does not seem to affect the reasonableness of the question.

If such an analysis is correct, once again a number of notorious problems become less puzzling. For one thing, the perplexing vagueness of the temporal intervals involved in the 'just after' meaning of *when* is understandable (see, for example, Ritchie, 1979, for a sensitive exposition of this problem). The temporal interval denoted will depend entirely upon the nature of possible consequential relations between the two events in question. Another problem for which the analysis seems to suggest a solution is the notorious tendency for the perfect to take over the function of the simple past tense, as it has in the evolution of modern spoken French, and for the reverse to happen, as in some American dialects of English in which the past tense does double duty for both perfect and simple past. Even apart from their inclusion in time adjuncts, references to past events nearly always involve some kind of causal or consequential relation—purely accidental temporal coincidences simply aren't as interesting and important to human purposes. When we refer to an event, we are therefore nearly always concerned with its consequences as well. It is not surprising that the simple past may usurp the consequent state-defining function of the perfect, nor that the perfect may take over the more purely temporal function that is usually assumed to be primary to simple tense.

Unfortunately, the account given above does not exhaust the complexities of the perfect in *when* clauses. For of course there *is* a difference in meaning between a perfect *when* clause and the corresponding *when* clause with simple past tense. For example, the following is a perfectly unremarkable statement:

(41)   When Jane spilled the coffee, Fred cleaned it up.

But the following is most unusual:

(42)   ?When Jane had spilled the coffee, Fred cleaned it up.

What is odd about (42) is that it seems to carry the implication that the spilling of the coffee was *predicted* by the speaker, perhaps because it was part of an intended or planned sequence. The implication is a curious one to make of such an event. It can be exposed even more clearly by contradicting it with an adverb like *accidentally* or *suddenly*: the addition makes the sentence even less acceptable:

> (43)   ??When Jane had accidentally spilled the coffee, Fred cleaned up the mess.

(Of course there is nothing wrong with such a proposition as a main clause:

> (44)   Jane had accidentally spilled the coffee.

The distinction brought out above was also latent between different versions of sentence (40).)

Since the distinction has once again to do with the role of the complement event in an overall plan or logical sequence, and since this idea has been associated both with the perfect itself *and* with the connective *when*, the question arises as to which of these two entities gives rise to it here. The answer is that it stems from the *when*, not from the perfect. To show this, it is necessary to step beyond the confines of reference to past events, and to consider for a moment the meaning of *when* clauses involving present (or rather, non-past) tense.

3.2   Reference to non-past time

A simple clause in the so-called present tense, with or without an auxiliary, most basically refers to the time of utterance.

> (45a)   I win!
> (45b)   The fish is eating the bait.
> (45c)   I have crossed the bar.

(As before, other uses of the present tense, such as the 'historic present', are ignored here.) All of the earlier remarks concerning the meanings of the auxiliaries in main clauses and the anaphoric nature of tense apply unchanged, with the single provision that the temporal referent to which the present tense most basically refers to the instant of the time of utterance.

However, in a *when* time adjunct, a present tensed clause apparently refers to anything *but* the time of utterance:

> (46a)   When I win, I shall buy champagne for everyone.
> (46b)   When the fish is eating the bait, I shall shoot it.
> (46c)   I hope to see my pilot face to face, when I have crossed the bar.

(Again, the meaning of *when* corresponding to *whenever*, seen in *When I take my sugar to tea I'm as happy as I can be*, is not considered here.) What all of these *when* clauses seem to share, regardless of their auxiliary, is the idea of the speaker's *certain prediction* of the proposition in question, whether or not he is correct in that prediction.

The idea of prediction invoked above is exactly the same as that which was needed to express the meaning of a past perfect *when* clause. The above sentences imply that the time at which the predicting is done is the present reference time (that is, the time of utterance). They also imply that the predicted situation is later than the reference time (that is, in the future). But certain past tensed clauses, including clauses in the past perfect, also denote situations. And the time at which the predicting is done is again the reference time, albeit the *past* reference time—if one has not been established then a past perfect *when* clause simply isn't acceptable. And the predicted perfective situation itself—that is, the consequent state of the event in question—is again to be found later than the reference time.

In fact it seems that *all when* clauses which include a clause denoting a *situation*, as opposed to an event (as defined in Section 1.5 of this paper, and in Steedman, 1977), imply that the speaker predicts or predicted the situation in question. For example, stative verbs in past tensed *when* clauses seem to behave very much like the perfect, for example displaying the same incompatibility with situation-type main clauses that was noted in example (39b):

(47a) When I knew the answer, I immediately phoned the Grange.

(47b) ?When I knew the answer, Fred was telephoning the Grange.

Even past progressive *when* clauses (which are also defined as situations) seem to share this property, although the effect is a subtler one, and was glossed over in the earlier discussion.

The idea of *prediction* is not unrelated to the idea of logical *consequence* invoked earlier, so we must be careful to distinguish them. It will be recalled that, whereas a simple past tensed main clause, such as *she won*, demands a prior temporal referent for its past tense, a simple past tensed *when* clause does not. The *when* clause is rather used to set up a *new* reference point, and to over-write any prior one. However, the 'predictive' *when* clauses, including the perfect, *do* require a previously established reference point, and, like main clauses, cannot be used without one. One may begin a conversation with *When Ann came to stay, . . .* (provided the hearer can identify the occasion in question), but may not *begin* with *When Ann had come to stay, ...* The reason is that the latter demands a reference time at which it could be predicted that the person in question *would* come to stay (or at least attempt to do so). It is only if this condition is satisfied that the usual process associated with a *when* clause can take over, and the consequent state in question can be found.

Thus we distinguish *two* components to the idea of cause and consequence which has so bedevilled the above discussion of the temporal categories. The perfect denotes the state of affairs that is *consequent upon* the event which the perfect dominates. On the other hand, the connective *when* with a situation as its complement seems to mean that the speaker can or could *predict* that situation. Since the most common basis for a prediction is that one knows the chain of causes and consequences of which it is a part, it is perhaps not surprising that these two aspects of temporal meaning, which are logically quite distinct, interact in such a complex fashion.

It might seem that this idea of predictability at a reference time, invoked to explain the behaviour of perfect *when* clauses, considerably complicates the idea of reference time itself. It is true that the notion that has been used so far, according to which the reference time of Reichenbach is represented as a reference event or 'window' on the time-line (together with the reference relation), will have to be elaborated once more. However, it will become apparent that the elaboration in question is exactly what is needed in order to explicate the further problem of the 'consequential' meaning of *when* clauses with simple past tense, originally introduced in example (2b).

3.3   When and the perfect

The extension to the theory that is implied by the preceding observations is simple in principle but complex in detail, and will be more fully developed elsewhere. The basic apparatus, consisting of a history, a data base describing the state of the world at any given instant, together with a set of housekeeping routines for the management of the data base, plus a body of world knowledge defined as inference procedures is still all that is required. However, the nature of the information represented in the history needs to be elaborated. In particular, it is no longer going to be adequate to represent the history of events as the single time-line implied in the preceding discussion. It will rather be necessary to represent it as comprising *several* time-lines, each associated with a single causal or consequentially related sequence of events leading towards the satisfaction of a particular goal, or intention. These sequences may from time to time intersect or diverge, and may be nested one within the other, the nested sequence representing the steps undertaken in achieving a sub-goal of the higher sequence. This representation has more of the character of a railway marshalling yard than the single main line of the earlier account. It embodies the idea that it is only events that are consequently related that necessarily have well defined temporal relations in memory. Purely coincidental relations in time are less useful, and may be only vaguely defined. The linguistic categories under discussion reflect implicitly such an organization of episodic memory, which is closely related to the notion of a script or plan advanced by Schank & Abelson (1977).

Consider, for example, the history of this type that is represented in Figure 5, which corresponds directly to a data structure in the program. This history might be paraphrased as follows:

'John, in order to compute the 99th prime number, logs on to the system, edits the
program which he needs, runs the program, and logs out again. Meanwhile, Betty,
in order to edit her own program, logs on at the same time as John and begins her
edit. At a point during the time that John is running his program, Betty stops
editing, and logs out. Moreover, the history represents the fact that it is John's
starting to run that for some reason causes Betty to stop her work and sign off'
Finally, while all this is going on, Ann, in order to print a program, signs on, prints
it, and signs off at the same time as Betty.'

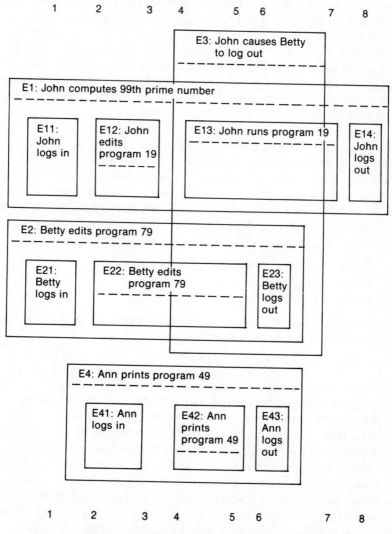

Figure 5   A 'history' of the model world showing causal sequences

Such a history is of course extremely simplified, for purposes of exposition. For example there is no representation of *why* John's actions cause Betty to stop what she is doing nor of the fact that John's editing *enables* his running, nor of the fact that Betty's editing is an incomplete period, or in Vendler's terms, an 'activity', unlike John's. In a more complete simulation these facts would be represented either in the history or in more general knowledge about the world. However, the example will serve the present purpose.

The definition of the perfect is straightforward in terms of such a representation. The perfect of a core event is true at some time if some event or situation which is consequent upon that event (that is, subsequent to the core event and on the same causal sequence) is in force at that time. For example, at the time 4 of the history we are considering the proposition *that Betty* has *logged in* is true, since the activity of her editing her program is in progress, and it is an activity which is on the same causal sequence as was her logging in (E2 in the figure). On the other hand, at time 7 the same proposition is not true, since although the core event occurred before that time, the entire causal sequence of which it was a part is over.

In order to explicate the effect of *when* clauses, including the so-called causal variety, and those including auxiliary *have*, it will be necessary to revise our view of Reichenbach's temporal reference point once more. The referent must not only include the 'window' defined by the core event itself. It must also include subsequent events in the same causal sequence. Consider for example questions about the history in Figure 5 which begin 'When John ran his program, . . .'. It is reasonable, given what we know, for these to continue as follows:

(48a)   . . . , was Ann printing?
(48b)   . . . , did he log out?
(48c)   . . . , did Betty log out?

On the other hand, in spite of the fact that Ann logs out at exactly the same time as Betty, it is *not* reasonable to go on

(48d)   . . . , did Ann log out?

Such a question implies or presupposes that John's running *caused* Ann's logging out, and that is not what this particular history describes.

What is the nature of the temporal referent to which these main clauses refer? Clearly, as before, it must define a window, or pair of time points between which the state of the world can be examined using the data base to represent successive instants. That much is necessary in order to know where to look in order to answer (48a). But, equally clearly, it must allow for the search to go beyond the confines of the events itself, if (48b) and (48c) are to be answered. However, the question of where that search may be permitted to look is equally clearly not merely a question of defining a fixed interval of time, not even one whose extent is allowed to depend upon the character of the reference event. Any purely temporal interval which allows the program to see as far ahead as Betty's logging out is going to allow it to see Ann's as well. It is therefore clear that the temporal referent must include some note of the particular sub-history upon which the event itself is found. The search later in the history for the main clause event must only take account of events—like John's and Betty's logging out—which are causally related to the reference event. It must be blind to all others.

We may therefore think for the moment of the temporal referent as a pair of points on the time-line as before, plus a note of the parent sub-history or sub-histories on which the reference event occurred. But how *far* along the parent paths is the search to be allowed to proceed? Obviously, it may not examine any *earlier* events on the parent paths than the reference event. It might appear that all we need is to search as far as the *next* event on the parent path(s). However, it will be recalled that certain events (such as the repetitions discussed in Section 1) may be compound. There is therefore no simple way to define such a scope. The current program therefore allows the search for main clause events to 'see' all events later in the causal sequence on which the core event is found.

With the new representation of the episode, the perfect in a *when* clause has exactly the same meaning as it does in a main clause. For example, if the *when* clause had been 'When John had run his program . . .', the referent that would have been set up would simply be a period comprising all instants at which the perfect itself was true—that is, all instants subsequent to the core event at which some event or situation arising from the same causal chain were in force. In order to express what has been referred to as the 'predictive' quality of the perfect *when* clause, it is clear that the search for these instants should be conducted with respect to an established temporal referent, rather than with respect to the whole episode. The resulting new temporal referent is therefore very similar to the one established by the related simple tensed *when* clause, except that it does not include the core event, but *only* its consequential state. Hence the puzzling fact that sentences (49a) and (49b) below mean something very similar, while sentences (49c) and (49d) do not is explained—cf. sentences (38) and (39) above:

    (49a)   When John ran his program, he logged out.
    (49b)   When John had run his program, he logged out.
    (49c)   When John ran his program, he was computing the 99th prime.
    (49d)   ?When John had run his program, he was computing the 99th prime.

Two further aspects of the meaning of *when* clauses must be mentioned. First, when the main clause is an event-description and the causal relation is presupposed, it is also presupposed that the relation is direct—that is, that the main event comes *next* on the path. This fact must be checked as part of the reference *relationship*[7]. Secondly, none of the above searching beyond the bounds of the original reference event is allowed in the case where the main clause is of the state-like 'situation' variety, nor do these carry any connotations of causation. It therefore follows that in the case of stative main clauses the search should be able to 'see' *all* the happenings in the history but should not proceed beyond the limits of the core event. That is to say that, for present purposes, *when* sentences with situation main clauses are very like the corresponding *while* sentences. It will be noted that such an account fails to explain the fact that most (but not all) sentences which have progressive or perfect main clauses with a perfect *when* clauses are anomalous (cf. Figure 1). That is to say that the program just described will produce the answer 'Yes' to the following questions about the history of Figure 5:

(50a)   ?When John had run his program, was he computing the 99th prime?

(50b)   ?When John had run his program, had he logged in?

However, not all such sentences are anomalous. In fact, they are acceptable just in case the imperfective or perfective situation described by the main clause is indeed a direct consequence of the core event of the *when* clause—for example:

(51a)   When John had run his program was he still computing the 99th prime?

(51b)   When John had run his program, had he finished computing the 99th prime?

However, at present, the program will accept all such sentences. The distinction in acceptability between (50) and (51), which appears to be intimately involved with further questions concerning the aspectual adverbials and verbs which appear in the latter sentences, will require further refinements to the definition of the consequential relation and its representation in the program.

To summarize this section: in order to account for the interaction of the perfect and causation in *when* clauses, a further elaboration of the concepts of episodic memory and reference time to include the idea of logical sequences of events has been necessary. Within this framework, the meaning of *when* clauses can be defined as follows. If the *when* clause is of the 'situation' variety, then the search for the new temporal referent is to be conducted within an establishing referent. If the *when* clause is of the 'event' variety, then the whole episode is searched. If the *main* clause is a situation, then the search for that situation is confined to the scope of the core event, and the whole effect is rather similar to that of a *while* sentence. If the main clause is an event, then the search for that event includes the consequences of the core event in the *when* clause.

4   CONCLUSION

In the preceding sections of the paper a model has been outlined of the way people answer questions about episodes. The discussion has concentrated on the function of *while* and *when* clauses. By successive refinements of Reichenbach's (1947) original notion of the temporal reference point that is established by such clauses, it has been possible to account for certain apparent ambiguities of tense, and of the progressive and the perfect, as being ambiguities of reference, arising from a single sense. The relation of causal or consequential meanings to more purely temporal ones has been discussed. In particular, the intimate relation of both the perfect and the connective *when* with causation and prediction has been examined. The tendency of simple past tense and the perfect not only to appear ambiguous, but also to take on each other's roles, has also been explicated in terms of the model.

The model hinges upon the idea that memory for episodes is linearly ordered, by analogy with the temporal sequences that it represents. The functions of tense, the auxiliaries, and the time adverbials are to direct the hearer's attention to certain points in such a structure, and to move the shared point of attention up and down the time-line that such a memory emulates.

The story has been a complex one. The reason has been that at every turn the idea of causation has intruded into the simple localist paradise of purely temporal descriptions suggested by the theories of Reichenbach and Isard with which the account began. Indeed, it seems that episodic memory should not be thought of as a single linear ordering of events, but rather as being further structured into sub-histories of events which are related as successive elements in causal chains constituting the plans and intentions of participants in the episode. Several such sub-histories will typically be in progress at any one time. Certain of the time adverbials, like *while* adjuncts, express purely temporal relations between events, and apply across different causal chains. Others, like *when* adjuncts, will have more to do with relations of sequence *within* such chains.

It is perhaps worth concluding by attempting to identify the significance of the computer in the development of this model, and for the study of deixis and reference in general. Any phenomenon in natural language which depends upon the changing context of a conversation presents the theorist with the problem of formalizing processes of change in the situation referred to. Deictic and anaphoric reference, including such reference to events, depends upon such processes of change in the context of discourse. A computer program expresses very directly the processes that result when it is run on the computer. For such a process, the idea of a context corresponds closely to that of the changing state of the variables which the program accesses during the computation, as Isard (1975) has pointed out. Programs therefore offer a helpful notation for precisely those pragmatic aspects of reference that are most intractable in non-procedural terms, and with which the meanings of the time descriptions considered here are intimately bound up.

NOTES

1. This work has continually been influenced by many discussions with Stephen Isard. He, Gill Brown, Jeb Ellman, Orvokki Heinamaki, Wolfgang Klein, Chris Mellish, Carlota Smith, and Cathy Urwin kindly read earlier drafts and made many helpful suggestions. Earlier versions were presented to the Max-Planck-Gessellschaft conference on Spatial Deixis, Nijmegen, March 1978, the Psycholinguistics Summer School, Mulsjo, August 1979, and the Semantics Workshop on Events, Situations and Actions, Austin, October 1980. The research was supported by a grant for computation from the SSRC and a Visiting Fellowship from the Sloan Foundation held at the Center for Cognitive Science of the University of Texas at Austin.

2. The word *meaning* will be used throughout the paper in an intentionally vague, common-language sense to refer indiscriminately to all aspects of meaning. When it is necessary to be more precise, such terms as *sense*, *reference*, and *denotation* will be used.

3. It should be remarked in passing that although a *when* clause is always evaluated before the main clause, and establishes the referent for its tense, it is not always the case that this referent endures for the tense of later 'naked' main clauses to refer to. The setting up of an enduring permanent temporal referent seems always to be markedly by an intonation break, whether the relative clause precedes or succeeds the main clause or is parenthetically embedded within the main clause as in

(i)   John, when he saw the expression on my face, made an excuse and left.

A *when* clause which is not set off from its matrix by intonation, does not set up a temporal reference point which outlasts the matrix sentence. An example is sentence (ii b) of the following exchange.

(ii a)   When John arrived, did Mary leave?
         NO.
(ii b)   Did Mary leave when Fred arrived?
         NO.
(ii c)   *Did Ann arrive?

Sentence (ii a) sets up the temporal referent of John's arrival, as usual. Had sentence (ii c) followed immediately, it would have been understood as referring to the same reference time. However, although the *when* clause of (ii b) sets the temporal referent for its main clause, it does not establish Fred's arrival as a *permanent* reference point, and so sentence (ii c) fails to refer to that time. (To make sentence (ii c) successfully refer to Fred's arrival, it would be necessary to include the word *then*, which explicitly refers to the most recently mentioned time, rather than to an established reference time. *Then* has rather the effect that the phrase *at that time* has, and itself may set up a new and enduring temporal referent.) What is more, sentence (ii b) seems to render the reference point set up by (ii a) inaccessible to the temporally anaphoric tense of (ii c).

   The above variety of functions that may be performed by *when* clauses are closely related to those involved in Halliday's (1967) constructs of theme and information. Elsewhere, Steedman & Johnson-Laird (1978) have related semantics of theme and information in general to the same fundamental characteristic of the human language-understanding mechanism that is exploited here, namely that it is a left to right process (albeit one that is under a hierarchical control), in which as much interpretation as possible is done as *soon* as possible. However, the present discussion is limited, like that of Isard (1974), to temporal relative clauses which establish an enduring temporal referent, that is to say to those separated from their main clause by one or more intonation breaks.

4. It will be obvious that the notion of cause or consequence is a complex one. For example, two events are held to stand in this relationship if the former merely *enabled* the occurrence of the latter, as well as when it actually caused it. Schank (1975) provides one possible taxonomy of the varieties of logical sequence of events in episodes.

5. This analysis is not meant to imply that *no* events involving repetition are represented as a whole in people's histories of episodes. Events like bands playing and programs running are perhaps prototypically single, non-repeated events. But activities like *talking to Mary* are likely to be repeated *en bloc*, not as a lot of individual utterances, and would not behave like examples (27) and (29).

6. The current paper will not deal with progressives of 'achievements', such as

    (i)   John was winning the race

which designate a prospective situation of activity leading up to the core event. While space prohibits any discussion of them here (but cf. Vlach, 1977; Dowty, 1979) it seems likely that the notion of causal or consequential sequences of events which is involved in the treatment of the perfect will be crucial to the analysis of these and the associated 'imperfective paradox' as well.

7. It is not quite clear whether this fact is in the domain of semantics or pragmatics. This detail is not currently implemented.

REFERENCES

Bennett, D. C. (1975). *Spatial and temporal uses of English prepositions*. London: Longman.

Bull, W. E. (1963). *Time, tense and the verb*. Berkeley: University of California Press.

Comrie, B. (1976). *Aspect*. London: Cambridge University Press.

Davies, D. J. M. (1973). *Popler 1.5 reference manual*. TPU Report 1, University of Edinburgh.

Davies, D. J. M., & Isard, S. D. (1972) Utterances as programs. In D. Michie & B. Meltzer (eds), *Machine intelligence 7*. Edinburgh: Edinburgh University Press.

Dowty, D. R. (1972). Studies in the logic of verb aspect and time reference. Unpublished doctoral dissertation, University of Texas, Austin.

Dowty, D. R. (1977). Towards a semantic analysis of verb aspect and English 'imperfective' progressive. *Linguistics and Philosophy*, **1.1**, 45–78.

Dowty, D. R. (1979). *Word meaning and Montague grammar*. Dordrecht: Reidel.

Geis, M. (1970). Time prepositions as underlying verbs. *Papers of the Sixth Regional Meeting of the Chicago Linguistic Society*. Chicago: Chicago Linguistic Society.

Halliday, M. A. K. (1967). Notes on transitivity and theme, II. *Journal of Linguistics*, **3**, 177–244.

Heinamaki, O. (1974). Semantics of English temporal connectives. Unpublished doctoral dissertation, University of Texas, Austin.

Hewitt, C. (1969). PLANNER: a language for proving theorems in robots. *Proceedings of the international joint conference on artificial intelligence*, Bedford, Mass.: Mitre Corporation.

Hornstein, N. (1977). Towards a theory of tense. *Linguistic Inquiry*, **8**, 521–557.

Inoue, K. (1975). Studies in the perfect. Unpublished doctoral dissertation, University of Michigan.

Inoue, K. (1979). An analysis of the English present perfect. *Linguistics*, **17**, 561–590.

Isard, S. D. (1974). What would you have done if . . . ? *Journal of Theoretical Linguistics*, **1**, 233–255.

Isard, S. D. (1975). Changing the context. In E. L. Keenan (ed.), *Formal semantics of natural language*. London: Cambridge University Press.

Isard, S. D., & Longuet-Higgins, C. (1971). Modal tic-tac-toe. In R. J. Bogdan & I. Niiniluoto (eds), *Logic, language, and probability*. Dordrecht: Reidel.

Kenny, A. (1963). *Action, emotion and will*. New York: Humanities Press.

Longuet-Higgins, H. C. (1973). The cat sat on the mat. Unpublished paper to the Edinburgh Wednesday Semantics Session.

Lyons, J. (1977). *Semantics* Vol. 2. London: Cambridge University Press.

McCawley, J. (1971). Tense and time reference in English. In C. J. Fillmore & D. T. Langendoen (eds), *Studies in linguistic semantics*. New York: Holt, Rinehart & Winston.

Miller, G. A., & Johnson-Laird, P. N. (1976). *Language and perception*. Cambridge, Mass.: Harvard University Press.

Partee, B. (1973). Some structural analogies between tenses and pronouns in English. *Journal of Philosophy*, **70**, 601–609.

Reichenbach, H. (1947). *Elements of symbolic logic*. New York: Free Press.

Ritchie, G. D. (1977). Computer modelling of English grammar. Unpublished Ph.D. dissertation, University of Edinburgh.

Ritchie, G. D. (1979). Temporal clauses in English. *Theoretical Linguistics*, **6**, 87–115.

Ryle, G. (1949). *The concept of mind*. London: Hutchinson.

Schank, R. (1975). The structure of episodes in memory. In D. G. Bobrow & A. Collins (eds), *Representation and understanding*. New York: Academic Press.

Schank, R., & Abelson, R. (1977). *Scripts, plans, goals, and understanding*. Hillsdale, N. J.: Erlbaum.

Smith, C. S. (1975). A new look at auxiliary *have* in English. *Proceedings of the Northeast Linguistic Society*, 1975.

Smith, C. S. (1978). The syntax and interpretation of temporal expressions in English. *Linguistics and Philosophy*, **2**, 43–99.

Steedman, M. J. (1977). Verbs, time and modality. *Cognitive Science*, **1**, 216–234.

Steedman, M. J. (1978). A procedural model of presupposition. In P. Seuren (ed.), *A symposium on semantics, Grammarij*, **9**, Nijmegen: Katholieke Universiteit.

Steedman, M. J., & Johnson-Laird, P. N. (1978). A programmatic theory of linguistic performance. In P. Smith & R. Campbell (eds), *Advances in the psychology of language: formal and experimental approaches*. New York: Plenum.

Vendler, Z. (1967). *Linguistics in philosophy*. Ithaca, N.Y.: Cornell University Press.

Verkuyl, H. J. (1972). *On the compositional nature of the aspects*. Dordrecht: Reidel.

Verkuyl, H. J. (1973). Temporal prepositions as quantifiers. In F. Kiefer & N. Ruwet (eds), *Generative grammar in Europe*. Dordrecht: Reidel.

Vlach, F. (1977). The semantics of the progressive. Manuscript, University of New South Wales.

Wason, P. C., & Johnson-Laird, P. N. (1977). A theoretical analysis of insight into a reasoning task. In P. N. Johnson-Laird & P. C. Wason (eds), *Thinking*. London: Cambridge University Press.

Winograd, T. (1972). *Understanding natural language*. Edinburgh: Edinburgh University Press.

Winograd, T. (1976). Towards a procedural understanding of semantics. *Revue Internationale de Philosophie*, **3-4** 117–118, 260–303.

Woods, W. (1968). Procedural semantics for a question-answer machine. In *Proceedings of the fall joint computer conference*. New York: Spartan.

Part 2

DISCOURSE ABOUT SPACE

Speech, Place, and Action
Edited by R. J. Jarvella and W. Klein
© 1982 John Wiley & Sons, Ltd.

Local Deixis in Route Directions[1]

WOLFGANG KLEIN

'Here comes the night'
(Van Morrison)

This study deals with the semantics of local deictics like 'here', 'there', 'left', 'right', etc., i.e. with expressions that are used mainly to refer to localities and whose reference depends in a systematic way on contextual factors like position of speaker, direction of gaze, and others. It is part of a larger project on the role of verbal and situational context in language behaviour (cf. Klein & Levelt, 1978). There are numerous contributions to a theory of context dependency (see, for example, Kratzer & von Stechow, 1976), and there are some instructive studies of local deixis in particular (e.g. Bühler, 1934; Fillmore, 1971; Atkinson & Griffiths, 1973; Miller & Johnson-Laird, 1976, Chap. 6.1; Clark 1977), but it is surely no overstatement to say that we are still far from an understanding how deixis—and local deixis in particular—really works in actual communication. It is obvious that what 'here' means in an utterance is largely determined by the context of that utterance. Sentences like 'Here are the tigers' or 'Come here!' seem to have an open slot, that is filled by contextual information when they are uttered; this contextual information may be given by prior verbal expressions, by succeeding verbal expressions, by common perception in the speech situation, by gestures, etc. Not very much is known about this process, about its components and how they interact. In this paper, I try to contribute to an understanding of this mechanism in two ways—one more theoretical, the other more empirical. In the first section, several problems are outlined which, in my view, are basic to the use of deictic expressions and of local deictics in particular. In Section 2, some results from an empirical study about the use of local deictics in route directions are reported.[2] The first part makes no claim to be a theory of deixis; rather, it forms a heuristic frame of analysis, and perhaps a starting point for such a theory.

1 COMPONENTS IN THE USE OF LOCAL DEICTICS

The following considerations focus upon 'here' and 'there'; but it should be clear that there are a number of other local deictics which are not dealt with here. A speaker who uses expressions like 'here', etc., in some speech situation refers to certain denotata. By saying 'It's pretty cold here', he may refer by 'here' to a room, to a corner of a room or to Siberia, depending on the particular context. A listener who wants to understand this utterance has to identify the specifically intended denotatum of 'here', just as he has to identify the denotata of proper names, of adjectives, or of verbs. But the identification problem is different in at least one respect: 'Siberia' in general denotes Siberia, but 'here' doesn't denote here. Solving the identification problem in deictic reference involves the solution of a whole series of sub-problems and at least the following ones: a common deictic space must be set up; a basic reference point ('origo') must be set up; speaker and listener must co-ordinate their perspectives; what 'here' and 'there' refer to must be delimited; the deictical oppositions of the language must be utilized; analogical deictic spaces must be established. The comments I shall make now on these problems treat them mainly as research problems, not as problems a speaker and listener have to solve together, though this is exactly what they do have to do in order to achieve successful communication.

1.1 Setting up deictical spaces

In general, the possible denotata of local deictics are localities, such as rooms, apartments, streets, cities, countries: they can be considered as subspaces of *deictic spaces*, such as the space of visual perception, or the space constituted by our geographical knowledge. But the denotata of local deictics need not be localities. When somebody says, 'Two problems should be kept apart here', he surely doesn't refer to a locality in the literal sense of the word, but to a very abstract 'place' in a train of thoughts. And if we read, 'In 1806, Shelley wrote his "Elegy"; here, the spirit of English romanticism found its. . . ', no locality is denoted, unless the denotatum of 'in this poem' is regarded as such. Uses of that type might be called 'metaphorical'; this is perhaps accurate, but it doesn't say very much: it is just a terminological immunization of the problem. What we have to account for is the fact that there may be very different deictic spaces; some of these uses may be primary in a diachronic or in an ontogenetic sense; others might be derived from the primary ones; but this doesn't obviate the fact that they all are at the disposal of a normal speaker, and that, in a specific communication situation, it should be clear which deictic space is being referred to. For instance, is it the space of visual perception, as in 'Here is my home', or the space that is constituted in our memory by our geographical knowledge, as in long-distance calls, when somebody says 'It's raining here', or even a much more abstract space, as in 'I can't go into detail here'? The deictic space of speakers and listeners need not be identical for a successful communication, but they must be sufficiently similar, and to make them so might well be a part of the communication; this is the case, for example, in route directions.

In its most general sense, a deictic space is nothing but a set of elements provided with some structure (an order or a topology); its subsets, or some of them, are the possible denotata. Deictic spaces may differ in (a) what is considered to be their elements, such as minimally discriminable units of perception, words (as in the Shelley example?), etc.; (b) subsets which are possible denotata, such as visual objects, poems, etc.; (c) kind of structure characterizing the deictic space; (d) number of dimensions: the space of visual perception is generally thought to be three-dimensional, a map that often serves as an analogical deictic space (cf. Section 1.7 below) is two-dimensional, a 'train of thought' might be considered as one-dimensional (it often is!), etc.; (e) kind of metric—if there is any: for most deictic spaces, we seem to have a concept of distance, but it is often doubtful whether it really fulfils the criteria of a metric. The concept of deictic space raises a number of problems for empirical research:

What then, are the deictic spaces used in actual communication, since the notions 'space of visual perception', 'geographical space', 'space of trains of thought', are somewhat fuzzy labels generated from specific examples? How do speaker and listener make sure that they are referring to the same, or a sufficiently similar, deictic space in a given situation? How are these different concepts of space interrelated, and, in particular, which structural properties are conserved in the transition from basic deictic spaces (visual perception, for instance) to more abstract ones?

Agreement upon the deictic space by speaker and listener is the first prerequisite for successful deictic reference; the intended subspace—locality or whatever—is now to be localized within this deictic space. This is done by a series of techniques, the first of which is to fix the basic reference point.

1.2 Fixing the basic reference point

Given a deictic space, one of its elements must be fixed as the basic reference point, in relation to which the denotata can be determined. In the unmarked case, this 'origo' (a term used by Bühler, 1934) is given by the position of the speaker: every participant of a speech situation brings his perspective with him, and it is that of the speaker that is crucial for the identification of denotata: 'here' denotes a space around the origo; 'there' denotes a space that does not contain the origo. This presupposes of course that the speaker (or his body, or perhaps his eyes) can be interpreted as an element of the deictic space in question, as, for example, in the space of visual perception. If this is not the case, some reference unit must be set up in the corresponding deictic space. This is often done in anaphorical uses of 'here', as in sentences like 'The reader is referred to Morton (1976); here, the problem of recursive reference is treated in full detail'.[3] On the other hand, an origo given by the speaker may be shifted. This is often done by pointing gestures: 'The picture here originally hung there' (pointing with a finger to some place), or in the case of analogical deixis (cf. Section 1.7 below): 'If the church is here' (pointing to some spot on the table), 'our home is just here' (pointing to another spot). The origo proper is not lost, it is just suspended in favour of another 'secondary origo', and it is always possible to go back to it without making this explicit.

Fixing the origo raises again a number of empirical problems. How is the (primary) origo precisely characterized—is it the speaker's body, his trunk, his eyes, his reach? How are secondary origins introduced, e.g. by pointing gestures with fingers, chin, eyes, by verbal means? How do children acquire the technique of origo shift?

Explicit origo shifting should not be confused with change of origo due to the speaker changing location during his utterance. If somebody moves through a room saying: 'From here, it's precisely one, two, three, four, five metres to here', the denotatum of 'here' changes within one speech act, and the origo is shifted, too, within that speech act. But it is still the basic type of origo implicitly given by the speaker's position. This constitutes a clear argument against the assumption that the origo is bound to the speech act. This seems to be the position held in Wunderlich (1971). If a speech act (or the speech situation that exactly corresponds to a speech act) is restricted to utterances of just one speaker whose position is unchanged, it doesn't matter, because both assumptions (origo bound to speech act; origo bound to position of speaker) coincide. But as soon as examples where this is not the case are taken into consideration, it becomes apparent that the speaker's position is crucial. Moreover, this view can easily be linked to the extended research on children's egocentrism and to adults' orientation: we learn to shift, but basically, we see, grasp, feel, structure, our surroundings from where we are.

1.3 Co-ordination

In the following, I shall only consider unmarked cases, i.e. cases where the origo is implicitly given by the speaker's (stable) position. The listener must take over this orientation; he must project it onto his own system of orientation, which is not at issue as long as he is listening. As soon as he starts speaking, roles are changed, and *his* orientation becomes central; the projection task becomes his. In many cases, the problem of co-ordinating two systems of orientation is trivial. The denotatum of 'here' often encloses both speaker and listener, and any difference in their position and hence in their orientation is irrelevant—though it exists. But there are many cases where the different position becomes important. A particularly clear example is telephone calls: 'The weather is wonderful here'—'Oh, here it's raining'. Of course this is not restricted to telephone calls, but also happens in face-to-face interaction. If somebody outside a house is speaking to somebody leaning out of the window, he may say 'It's cool here', and the other speaker may respond: 'Oh, you should feel it in here!' In cases like this, the denotatum of 'here' centres so narrowly around the respective origo that it doesn't include the position of the respective listener. This point becomes move obvious, if not only the position of the speaker, but also his direction of gaze is important, as with the local deictics 'left' and 'right'. If speaker and listener are facing each other, one's 'left' is the other's 'right'. In this case, the co-ordination is very simple;[4] it is more complicated if there is an angle of 90° between the two directions of gaze, because then, the speaker's 'left' is the listener's 'right', if the listener is to the speaker's left and the locality referred to is between them; if it is not between them, it is to the left of both listener and speaker. Things are much more unclear with 'here' and 'there', in cases when a non-trivial co-ordination is necessary: the speaker's 'here' is often the listener's 'there', one of the speaker's 'there's is the listener's 'here', the speaker's and the listener's 'here' may overlap without coinciding totally, etc. These mappings are very complex, and they become still more complex if shifted origins are considered. This leads to research problems such as : How do these mappings work in the unmarked case where speakers change position? How do they work in the case of shifted origo?

1.4   Delimitation

Fixing the origo of a given deictic space and mapping the two systems of orientation doesn't guarantee that the subspaces—the denotata—can be identified. The denotatum of 'here' is indeed not the origo itself, but some space enclosing the origo. Saying 'it's cold here' means 'it's cold within some area around the speaker', and neither the origo nor the word 'here' indicate how far this area reaches. The boundaries are fixed by the context of the utterance. This delimitation follows certain principles. 'Here' may refer to the chair on which I am sitting, to the room where I am, to the house where I am, to the street, the city, etc., in widening circles around the speaker which may or may not include the listener.[5] But it is very unlikely that a particular 'here' will be used to refer to a chair (with speaker) and the surrounding space at an exact distance of 69.3 cm, or to the room and two adjacent rooms—unless they form a cognitive unit in some sense, such as the reach of the speaker, or in the second example, an apartment. In many cases, the delimitation is immediately supported by some verbal means, e.g. 'here in this tiny cabin, he spent half a year', or 'here in Heaven, they sing too much'; but this does not have to be the case. We often reconstruct the borders of 'here' (and other local deictics) by our knowledge of the world. If somebody says 'I'm sitting very comfortably here', our general knowledge tells us that 'here' does not refer to the Earth, whereas in 'there is no justice here', it doesn't refer to a chair.

Obviously, the delimitation is not always very sharp; the borders are often diffuse. But fuzziness of denotata is not a specific problem of local deixis. The central empirical problems raised by the necessity of delimitation are: What are the possible borders within a given deictical space (a room might be a denotatum, but not a room and half of the next)? How is the delimitation established in a given speech situation—by verbal context, by components of our factual knowledge, by gestures?

1.5 Deictical oppositions

Deictic space, origo, co-ordination, and delimitation make it possible to identify the denotatum of 'here' in a given context—it is a subspace of the deictic space including the origo within certain boundaries. But 'here' is not the only local deictic expression. It belongs to a certain system that, according to the language, may have two ('here'–'there'), three ('hier'–'da'–'dort', 'aquí'–'allí'–'allá'), or even more components. And there are, of course, other groupings of deictical expressions, like 'left'–'right' which form their own system. Several proposals have been made to characterize the oppositions of such deictic systems in different languages, such as 'proximal' versus 'non-proximal' for English (e.g. Clark 1977), or 'proximal'–'middle'–'distal' for Bella Coola (Davis & Saunders, 1975), or the traditional 'near the speaker'–'near the listener'–'near the third one' in Latin grammar for 'hic'–'istic'–'illic'.

But even in the comparatively simple 'here'–'there' system of English, things are sometimes rather complicated, because what 'proximal' and 'non-proximal' mean again depends on the context. It is apparently possible to say 'here comes my mother', when she is at a distance of 100 metres, but one can also say 'there is my mother', when she is at a distance of 10 metres. 'There' can be used if the denotatum is closer to the speaker than to the listener (but 'distant' from both), but it can also be used precisely in the sense of the opposition 'speaker–here' versus 'listener–there' (e.g. 'You can't see it from there, only from here'). The system seems to work roughly as follows: in a given situation, a 'here' always denotes a subspace of a deictic space around an origo (shifted or unshifted); the rest of the deictic space is—in that situation—open for possible denotata of 'there': 'there' denotes some subspace of the complement of a 'here'. Precisely what it denotes is then marked by three characteristics: (a) negatively by the respective denotatum of 'here'—if no 'here' is used in that particular situation, the whole deictic space is open for 'there', except that it must not include the origo;[6] (b) by some additional information concerning the location within the space, e.g. some pointing gesture, some verbal expression—as in the case of anaphoric or cataphoric 'there'—by shared perception, etc.; (c) by some additional information concerning the delimination (as in the case of 'here').

If the opposition is understood in this way, the 'proximal'–'non-proximal' distinction is just a special case. The situation is much more complex with three-step systems, as 'hier'–'da'–'dort' in German, where 'da'—apart from its other meanings—competes both with 'here' and 'there': 'Ich bleibe ein paar Minuten da' versus 'das Buch muß irgendwo da (pointing with the finger) gelegan haben'. These systems differ from language to language, and the analysis of their constitutive oppositions is one of the research problems raised by them. The other one is by what means a speaker makes clear in a given speech situation where his 'there' is located and what its borders are (cf. (b) and (c) above).

Basically, we now have all the components that usually interact to determine what is referred to by 'here' or 'there'. This mechanism of deictic reference with shared deictic space, origo fixing, co-ordination, delimitation of subspaces, and deictic oppositions looks rather complex, but I don't see what could be omitted from it. On the contrary, the system becomes even more complicated if we take into account some other everyday uses, namely those that involve analogical deictic spaces.

1.7 Analogical deixis

If somebody points to a red spot on a map and says: 'Here is my home', he wants to say 'At the place that in reality corresponds to this spot . . .', and he is normally understood that way. In this case, we have two deictic spaces involved: the map, and the geographic space represented by the map. The map functions as an analogue, and by pointing to an element of the map, I am referring to the analogous place in the 'real space'. The mapping is here (!) clearly given by the given projection. But analogical deixis is also possible when the mapping is not given by some geometrically defined relation, but by some—perhaps vague—resemblance. If somebody points to his own shoulder and says: 'The bullet hit him here', he refers to the corresponding part of the body of some other person. In the same way, it is possible to refer to 'generic places'. If a professor of medicine says in a lecture: 'The needle must be inserted precisely here', pointing on some part of his own hand, he doesn't actually refer to the part of his hand he is pointing to—he would be astonished if the students all wanted to inject him *there*—nor to the corresponding part of some other specific person, but to the part of the 'generic hand', of which he used his own as an instance.

The central empirical problem of analogical deixis is the kind of mapping between the deictic spaces involved. It is apparently possible to say 'The bullet hit Charlie here' (pointing on one's shoulder), even if Charlie is not a human being, but a grizzly bear; it's impossible, however, if Charlie is a snake.

This seems the right point to close these comments on the mechanism of local deictic reference. Perhaps they raise more problems than they clarify, but they may serve as a basic framework for further analysis. In the following, some results concerning the use of deictics in route directions are outlined. Though there will often be no explicit reference to the conception, the whole study should be seen in the context of this framework.

2   USING LOCAL DEICTICS IN ROUTE DIRECTIONS

2.1   Route communications

In English, there seems to be no standard term for the complex co-operative verbal action that consists of asking for route directions and giving them—as for instance 'Wegauskunft' in German; in the following, I will call this action 'route communication'. It is a very common type of complex verbal action. By complex verbal action, I understand activities like giving a talk, recounting a narrative, explaining a game, describing an apartment, arguing together, etc. In general, several participants—at least two—are engaged in such an action, but their role might be different. According to that, I classify them as basically monological or basically non-monological (giving a talk is basically monological, arguing together is basically non-monological); a complex verbal action might indeed be composed of several passages, some of them being monological, some not. A second subdivision follows the type of information to be presented or elaborated: it may prestructure the verbal planning to a high or a low degree. Narratives are strongly prestructured by the temporal order of events, explaining games weakly structured; that's why most people soon get confused when they try to explain a complex game. In the weakly prestructured case, people typically try to introduce some temporal ordering, e.g. by following the running of the game, by imaging a tour through an apartment (Labov & Linde, 1975), etc. Route communication shows a clearly asymmetric role of its participants that is reflected in the verbal tasks they have to carry out: the person who asks for directions (henceforth F) wants to know something, and he tries to get this information from somebody he takes to be competent and willing to give it (= A). F's initial tasks are: (a) getting into contact with A; (b) making clear what he wants; (c) succeeding in getting A to take over the task of giving him directions. If he succeeds, it is up to A to make clear to F how to reach his destination; he has the task of (d) describing the way (route directions proper); (e) making sure that F understands. It is then up to F, who set the task, to take it back and to conclude the interaction. F then has the task of (f) attesting to A that his job is done; (g) acknowledging

A's help; (h) ending the contact. As a rule, these three groups of tasks correspond to a clear interactional scheme of successful route communication. In the first part ('introduction'), F is dominant from an interactive point of view: (a)–(c) are carried out. In the second part ('central sequence'), A takes over and becomes dominant: (d) and (e) are solved. In the third part ('conclusion'), F is dominant again: (f)–(h) are carried out. There may be deviations. If F is successful with (a), but not with (b), everything drops until (h). There may also be overlaps or repetitions, but typically a route communication follows this scheme.

Route communications are interesting from an interactive, a cognitive, and a linguistic point of view. They are all closely linked, of course; but in the following, I shall concentrate on the third aspect, with some remarks on the second one, where necessary; almost nothing will be said about the interactive aspect. Only point (d), the route directions proper, are dealt with here, because it is the most yielding in the present context. (For a more detailed analysis of route communications, see Klein, 1979).

The study is based on 40 route communications in natural context. They were gathered in May 1977 in the inner city of Frankfurt/Main by students (cf. Figure 1). At the upper Zeil (a), the main shopping street, or at the

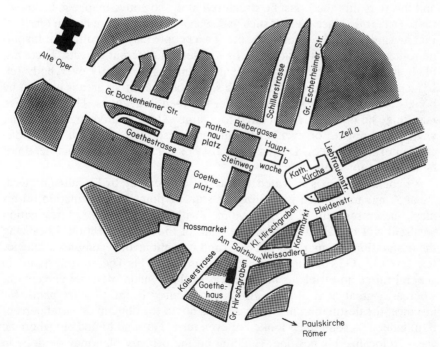

Figure 1   Simplified map of a part of central Frankfurt

Hauptwache (b) (a small historical building from the early eighteenth century) people were asked either for the 'Alte Oper' or the 'Goethehaus', both well-known landmarks in Frankfurt. The whole action was covertly recorded using a Nagra SNN audio tape recorder. Approximately 100 route communications were recorded, some of them very noisy because of the traffic. The first 20 for each destination (Alte Oper, Goethehaus), if fully understandable, were selected and transcribed for further analysis; they are labelled as O1–O20 and G1–G20; a selection is given in the appendix. The transcription is in standard orthography, with some slight touches of dialectal pronunciation for some speakers. Pauses and parallel speaking were transcribed as accurately as possible. Sometimes, more than one person answered; in this case, indices are used: A_1, A_2, etc.

2.2 Planning the description

In order to describe how to go from the starting point to the destination, A must have some cognitive representation of the area in question. In general, he owes his knowledge to his own previous experiences, e.g. he remembers what he has seen and heard and how he moved, or how the streetcar moved, and this remembrance must be structured into a cognitive map, e.g. he knows that at a certain place there is such and such a building where he can turn left, that he can't cross the steet there, etc. Two people may have different favourite routes, and their attention may be focused on different objects. There are likely to be objects which are salient landmarks for nearly everybody (cf. Lynch, 1960), but whether the image somebody has of an area is marked by book stores or fashion shops will differ between individuals. Thus, cognitive maps may be differently structured to a large extent. Moreover, they can be vague, incomplete, or even wrong in some respects (see, for a recent discussion of this concept, Downs & Stea, 1973, 1977). This can, but need not be, relevant for route directions.

A's cognitive map is activated, at least to some extent, by F's initial request. What A has to do then is localize the starting point and destination on his map. Such a segment of a cognitive map with starting point and destination localized will be called the 'primary plan' of the route direction. Localizing the destination is sometimes not easy, and it might involve complex strategies (cf. text O3, G2, or the fantastically complex G1). The starting point in general raises no problems because it is in the domain of visual perception, whereas a great deal of what else is represented in the primary plan—for instance, the destination in most cases—is not in the domain of visual perception; indeed, A sometimes looked or even turned around to find out where he was—to localize his position. Building up the primary plan may be done in advance, or step by step. Consider G11:

F Entschuldigung, können Sie mir bitte sagen, wo's zum Goethehaus geht?
   Excuse me,   could you tell me how to get to the Goethehaus?
A

F   Ja
                               Yes
A [3 seconds] Goethehaus?   ja, gehen Se da rauf, immer geradeaus,
               Goethehaus?   yes, go up that way, always straight on,

   erste Straße links, erste Straße rechts
   first street to the left, first street to the right

F erste links, erste rechts   dankeschön.
   first left,   first right   thank you
A   ja
                           yes

A makes a planning pause after the question: then he reaffirms himself that
he has correctly understood the question, indicating that he is able and
willing to answer; and then, he carries out his description in one stroke.
When speaking, he apparently has a sufficiently clear primary plan; he is an
'advance planner'. His counterpart may be called 'stepwise planner'. A clear
example is in G15:

F

A Ja; [10 seconds] hier die Zeil runter, auf der andern Seite, ja
   Yes;   here down the Zeil, on the other side,   yes
F

A [14 seconds] praktisch gehen Se jetzt hier an [13 seconds] eh [3 seconds]
                in fact   you go along here now   er
F

A Sie müssen wohl von hinten rüber, weil da ne Ampel ist, ja;
   you probably have to cross over from there, because lights
F

A   da hinter der Kirche lang; dann gehn Se
   are there, yah; there along behind the church; there you go
F

A   rechts die Straße wieder grad runter und dann müssen Se
      down that street to the right again and there you have to
F

A   bis zur [2 seconds]wie heiß'n das? auf der linken Ecke [4 seconds]
      go to the   what's it called again? The left corner
F

A   bis die ne Rolltreppe kommt, da is Möbel Mann, diese Straße
      till you reach the an escalator, there's Möbel Mann, that street
F

A
      müssen Sie links rein; und die erste wieder rechts;
      you have to go in to the left; and the first one again to the right;
F   gut, dankeschön
      okay, thank you
A   also, auf der einen Seite ist, eh
                           well, on the one side, there is, er
F

A   Neckermann, Reisebüro, und auf der andern Straßenecke ist
      Neckermann, a travel agency, and on the other street corner there is
F

A   Möbel Mann; *die* Straße links rein und dann die erste
      Möbel Mann; *that* street you go in to the left, and then, it's the first
      rechts.
      right.

Though reflecting at the beginning, A has no clear plan when he starts speaking. He soon comes to a point that is problematic; he then reflects on the situation—he tries to elaborate his primary plan there—restarts at the beginning, arrives again at the point of confusion, reflects again, and then advances a little bit further, until the next unclear position is reached; he tries to picture the situation there to himself, and then is able to continue to the end. After that, he has no difficulty in recapitulating a part of his description; the plan being there, he is able to repeat, vary, or extend his description. He doesn't work out a complete plan in advance, but starts speaking as soon as he has got the first bit ready, and he then goes on step by step. Planning in advance and planning stepwise are complementary techniques, and it is an open question whether they represent individual styles or whether their use simply depends on the particular task. Having a gap in the conversation—and a long planning pause is such a gap—is awkward, and it may well be that A in G15 starts simply because he doesn't like the propsect of a gap.

The primary plan, whether built up in advance or stepwise, is a first condition for a successful description. But less than the whole primary plan is reported, of course; this would contain a lot of information that is superfluous for the purpose of the required route directions. The speaker must select from it and arrange those pieces of information he thinks to be relevant for the listener. He has to form a 'secondary plan' which will immediately underlie the linearized sequence of verbal expressions, with which he describes the route. The organizing principle of this secondary plan is that of an 'imaginary journey' through the primary plan from starting point to destination. During this journey, certain points of the primary plan are selected and marked; this series of 'fixed points' forms the skeleton of his description. His directions have three components: fixed points are introduced, directions relative to the fixed points are marked, and actions (or events) are indicated. Consider the following passage from O4:

```
F   [...]                                                    ja
                                                             yes

A       Ja, [5 seconds] jetzt gehn Sie vor, bis ganz vorn hin
        Yes,            you go on here,   until right before
F                                    ja
                                     yes

A   bis Sie an den Kaufhof stoßen      dann gehen Sie links rein,
    till you run into the Kaufhof      then you go there to the left
F                       ja
                        yes

A   dann ganz links, dann kommt erst die Schillerstraße,
    the Biebergasse     well you go on here and then you stick
F


A   dann ganz links, dann kommt erst die Schillerstraße,
    to the left,      then you come first to the Schillerstraße,
F                         mhm
                          mhm
A   die überqueren Sie      da is vorn an der Ecke is ein
    there you cross over    there is on the corner there is a
F


A   Herrenboutique, da gehn Sie dran vorbei.
    men's shop,     there you go right past.
```

The first fixed point after the starting position is the Kaufhof (a big department store); here, the walker has several possibilities, one of which is marked:

'links rein'. In other cases, possible alternatives are explicitly excluded. This is not done in the present example; here, only the right direction is indicated as such, in fact, given twice: once by the deictic statement 'links rein', and then by the additional information 'die Biebergasse'; A has incorporated a unit of his primary plan that is not absolutely necessary but which provides additional help. Then, the route is repeated until a new fixed point is reached: Schiller-straße. In this way, point after point is selected, verbally introduced, and this skeleton is completed by commentary or additional information that helps to make sure that F gets the message. And he has got it if he has succeeded in building up a rudimentary image of the area, one that essentially consists of a series of selected points, and if he knows what he has to do at these points.

This information is given by three types of descriptive expressions[7] that the speaker uses: expressions that introduce fixed points, deictic expressions that link certain fixed points, and expressions for what F has to do there or what happens there; in a sequence like: '. . . until you get to a small house with green shutters; there, turn left', a fixed point ('a small house with green shutters') is introduced; the local deictic 'there' refers to that fixed point, or rather to a locality close to that fixed point, and then the listener is told what has to be done at the denotatum of 'there'.

2.3   Local deixis

After these general considerations on planning, let me turn to the specific problem of deictic reference in route directions. It is characterized by two specific features:

(1) Speaker and listener do not share a deictic space at the beginning. They share a perceptual space, but this is not enough. The listener at first doesn't have available the deictic space represented by the speaker's cognitive map of the area in question. Hence, A has to provide F with the idea of such a deictic space, or the indispensable elements of it; and this is what is achieved by introducing fixed points and giving additional information.

(2) The origo is given by the location of the speaker which, in this case, doesn't differ crucially from that of the listener. But then, the location of the speaker and listener—of the imaginary walker—is constantly shifted, or rather thought of as shifting during the imaginary walk.

In general, there is no problem of co-ordination: the orientation of A and F in the imaginary walk is thought to be identical, and at the starting point, it either differs in a trivial way that doesn't affect the use of deictics, or A changes his position or his direction of gaze (or causes F to do so) to this effect. The delimitation is generally based on factual knowledge; it is rarely explicitly specified. The deictic oppositions are as usual, and analogical deixis is rarely used. In the following, I shall concentrate on the two points mentioned above: building up a rudimentary deictic space that mainly consists of a series of fixed points, and the moving origo and its function for the identification of denotata. The fixed points used are streets, places, buildings, etc. There are essentially four ways for a listener to recognize what the speaker intended as a fixed point:

(1) On the basis of his previous knowledge, the speaker expects that the listener simply will know some landmarks, or he can check this by questions like: 'Do you know where . . . is?'—'Yes'—'Okay, there it's . . .'.

(2) On the basis of visual introduction, mainly by pointing gestures, e.g. in G17, where A says: 'Sehen Sie dieses Schild Bill-Binding da oben ja?'—F: 'Ja, ja'—A: 'Okay, und dann da geradeaus'. This is only possible for the space of visual perception, of course.

(3) On the basis of (non-deictic) descriptions, such as in G6: 'bis Sie an den Platz kommen, wo eh son'n großes Brunnen rausspringt, da gehn Se links runter', or G16: 'Um wenn Se e Stück drin sin, wo die Leute da sitze, dann . . . .'

(4) On the basis of indications relative to a previous fixed point; this is often done with expressions like 'the first . . . after', 'the next . . .', etc., e.g. in G16: 'da gleich bis zur nächste Ampel'. This strategy is very frequent, and some speakers, as A in G11, use it exclusively: the first reference point is that starting point, and all other indications of fixed points are related to this first one.

Typically, these possibilities are used in combination with each other. In the following, one example (from G10) is considered in some detail. F's reactions are omitted; the fixed points are underlined:

A₃ Am beste is, Sie gehn jetzt *auf die anner Seit*; *un hinner der Kirch* überqueren Sie *die Straß*, ja? Dann gehn Se *an de Kaiserstraß* e Stück erunter, bis Se an *de nächst Ampel* komme; da gehn Se links erein un dann sind Se gleich *dort*; da links, gell, da links erein, e Stück, un *da geht links e Straß un rechts*; die rechte Straß, das is der *Große Hirschgraben*; da kommt gleich 's *Goethehaus*.

[You best go to *the other side* now; and behind the church, you cross *the street*, okay? There you go a bit down the Kaiserstraße, till you get to the next light; there you turn left and then you are almost *there*; there to the left, all right, there to the *left*, a bit, and there *to the left* and *to the right* is a cross street; the street on the right, that's the *Große Hirschgraben*; shortly after that is the *Goethehaus*.]

'Die anner Seit' (= the other side) is a type 4 expression, combined—as often happens—with non-deictic information; it refers back to the original location:

that side which is not here.[8] The next fixed point 'hinter der Kirch' (= behind the church) is visual with a deictic component: 'behind'. What is meant is 'behind the church that is before our eyes'. The next one is 'die Straß' (= Katharinenpfad); it is again a type 4 expression: 'die Straß' here means: that street that you will reach if you go on behind the church. The next fixed point, 'an de Kaiserstraß', has a peculiarity: an expression may be used this way only if the denotatum can be assumed to be known to the listener, i.e. the way in which the fixed point is introduced corresponds to type 1. But A can't assume that F knows the Kaiserstraße; either he assumes it nevertheless, or he assumes that F is able to read a street sign, i.e. that he is able to acquire the necessary knowledge. There follows again a fixed point of type 4, 'die nächst Ampel'. The next point, 'dort', is clearly deictic, but it doesn't fit the general pattern: it is the first marking of the final destination; it means 'there, where you want to go', rather than 'at the traffic lights'. (Incidentally, this is one of the rare cases where the strictly serial order of the fixed points is given up.) The lights are taken up by the deictic expression 'da links, gell, da erein', which, however, doesn't introduce a new fixed point. Again, this is done by an expression of type 3: that place, where there is a street to the left and a street to the right. This expression also contains a deictic component, and it could be argued that it is a combination of types 3 and 4. With its aid, the next and—apart from the destination itself—last fixed point is introduced: 'der große Hirschgraben'. All that remains is the final marking.

Such a series of fixed points, together with some additional information perhaps, forms a rudimentary picture of a deictic space; the picture is completed if the imaginary traveller becomes a real one, and it is sufficient to set up—by means of local deictics—a lot of localities where certain actions are to be performed.[9] This is done by the deictics 'hier', 'da', and 'dort'. 'Here' is usually used to refer to a space around the initial location whose borders are not specified—because there is no need to do so. The denotatum of 'dort' and 'da' (in local sense) is *not* the fixed point with which it is used: 'bis Se an de nächst Ampel komme; da gehn Se links rein'. 'Da' refers to the space around the imaginary position of the speaker at the fixed point in question. No delimitation is used; it is expected that F will draw the borders from his factual knowledge.

How this mechanism works is perhaps more clearly to be seen with the deictics 'left' and 'right', whose denotatum not only depends on the—real or imaginary—position of the speaker, but also on his—real or imaginary—direction of gaze. There is one case in the data where the *same* street, the Biebergasse or its continuation, the Freßgasse, is described in relation to the *same* fixed point one time as to the left (O1),

A   Hier vor bis zum Kaufhof [. . .] und da halten Sie sich rechts, geradeaus durch die Freßgasse the other time as to the right (O4),

A   Jetzt gehen Sie vor, bis ganz vorn hin, bis an den Kaufhof stoßen, dann gehen Sie links rein, die Biebergasse

This is simply due to differences of position and their consequences. In O1, the original position is in the *Zeil* (see Figure 1); speaker and listener gaze in the direction of the Hauptwache. If F is thought to move in this direction and if—and this seems most natural—he maintains his direction of gaze, the Freßgasse (or the Biebergasse) will be to his right, as soon as he arrives at the fixed point 'Kaufhof'. In O4, the original position is south-east of the *Hauptwache*; speaker and listener gaze towards the Kaufhof, and at this fixed point, the Kaufhof, the Biebergasse is to the left. What 'left' and 'right'—and analogously 'dort', 'da', 'hier'—mean is determined by the origo and by the direction of gaze. In route directions, both position and direction underly a constant imaginary change. In this case, the determinants of local deixis are set up by the explicitly fixed points, on the one hand, and by the normal and expected course of events—of walking and looking in an imaginary space.

NOTES

1. I wish to thank V. Ehrich, R. Jarvella, A. Kratzer, W. Levelt, M. Miller, E. Schegloff, M. Silverstein, J. Weissenborn, and D. Wunderlich for helpful comments and criticisms on earlier versions. Special thanks go to Elena Lieven, who has made numerous stylistic corrections; if my English is understandable, it is mainly to her merit.

2. This study is described in greater detail in Klein (1979). It not only concerns the use of deictics, but also interactive and cognitive aspects of the complex verbal action of asking for the way and giving route directions.

3. I don't see any substantial difference between deictic and anaphoric use of 'here' (and, in a similar way, of 'he', 'that', etc.) Anaphorical (and in the same way cataphorical) use is just that special case of deictic reference where the reference unit is *verbally* introduced into the context, whereas in other cases it is there by gestures, by shared perception, or by shared knowledge.

4. This may lead to some confusion with people who professionally take over the listener's orientation, such as opticians and ophthalmologists. The usual method of co-ordinating perspectives then leads to wrong results. On the other hand, it seems that in imperatives, it is generally the listener's perspective that is decisive: 'turn right!' always means 'turn right from your perspective!' This is true at least in route directions.

5. It is precisely this idea that makes the assumption of deictic spaces being provided with a topological structure so tempting. Where a structure defined, the possible denotata could be identified with the neighbourhoods or rather a subset of the neighbourhoods. If it is some distinguished element of the topological space, the possible denotata of 'here' could be a subset of all those neighbourhoods that contain x as an element. But suggestive as this idea may be—it does not give us the topology.

6. This is somewhat simplified, since 'there' cannot be applied to places with objects which the speaker is touching. I cannot say 'the book there' when touching it. Touching turns everying into here.

7. The expressions used in the route directions may be subdivided into three classes, according to their function: descriptive expressions, commenting expressions, and interactive expressions. The speaker may comment upon what he says, or on the difficulty of the task or route; typical are expressions like 'oh, that's quite near', 'well, it's complicated', etc. With interactive expressions, A checks whether F got the message or simply whether F is still following his explanations, and F signals that he is still 'receiving' and that A can and should continue; a standard technique is 'mhm' with question intonation on A's side and with affirmative intonation on F's side (for some details see Klein, 1979, pp. 33–37).

8. It is precisely the deictic character of the word 'other' that is used in the famous riddle about the village of liars, the village of truth-tellers, and the cross-roads where somebody from one of the villages—it is not known which one—is sitting. If one has to discover using only one yes/no question whether the village of the truth-tellers is to the left or to the right, one must ask: 'Would somebody from the other village send me left for the village of the truth-tellers'. The reference of 'somebody from the other village' is different depending on the person sitting there.

9. A similar result can be obtained by using temporal deictics; they are determined by the sequence of actions: 'dann' means 'at the moment after you have done what I previously said'. I don't consider these uses here.

REFERENCES

Atkinson, M., & Griffiths, P. D. (1973). Here's here's, there's, here and there. *Edinburgh Working Papers in Linguistics* 3 (mimeo).

Bühler, K. (1934). *Sprachtheorie*. Jena: Fischer.

Clark, E. (1977). From gesture to word: on the natural history of deixis in language acquisition. In J. S. Bruner & A Garton (eds), *Human growth and development: Wolfson College lectures, 1976*. Oxford: Oxford University Press.

Davis, P. W., & Saunders, R. (1975). Bella Coola nominal deixis. *Language*, **51**, 845–858.

Downs, R., & Stea, D. (eds) (1973). *Image and environment*. Chicago: Aldine.

Downs, R., & Stea, D. (1977). *Maps in minds*. New York: Harper & Row.

Fillmore, C. (1975). Santa Cruz lectures on deixis, 1971. Bloomington, Ind.: Indiana University Linguistics Club.

Klein, W. (1979). Wegauskünfte. *Zeitschrift für Literaturwissenschaft und Linguistik*, **33**, 9–57.

Klein, W., & Levelt, W. J. M. (1978). Sprache und Kontext. *Die Naturwissenschaften*, **65**, 328–335.

Kratzer, A., & von Stechow, A. (1976). Äußerungen und Bedeutung. *Zeitschrift für Literaturwissenschaft und Linguistik*, **23/24**, 97–130.

Labov, W., & Linde, C. (1975). Spatial networks as a site for the study of language and thought. *Language*, **51**, 924–939.

Lynch, K. (1960). *The image of a city*. Cambridge, Mass.: MIT Press.

Miller, G. A., & Johnson-Laird, P. N. (1976). *Language and perception*. Cambridge, Mass.: Harvard University Press.

Wunderlich, D. (1976). *Studien zur Sprechakttheorie*. Frankfurt/Main: Suhrkamp.

APPENDIX: SELECTED TRANSCRIPTIONS

O2

F   Zum alten Opernhaus
To the old Opera House

A Ja?   jaaa [10 seconds] da gehen Sie jetzt bis
Yes?   *yahhh*   *you go now as far as*

F   ja   oben drüber, ja
yes   *above there, yes*

A zur Zeil   oben drüber, nicht unten durch
the Zeil   above there, not below

F

A oben drüber, gehen durch die Goethestraße durch, und dann kommen
above there, you go through the Goethestraße, and shortly you

F   dankeschön
thank you

A Sie direkt an die alte Oper   bitte, Wiedersehen
will be at the old Opera   you're welcome, see you.

O17

F Entschuldigen Sie, können Sie mir sagen, wie man zur alter Oper kommt?
Excuse me, could you tell me how to get to the old Opera?

A

F

A na, oh ja doch [2 seconds] Sie können [2 seconds] hier rauf [2 seconds] bis
well, oh yes,   you can   here that way   till

F   jaha
yah uhhuh

A [6 seconds] ehm, ich muß auch erst überlegen   weil's von bissel
ehm, let me think first myself   'cause it's been

F   ja
yes

A verbaut wurde; [4 seconds] Sie gehen jetzt hier eh zur Ecke   dann
changed a bit here   now you go here to the corner   then

F

A links oben über den Platz, dann gehn Sie geradeaus, das ist die
to the left up above across the square, then straight on, that's the

F   ja
yes

A Goethestraße, also nicht diese, sondern die nächste dann rauf, und dann
   Goethestraße, that is not this one but the next one, up it then, and then
F   mhm
                       mhm
A stoßen Sie direkt   das ist dann auf der rechten Seite ist dann die
   you run immediately into that is on the right side then is the
F   mhm   gutt, dankeschön
               mhm   *okay, thank you*
A alte Oper   das sehen Sie schon;   bitte
   old Opera   *you'll see it then*   *you're welcome.*

G2

F Können Sie mir sagen, wie man zum Goethehaus kommt?
   Could you tell me how to get to the Goethe House?
A   Goethehaus?
                                                        Goethe House?
F   nee, Großer Hirschgraben war das, glaub ich
               no, it was Großer Hirschgraben, I think
A keine Adresse?   bitte?
   no address?   *sorry?*
F Großer Hirschgraben, die Straße [5 seconds] Wissen Se nicht,
   Großer Hirschgraben, the street   You don't know,
A fragen wir nochmal.
   we'll ask somebody else.

G4

F Können Sie mir sagen, wie man zum Goethehaus kommt?   Zum
   Could you tell us how to get to the Goethe House?   *To the*
A   wie?
                                                        what?
F Goethehaus   Goethe
   Goethe House   *Goethe*
A   Güterhaus?   hm, das ist hier etwa, Goethe,
               Goods House?   *hm, that's here somewhere, Goethe,*
F

A Goethe, Goetheplatz, Goetheplatz und Goethehaus, he,
   Goethe, Goethe place, Goethe Place and Goethe House, hey,
                                           ja, ja, ja,
                                           oh yes, sure,

ich glaube da is da, oder? ganz in der Nähe davon
I think it's there, or? around here somewhere

F

A wenn Sie hierher, also wenn Sie jetzt über die Straße gehen,
if you here, well, if you cross the street now,
F   ja
                                                                 yes
A ja und dann gehn Sie gerade, ich glaube da wo ist die Kirche
okay, and then go straight on, I think there where is the church
F   ja, danke   okay.
                                     yes, thanks   *okay.*
A da muß sie[!] irgendwo sein   bitte.
there she   must be somewhere   *you're welcome.*

G17

F Entschuldigung, können Sie mir sagen, wie man hier zum
Excuse me, could you tell me how to get to the
A

F Goethehaus kommt?
Goethe House here?
A   ja: Moment   [2 seconds] okay [1 second]
                           yes, just a moment   *okay*
F   ja
                                           yes
A du mußt hier durch, ja?   und [4 seconds] okay,
you have to go through here, alright?   *and*   *okay,*
F

A wie am besten, ja; hier durch, ja? is auch eine Straße; sehn Sie
what's the best, yes; through here, okay? there is another street; do you see
F   ja, ja
                                           yes, sure
A dieses Schild Bill-Binding Bier da oben, ja?   okay, und dann da
this sign Bill-Binding Beer up there, yeh?   *okay, and then*
F   mhm
              mhm
A geradeaus   und jetzt is es entweder, es gibt eh zwei kleine Gasse,
straight on   *and now it's either, there are er two small side streets,*
F

A   ja, eh immer geradeaus, und dann kurz vor Berliner Straße,
    yes, ah, you keep going straight, and then shortly before the Berliner Straße,
F

A   eh eh, irgendwo in dieser Richtung, das weiß ich auch nicht so weit
    ah ah, somewhere in that direction; I'm not quite sure, either so far
F   is gut, danke
    that's fine, thanks
                        fünf Minuten, ja? auf der rechten Seite
A   *in five minutes, okay? on the right side,*
F   ja, is gut,   vielen Dank
                               yes, that's fine, thanks a lot
A   eh aber zuerst hier runter   okay.
    but first down here   *okay.*

Speech, Place, and Action
Edited by R. J. Jarvella and W. Klein
© 1982 John Wiley & Sons Ltd.

How to Get There From Here[1]

DIETER WUNDERLICH and RUDOLPH REINELT

We are often confronted with the unforeseen task of telling a stranger how to reach his destination. Just as often, we may seek out a passer-by to give us directions if we ourselves are not familiar with some vicinity. The present paper deals with the question of how people cope with this task in a satisfactory way. Our interest in this question stems from the observation that in situations of this type, the 'informant' will often produce and repeat certain reduced forms of speech.[2] At the same time his actions of this kind seem to be tuned to the confirmatory behaviour of the 'questioner', as he tries to take in the information given. To put it more generally, each party behaves in a way that is conducive to satisfactory performance of the task at hand. We make the assumption here that both the 'informant' and 'questioner' are able to do this because they have learned certain strategies for interaction in accordance with a general scheme for pursuing such a task.

The research reported here takes up some ideas present in the work of Jochen Rehbein (1977, pp. 282–290) and Wolfgang Klein (1977; this volume). Those points to which we subscribe will be considered rather briefly, however, In somewhat more detail, we will discuss issues we consider more controversial.

In a situation of the kind described above, the task of giving directions as a whole can be divided into three subtasks. One subtask is cognitive, another is interactional, and the third is linguistic. Let us first state these in rough detail.

The cognitive task. Here, the 'informant' has to activate a cognitive map of the relevant spatial area, he needs to identify within this the location of the encounter (which will almost always be the starting point for the route described), he needs to identify the location the 'questioner' is interested in (the end point of the route), and he has to select a suitable way of connecting these points or places. On the other hand, the 'questioner' has to mentally construct a plan of the route described and memorize its crucial parts.

The interactional task. The 'questioner' has to initiate and, finally, to terminate the verbal exchange. He has to clarify his request and his possible preferences regarding expense of time, means of transportation, and the like, and he has to confirm the information given. The 'informant', on the other hand, has to give a comprehensible outline of the route. He has to repeat parts of it, add comments, and provide any other information which might be helpful.

The linguistic task. The 'informant' has to produce a concise description of the selected route. He has to mark out its stages and to clarify how to continue on at choice points along the way.

While these different tasks are interconnected, they can be dealt with from different theoretical points of view. Whereas Klein has been mainly concerned with the ties between cognitive and linguistic processes, we are interested in addition in some of the bonds between interactional and linguistic devices. Our approach in this regard more resembles Rehbein's, though he considered above all the role of getting directions in the overall process of finding one's way.

Our own investigation is based on a corpus of more than 80 tape-recorded route directions. To ensure generality, we chose various points of origin and various destinations. A given destination was requested from different origins. The route directions were collected mainly in the city of Düsseldorf, but also in Krefeld and Mainz. The locations requested included such things as a youth hostel, local court, police headquarters, central station, tax office, university, museum, department store, and remote streets. Generally, when making the request the questioner did not know the way to the destination. Also included were some cases where two persons in each other's company were addressed and asked for directions. Although these cases are of particular interest, especially regarding mutual suggestions and corrections, we will not consider them here. (A case of this kind is described in Wunderlich, 1978, p. 64 ff.) The data collection and transcription for this study was carried out mainly by Gabi Müller and Rudolf Reinelt. Reinelt also elaborated some of the results on linguistic devices.

The first major section of the paper will deal with the overall scheme of giving directions. Every such discourse event consists of several clearly marked phases, only one of which is the actual route-description. The second major section covers the three dominant parts of a route-description, which are shown to be distinguishable in terms of characteristic verbal devices used.

THE INTERACTIONAL SCHEME OF GIVING DIRECTIONS

Parts of the interactional scheme

First, let us introduce some terminological notions. Let A be the person (or the group of persons) who wants to be given directions (the 'questioner'), and B be the passer-by (or the group of passers-by) giving the directions (the 'informant'). The complete discourse emerging from the first initiative of A up to the final leave-taking of A and B will be called *route-information*. It consists of several phases in which A and B play different roles according to their respective tasks mentioned above.

One of these phases is called the route-description. B gives a description here of how to get from the *starting point* (the place where the encounter takes place) to the destination. As we will see, this description always takes the form of an imaginary wandering, or tour along the route. B uses certain 'landmarks' as *intermediate destinations*, with respect to which the following moves are defined. The desired location may, then, be called the *final destination*. It is surrounded by a certain immediate environment, in which the final steps will be obvious. Likewise, the starting point can be viewed as being enclosed in the space of visual perception, within which an *initial destination* may be marked off.

When complete (and to be successful), the route-information consists of four sections, which are performed successively. There is, however, a possibility of re-entering an already completed phase, particularly in the case of self-corrections, or in case the question of alternative routes is raised. The four phases may be called *initiation, route-description, securing,* and *closure*.

Phase I: Initiation

Phase I is always initiated by A, and always ended by B's starting of a route-description.

(a) A turns to a passer-by B and asks him for the way to the desired location x. Generally, A uses a routine formula, e.g. the tripartite formula

'Entschuldigen Sie bitte, können Sie mir sagen, $\left\{ \begin{array}{l} \text{wie ich zu } x \text{ komme?'} \\ \text{wo } x \text{ ist?'} \end{array} \right\}$

'Excuse me, please, can you tell me $\left\{ \begin{array}{l} \text{how I can get to } x\text{?'} \\ \text{where } x \text{ is?'} \end{array} \right\}$

The first phrase serves to attract B's attention, the second to introduce the task requested of B, and the third for A to say where he wants to go. In any case, the question will be understood to mean that A wants to go immediately from the place where he is now to x.[3] Hence the place of the encounter can serve as a spatial *origo*.

(b) B reacts by indicating that he has understood the request. Several ways of reacting are open to B. He may simply start the route-description, thus initiating the next phase. (This happened in six of our cases.) More likely, however, is that B will repeat the name of x, or that he will show an expression of surprise or reflection, or some indication that he is planning a description. B may also ask for clarification of the task. He may demand further

	A = 'questioner'	B = 'informant'
Phase I	INITIATION (a) Initial question (c) Reconfirmation	(b) Confirmation of the task
Phase II		ROUTE-DESCRIPTION
Phase III	←————— SECURING —————→	
	Confirmation	Repetition, completion
Phase IV	CLOSURE (a) pre-closing (b) separation	

Figure 1   The distribution of verbal tasks in a route-information

specification of the place, or of the means of transportation, or may ask what it is that A wants at x.

B may also correct implicit assumptions of A concerning the approximate direction or distance to x, or indicate the complexity of the task, or that the distance to be covered is great. He may evaluate what he's going to do in advance. For example, he may mention several alternatives, or indicate that he doesn't know a good way to the destination. Finally, B may offer to come along.

(c) Depending on B's reaction, A may reconfirm that B has properly understood the request, or he may supply B with a specification of his goal, with his personal preference concerning transportation, etc.

Parts (b) and (c) of the initiation phase may lead to a repetitive exchange of turns, but they may also be omitted. In any event, this phase has ended when B starts the route-description.

If B does not know x or the way to get there, the initiation phase can be extended considerably. If B reacts by expressing his ignorance (combined with explanatory or apologetic expressions), it is possible that A maintain his initiative, e.g. by putting his question differently. B may then offer some compensation by giving a vague direction, suggesting that A ask somebody else, or looking for another passer-by.[4] In this case it is A who has to bring the verbal exchange to an end. Thus, in the unsuccessful case, an initiation is followed directly by closure.

Phase II: Route-description

Phase II is always initiated and terminated by B. In complying with A's request, B will give a description of the path to be followed, which begins with the starting point or an initial destination within the visual field, and ends with the final arrival (e.g. 'Und da ist es dann'—'and there it is'). B may give his description continuously, in one piece, or he may develop it step by step, interrupting himself for planning pauses, self-corrections, consideration of alternatives, or by re-entering phase I (b). Here, some turn-taking is possible, depending on the individual style of B in presenting his directions, and on supplementary questions or intermediate confirmations on the part of A. The way to be covered is clearly partitioned by verbal means into different sections.

The route-description is finished when B has for the first time stated that the final destination has been reached. In subsequent parts of the discourse some sections of the route, or even the whole route, may be repeated, extended, or specified. In a sense, B then re-enters phase II, and can end again by re-stating the arrival. Non-initial route-descriptions are, however, less organized by purely linguistic means, and more sensitive to B's confirmatory behaviour. We hence can identify another phase of the route-information (contrary to Klein's (1977) assumptions).

Phase III: Securing

Phase III is not obligatory in the complete route-information, although it is found in almost all of the data we have collected. Phase III is either triggered by the behaviour of A, when he does not yet initiate a closure, or it is initiated by B, when he wants to make sure that A has understood his directions. Generally, A is expected to confirm the directions given, in one way or another, e.g. by repeating crucial parts of them. If A fails to do so, and also hesitates to initiate a closure (thus signalling the successful completion of the task), or if A's confirmation is not convincing, B will continue to feel obliged to provide the desired information.

Several variants of securing provisions can be found: B may summarize, repeat, paraphrase, or complete crucial parts of the description, or conditions for the decisions that have to be taken. He may even recapitulate the whole description. He may also give supplementary hints about distances and durations.[5] He may refer to possibilities of re-enquiry, or to points he himself is not sure of. Finally, he may assure A that he will easily find his way.[6] The securing is completed as soon as A initiates the closure.

Phase IV: Closure

Phase IV is always initiated by A, because only A can state that the request has been satisfactorily fulfilled. A alone is in a position to remove the obligation under which B has been placed by his request. The most prominent way to initiate a closure is an expression of gratitude. But A may also announce or indicate that he will carry out the suggested action. In a sense, thanks or announcements are only pre-closing signs since B can react by re-entering phase III. (In this case A has to re-initiate a closure.) The closing itself is generally also initiated by A, who turns away from his addressee.

An illustrative example of a complete route-information is given in the appendix.

From the point of view of the on-going interaction, phases I and III are the most important. The delaying provisions in phase I show that B needs sufficient certainty in regard to his task, given A's expressed aim. Correspondingly, in phase III, B will want to ensure that A has understood the crucial parts of his directions. The structure of phase III, however, is not very systematic. It depends on the particular route-description as well as on the point where A initiates a closure. A delay of closure will lead B to repeat the crucial parts of the description in increasingly reduced form, or be forced to provide further specification. Both can be observed in our example. If A delayed the closure still further, B would probably not know what to do.

From the point of view of seeing spatial descriptions in contrast, phases II and, to some extent, III are the most important. Phase III, however, exhibits few new verbal devices, and is much less structured than II. We will therefore restrict ourselves in the next section to a discussion of the verbal devices exhibited in the route-description itself. It should remain obvious, however, that a route-description itself is always embedded in an interactive setting which arises with a selection and variation among linguistic devices, and that, secondly, route-descriptions as a rule only follow a securing of the task and precede a securing of its results.

AN ANALYSIS OF ROUTE-DESCRIPTION

Definition and selection

In this part, we consider those elements of route-information which constitute linguistically complete route-descriptions. As we have seen, a route-description begins after the first phase, in which the task for B, the informant, has properly been settled. It is always initiated, and also terminated by B. In this stage, pauses for planning, self-corrections, supplementary remarks, etc., are possible at any time. These will not be discussed here.

Let us first take a look at some examples of cases where a route-description is given without interruption. There are, of course, more complex examples. The elements of a complex route-description, however, can be derived in a straightforward way from more simple ones.

(1)

a Wenn Sie hier geradeaus gehen, ('If you go straight on here,
b die nächste Haupstraße—wo die/ at the next main street— where
diese erleuchteten Hinweisschil- the/these lighted directional signs
der stehen— are—
c da is dann das Polizeipräsidium. there are the police headquarters
then.')

(2)

a Gehn se hier rechts rum, ('Turn right here,
b nächste Straße links dann ähm next street to the left, then um
ja eigentlich immer dem großen that's right always follow the
Autoverkehr nach, kommense heavy traffic, you come upon the
auf die Rheinbrücke drauf, ja? Rhine bridge, o.k.?
c und direkt am Fuße der andern and right at the foot of the other
Rheinbrücke is die Jugendher- (side of the) Rhine bridge is the
berge. youth hostel.')

(3)

a Gehn Sie hier vorne unter den ('Go here in front under the
Tunnel, tunnel,
b dann kommse da wieder hoch, then you come up again there,
un immer geradeaus, diese and always straight ahead, this
Richtung, direction,
c kommse direkt vor dem Haupt- you come out directly before the
bahnhof raus. main station.')

(4)

a Gehn Sie geradeaus, ('Go straight on,
b und dann rechts die Kruppstraße and then to the right down the
runter, immer geradeaus, Kruppstraße, always straight on,
c dann vor der Brücke auf der then in front of the bridge on the
linken Seite da is das Finanzamt. left side there the tax-office is.')

(5)

a Wenn Se hier runtergehn, ne ('If you go down here,
b kommse unten anne Ampel, ne, you come to a traffic light,
und dann links runter die and then down to the left

Straßenbahnschienen nach	following the tramline
c bis unten auf de/vor de Brücke	until below on the/before the
links da is et Finanzamt.	bridge, on the left there is the
	tax-office.')

Almost all of our examples of route-descriptions can be partitioned into three segments. These have been indicated by the letters a, b, and c. For each segment, some parts of the route as well as some of the linguistic means used are characteristic. We will establish this more generally.

As for verbal devices, we can distinguish *nominals* (e.g. *Ecke, Tunnel, Kruppstraße*), '*directives*' (e.g. *hier, und dann, immer geradeaus, bis*), *position markers* (e.g. *an, links, drüben, nächste*), and *verbs of movement* (e.g. *gehen, sich halten, kommen*). Every segment of a route-description is marked by special verbal elements.

Constructional units

(a)   The initial route

The route to be described begins at O, the place where the two speakers are. This place can be referred to using the word *hier* ('here'). Since walking, or

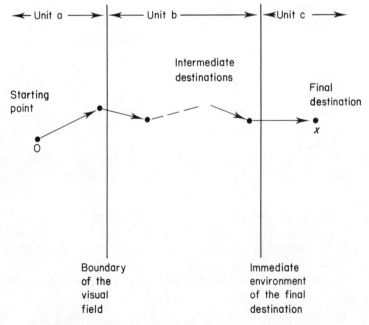

Figure 2   The constructional units in a route-description

going somewhere, is always a spatiotemporal activity, one can also refer to its beginning by *jetzt* ('now'), under the (*always* made) assumption that A, the questioner, wants to start immediately.

Almost every route-description commences with an initial route, whose prominent points are still within the visual field. These initial directions can be indicated by the use of *hier* in combination with a position marker: *hier durch* ('through'), *hier links* ('left'), *hier rum* ('around', 'about'), *hier runter* ('down'), *hier drüben* ('over there'), *von hier gleich* ('soon'). The word *hier* becomes thus the characteristic 'directive' for the initial route, often combined with a pointing gesture. Such a gesture introduces a vector. In its deictic field are all the places along the vector, i.e. within one spatial direction. *Hier*, if combined with such a gesture, denotes a place near the speaker along this vector (Wunderlich, 1979).

In some cases, different points within the visual field are distinguished. In these cases *da* and *hier* are opposed to one another. They then denote places in different directions, and *da* is understood as denoting a more remote place than *hier*.

> Der kommt von da, fährt hier rum, und fährt dann über die Rheinknie-brücke rüber.
> ('It comes from there, goes around here, and then goes over the Rhine Knee bridge')

> Ja, von hier am besten oder hier vorne, drüben da hinterm Kirchplatz, hier ist direkt ne Haltestelle.
> ('Yes, from here the best, or in front here, over there behind the churchyard, right there there is a bus stop')

(b) Intermediate routes

After the initial route, but before the destination is reached in the description, some points of orientation are usually mentioned. These are intended to guide the questioner in finding his way along the route if he needs to change direction, and the final destination is still out of sight. If no change in direction is required, the use of the single formula *immer geradeaus* ('always straight ahead') will suffice.

To provide the requisite orientation, the informant will construct a pathway bordering on buildings, public squares, bridges, street crossings, etc. Such objects usually have characteristic features which make them easily recognizable. The success of a route-description depends to a large extent on the appropriate choice of these 'landmarks'. In addition, certain objects like traffic lights, busy intersections, tramlines, etc., may be used for orientation.

Some landmarks extend over a considerable distance, whereas others do not. In the first category we have streets, roads, tunnels, subways, bridges, and the rails of the tramway. Nearly all other objects belong to the second class. This distinction affects the choice of verbs of movement, 'directives', and position markers. We may, for instance, 'follow a street', 'go through a tunnel', or, alternatively, 'go up to a certain place', 'turn left at a crossing', etc. Generally, descriptions mention both kinds of objects. The extended landmarks themselves are partial routes one has to follow, whereas non-extended landmarks (or their meetings with extended ones) constitute the decision points.

In a route-description these non-extended landmarks usually function as intermediate destinations. The informant attempts to develop an image of the actual route—we therefore speak of an imaginary wandering—and to communicate this image to the questioner. In doing so, he will try to set up a perspective at each landmark of his route-description. The questioner is meant to follow the route up to this landmark and to decide there on a direction (a new one or continuation of the old). One move serves then as the intrinsic basis for the next. All secondary deictical[7] means are applicable (like *rechts, links, geradeaus, kommen,* etc.)

A special problem is the means of transportation. In order to use a bus, one has to know where to get on, the line number, the direction, and where to get off. In such cases the orientation as defined by the preceding move may be lost, and the informant may think it necessary to re-introduce explicitly the intrinsic basis (cf. the following example):

> und dann gehn Sie die Alleestraße gradeaus so wie Sie ausgestiegen sind ('and then you follow the Alleestraße straight on, in the direction of your descent from the bus').

(c)   The final route

The final destination must be taken up at the end of each route-description. Without it, the route-description seems somehow defective. The questioner wants to arrive at his destination, and will expect the description to get him there. However, it will generally suffice that the description reach a point from where the final steps are obvious. The destination itself should become visible and recognizable from the description, or at least easy to find.

In a few cases in our corpus where the final destination could be identified only by means of very complicated explanations, the informant provided an intermediate destination as a substitute, and instructed the questioner to ask again there.

A route-description is completed when the informant comes to the final destination for the first time. After this a securing phase can follow, which is often linked to the actual route-description by the marker *also* ('thus', 'so').

The final arrival is stated by means of more or less routinized forms. These are

(1) *da ist* + *x*

e.g. *x* = *es, das Finanzamt, die Jugendherberge*, . . . ('it', 'tax office', 'youth hostel', . . .);

(2) Movement verb + $\left\{ \begin{array}{l} genau \\ direkt \end{array} \right\}$ + preposition + *x*

e.g. Kommse direkt vor dem Hauptbahnhof raus ('You'll come out right at the main station').

Verbal devices

We consider here only verbal means which are functionally relevant for a route-description. These will serve to lead the questioner from one point to the next, and, finally, to his destination. They can be classified into four categories. Rather than being syntactically based, the criteria rest on functional aspects that are peculiar to a route-description. In the following, we list the specific functions of the words being used, not aiming at a general semantic description.

(a) Nominals

The informant chooses several objects as points of orientation. They can be identified by proper names provided there exist appropriate signs or inscriptions along the route. They can also be identified by features which are covered by a common noun or a specifying attribute (e.g. *Ecke, Tunnel, Ampel, breite Straße*). Description (1) on p. 189 is an example where the informant apparently considers a common noun (*Hauptstraße*, 'main street') to be insufficient for a correct identification, and therefore adds a relative clause (*wo diese erleuchteten Hinweisschilder stehen*, 'where these lighted directional signs are').

(b) 'Directives'

Particular words are characteristic of each of the constructional units. In a way, it is these words which direct the questioner's attention. We will call them 'directives'.[8] There are only a small number of such words.

The starting point or the initial route is generally indicated by *hier* ('here'). *Hier* cannot be used to denote anywhere else.[9]

Further sections of the route are generally indicated by (*und*) *da*, ('(and) there') or (*und*) *dann* ('(and) then'). These words serve to organize the full route-description into smaller, identifiable parts. Their spatial and temporal aspects, however, are not always distinguishable; in most cases an exchange of *da* and *dann* is possible. Since every movement is a spatial-temporal event, they don't need to be distinguished. The spatial aspect concerns the new part of the route to be covered, or the new object mentioned. The temporal aspect concerns the new phase in wandering from one point to another.

The use of *immer* ('always) is restricted to intermediate routes. *Immer* indicates continuing movement in one direction as far as the next point to be mentioned. Thus *immer* occurs mainly with extended landmarks, such as streets. Clearly, *immer* emphasizes the temporal aspect of a movement.

The word *bis* ('until') is used to mark the end of a part of the route at a particular place. It indicates a continuity in approaching this place and thereafter a change in direction, unless it relates to the final destination.

Direkt and *genau* ('directly', 'exactly') indicate the immediate environment of a location. These words occur mostly in connection with the final destination, and serve to assure the questioner that the final phase of the tour will not be problematic.

Gleich ('soon') has a special use. It always implies a certain distance between two points, which needs to be covered. The greater the informant's uncertainty when he uses *gleich*, the further away the respective part will be from the starting point. But, at the same time, the informant appears to want to assure the questioner that he will reach his destination.

(c)   Position markers

Almost always, directives occur together with position markers (prepositions, particles, or adverbs), which specify their function with respect to the points of orientation or destinations given.

As far as the initial tour within the visual field is concerned, most position markers specify the deictic use of *hier*. Some of these words are deictics themselves. For example, *drüben* ('over there') is a primary deictic;[10] *rechts* ('on the right'), *links* ('on the left'), *rauf* ('up there'). and *runter* ('down there') are secondary deictics (see note 7).

The secondary deictics can also be used in later parts of the route-description. Upon reaching its destination, every movement along a partial route defines a new perspective which can be taken there. If position markers, like *vorne* ('in front'), *hinter* ('behind'), *durch* ('through'), can be used either intrinsically—as defined by the respective objects mentioned—or deictically, normally the latter will be used. That is, these markers will be used with respect to the momentary position of the imaginary wanderer (i.e. to the position anticipated of the questioner at the respective time).

In addition, we have non-deictic position markers, which denote spatial relations between objects, like *an, zu, bei* ('at', 'to', 'by').

Another distinction has to be made between those position markers which are static (e.g. *hinter, vor, rechts, zu*), and those which are directional (e.g. *geradeaus* ('straight ahead'), *rauf, runter, rum, durch*). This distinction corresponds to the nature of the directives and verbs of movement with which they can be used.

(d) Verbs of movement

While directives and position markers can be left out only under certain conditions, verbs of movement can always be omitted. Moreover, only a small number of verbs occur in contexts of this kind. The most common ones are: *gehen* ('go'), *laufen* ('run'), *fahren* ('go', 'drive', 'ride'), *kommen* ('come'), *folgen* ('follow'), *sich halten* ('keep').

Gehen indicates travel by foot, and occurs mainly in the description of initial routes, but also in later sections. In contexts of the sort under consideration here, *laufen* does not differ from *gehen*. It does occur more often in connection with intermediate or final routes. *Kommen* is always used together with a destination. It introduces a perspective shift. *Fahren* is used when vehicles or transportation are involved. *Folgen* and *sich halten* occur only with continuative objects. In the context of *folgen* this object must be specified, whereas with *sich halten* reference to the direction is sufficient. The use of these verbs varies on an idiolectal basis.

A minimal standard model of route-description

As we have seen above, the choice of nominals and position markers essentially depends on the local properties of the environment. Verbs of movement are optional. Hence we can conclude that the effective performance and sequencing of a route-description is mainly achieved by means of 'directives'. These are very sensitive to the constructional units mentioned above.

We may specify the sequencing of a route-description by showing its minimal parts. This will provide us with a standard model of route-description.

(1) Almost all route-descriptions begin with the word *hier*, mostly in combination with a position marker. These words indicate the initial route.

(2) Every subsequent step is indicated by *und dann* or one of its variants.

(3a) A change of direction is indicated by a position marker used in a secondary deictical way.

(3b) An indication comes that a certain direction should be followed continuously. This is mostly done by the word *immer* in combination with a position marker *geradeaus, rechts, links*. Every such indication may leave open alternatives and thereby create complications, e.g. at crossings where it is not clearly definable which road is to be regarded as continuing straight on.

(3c) Given that no such problems turn up, the questioner may come to a point which is still clearly not his destination but still of some significance. The informant construes these points as intermediate destinations. The directive used in this case is *bis* in combination with a nominal (and a preposition like *zu, an,* which has no significant effect). It indicates continuation until the location referred to by the nominal is reached. At this place a change of direction is possible as well as maintenance of the present one. Of this latter possibility, however, use is only rarely made.

(3d) The provisions (3a)–(3c) can be applied iteratively.

(4) Approaching the final destination the questioner is given another hint: the immediate environment of the final destination is specified by *direkt* or one of its variants, followed by the name of the desired location.

We can conclude from this standard model that different points will be identified with different means. The route-description has two prominent points: the starting point and the final destination. Between these points lies an area of relative uncertainty, and proper choice of intermediate destinations as well as of position markers helps to disambiguate the situations the questioner may meet.

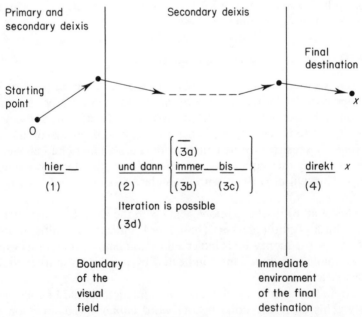

Figure 3.   The minimal model of route-description. The dashes shown have to be filled by appropriate position markers and nominals

What is certain and uncertain about a route described also determines the choice of constructions at the informant's disposal. Near the beginning and near the final destination only a very small and limited class of words, connected in highly routinized formulae, may be used. But in the space to be covered in between many words and constructions can be applied to describe the course to be followed.

So we propose the model shown in Figure 3.

Any actual route-description may differ from this model in a limited way, especially when transportation is used or a particularly long or short distance is to be covered. But in a way all route-descriptions can be fitted into this general scheme.

NOTES

1. We would like to thank Gabi Müller for collecting and transcribing some of the route descriptions reported, and Florian Coulmas for some initial help in editing our English manuscript. Our major debt, however, is to our fellow citizens who willingly served as our informants, and provided the descriptions of which we present an analysis.

2. Here we do not only mean the *empractical* use of language in the sense of Karl Bühler (1934, p. 155 ff.). A typical example of such a use would be the following. A and B are walking in the same direction; A catches up with B and asks:

Hier geht's doch zum Hauptbahnhof?
('This is the way to the main station?')

B answers:

Immer gradeaus.
('Straight on')

B's answer must be interpreted in the context of the common movement; this very movement defines the direction which has to be followed.

We rather mean something like B's productions in lines (11)–(13) of the following example:

(1)	A:	Entschuldigung	('Excuse me,
(2)		wissen Sie, wo die Einsiedelstraße ist? [. . .]	do you know where the Einsiedelstraße is? [. . .]
(3)	B:	Da müssen Sie hier	You have to go here,
(4)		die nächste Straße links rein	turn left into the next street,
(5)		dann halten Sie sich wieder links,	then go to the left again,
(6)		kommen Se da unter de Unterführung durch	go through the pedestrian underpass,
(7)		und dann auf der rechten Seite	and then on the right side
(8)		kommt die Paulsmühlenstraße,	will come the Paulsmühlenstraße,
(9)		da is die Einsiedelstraße, ja?	there is the Einsiedelstraße, you see?
(10)	A:	Ja, . . .	Well, . . .
(11)	B:	Also links,	So, to the left,
(12)		nochmals links	again to the left,

(13)	unter de Brücke durch	through beneath the bridge,
(14)	die Querstraße is die Einsiedel-straße	the cross-street is the Einsiedel-straße.
(15)	A: Gut, dankeschön.	Okay, thank you.')

Here, B produces a list of catchwords only after having given a full route-description, being provoked by A's hesitation to close down the exchange.

Another case of route-information, in which, provoked by the needs in the discourse situation, a variety of so-called foreign talk was produced, has been discussed elsewhere (Wunderlich, 1976, p. 364 ff.).

3. Some confusion may thus arise if A is already at x (see, for example, Wunderlich, 1978, p. 70), or if A wants information only for later use.

4. Surprisingly enough, even if B is fully incapable of providing the service requested, he will consider himself socially obligated to accept the task. This often leads to total nonsense. Some unsuccessful attempts at getting route directions have been described in Wunderlich (1978, p. 72 ff.).

5. Generally, distances and durations of movement are not referred to during the route-description itself, but rather before or after.

6. Quite often, assurances of this kind as well as statements of uncertainty, or occasionally general evaluations of the route to be taken, serve to frame the route-description itself (see also Wunderlich, 1978, p. 55 ff.).

7. The distinction between primary and secondary deictics could possibly be drawn along the following lines. Primary deixis only concerns the speaker, or the speech event, as such (with its local, temporal, and personal aspects), whereas secondary deixis concerns the body of the speaker and its possible positions within the spatial area. This may explain why, with regard to those parts of the route that are out of sight, only secondary deixis is possible. It is not the speaker, or hearer, who is transferred, but his bodily position.

8. The use of the term 'directives' here is quite different from that of Searle, who classifies speech acts under this label.

9. It is not quite clear for us why, with respect to later parts of the route, even a transferred use of *hier* is impossible. The only explanation we have is this. The informant already has used *hier* with respect to the initial route; any further use could still make sense regarding the speech situation itself, and thus need not induce a shift of perspective.

In other contexts, however, transferred uses of *hier* are quite often observed. Compare these examples of Klein's (1978, p. 27):

  (i) Bald darauf kam Caesar nach Rom. Hier hatte sich eine starke Fraktion um Pompeius gebildet.
  (ii) Bald darauf kam Caesar nach Rom. Dort hatte sich eine starke Fraktion um Pompeius gebildet.
     ('Soon after that, Caesar came to Rome. Here/There a powerful fraction had been grouped around Pompeius.')

Contrary to Klein's considerations, the analysis of (i) against (ii) seems to be clear to us. In (ii) *dort* is used anaphorically, and can be substituted by *in Rom* without any change in meaning. Both sentences of (ii) are produced under the same perspective. If we would, however, substitute *hier* by *in Rom* in (i), we would get the same reading as in (ii), i.e. we would have changed the meaning of (i), since in (i) we do have a shift in perspective. In the first sentences of both (i) and (ii) a terminated movement is described. Every such description introduces with the destination point of the movement a (potential) new *origo*. This may or may not be made use of. If there is a subsequent deictic expression which refers to one of the components of an *origo* (its local or temporal component), then it refers to the respective component of the new *origo*, given that the reference to the corresponding component of the speech situation itself makes no sense. This explains the shift in perspective in example (i).

Differently from the transferred use just mentioned, the informant can, however, use *hier* with respect to any part of a route, if he has a map or other graphic material at hand at which he is pointing with the tip of his finger (see Klein, 1978, p. 29; Wunderlich, 1979, p. 166).

10. *Hier drüben* deserves special consideration. If we took *hier* as referring to the place where the speaker is, and *drüben* as referring to a place which is separated by a barrier from the place where the speaker is, we would find ourselves in a contradiction. The utterance of *hier*, however, will almost always be accompanied by a gesture or a particular direction of gaze, which introduces an *origo* which is not identical with the place where the speaker is. Hence one can refer with *hier drüben* to a non-empty intersection of two places.

REFERENCES

Bühler, K. (1934). *Sprachtheorie*. Jena: Fischer.

Klein, W. (1977). Wegauskünfte. Max-Planck-Insitut für Psycholinguistik, Nijmegen (mimeo).

Klein, W. (1978). Wo ist hier; Präliminarien zu einer Untersuchung der lokalen Deixis. *Linguistische Berichte*, **58**, 18–40.

Rehbein, J. (1977). *Komplexes Handeln. Elemente zur Handlungstheorie der Sprache*. Stuttgart: Metzler.

Wunderlich, D. (1976). *Studien zur Sprechakttheorie*. Frankfurt: Suhrkamp.

Wunderlich, D. (1978). Wie analysiert man Gespräche? Beispiel Wegauskünfte. *Linguistische Berichte*, **58**, 41–76.

Wunderlich, D. (1979). Meaning and context-dependence. In R. Bäuerle, U. Egli & A. von Stechow (eds.), *Semantics from different points of view*. Berlin: de Gruyter.

APPENDIX: AN EXAMPLE OF A ROUTE-INFORMATION

The whole discourse has been partitioned into four phases according to the interactional scheme described in the text. The arabic numerals indicate our segmentation into smaller units. We give an approximate translation.

I – Initiation

1A: Entschuldigen Sie bitte, können Sie uns sagen, wie wir zur Uni kommen?

('Excuse me, please, could you tell us how to get to the university?

2B: Zur Uni—ja

To the university—yes

3	am besten mit der Straßenbahn	best is by tramway
4	das ist noch'n ganzes Ende	it's a long way
5	also, das sind ungefähr . . .	that's about . . .
6	Sie wollen dann zur/zum Haupt-gebäude sicher	You certainly want (to go) to the main building
7A:	Ja	Yes
8B:	Und das ist also, das ist sicher noch von hier 2½ km, 2½ bis 3 km.	That's about, that's surely 2½ km from here, 2½ or 3 km
9A:	Hm	Hm
10B:	Mindestens	At least.
11	Da fahren Sie am besten	Best you go,
12	ja, also am allerbesten wäre	well, best of all will be

II – Route-description

13B:	Sie gehen jetzt hier gradeaus,	You now go straight ahead
14	über diese Kreuzung	across this crossing
15	äh bis zur zweiten Kreuzung	up to the second crossing
16	und da is links ne Haltestelle	there on the left is a bus stop
17	und da fahren Sie mit der Buslinie 61	and then you take line 61
18	die fährt genau zur Uni.	it goes directly to the university.

III – Securing

19A:	Ja	Well
20B:	Das wäre da beste, Buslinie 61 zur Uni	That would be best line 61 to the university
21A:	Hm	Hm
22B:	Hier—an der zweiten Kreuzung	Here at the second crossing
23	in der Richtung geht es	this way
24A:	Ja	Yes
25B:	Also jetzt nicht hier, sondern da, die zweite,	So now not here, but over there, the second one,
26	Sie könn'n auch so'n bißchen schräg hier gehen gleich	You can also go just a little diagonally from here
27A:	Ja	Yes
28B:	Und dann mit der Buslinie 61	And then by bus line 61

IV – Closure

29A:	Ja, danke	Well, thank you
30C:	Gut, versuch'n wir's mal	Well, let's try then

31B:	Da geht am schnellsten und am einfachsten	This is the fastest and the easiest
32A:	Ja	Yes
33C:	Danke	Thank you.')

(B is accompanied by C.)

Let us briefly comment on the phases of this exchange.

I – Initiation

B needs some steps to secure his task by checking transportation, destination, and distance. As far as A does not refuse his suggestion, B can legitimately assume that he has correctly taken up the task. Meanwhile, he is able to plan his route-description. The repetitions in 11–12 are typical effects of verbal planning. Another indicator of B's planning process is the change in the recommended transportation from tramway to bus (see lines 3 and 16–17).

II – Route-description

The description consists of three parts. The first one remains within the visual field and uses deictic indicators. It ends with 15—this can be inferred from the deictic indicator in 22. The second part includes intermediate points, or sections, outside of the visual field and not yet within the environment of the final destination, i.e. the bus stop and going by bus. The last part states the arrival at the final destination, i.e. the university.

III – Securing

Obviously, B provides new information herewith, however, only slightly improving the direction already given. While the route-description itself is rigidly composed in the temporal order of the sections of the route, the securing is not. It alternates between the most crucial point, that is the number of the bus line, and the description of the initial route within the visual field. Any further statement about the final destination is omitted. Moreover, an assurance of the best alternative is only found in phases I and III, not in II. The securing is thus clearly marked off against the route-description itself.

Speech, Place, and Action
Edited by R. J. Jarvella and W. Klein
© 1982 John Wiley & Sons Ltd.

Language and Geographic Orientation for the Blind

MICHAEL BRAMBRING

It is a matter of daily necessity for those who are blind to find their way through the cities and towns in which they live or work. Systematic mobility training, developed in the United States following the Second World War (Hoover, 1950), has made it possible for increasing numbers of blind persons to walk along city streets without the aid of someone who can see. My own interest in studying geographic orientation in the blind is largely a consequence of this kind of mobility training, since only a blind person who has become fairly mobile will have the desire to increase his radius of locomotion with suitable help, and try out new ways to reach destinations on his own. Until now, however, such attempts have often failed, partly because of an inability of people who can see to give those who cannot the kind of information they would need to succeed in this endeavour.

The present paper examines some of the problems of providing the blind with useful geographic information about their environment. It analyses descriptions of routes familiar to the blind, and compares these with descriptions by people who can see. The comparative nature of the investigation is intended first to ascertain whether blind and sighted persons' way descriptions differ with respect to the type and quantity of information used to communicate particular routes, and secondly to estimate those kinds of information the blind may need for successfully being oriented in, and navigating through, their spatial environment.

LOCOMOTION IN THE BLIND

There are two main problems in street locomotion for the blind: (1) the reliable perception of objects; and (2) adequate orientation (Foulkes, 1971; Warren & Kocon, 1974; Welsh & Blasch, 1980). Each of these problems can be seen as having two aspects (see Figure 1).

The perception of objects includes (a) the perception of obstacles, and (b) the identification of landmarks. By obstacle perception, I mean that the blind

203

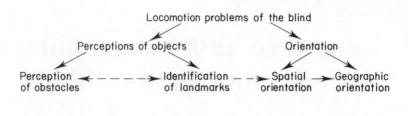

Figure 1   General problems of locomotion of the blind

person be able to detect and recognize potentially dangerous objects (for example, trashcans and steps) early enough to avoid them. Identification of landmarks, on the other hand, should entail that a blind person be able to determine his location at different points along a particular route. Objects in the perceptual surround thus can be both obstacles and landmarks. However, while the perception of obstacles is of central importance to the blind person's safety, his identifying objects as landmarks is essential to his spatial and geographic orientation.

Concerning adequate *spatial* orientation, we need to define an ability of a person to estimate his own position with respect to the immediate surroundings, for example to determine directions and ascertain distances (cf. Klix, 1971). *Geographic* orientation, in contrast, is more a matter of the ability to classify one's position in regard to topographic, that is, not directly perceivable space, illustrated by success in finding one's way around in unfamiliar terrain, or being able to describe or draw one's topographic surroundings (cf. Howard & Templeton, 1966; Downs & Stea, 1973, 1977; Gould & White, 1974).

At the beginning of the century, there was still a controversy, in continuation of the nativist/empiricist debate in modern philosophy (starting, for example, with Locke, Berkeley, and Diderot), as to whether a blind person has any kind of spatial concept at all (cf. Morgan, 1977). In particular, von Senden (1932), who had studied 66 cases of persons born blind whose sight was restored by surgery, came to the conclusion that the blind have no true conception of space. More recent studies, for example on intermodal transfer (cf. Ettlinger, 1973) and on intersensorial substitution (Bach-y-Rita, 1972, 1980), show, however, that information from various sensory modalities can lead to analogous spatial perceptions.

The few comparative investigations available on the geographic orientation of blind and sighted persons (McReynolds & Worchel, 1954; Khopreniva, 1960) show that the blind, just like sighted persons, can give directional information on the striking points about a city, or of other cities. Likewise, studies on the quality of blind people's street locomotion with the aid of tactile maps or verbal descriptions (Leonard, 1966; Bentzen, 1972; Blasch, Welsh, & Davidson, 1973; Brambring, 1977) demonstrate that they are capable of orienting themselves geographically. It is evident, however, that people who are blind have greater difficulty in becoming oriented on the street. Their main handicap is that they do not have a grasp of large spaces, and thus cannot help themselves to become oriented by the use of distant characteristics of or objects in the locality, such as church steeples and tall buildings.

DESCRIPTIONS OF ROUTES

The most common means of imparting geographic information is verbal description. The blind child obtains it from parents or siblings, the blind schoolchild from teachers or fellow pupils, the blind adult from members of his family or fellow workers. The sighted person knows from experience how unreliable verbal communications about the geographic environment can be. Practically everyone, at some time or another, has been thoroughly confused in a strange locality by residents who forgot in their descriptions to mention side streets, or neglected to say that on a particular street there was only one-way traffic. It is presumably much more difficult still for sighted persons to give adequate verbal information to the blind about spatial surroundings, since, as a rule, the sighted have little or no understanding of the special problems of locomotion with which the blind are faced, or how they are solved. They do not know, for instance, that changes in the consistency or composition of the ground surface, or reflections of sound, can be especially precise means of orientation. A study by James, Armstrong and Campbell (1973) showed that even professional mobility trainers for the blind do not agree on how a particular route can most clearly be described. These authors asked 21 mobility trainers to compose a written description of a particular route for a ficticious blind client. The amount of variation in the descriptions was considerable. Their overall length varied from 76 to 670 words, the number of separate instructions given from seven to 18. Some trainers considered information on distances to be fully superfluous; others considered compass directions to be of importance. There was unanimity only with regard to street names.

In the present research, blind persons themselves were asked about relevant information with respect to their routes, on the reasonable assumption that those who are most immediately involved should be able to give the most valid and reliable answers. In the first of two studies reported, four blind students were asked, on several occasions, to describe their daily route from their dormitory to the nearest bus stop. In the second study, nine sighted and nine blind subjects, matched on various criteria, each described two different routes.

Both sets of data obtained were evaluated with regard to their relevant psychological implications, namely in regard to the above-mentioned problems of locomotion of the blind. In the second experiment, a further, differentiated evaluation of the language used was carried out, based on linguistic analyses of interaction sequences involving the requesting and giving of street directions (Klein, 1978; Wunderlich, 1978; see also these authors' contributions to the present volume). Klein (1978) distinguishes between route information and route description. The former includes the entire sequence of activity, from the establishment of contact with a potential informant until the two parties go their separate ways. Route description is then the explanation given of the route itself, i.e. that part of the social encounter in which the person familiar with the route elucidates it. Here, Klein distinguishes three kinds of statements: (a) descriptive statements which serve as a linguistic transliteration of the instructions pertaining to the activity to be performed; (b) commentarial statements which serve as an evaluation or repetition of what was said; (c) interactive statements which serve to establish a social relation between questioner and answerer. For the actual description of the route, Klein (1978) distinguishes three categories: data on distance, data on direction, and data on fixed points as constructional units. According to him, a route description is equivalent to an 'imaginary walking tour' (p. 18) from the point of departure via various fixed points to the goal. Except for the categorization of fixed points, however, Klein gives no precise evaluational criteria, nor does he test his scheme of classification empirically.

Wunderlich (1978) divides route information into a minimum of three and a maximum of four phases. In their simplest form, these phases are (1) the introductory phase, i.e. clarification of the problem; (2) the route-description phase, i.e. the stepwise elucidation of the route; and (3) the final phase, i.e. confirmation that the questioner has understood. As with Klein (1978), Wunderlich (1978) gives neither precise evaluational criteria nor a statistical test of the quality of the classification scheme proposed.

STUDY 1: ROUTE DESCRIPTIONS GIVEN BY BLIND PERSONS

Our first study analysed verbal information which the blind give for a route which they know well. Here, we were interested in the kind and amount of information provided, as well as the relationship between this information and positions or places along the route in question. Moreover, we wished to examine the extent of agreement between various blind subjects in providing geographic information as data.

Four blind students in their mid twenties participated in the experiment. All were native German speakers living and studying in the city of Marburg. On four different days, each subject was asked to describe the route (c. 400

metres) from their common dormitory to the nearest bus stop while following this route. Tape recordings made were transcribed and evaluated for content with respect to the general problems of locomotion of the blind discussed above. The evaluation of the 16 descriptions was carried out by independent, competent judges. The objectivity of these evaluations, however, was not separately tested. The catalogue of descriptive designations developed included the following four general categories (cf. Brambring, 1977):

(1) *Data on distances.* Statements were designated as containing data on distances if distance information was expressed either directly (*ungefähr 6–8 Meter bis zur Straßenecke*/'about 6–8 metres to the next corner'), or indirectly (*ich gehe geradeaus bis zur Ecke*/'I go straight ahead until the corner').

(2) *Data on direction.* Statements were designated as containing data on direction if they expressed an actual change or actual correction in direction, e.g. *ich wende mich um 90 Grad*/'I make a 90 degree turn' (change of direction) or *ich gehe zwei Schritte nach rechts*/'I take two steps to the right' (correction of direction).

(3) *Data on landmarks.* Objects described were designated as landmarks if they served an orienting purpose and were not mentioned as something to be avoided, e.g. *die Unregelmäßigkeiten des Bürgersteigs fallen an dieser Stelle besonders auf*/'the irregularities in the sidewalk are especially noticeable here' (structure or surface of the ground) or *auf der linken Seite neben mir im Augenblick nur Wand, dann Eingang und wieder Wand*/'at the moment there is only a wall beside me on the left, then comes an entrance, and then wall again' (objects as guidelines).

(4) *Data on obstacles.* Objects mentioned were designated as obstacles if mentioned by the subjects as something to be avoided, e.g. *hier muß ich mehr links gehen, um nicht an die Parkuhren zu rennen*/'here I have to go more to the left, in order not to bump into the parking meters'.

Table 1 Geographic information given by the blind in route descriptions (dormitory to bus stop)

Information type	Number of distinct items	Percentage of unique and shared references			
				Shared by	
		Unique	2 speakers	3 speakers	4 speakers
Data on distances	15	46.7	26.7	20.0	6.7
Data on directions	13	30.8	23.1	15.4	30.8
Data on landmarks	69	37.7	17.4	21.7	23.2
Data on obstacles	19	68.4	15.8	10.5	5.3

The total frequencies are based on data from four subjects over four trials.

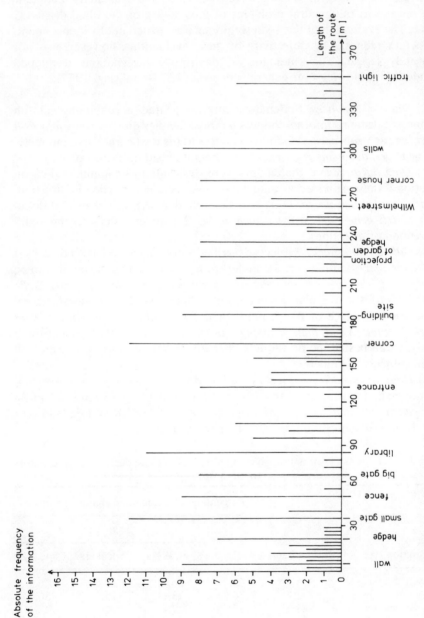

Figure 2   Distribution of information regarding specific landmarks in relation to the route described. The abscissa shows distances in 30 metre intervals, the ordinate frequency of mention (total possible = 4 subjects × 4 trials)

A given utterance could contain more than of these types of information, but only one category was used to code each partial statement made in it.

The results of this analysis are presented in Table 1. As Table 1 shows, the four subjects produced 116 distinct items of information during their four walks, i.e. approximately seven items per route per person, or the equivalent of one item about every 60 metres. It can be seen from the table that landmarks were by far the most frequently named items. As we have suggested, recognizing these objects can serve to estimate relative position along the route. The verbal descriptions given are in relatively high agreement with respect to directional information, whereas the data on obstacles, on the other hand, appear to be more idiosyncratic and limited to particular individuals.

The results point to the special importance of landmarks for the blind during street locomotion. This conclusion is further underlined by the distribution of landmarks mentioned in relation to the route (see Figure 2).

Figure 2 shows that the number of landmarks mentioned in individual sections of the route varied considerably. They were frequent between 0 and 30 metres, between 150 and 180 metres, and between 240 and 270 metres. But these sections of the route also had something else in common: in them, the blind person had to change direction or cross a street. From this, it can be inferred that the blind need more orientation information about such 'neuralgic' points if they are to continue in safety. This fact should be given due consideration in describing routes to blind persons, and in the construction of maps for the blind.

STUDY 2: A COMPARISON OF ROUTE DESCRIPTIONS BY BLIND AND SIGHTED PERSONS

In a second study conducted, the task of the participants was to describe two different routes 500–1000 metres long, beginning at the place where they lived and having well-known places in the city of Marburg as their destination (e.g. city hall, library, student cafeteria, etc.). Both blind and sighted German subjects were tested, and in a yoked manner. Nine blind persons aged 25 years were asked to describe their two routes in such a way that another blind person could negotiate them safely. For comparison, nine sighted persons were asked to describe the same routes for another sighted person.The sighted subjects were chosen such that they lived in the same residential building as one of the blind subjects, and were comparable to him or her in age, sex, and education. Thus, a total of 36 route descriptions were collected, two each from 18 different subjects. Owing to a technical fault, two descriptions, one from a blind and one from a sighted subject, could not be evaluated.

Transcriptions of the remaining 34 route descriptions were first classified according to the scheme used in Study 1. These results are presented in Table

Table 2   Geographic information given by blind and sighted subjects in describing two routes each

	Group			
	Blind		Sighted	
Information type	Median	Range	Median	Range
Data on distance	26.7	30–97	8.7	10–31
Data on directions	14.0	16–54	5.5	4–15
Data on landmarks	46.5	33–149	18.5	19–52
Data on obstacles	4.0	0–45	0.1	0–1

Based on nine subjects per group. Group median based on mean per subject over the two routes. Range based on sum of information per subject for the two routes.

2. Table 2 indicates that the blind subjects tested gave a great deal more information that the sighted subjects in all four categories ($p < 0.001$ by Mann–Whitney U-tests in all cases). In the case of distance, directional, and landmark information, the blind gave nearly three times as many mentions per route as the sighted. For the seeing subjects, data on obstacles are almost entirely absent: one subject mentioned one obstacle on one route. The results indicate that the blind require considerably more information for geographic orientation than the sighted, and raise two problems for getting and mastering it. The process of acquiring the needed information will consume more time, and require a greater mnemonic effort.

The second step in evaluating the results of Study 2 was a re-analysis of the data collected in accordance with a more detailed linguistic scheme of classification. This analysis was aimed at answering the question of whether, in describing routes, the blind use different linguistic elements or entities than sighted persons. The scheme used was based on models given in Klein (1978).

The re-analysis consisted of two parts, or phases. In the first part, we examined whether the total route described could be divided into delimitable sections by individual judges. In this task, the judges were to divide the overall route description into as many small sections as possible, in such a way that each section formed a meaningful unit with clear boundaries. Such a section was considered to be delimitable if a caesura was made at these points in describing the route. In the simplest case, this meant giving a new point of departure.

Example: *An der Ampel rechts bis zur nächsten Straße*
        'At the traffic light turn right and go to the next street'
        'At the traffic light' = point of departure
        'turn right' = statement of direction
        'to the next street' = goal, or new point of departure

As this example suggests, the smallest sections of a route described frequently coincided with (a) a point of departure, (b) a direction mentioned, and (c) a goal, which subsequently became the new point of departure.

The sections of descriptions, however, were not always as clearly arranged as this example suggests. Sometimes there was no explicit description of the point of departure, the direction intended, or the precise goal. In such cases, the point of departure was usually defined by the word *dann* ('then'). Sometimes the point of departure was not even replaced by *dann*, and could be inferred only from context. Similarly, often an explicit statement of the goal was missing, and a section was considered to have reached its end if a new point of departure was mentioned, or at least a new direction.

Example: *An der Ampel rechts, dann links bis zur Schule*
'At the traffic light go to the right, then turn left and proceed until you come to the school'
'At the traffic light' = point of departure
'go to the right' = statement of direction
'then' = new point of departure
'turn left' = statement of direction
'(and proceed until you come) to the school' = goal

In this example, *dann* implicitly defines a new point of departure, since it was used to designate the next street. The following illustrations also give a complete description of a delimitable section of a route: *die Treppen runter*/'down the steps'; *über die Straße*/'across the street'. The particular characteristics of the locality usually made it clear where a new section began, and where it ended. However, no section was ever described by a body rotation alone, such as *du drehst dich um 90 Grad nach links*/'turn 90 degrees to the left', since the momentary location being projected was not shifted. Usually, such expressions were followed by a supplementary *und gehst dann geradeaus*/'and then go straight ahead'. In contrast, the expression *du gehst nach links*/'turn to the left' was used to describe an entire section when followed by a *dann* used to introduce the next section, as in the second example above.

The route subdivisions were marked by six advanced psychology students serving as judges. To determine the reliability of these judgements, each route description was scored by at least two different persons. Inter-judge agreement averaged 86%, and ranged for pairs of judges from 75% to 94%. These figures indicate that the independent judges used were in quite close agreement on the subdivisions needed. Using this scheme, there were 129 subdivisions in the descriptions produced by the sighted persons and 283 subdivisions for the blind subjects. The average overall length of the routes was about 690 metres, meaning that for the sighted subjects, one subdivision corresponded to about 90 metres, and for the blind subjects, to about 40 metres. The complexity of the descriptions varied with both the person providing them, and the route being described.

In the second part of the re-analysis, the route descriptions were classified in terms of five linguistic categories, as follows:

1 *Designation of points of departure for route descriptions.* Points of departure can be defined by naming a particular object, or by implicitly describing the new point of departure by means of spatial and temporal deixis.
   1.1   Points of departure defined by naming of objects.
      1.1.1   The point of departure is an explicitly named object, and is assumed to be known, e.g. 'in front of the City Hall', 'in Gutenberg Street'.
      1.1.2   The point of departure is determined by pointing to an object, e.g. 'you see that house over there. . . .'
      1.1.3   The point of departure is determined by an object which depends upon the previous route, e.g. 'the next street', 'the third traffic light'.
      1.1.4   The point of departure is determined by an object which is defined by characteristic features without reference to the previous route, e.g. 'at the fountain', 'beginning at the thoroughfare'.
   1.2   Points of departure defined without naming of objects.
      1.2.1   The point of departure is established by spatial deixis, e.g. 'here', 'there'.
      1.2.2   The point of departure is established by temporal deixis, e.g. 'then', 'first', 'afterwards'.
      1.2.3   Points of departure are defined by enumeration, e.g. 'and always straight ahead', 'around to the left, right and. . . .'
2 *Designation of directions.* Statements are designated as data on directions if they either give a direction explicitly, or if the direction can be deduced from the given position.
   2.1   Explicit data on directions.
      2.1.1   Explicit instructions based on the previous direction, e.g. 'to the right', 'to the left', 'straight ahead'.
      2.1.2   Explicit instructions based on body rotation, e.g. 'turn 90° to the right, and then start walking. . . .'
   2.2   Implicit instructions based on the particular locality, e.g. 'then go down the steps', 'continue down the street. . . .'
3 *Designation of distances.* Statements are designated as data on distances if they contain information on some number of metres or steps, or length of time.
   3.1   Precise or approximate statements on distance.
      3.1.1   Precise statements on distance, e.g. '5 stairs', '10 metres'.

3.1.2   Approximate statements on distance, e.g. '10 or 20 metres', 'about 5 minutes', 'around 20 steps'.

3.2   Vague or lacking statements on distance.

   3.2.1   Vague statements on distance e.g. 'not far'.

   3.2.2   No statement on distance.

4   *Designation of destinations.* Destinations can be designated by naming objects, analogous to points of departure; if no object is named, it is impossible to define the destination.

4.1   Destinations defined by naming of objects.

   4.1.1   The destination is explicitly named, and is assumed to be known, e.g. 'until you come to the City Hall', 'until you reach Gutenberg Street'.

   4.1.2   The destination is defined by pointing to an object, e.g. 'over there you see a house; that's it'.

   4.1.3   The destination is defined by an object which depends upon the previous route, e.g. 'to the next street', 'to the third traffic light'.

   4.1.4   The destination is determined by an object which has characteristic features without reference to the previous route, e.g. 'until you come to the fountain', 'until you reach the thoroughfare'.

4.2   No data on destination.

5   *Comments.* Statements are designated as comments if they consist of an evaluation or an additional, redundant explanation of the first four categories.

   5.1   Redundant comments, e.g. 'then you go past (hesitation), *and the next street is the Biegenstraße* (which is redundant)'.

   5.2   Evaluative comments, e.g. 'it's not hard to find', 'there you have to pay close attention'.

Judgement by means of this more elaborate classification scheme was again made by the six independent judges, with each transcription again scored separately by at least two persons, with the subdivisions in it already marked. For each subdivision, a judge was to decide whether it could be designated as belonging to any of the five categories, and if so to which. The average percent agreement between judges was again high. The overall mean agreement was 84.7%. Most agreement (95%) was found for information on direction, least agreement for points of departure (72.3%) and destinations (79.5%), which were often mutually confused, and could perhaps better be collapsed with each other into a single category.

Tables 3–6 present the results of this frequency analysis for both groups of subjects tested. For points of departure, the relevant data shown in Table 3. As Table 3 shows, both blind and sighted subjects described points of depar-

Table 3   Points of departure given in the route descriptions collected

Determination of departure by means of	Group			
	Sighted		Blind	
	Frequency	Percentage	Frequency	Percentage
(1) Naming of objects				
(a) Explicitly named object, assumed as known	7	5.4	8	2.8
(b) Pointing to an object	0	0.0	0	0.0
(c) Dependent on previous section of route	8	6.2	16	5.7
(d) Independent of previous section of route	9	7.0	20	7.1
Sum	24	18.6	44	15.6
(2) Naming no objects				
(a) Spatial deixis	21	16.3	38	13.4
(b) Temporal deixis	19	14.7	86	30.4
(c) Enumeration	65	50.4	115	40.6
Sum	105	81.4	239	84.4
Total sum	129	100.0	283	100.0

The data are based on nine subjects for each group.

ture mainly without naming any concrete object. This difference is significant in both groups separately ($p < 0.01$ by Wilcoxon tests). In the category 'naming of objects' it is striking that sighted persons more frequently assume objects as being known than the blind do, although the difference is not statistically reliable for the present sample. In the category 'no naming of objects' the sighted subjects defined points of departure proportionally more frequently by means of *spatial* deixis and enumeration, and the blind more frequently by *temporal* deixis. However, only the more frequent use of temporal deixis by the blind is here statistically reliable ($p < 0.01$ by matched pairs sign test by subjects).

The designations of statements on direction and distance are summarized in Table 4. Table 4 shows that the two groups of subjects used direct and indirect statements on direction with approximately equal frequencies. It is striking from the table that the blind subjects but not the sighted ones used instructions involving body rotation ($p < 0.05$, again by matched pairs sign test by subjects). Still further, Table 4 shows that, almost without exception, the seeing subjects gave no precise or approximate information in their statements on distance, while blind persons did so about one time in five ($p < 0.01$, again by sign test). Even among the blind, however, such informa-

Table 4 Distances and directions given in the route descriptions

| | Group | | | |
| | Sighted | | Blind | |
Type of data	Frequency	Percentage	Frequency	Percentage
(1) Explicit data on directions				
(a) Based on previous				
direction	75	58.1	142	50.2
(b) Based on body rotation	0	0.0	16	5.6
Sum	75	58.1	158	55.8
(2) Implicit data on directions				
based on particular locality	54	41.9	125	44.2
Total sum	129	100.0	283	100.0
(1) Precise or approximate data				
on distances				
(a) Precise statements on				
metres, steps, or time	0	0.0	30	10.6
(b) Approximate statements				
on metres, steps, or time	2	1.6	29	10.3
Sum	2	1.6	59	20.9
(2) Vague or lacking data on				
distances				
(a) Vague statements on				
distances	16	12.4	25	8.8
(b) No statements on				
distances	111	86.1	199	70.3
Sum	127	98.5	224	79.1
Total sum	129	100.0	283	100.0

The data are based on nine subjects for each group.

tion was consistently less frequent than vague information, or nothing being said about distance ($p < 0.01$ by sign test).

Table 5 presents the data with respect to goal points obtained. It reveals a tendency for the sighted subjects more regularly to choose an object in defining goal points than the blind ($p < 0.01$ by matched pairs sign test). Within the subcategories of 'naming of objects', however, there are no significant differences between the two groups.

Finally, Table 6 shows the use of evaluative and redundant comments by subjects in the two groups. It is evident from the table that the blind subjects used more comments in general of both kinds ($p < 0.05$ for both types

Table 5   Determination of goal points in the route descriptions

| Determination of goal points by means of | Group | | | |
| | Sighted | | Blind | |
	Frequency	Percentage	Frequency	Percentage
(1) Naming of objects				
(a) Explicitly named object, assumed as known	21	16.3	24	8.5
(b) Pointing to an object	0	0.0	0	0.0
(c) Dependent on previous section of route	22	17.1	32	11.3
(d) Independent of previous section of route	44	34.1	87	30.7
Sum	87	67.5	143	50.5
(2) No determination of goal points by objects	42	32.5	140	49.5
Total sum	129	100.0	283	100.0

The data are based on nine subjects for each group.

Table 6   Evaluative and redundant comments in the route descriptions

| Type of comment | Group | | | |
| | Sighted | | Blind | |
	Frequency	Percentage	Frequency	Percentage
(1) Evaluative	1	0.8	25	8.7
(2) Redundant	40	31.3	134	47.5

The data are based on nine subjects for each group.

summed together by sign test). Separately, however, only the difference for evaluative comments is significant ($p < 0.01$). The sighted subjects injected commentary of these two kinds into about one-third of the subdivisions they produced, as opposed to more than half of the sections for the blind subjects' descriptions.

CONCLUSIONS AND SUMMARY

In summary, the findings of this re-analysis can be interpreted as providing good insight into the problems of the blind in comparison with sighted persons in regard to street locomotion. The linguistic analysis of route descriptions given by blind persons reveals that they use less information from the environment and more information relating to their person. This interpretation is suggested by the way in which points of departure and destinations were determined for the individual sections of the route. Blind persons less frequently name objects in defining such points, probably because they cannot test this kind of information visually, and it is thus unreliable for them. They tend to use more temporal and less spatial deixis in defining new points of departure. It is particularly characteristic that they make explicit statements about distances more frequently than sighted persons, whereas the latter obviously can do without such information, since it is implied in the description of characteristic features of the surroundings. The blind, on the other hand, obviously have greater need of information that is person-oriented, i.e. that can be checked by the particular person. This is shown by the precise statements made in regard to distances, which permit correct estimates independently of the environment, and also by the information given involving body rotation, to which sighted persons never refer.

The difference between route descriptions given by blind and by sighted persons can be cautiously characterized thus: sighted persons give environment-oriented descriptions, whereas the blind tend to use person-oriented descriptions. In other words, sighted persons make more use of external characteristics for orientation, and the blind tend to rely more on internal characteristics.

In regard to the amount of information given in describing a route, there is naturally a major difference between sighted and blind persons. The latter provide more than twice as much information as the former, and their subdivision of routes is correspondingly more than twice as detailed. This implies that blind persons may need far more fixed points in such descriptions in the sense of Klein (1978). The additional comments made apparently serve partly as further verification, and possibly to help the listener construct the more fine-grained plan of the route which is being offered. Evaluative comments also appear to have a verifying sort of function, and have, as we have seen, mainly to do with warning against possible dangers. As was shown in the earlier classification scheme data, such comments are extremely rare in sighted persons' descriptions of walking routes, but fairly frequent in those of the blind.

From a certain methodological viewpoint, namely the objectivity of the judges, the classification scheme elaborated here proved to be quite useful. To test its more general validity, however, it would be necessary to examine whether the categories as developed are able to capture relevant dimensions of descriptions of routes varying in complexity, and using other modes of locomotion, such as travel by car or bicycling.

REFERENCES

Bach-y-Rita, P. (1972). *Sensory substitution*. New York: Academic Press.

Bach-y-Rita, P. (1980). Brain plasticity as a basis for therapeutic procedures. In P. Bach-y-Rita (ed.), *Recovery of function: theoretical considerations of brain injury rehabilitation*. Bern: Huber.

Bentzen, B. L. (1972). Production and testing of an orientation and travel map for visually handicapped persons. *New Outlook*, **66**, 249–255.

Berkeley, G. (1948). New theory of vision. In A. A. Luce (ed.), *The works of George Berkeley*, Vol. 1. London: Nelson.

Blasch, B. B., Welsh, R. L., & Davidson, T. (1973). Auditory maps: an orientation aid for visually handicapped persons. *New Outlook*, **67**, 145–158.

Brambring, M. (1977). Geographische Informationen für Blinde. *Zeitschrift für experimentelle und angewandte Psychologie*, **24**, 1–20.

Diderot, D. (1961). Lettre sur les aveugles, à l'usage de ceux qui voient. In T. Luecke (ed.), *Philosophische Schriften*, Vol. 1. Berlin: Aufbau-Verlag.

Downs, R. M., & Stea, D. (eds) (1973). *Image and environment*. Chicago: Aldine.

Downs, R. M., & Stea, D. (1977). *Maps in minds*. New York: Harper & Row.

Ettlinger, G. (1973). The transfer of information between sense-modalities: a neuropsychological review. In H. P. Zippel (ed.), *Memory and transfer of information*. New York: Plenum Press.

Foulkes, E. (1971). The perceptual basis for mobility. *Research Bulletin*, American Foundation for the Blind, **23**, 1–8.

Gould, P., & White, R. (1974). *Mental maps*. London: Penguin.

Hoover, R. E. (1950). The cane as a travel aid. In P. A. Zahl (ed.), *Blindness: modern approaches to the unseen environment*. New York: Hafner.

Howard, I. R., & Templeton, W. B. (1966). *Human spatial orientation*. London: Wiley.

James, G. A., Armstrong, J., & Campbell, D. (1973). Verbal instruction used by mobility teachers to give navigational directions to their clients. *New Beacon*, **57**, 86–91.

Khopreniva, J. G. (1960). Effect of a 180° turn on the topographical representations of the blind. *Dokladỹ Akademii Pedag. Naute.*, *ESFSR*, **2**, 115–116.

Klein, W. (1978). Wegauskünfte. In W. Klein (ed.), *Sprache und Kontext*. Göttingen: Vandenhoeck & Ruprecht.

Klix, F. (1971). *Information und Verhalten*. Berlin: Verlag der Wissenschaften.

Leonard, J. A. (1966). *Aids to navigation. A discussion of maps for blind travellers*. London: St Dunstan's.

Locke, J. (1902). An essay concerning human understanding. In J. A. John (ed.), *The philosophical works of John Locke*, Vol. 2. London: Bell.

McReynolds, J., & Worchel, P. (1954). Geographic orientation in the blind. *Journal of General Psychology*, **51**, 221–236.

Morgan, M. J. (1977). *Molyneux's question. Vision, touch, and the philosophy of perception*. Cambridge: Cambridge University Press.

von Senden, M. (1932). *Raum- und Gestaltauffassung bei operierten Blinden vor und nach der Operation*. Leipzig: Barth. English translation: *Space and sight*. London: Methuen, 1960.

Warren, D. H., & Kocon, J. A. (1974). Factors in the successful mobility of the blind: a review. *Research Bulletin*, American Foundation for the Blind, **28**, 191–218.

Welsh, R. L., & Blasch, B. B. (eds) (1980). *Foundations of orientation and mobility*. New York: American Foundation for the Blind.

Wunderlich, D. (1978). Wie analysiert man Gespräche? Beispiel Wegauskünfte. *Linguistische Berichte*, **58**, 41–76.

Speech, Place, and Action
Edited by R. J. Jarvella and W. Klein
© 1982 John Wiley & Sons Ltd.

The Structure of Living Space Descriptions[1]

Veronika Ullmer-Ehrich

Spatial descriptions have until recently been investigated mainly by psychologists, for whom the focus of research has lain principally on endogenous factors in spatial perception and the mental procedures used in organizing material being perceived into a coherent cognitive scheme (Canter, 1977; Downs & Stea, 1973a; Lynch, 1960). Although the data for work in this tradition are to a large extent drawn from verbal descriptions, their linguistic properties as such have never been of primary interest. In linguistics, on the other hand, the syntax and semantics of spatial expressions have been the primary objects of study (see Leech, 1969; Saile, 1977), whereas little attention has been given to the way these expressions are actually used when people communicate about space. With concern for discourse on the increase in both disciplines, attempts to work in a more integrated fashion may be a natural outcome. This paper is intended to relate some analyses of meaning and form in spatial expressions to an analysis of their use in a specific type of discourse. The paper is based on observational data and (admittedly soft) techniques of discourse analysis.

Cognitive psychologists have introduced the notion of a cognitive map as an explicative analogon in which the structural properties of internal space representation are reconstructed in terms of the structural properties of cartographic maps (see Lynch, 1960; Downs & Stea, 1973a,b; Canter, 1977). As a heuristic concept this notion is also useful for the linguistic analysis of communication about space, since giving a verbal description of spatial information, like drawing a map, requires the solution of basically the same sorts of problem:

(1) *The selection problem.* From the wealth of information about a certain area, those parts need to be selected for a map which are relevant to the map's purpose: for a road map, different items will be selected than for a meteorological map. As far as verbal behaviour is concerned it is, of course, the purpose of a conversation which determines what will be mentioned and what will not.

(2) *The transformation problem.* The fact that maps are two-dimensional requires a transformation which 'maps' the three dimensions of space onto the plane format of maps. For a verbal description, a transformation onto the one-dimensional, *linear* order in speech is required. In other words, the transformation problem is linguistically a problem of linearization.

(3) *The symbolization problem.* To construct a map, one has to decide on the graphical representation of the bits of information to be represented. Roads will, for example, be distinguished from rivers by colour, villages from towns by size. Giving a verbal description obviously also makes it necessary to solve the symbolization problem; one has to choose appropriate words and sentence forms to convey the information in question in a comprehensible way. In other words, on the level of verbal behaviour the symbolization problem is a problem of formulation.

The format organizing the internal representation of spatial information is widely debated in psychology. There, a primary issue is the question as to whether spatial knowledge is represented in a proposition-like or in an image-like format (see Pylyshyn, 1973; Kosslyn, 1977; Wilton, 1977; Wilton & File, 1977). That issue, however, will not be of concern here, since the analysis to be given is restricted to the purely linguistic properties of the descriptions at hand without conclusions being drawn as to their psychological counterparts. Correspondingly, 'linearization' and 'formulation' are both treated as linguistic concepts referring to the macrostructural *linear* organization of discourse on the one hand and to lexical and grammatical properties of microstructures provided by singular utterances (i.e. *formulations*) in a discourse on the other. This restriction, which is mainly a methodological one, does not exclude a psychological interpretation of the results. A psychological approach to the same (kind of) phenomena is highly desirable (and does in fact exist—see Levelt, 1979) but in the present case must be regarded simply as a *desideratum*.

Linguistic analyses of spatial descriptions have until now been confined to apartment layouts and route directions (Linde, 1974; Linde & Labov, 1975; Klein, 1977; Wunderlich & Reinelt, this volume). Single room descriptions are not just a further example. Rather it is assumed that they differ in at least two essential respects from these other cases.

(1) Route directions are directive in nature. They serve to orient the intended actions of the person receiving them. Hence the participants of any route direction exchange need to heed certain interaction constraints, which provide for descriptions being neither overly specific nor under-determined in terms of what at each stage in the conversation the receiver needs to know in order to allow him finally to find his way. Apartment descriptions of the type collected by Linde as well as the student room descriptions in the present study are illustrative in nature. Like route directions they serve to supplement the addressee's knowledge, but they are *in the first place* not intended to guide

his actions. They may therefore be more detailed on the one hand but will certainly be less dialogical on the other. It is, moreover, likely that there will be characteristic formulation properties which show up in single room descriptions but not in apartment descriptions or route directions.

(2) Usually, one needs to have followed a route or walked through the rooms of an apartment to be able to describe either of them. Single rooms, which can be observed from a constant point of view, do not impose these preconditions on descriptions of their furniture arrangement. This will have special consequences for the way in which they are described, especially with regard to the linearization properties in the discourse, and in view of the fact that an *imaginary tour*, somehow reflecting the speaker's primary experience, has been shown to be an organizing principle for apartment descriptions and route directions.

A further issue of this paper with respect to formulation is the question as to how speakers make use of prepositions like *vor* (in front of), *hinter* (behind), and *neben* (beside), and adverbs like *vorn* (in front), *hinten* (back), *links* (to the left), and *rechts* (to the right). As is well known, these expressions can be used in either a deictic or an intrinsic perspective (see Fillmore, 1975). In the deictic perspective speakers make their own bodies, their visual orientation, or that of the hearer the reference point of the description. In the intrinsic perspective, the intrinsic front of one of the described objects is made the point of reference. What has to be counted as the intrinsic front of an object (provided it has one at all) depends on the object's functions. Furniture is obviously functional in nature. The front of, for example, a cabinet (or of any other non-circular container) is that side, where its openings to storage space (doors, drawers, etc.) are located. Now, the deictic perspective being bound to one's visual orientation, is essentially perceptual whereas the intrinsic perspective, being bound to the described object's use, is essentially functional (Miller & Johnson-Laird, 1976). This fact provides another motivation to study room descriptions. Rooms usually contain various objects related to each other in terms of function as well as in terms of space. Hence, describing how these objects are arranged basically allows for taking either a deictic (perception-oriented) perspective or an intrinsic (function-oriented) perspective. In this paper it will be asked how these different perspectives are actually used and what parameters determine the choice between them.

DESCRIPTION OF THE DATA

The study reported is based on 20 extended interviews collected at the University of Düsseldorf in 1977. The subjects were students who lived in two different student residence halls near the university campus outside the city. Each interview lasted at least one hour and touched on subjects' living conditions in various respects, furnishing and furniture arrangement of their rooms being only one of them (others were, for example, social activities, shopping possibilities, etc.). The real purpose of the investigation was not made transparent to subjects, but was vaguely described as being a sociological/planological one. This procedure was intended to motivate students to give an extended account of their living situation. Furthermore, it was hoped that subjects would not think that they had to conform to any (hypothetical) high standard of verbalization. The interview situation was kept rather informal. Subjects talked freely and introduced conversational topics they were interested in (e.g. women's emancipation). Hence, each interview developed differently. Nonetheless, in order to make them comparable, the interviewer asked the same questions of each subject, though sometimes in different orders. At some point, where it appeared appropriate with respect to the stage of the conversation, the following questions were asked: 'What is your room like?' (unmarked question) and 'Could you describe the furniture arrangement to me?' (marked question). The analysis given in the present paper is based on the answers received to these questions.

Subjects knew that the conversation was being taped but did not seem to be bothered by this. Some of them obviously enjoyed the opportunity to talk to someone about their problems. In all cases, the interview was closed by requesting subjects to draw the furniture arrangement of their rooms. The drawing task in no case immediately followed the verbal description given of the room and can thus be supposed to have been independently solved. Hence, it is possible to check the verbal descriptions against the drawings. Although drawings are but another type of symbolic representation, which can in no part be considered as 'real' counterparts of verbal representation, a comparison between the two kinds of symbolization may reveal some properties which are characteristic for verbal versus non-verbal forms of representing spatial knowledge.

Some descriptions as well as some of the drawings are presented below. In the transcriptions, some aspects have been omitted which are not taken up by the analysis given here. In particular, any suprasegmental information as well as interactive signals like *hm* and *ja* given by the interviewer are left out. This simplification, though unwise in some other imaginable cases, seems justified here because the investigation is above all concerned with aspects of language production *within* an extended piece of (more or less monological) discourse, and not with interactive devices used in conversation.

COMMUNICATIVE ASPECTS OF SPATIAL DESCRIPTIONS

As with other types of discourse, spatial descriptions usually serve some communicative purpose, such as the giving of evidence in, say, automobile accidents (illustrative purpose) or the giving of technical working instructions (directive purpose). Communicative purpose may be exhibited either by the type of conversational exchange in which participants are engaged or, more specifically, by the form and content of some question. In general, the type-of-conversation parameter is stronger then the preceding-question parameter. For instance, the interview as it has been used in the present study does not as such demand any spatial description at all. Accordingly, subjects failed to give route directions, even when they were explicitly asked questions like 'How does one get to the shopping centre?' or 'How do you get downtown?' This failure is by no means due to a communicative mismatch but originates from the fact that in the given situation, the interviewer obviously has no real need for getting anywhere. So subjects try to make their replies informative according to the purported sociological aim of the study, giving answers like 'You can easily go by bike'. Illustrative examples are (1) and (2).

(1) A Das ist also etwas das mir an dem ganzen Campus überhaupt nicht gefällt, daß das eben so isoliert ist alles, daß man da praktisch ne Stadt für sich bildet, daß da zum Beispiel also keine Geschäfte sind, das ist also für mich, irgendwie ist das bescheuert, ich kann mir nicht helfen, die bauen da zwar nen Buchladen, ja und aber wenn Sie zur nächsten Bäckerei wollen, da müssen Sie wer weiß wie weit fahren, ich glaube die nächste Bäckerei ist ne Viertelstunde entfernt, und der nächste Lebensmittelladen, wo man halbwegs günstig einkaufen kann, der ist am Karolingerplatz eben, das sind also zwanzig Minuten, das sind, im Grunde genommen ist das Unfug, das geht irgendwo nicht, wenn Sie mich fragen.

Well this is something about the whole campus which I don't like at all, that everything is just so isolated that it is basically a city in itself, that there for instance are no shops, for me this is somehow it is crazy, sure, they build a bookshop there, but if you need to go to the bakery, you have to drive I don't know how far, I think the nearest bakery is a quarter of an hour from here, and the nearest grocery where you can shop half decently, that is at the Karolingerplatz, that's twenty minutes away, that is basically it is really a nuisance, it simply doesn't work, if you ask me.

Q Wie kommt man da hin zum Karolingerplatz von hier aus?

How do you get to Karolinger-platz from here?

A *Ja mit der Straßenbahn, oder wir machens jetzt so, wir ham das ein bißchen organisiert, die Leute, die n Auto haben, die fahrn da eben einmal die Woche hin.* (T1)

Well, by trolley line, or we do it like this now, we have organized a bit, the people who have a car go there once a week.

(2) Q Wie kommt man denn eigentlich   How do you get downtown from
        vom Heim in die Stadt?   the hall?
     A In die Stadt? Ja, mit der Straßen- Downtown? Well, by trolley line.
        bahn, die hält ja gleich Uni-   It stops nearby the medical
        kliniken, Moorenstraße.   school, Moorenstraße.
     Q Ach so.   I see.
     A Da kommt man in die Stadt, oder   That's how you get downtown, or
        man kann auch hin laufen.   you can walk there.
     Q Und wenn man in die Altstadt   And if you want to go to the old
        gehen will oder so?   city?
     A *Ja, da lauf ich meistens hin, ich*   *Yeh, there I usually walk, I am in*
        lauf überhaupt ziemlich gut und   *general a good walker, that*
        gern, das macht mir nichts aus.   *doesn't bother me.*
     Q Ja, wie läuft man da hin?   Yes, how do you walk there?
     A *Einfach Richtung Norden, immer*   *Simply by going northward,*
        geradeaus. (T3)   *always straight ahead.*

Correspondingly, subjects answered the unmarked question ('What is your
room like?') by simply enumerating the pieces of furniture in their rooms and,
eventually, evaluating them. (3) and (4) illustrate answers to questions of the
unmarked/marked types given by the same person.

(3) Q Und wie sind Zimmer überhaupt   And what are the rooms like as a
        so? Oder Ihr Zimmer?   whole? Or your room?
     A Hm ja, so von der Einrichtung,   Hm, as regards the furnishings,
        wir ham also ne Couch und dann   we have a couch and then so so
        so-so mit Bettkisten unten zwei   with bedboxes underneath, two
        schöne weiße Tische, zwei große   nice white tables, two working
        Arbeitstische und noch son klei-   tables, and then, well a smaller
        neren Tisch, unsere weißen   table, our white book shelves
        Regale an einer Wandseite, und   along one wall, and then there is
        dann is n Schrank, und dann eben   a cabinet and then the kitchen
        die Kochnische mit diesem eh   counter with this er refrig with
        Kühlschr mit m Kühlschrank da.   the refrigerator there, and well I
        Und ja ich mein, wenn man da,   think, if you go there, when I first
        als ich zuerst in das Zimmer rein- came into the room, I found it
        kam, fand ich also unheimlich   unbelievably bare, everything so
        öde, alles so weiß, die Wände   white, the walls white and the
        weiß und der Boden weiß na ja.   floor white, well, then there's a
        Dann hat man also ne schöne   nice red couch, red somehow a,
        rote Couch, rot irgendwie ne,   striped in different reds and then
        verschiedene Rots gestreift, und   orange cushions, well it didn't fit
        denn orangene Bettkissen, also   together at all but I mean you
        das paßte alles überhaupt nicht   furnish the room to your own

zusammen, aber ich mein man richtet sich dann die Zimmer alle ein nach seinem eigenen Geschmack, und ich hab n Teppich reingetan, auf die weißen Tische kamen irgendwie Deckchen drauf, oder man tut sich da so die ganzen Arbeitssachen drauf, dann sieht mans nicht mehr, und manche Leute ham sich so andere Schränke und so reingekauft, ds hab ich also nicht für nötig empfunden, weil irgendwie sah ich das nich ein, daß ich da also ich hab nich so viele Sachen da wie andere Leute, und ich mein von der Ausstattung, die sind unheimlich praktisch würd ich sagen, sind sie von der was eben da is, sind sie eben unheimlich praktisch, das is also von daher gesehen relativ positiv, mm ich mein man hat nicht viele Möglichkeiten das umzustellen, aber wenn man jetzt so in verschiedene Zimmer reinguckt, man sieht doch, was alles so für Va Variationsmöglichkeiten bestehen. (T8)

taste, and I brought in a carpet, on the white tables came a kind of cloth, or you put all your working things there, then you don't see it anymore, and some people bought other cabinets and things, that I didn't consider necessary, because somehow I didn't see why, that I, well I do not have that much stuff there as other people, and I think the furnishings, they are really functional, I'd say, they are, from what's there, they are just really useful, that is, well seen like that relatively positive, mm I mean you don't have much choice in rearranging things, but if you look into different rooms, you will still see, how many va possible variations there are.

(4) (Schließt unmittelbar an (3) an)
Q   Wie ist das bei Ihnen gestellt?
A   Ja, ich hab meine Arbeitstische praktisch an ner am Fenster, eh, an der, an einer Wand, ja da sind die Regale, da kann man praktisch nichts anderes machen, und an der gegenüberliegenden Seite vom Fenster ist, da steht die Couch, is praktisch so wies auch am Anfang war, und dann ist noch an die Couch angeschlossen, so ja so ne ziemlich unkom-

(immediate continuation of (3)).
How did you organize it?
Yes, I have my working tables almost at one at the window, er, at the at one wall, well, there are the shelves, you practically can't do anything else there, and against the wall opposite the window is that's where the couch is, it's practically as it was in the beginning, and then still connected to the couch is sort of, yes, sort of a rather uncomfortable

fortable Sitzgelegenheit, das ist
praktisch so ja so n Element noch
irgendwie, und das is praktisch
so ja an der Wand, an der
gegenüberliegenden Seite vom
Regal. (T8)

sitting area that is practically
sort, yes sort of an element still
somehow, and that is practically
so yes on the wall which is on the
opposite side of the shelf.

These examples show that not only the discourse subtypes (enumeration versus spatial description) but also the selection of singular items (in this case pieces of furniture), and the order in which these are mentioned, may depend on the question which has been asked and are thus a function of the dialogue. It is, I think, rather the type and the stage of the discourse and not so much the form or even the content of the question being asked which primarily determines the content of the answers. For a different dialogue situation, say for a conversation between architects, even the unmarked question will probably yield a spatial description as reply. In any case, the examples cited give support to the hypothesis that a verbal description as part of a conversation is not just the linguistic materialization of some fixed internal representation of (non-linguistic) knowledge of the world, to which it simply adds grammatical form, but that the processing of non-linguistic information (about some state of the world) in speech (-production) encompasses the processing of conversational knowledge as well.

THE OVERALL STRUCTURE OF LIVING SPACE DESCRIPTIONS

In principle, there are at least two different ways for giving a verbal description of the arrangement of some furniture. One of the possible techniques is to use the room in which the conversation takes place as a model for the room that is to be described. Using the second technique, the description takes the form of an imaginary tour around the walls of the room in question. (5) illustrates the modelling technique, while (6) is an example for the tour-representing technique.

(5)   Wenn man, man käm jetzt hiér
      rein (setzt seinen Stuhl so um, daß
      er die Tür, die sich ursprünglich
      rechts von ihm befindet, im
      Rücken hat), oder man käm hiér
      rein, so, dann ist da das Bett in dér
      Ecke, da ist auch n Fenster, n altes
      Fenster, noch so unterteilt, in dér
      Ecke ist der Schreibtisch, mußt ich
      leider im Augenblick n bißchen
      dáhin stellen, weil da jetzt ne
      Wasserleitung verlegt worden ist,

      If you, you came in hére now
      (moves his chair so that he has
      the door, which originally was to
      his right, to his back) or you
      came in here, like this, then there
      is the bed in thát corner, there is
      also a window, an old window
      divided into parts, in that corner
      is the desk. Unfortunately I had
      to for the time being move over
      thére because there was a water
      pipe being laid in this room stick-

die im Raum ist, so von der Wand absteht, der Schreibtisch nicht mehr ans Fenster paßte, und eh hier links ist dann sozusagen die Sitz, ne Sitzecke, wo noch so ne alte Couch steht, n paar Stühle drum rum, und da drüben auch n sideboard, Teppich, n Bastteppich ist auch noch drin, und ich hab noch son großen Ledersessel, hab ich geschenkt bekommen. (T11B)

ing out from the wall, the desk didn't fit at the window any more, and er hére to the left is then so to speak the seat, a sitting area, where there is still an old couch, a couple of old chairs around it, and over thére also a sideboard, carpet, a bast carpet is in there too, and I also have a big leather armchair, that I was given as a present.

(6) Also, das Zimmer zu Hause, das auch, wenn man, s ist auch nicht schlauchförmig aber auch ziemlich rechteckig, eh an der eh die Tür ist an einer Schmalseite, wenn man reinkommt rechts davon ist auch das Bett, dann steht da so son Blechregal, wie man dat so im Keller hat für die Einmachgläser oder so, hab ich n paar Bücher drauf, aber auch nicht viel, weil ich ja die meisten hier hab, ne, ja hm denn is da son ganz kleines Bücherschränkchen, und damit wär die eine Wand abgedeckt, die rechte lange Wand, dann kommt das Fenster, an der linken Wand ist ne Couch, und davor n Tisch, n einfacher Tisch, da les ich schreib ich, ess ich, ja und dann neben der Couch is son kleines Öfchen, und das wars schon. (T6)

Well, the room at home, that also, if you, it is also not elongated, but also rather rectangular, er at the er door is on a narrow side, as you enter to the right of it is also the bed, then there is a metal shelf like you have them in a cellar for home canning jars or so, I have some books on it, but not a lot, because most of them I have here, a ya hm, then there is a very small bookcase and that covers that wall, then comes the window, on the left wall there is a couch and in front of it a table, a simple table, there I read, I write, I eat and then beside the couch is a small stove, and that's all.

The modelling technique seems to be a most natural and comprehensible way to give a room description as part of a face-to-face conversation. But actually only one instance of this type, the one just cited, has been obtained. It is an open question whether the tour-representing technique in fact is the more common and conventional one or whether the present results are biased by, for example, the fact that the interviews were being taped. Speakers, for instance, might have been aware of the fact that a tape recording of the modelling technique would be of no use in reconstructing the room arrangement without further orienting information. In other words, the modelling technique is more context dependent than the tour-representing one. This difference linguistically relates to the kinds of deictical expressions used with either technique. Modelling descriptions express spatial information mainly by using adverbs of the *primary deixis* system (*here* and *there*) uttered with heavy stress, and accompanied by pointing gestures, whereas touring descriptions mainly contain spatial expressions of the *secondary deixis* system (*left, right, front, back*), which of course allow for but do not demand pointing gestures to make the description comprehensible. Primary deixis elements like *I, you, here, there,* and *now* are conceptually related to the basic co-ordinates of communication (speaker, hearer, place and time of utterances) and they are either used as linguistic 'pointers' to these co-ordinates or at least accompany real (gestural) pointing (see Wunderlich, 1971; Clark, 1977). Secondary deixis elements do not refer equally to basic communication co-ordinates. Although the left/right orientation is of course present in each conversation, it is in itself not a defining element of communication as such. However, the actual interpretation of secondary deixis expressions for a given utterance and in a given situation often depends on the visual perspective of speaker and/or hearer and is therefore contextually determined as well. On the other hand, the system of secondary deixis allows one to treat an arbitrary individual being neither present in nor essentially bound to the actual speech situation as a *reference point* (*origo*) for locating certain other individuals. The system of secondary deixis therefore is highly important for communications about spatial environments which are not identical with the environment of the conversation itself. Being less bound to the actual situation than the primary system, the secondary system ensures that descriptions given on particular occasions will remain comprehensible at other times and places.

In what follows I will first give an account of the general structure of student room descriptions. An illustrative example is given by text (7), together with the drawing belonging with it (Figure 1).

(7) Q Können Sie mir son bißchen das ganze Arrangement verdeutlichen?

Could you make the whole arrangement a little bit clearer to me?

A Ja, wenn man mal davon ausgeht, daß eh dieser Raum in etwa quadratisch ist (form of the room)

Well, if you assume, that this room is about square

Und eh ich beginne mal mit der Erklärung, wo man zur Tür reinkommt, (reference frame)

And er, I'll begin my account from where you enter the door

dann ist also auf der rechten Seite bis zum Fenster geradeaus ist die Regalwand, unter der Regalwand steht in der Nähe des Fensters mein einer Schreib-

then there is on the right hand side up to the window straight on is the wall with the book shelves, under the shelves near the window is one of my desks, then

tisch, dann n Stück weiter, noch unterm Fenster hab ich n privaten Sessel reingebaut, der sich also ausgezeichnet eignet, wenn man bloß was zu lesen hat, daß das Licht von hinten scheint, und neben dem Sessel bis in die Ecke steht dann der zweite Tisch mit dem Fernsehgerät drauf und dem ganzen Plunder, und dann gegenüber des, gegenüber vom Regal an der Wand, eh da beginnt also dann die Eckkombination und zieht sich also auch an der verbleibenden Wand noch lang, und hinter dieser verbleibenden Wand ist also dann diese Naßzelle. (T10A)

a bit further on, still under the window, I have built in a personal armchair, which is excellent when you merely have something to read, since the light comes in from behind, and next to the armchair as far as the corner there is then the second table with the tv on it and all the junk, and then opposite this, opposite the shelves on the wall er there the sitting area begins and continues along the last wall and behind this last wall is then this shower stall.

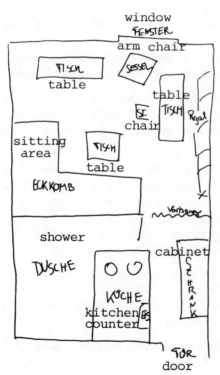

Figure 1 The room diagram drawn by the speaker of text sample (7)

Such a living space description usually begins with the introduction of a *reference frame* in terms of which certain places or regions can be identified and related to each other. The co-ordinates of this frame are the *reference place* and the *reference orientation*. By reference place I mean a designated locality that serves as origo for the localization of further places. (In my data as well as in those of Linde and Labov this is most often the entrance.) By reference orientation I mean the (hypothetical) visual orientation of a potential observer with respect to the reference place. Reference place and reference orientation are conventionally given by a conditional clause:

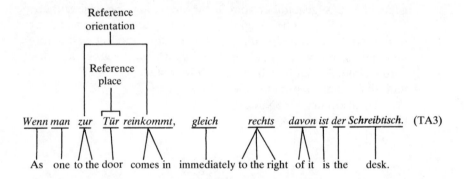

Normally, entering a room means to enter it through the door, therefore the reference place may be omitted if the orientation has been specified:

> Wenn man da reinkommt, haben wir also direkt rechts oder links, ist verschieden, haben wir einen Schrank, einen Kleiderschrank (T12).
> (As you enter we have directly to the left or to the right, it depends, we have a cabinet, a wardrobe closet).

Of course, the orientation is in some way given by inference alone, which is based on our common knowledge about people's usual way of moving: entering a room usually means to enter it forwards such that the perception apparatus is directed ahead into the room.

Besides reference place and reference orientation often the shape and/or size of the room is mentioned in a room description:

> Eh, also dieser Trakt ist abgetrennt von dem Zimmer, das ist also ganz, das ist also relativ quadratisch. (T7A)
> (Er, well, this part is separated from the room, as a whole it is completely, it is relatively square).

> Ja wenn man also einmal davon ausgeht, daß eh dieser Raum eh in etwa quadratisch ist. (T10A)
> (Well, if you assume that er this room is er about square . . .)

This seems to be specific for the representation of spatial configurations which can be looked over from an unchanging point of view. Linde and Labov, at least, quote similar findings only for the mentioning of individual rooms, whereas an apartment as a whole is in general not described with respect to shape, at least not in descriptions which follow a touring strategy. This is not surprising in view of the fact that normally one does not have the opportunity to see all the rooms in an apartment at once.

Once reference place and reference orientation have been specified, the furniture arrangement in a room is described as an imaginary *gaze tour* along its walls. The tour reconstructs what would be seen if one were gazing into the room and bringing one piece of furniture after another into focus. That the description takes the form of an imaginary gaze tour and not of an imaginary person's walking tour can be derived from the following four linguistic observations:

(1) In the case that a deictical perspective is used, the reference frame which has been introduced is held constant throughout the description. There are no secondary *origins* serving as reference points for the interpretation of spatial deictics (see example (8)).

(8)   Ja also die Tür is an der Stirnwand ne, genau in der Mitte, da is links direkt hinter der Tür is s Waschbecken, dann kommt dieser große Kleiderschrank direkt anschliessend, dann is etwas Raum ne, also n Meter fünfzig etwa, dann kommt der Schreibtisch, der steht links in der Ecke unterm Fenster, das Fenster is also links in der Ecke bis reichlich über die Hälfte nach rechts, das Fenster is ziemlich groß [. . .] ja und dann neben diesem Schreibtisch auch direkt anschließend steht dann hinten an der anderen kurzen Wand des Zimmers, also das Zimmer is also zweifünfzig, steht dann der andere Schrank so bis in die Ecke ran, da vor diesem Schrank stand dann früher noch dieser kleine Tisch und der Stuhl, die ich beide in den Schrank verfrachtet hab, den

Well, the door is on the front wall, right in the middle, there is on the left directly behind the door is the wash basin, then comes this big wardrobe directly adjoining, then there's some space, about one metre fifty, then comes the desk, it is on the left in the corner under the window, the window goes from the left-hand side in the corner considerably more than halfway to the right, the window is rather big . . . yes and then beside this desk also directly adjoining there is in the back on the other short wall of the room, the room is about two-fifty, there is the other cabinet going to about the corner, there in front of this cabinet then used to be this small table and the chair, which I both loaded into the wardrobe cabinet and then on the right wall, and as you enter the

Kleiderschrank, und dann an der rechten Wand und wenn man zur Tür reinkommt eh, steht dann das Bett bis rechts in die Ecke neben der Tür, s is also n ziemlicher Schlauch das Zimmer, ne. (T2)

door er there is the bed going right up to the corner next to the door, it is pretty elongated that room, you know.

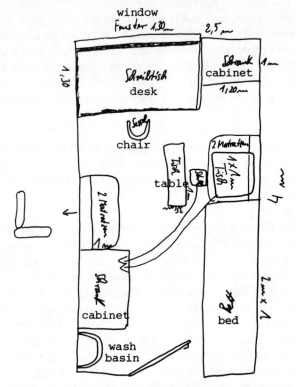

Figure 2   The room diagram drawn by the speaker of
text sample (8)

Due to the walking tour format, the use of deixis in route directions is entirely different. During a walking tour the orientation changes each time the tour subject makes a turn. Thus describing a certain environment using that format makes it necessary to shift the origo to refer to orientation changes. A good example is the description O4 in Klein (this volume).

(2) Route directions using the walking tour format introduce the addressee as the one who makes the imaginary tour. Correspondingly, the subject-NPs of the individual sentences making up the entire description almost always refer to the addressee (see for example G15 in Klein, this volume). Living-room descriptions of the gaze tour format, in which the subject is a generic observer (called *man* in German) keeping a fixed position, show a different

pattern of sentence subject selection. It is not the addressee but the individual pieces of furniture which are referred to by the respective subject NPs. In other words, a gaze tour describes a certain environment as if certain objects belonging to that environment would come in turn into view.

(9) Ja eh wenn man zur Tür reinkommt, gleich rechts davon ist der Schreibtisch an der Wand, im Anschluß daran ist das Bett, und dann kommt schon die Ecke zum Fenster, und da ist zwischen Fenster und Wand dieses Bücherregal, und an der anderen Seite, ja da is nich mehr viel Platz, da schließt sich da die andere Längswand an, da hab ich die Schlafcouch stehen, zwischen Schlafcouch und Bücherregal den Eßtisch, an die Schlafcouch ran kommt der Kleiderschrank, neben m Kleiderschrank steht der Kühlschrank, und dann inner Ecke kommt das Waschbecken. (T3)

Well, er as you enter the door, immediately to the right of it is the desk against the wall, connected to it is the bed and then comes the corner going up to the window, and there between the window and the wall is this bookshelf, and on the other side, um, there isn't much space left, there the other long wall is connected, there I have the couch bed, between couch bed and bookshelf the dining table, by the sleeping couch comes the wardrobe, beside the wardrobe is the refrigerator, and then in the corner is the wash basin.

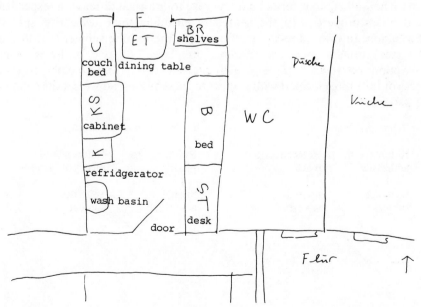

Figure 3   The room diagram drawn by the speaker of text sample (9)

(3) Descriptions in the gaze tour format show a specific pattern of verb selection. The main verbs used in VPs locating those individuals which are referred to by the respective subject NPs almost always describe states, whereas in route directions of the walking tour format main verbs usually describe accomplished actions (of the tour's subject). (See again (9) and for comparison G15 in Klein, this volume.) The spatial adverbials complementing the respective main verbs accordingly differ between local prepositional phrases in gaze tour descriptions and directional prepositional phrases in walking tour descriptions. A more involved case is the analysis of *kommen* (to come), which frequently occurs in both kinds of descriptions. *Kommen* can be used to describe either actions or events. (Action: *Er ist freiwillig gekommen* (He came voluntarily). Event: *Unversehens kam der Winter* (Unexpectedly, the winter came).) *Kommen* never describes states. In this respect the frequent use of *kommen* seems to be inconsistent with the state-describing nature of the gaze tour format. In fact, I consider the occurrence of *kommen* not as specific for gaze tours versus walking tours or vice versa but for tours as opposed to non-tours. In any case, a tour is a *temporally ordered sequence of events* (no matter what the nature of these events is like). In walking tours, this sequence is given by the subject's imaginary movements, one coming after the other. In gaze tours, the sequence is given by the chain of objects (imaginarily) coming into view one after the other. That the gaze tour represents a temporal sequence, too, is linguistically expressed by temporal adverbs used in combination with *kommen*, which together indicate the transition from one stage in the tour to the next.

(4) The walking tour format and the gaze tour format differ with respect to word order properties in the sentences encoding their respective spatial information. In route directions reference to the touring subject (i.e. to the addressee) usually precedes reference to places, whereas in living-room descriptions reference to places usually precedes reference to the objects (i.e. pieces of furniture) located with respect to these places. So we get the following patterns:

Route directions   *Living-room descriptions*

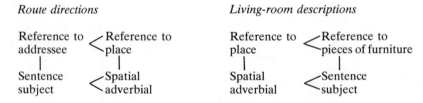

Here are some examples:

Route directions (Klein, this volume, O2)

Da	*gehen*	*Sie bis*	*zur*	*Zeil*
There	go	you	to the Zeil	

Subject   Spatial adverbial
(directional)

Und dann kommen Sie	*direkt*	*an die alte Oper*
And then come	you	directly	to the old opera

Subject   Spatial adverbial
(directional)

Living-room descriptions (T6A)

Wenn man zur Tür reinkommt,	*ist rechts*	*sofort*	*die Kochnische*
As you enter the door	is to the right	immediately	the cooking facilities

Spatial adverbial   Subject
(locative)

Dann kommt rechts	*dahinter*	*der Eingang zur Dusche*
Then comes to the right	behind it	the entrance to the douche

Spatial adverbial   Subject
(locative)

The difference between the two patterns may perhaps be explained by a universal which asserts that in unmarked cases reference to persons always precedes any other kind of reference (see Givón, 1976). But this account does not explain why in living-room descriptions we hardly find any 'subject < locality' utterances, although in German this word order is as common as the opposite one. On the other hand, the well-known *givenness* and/or *aboutness* accounts for topicalization seem to fail. The *givenness* account roughly says that in general given information precedes new information (see Clark & Haviland, 1977). If one looks at the distribution of definite/indefinite NPs in the data, one will find that the subject NPs in non-prior position are mostly definite. In fact they refer to items (pieces of furniture) which in the context of the interview have always been mentioned before (when subjects answered the unmarked question by giving an enumeration). This means that the NPs in question are to be taken as *referentially given*. Since we can certainly not adopt an analysis in which both parts are given, we might assume that the spatial adverbials, referring to the respective localities of the NP objects, convey *new* information. But in this case we would have the reversed *given-new*-order.

The *aboutness* account says that the topic of a sentence is what the sentence is about, and it (sometimes tacitly) assumes that topics precede non-topics. What a living-room description indeed is about is the spatial arrangement of the furniture and thus the localities of its separate elements. In this sense the *aboutness* account seems to fit the observed patterns. But route directions can also be said to be 'about' localities, in the sense that they direct a given addressee through a spatial environment which is defined by its individual landmarks and paths. Thus we would at least have to say that the human/non-human distinction takes precedence over the aboutness property, but the generality of this statement also seems to be doubtful.

I believe the different word-order patterns can be explained in terms of the different tour formats. The walking tour leads through an environment which could never be in full view of the addressee, whereas the *gaze tour* leads through an environment which could be scanned. Thus, once the direction of the gaze tour has been specified, the sequence of points on the tour is predictable, such that the discrete places filled by certain objects can be considered to be *potentially given*. The discourse focuses on the question as to which objects actually fill the predictable places. This is why the subject NPs are in nonprior positions. In other words, referential givenness and focushood may overlap. This means that the topic/comment distribution does not uniquely correspond to a *general given/new* distribution. I therefore propose to distinguish primarily between focus and non-focus constituents. Non-focus constituents generally have to be predictable in a way which is comparable to the predictability of localities on a gaze tour. Focus constituents, no matter whether they are *referentially given* or not, refer to individuals or to properties which in a given context are not similarly predictable. Distinctions such as this are by no means original (see Kuno, 1975; Dik, 1978) and they are considerably vague. Much more theoretical and empirical research will be necessary before more satisfying conclusions can be drawn. However, the main point I want to make here is that it is the overall (cognitive) format of a discourse which determines the word-order properties of its individual utterances rather than the referential givenness of things referred to in these utterances.

The overall organizing principle for living-room descriptions, the gaze tour, has been reconstructed here in terms of characteristic formulation properties of the separate utterances making up its parts. The microstructural organization of a discourse has been treated as being interdependent with basic features of its microstructures. The gaze tour is an analytical concept covering a range of rather simple linguistic means which serve to fulfil a rather complex linguistic task. This concept, however, may not refer to mental processes organizing the internal representation of spatial knowledge. Whether people's mental access to the relevant kind of knowledge is provided for by carrying out a gaze tour in the mind would have to be demonstrated by independent non-linguistic tests.

THE LINEARIZATION STRUCTURE

Two different linearization principles have been found which I call *Round About* versus *Parallel Line*. Subjects who linearize information about a living-room layout according to the *Round About* principle describe the furniture arrangement by 'gaze touring' their way around the room along *adjacent* walls. People who follow the *Parallel Line* principle 'jump', i.e. they describe the arrangement by 'gaze touring' through the room along two or three parallel lines, whose order of mention need not reflect spatial connectivity. That is, the distinctive feature between *Round About* and *Parallel Line* strategies is the spatial connectedness of the lines along which the description proceeds (cf. Figure 4, also example (10) and Figure 5).

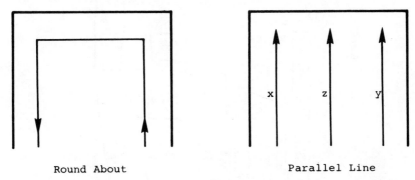

Figure 4   Schematic diagram of round about and parallel line room description strategies

(10) *Round About*

Ja eh wenn man zur Tür reinkommt, ist rechts sofort die Kochnische [. . .] ja die ist so einmeterzwanzig ungefähr breit die Kochnische, dann kommt rechts dahinter der Eingang zur Dusche [. . .] ja und dann kommt das Zimmer, das ist ungefähr zwölf Quadratmeter groß, da steht auf der rechten Seite das Bett, das ist ein mal zwei Meter groß, und dann ist eben um die Ecke gewinkelt angebaut dieser Nachttisch mit m Sessel, hm und als ich einzog standen die beiden

Well, er, as you enter the door immediately to the right there is the kitchen counter [. . .] yes it is well about one metre twenty wide the kitchen counter, then comes right behind it the entrance to the shower [. . .] yes and then comes the living room, and that is about twelve square metres, there on the right-hand side is the bed, that is one by two metres big, and then built right into the corner is this nighttable with a chair, hm and when I moved in, the two desks stood directly under the window,

Schreibtische direkt unterm
Fenster, und der andere Schrank
ist gegenüber von der Kochnische,
und da sind auch noch zwei
Kleiderhaken, ich könnt Ihnen
das aufzeichnen, aber ich weiß
nicht ob Ihnen das viel nützt. (T6)

and the other cabinet is opposite
the kitchen counter, and there
there are also two clothes hooks, I
could draw it for you, but I don't
know if it's of any use to you.

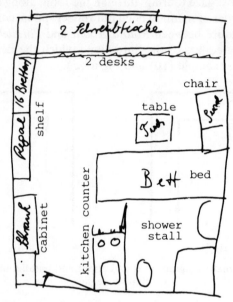

Figure 5   The room diagram drawn by the
speaker of text sample (10)

(11) *Parallel Line*

Man kommt also rein

y-line → dann is rechts der Schrank

x-line → links is die Küche und daran anschließend praktisch die
Duschzelle
und durch diesen engen Gang, der da noch bleibt, kommt
man ins Zimmer da steht dann an der Duschwand bei mir
steht das Bett, einige hams umgestellt, aber ich habs so
gelassen

z-line → man kommt also, man guckt auf das Fenster, wenn man
reinkommt

y-line → und rechts sind die Regale, das ist auch eine ganze Wand, die
sind immer jeweils gegenläufig angebracht

z-line → und ich hab dann den Schreibtisch direkt unterm Fenster
stehn
y-line → und den anderen Tisch rechts dadran unter den Regalen
x-line → hinten in der Ecke hat ich also wie gesagt, hat ich lange
Regale drin, jetzt hab ich da den Tisch stehn (T9A)

(You come in, then there is the cabinet on the right, on the
left is the kitchen, and nearly connected to it the shower stall,
and through this narrow passageway which is left you come
into the actual room, that's where on the shower wall in my
room is the bed, some people switched this around, but I left
it like that, so you come in, you see the window ahead, as you
come in, and to the right are the book shelves, that is also a
whole wall, and then I have the desk directly to the right of it
below the shelves. In the back in the corner in it I had as I
said, shelves for a long time, now I have the table there.)

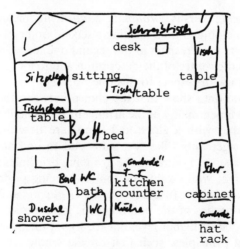

Figure 6   The room diagram drawn by the
speaker of text sample (11)

The observational data collected don't reveal which parameters govern the
choice between either of these linearization principles (or whether there are
any such parameters at all). In an experimental control study, Ullmer-Ehrich
and Koster, however, found the following. There are two different but
interdependent levels of linearization. On the lower level, information about
singular sub-areas of the overall spatial arrangement is linearized. On the
higher level, these sub-areas are bound together to give the overall structure.
Round About and *Parallel Line* belong to the higher level of organization. On
the lower level again two different linearization principles were found, which

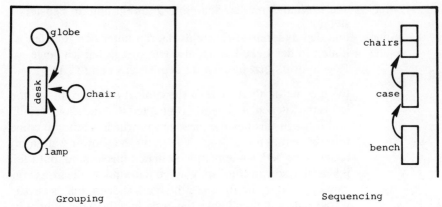

Figure 7   Schematic diagram of grouping and sequencing linearization principles

we called *Sequencing* versus *Grouping*. *Sequencing* means beginning the description with one object, then locating a second object with respect to the first one, a third one with respect to the second one, etc. *Grouping* means to take one object as the centre of the description and to locate all other objects within the sub-area with respect to this one object.

The experimental data show that the choice between these techniques is determined by the functionality of the arrangement. Functional arrangements (like a desk together with a globe and lamp) are described by *Grouping*, dysfunctional arrangements (like two sofas end to end and a cabinet) are described by *Sequencing*. Following the grouping principle induces the selection of *Parallel Line*, while following the sequencing principle induces the selection of *Round About*. In other words, *Grouping* and *Sequencing* are determined by properties of the non-linguistic input structure. *Parallel Line* and *Round About*, being higher level linearization principles, are determined by the lower level principles, such that on the whole we get a bottom-up organization in linearization.

SOME ASPECTS OF FORMULATION: PERSPECTIVE SHIFT AND THE USE OF DEIXIS

In this section, I will discuss how people actually use expressions of secondary deixis. I will consider some determinants of the choice between the deictic and the intrinsic perspective as well as the distribution between spatial and temporal deictics. One may argue that the deictic perspective, making the speaker's current orientation the reference point of some indication, can be of no relevance here, since the descriptions in question do not refer to the spatial environment of the on-going conversational exchange. In fact, the spaces subjects describe need to be recalled from long-term memory. For the present purpose, the deictic perspective therefore is to be understood as the as-if-perspective of the imaginary gaze tour or—to put it in Bühler's terms—as a *Deixis am Phantasma*. The concept of an intrinsic perspective has its problems as well. On the one hand, it is the essential nature of the intrinsic perspective that the reference point of some indication is given by an intrinsic part of one of the objects located with respect to the others. On the other hand, descriptions given in the intrinsic perspective can still be ambiguous with respect to the speaker's actual or imaginary orientation. Take the expression *to the left of the sofa* in its intrinsic interpretation. Does it refer to what is to the left if you were sitting in the sofa or if you were facing it? (See illustration below.) Both interpretations are, of course, equally appropriate. Orienting information is relevant even for the so-called intrinsic perspective, making the distinction between deixis and intrinsics at least somewhat vague. This fact suggests that one ordinarily deals with deixis alone and merely distinguishes the cases where primary reference orientation is maintained from those where it is shifted. I will, however, continue to distinguish deixis and intrinsics because, as will be shown below, it also helps to explain the distribution of spatial versus temporal expressions. One of the questions asked in the present study was how—if at all—speakers indicate in which of the two possible ways they

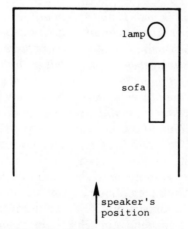

Figure 8 The speaker can take three perspectives of the position of the lamp shown with respect to the sofa: lamp to the right of the sofa, lamp to the left of the sofa (both intrinsic perspectives), and lamp behind the sofa (deictic perspective)

are talking. Are there any specific markers or organization principles accompanying eventual perspective shifts? Miller & Johnson-Laird (1976) state that 'usually intrinsic interpretations dominate deictic ones. If a deictic interpretation is intended when an intrinsic interpretation is possible, the speaker will usually add "from my point of view" ' (Miller & Johnson-Laird, 1976, p. 398). This statement, which certainly applies to isolated utterances, has to be modified with respect to complex discourses.

Students describing their living-quarters usually start their description with a deictic perspective and they maintain this perspective throughout the description. Shifts to an intrinsic perspective only occur when subregions of the entire environment are described by (more or less independent) *inserts* (Schegloff, 1972) to the entire description.

(12)   Eh also, wenn man die Tür aufmacht, *dann ist jetzt rechts die Kochnische mit oben drüber nem Hängeschrank über der Kochnische, dann ist da ne Ni ne Nirostaspüle unt eh unter diesem Hängeschrank, links davon ist der eingebaut in diese Kochnische ist Herd mit zwei Kochplatten, eh eingebaut in diese Kochnische ist rechts unten son ja man kann sagen son kleiner Abstellschrank, wo man also Scheuermittel und son Kram alles reingeben kann, und außerdem ist da noch son kleiner Abfalleimer, also in diese Ab diese Abstellnische, und links davon ist der Kühlschrank*, der hat eh ja wieviel Liter weiß ich jetzt nicht, vielleicht soo groß in etwa, und eh hat den Vorteil hat ne Abtauautomatik, die empfinde ich immer als besonders praktisch, man schaltet abends einfach bloß diesen Knopf ein, ja und am nächsten Morgen läuft er ist er abgetaut und läuft bereits wieder, man muß sich also gar nicht darum kümmern, das ist schon schön. Dann jetzt weiter, auf der rechten Seite, wenn man rein-

Er well, if you open the door *then to the right is now the kitchen counter, with a cupboard above the kitchen counter, then there is a Ni a Nirosta sink below this cupboard, to the left of it built into this kitchen counter is the oven with two cooking plates, er built into this kitchen counter at the right bottom is well you can say a small cupboard where you keep scouring agents and the like, and furthermore there is a small trash can in this pl in this place, and to the left of it is the refrigerator*, it has er ya how many litres I don't know by now, perhaps about this big, and er it has the advantage of having an automatic defroster, this is always useful, I think, you simply push this button in the evening, and the next morning it's running it is defrosted and already running again, you don't have to concern yourself· with it, that's really nice. Now further on the right-hand side when you come in, where this is a mirror image in some of the rooms, you have to imagine it so, that the rooms are all built the same, but with some of them it is

kommt, eh wobei das in einigen Zimmern spiegelverkehrt ist, man muß sich das also so vorstellen, daß die Zimmer zwar im Prinzip alle gleich aufgebaut sind, eh bei manchen ist das ganze genau symmetrisch so spiegelsymmetrisch, das is also wenns hiér der Wohnraum is, dann hiér beispielsweise und hier die hiér der Eingang, dann ist es bei andern genau umgekehrt, dann ist hiér der Eingang und hiér der Wohnraum, das ganze ist dann spiegelsymmetrisch, eh auf der linken Seite ist dann bei mir eh die Gardrobe, das sind also drei Haken, und dann kommt der Kleiderschrank, der ist *eh wie groß ist der, der ist zwei Meter hoch, em der steht links, auch so für Mäntel und solche Sachen, und rechts sind eben die Ablagen, ja wie halt son Kleiderschrank* aussieht. Hm ja und dann gehts also direkt eh auf der rechten Seite diesmal in die Naßzelle rein, dann ja soll ich die auch noch beschreiben? Da is also rechts die Toilette, [. . .] (T1)

exactly symmetrical as in a mirror, that is if the living room is hére, then hére for example and here the entrance is hére, then it is exactly reversed in others, then the entrance is hére and the living room hére, everything is then a mirror image, er on the left of my room is the hat rack, it consists of three hooks, and then comes the wardrobe, it is, er *how big is it, it is two metres high, em it is on the left, also for coats and such things and on the right are the shelves, er well whạt a wardrobe* is like, and then directly er on the right this time you get into the shower stall, shall I describe that, too? There is to the right . . . .

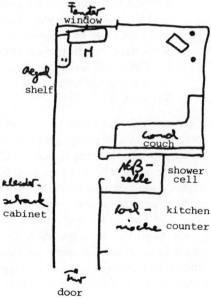

Figure 9　The room diagram drawn by the speaker of text sample (13)

In this example, cooking convenience, hat rack, and shower stall are first located in the deictic perspective and then described with respect to their internal layouts in the intrinsic perspective. The expressions of secondary spatial deixis used intrinsically often combine with an anaphor like *davon* pointing back to some element already mentioned which belongs to the same subregion of the environment as the object to be located with respect to this element. Shifting back to the deictic perspective is marked by *und dann* (and then), where the temporal element indicates the next step of the tour. Sometimes these markers are accompanied by a resumption of the primary reference frame ([. . .] 'Wenn man zur Tür reinkommt', [. . .]).

(13) Wie gesagt, die heizen ja meist unheimlich stark, *ja und dann* neben diesem Schreibtisch auch direkt anschließend, steht dann hinten an der anderen kurzen Wand des Zimmers, also das Zimmer ist also zweifünfzig, steht dann der andere Schrank so bis in die Ecke ran, *da vor diesem Schrank* stand dann früher noch dieser kleine Tisch und der Stuhl, die ich beide in den Schrank verfrachtet hab, den Kleiderschrank, und *dann an der rechten Wand wenn man zur Türe reinkommt* eh steht dann das Bett bis rechts in die Ecke neben der Tür, s ist also n ziemlicher Schlauch das Zimmer, ne. (T2)

As I said they mostly heat incredibly well, *yes and then* next to this desk also directly connecting, there is in the back on the other short wall of the room, the room is about two-fifty, there, is the other cabinet then going up to the corner, *there in front of this table*, used to be this small table and the chair, which I both loaded into the case, the cabinet, *and then on the right wall as you enter the door* er there is the bed then up to the right corner beside the door, it's pretty much a tube that room, you know.

It seems suggestive to me to interpret the explicit resumption as a step back to some node in a branching structure and the temporal indication as a move forward along a looping structure. If this idea were right, it would be interesting to find out whether and how branching and looping correspond to the different description formats (*Round About* versus *Parallel Line*). Since explicit resumption and temporal indication, however, can occur in combination, one has to be wary of psychological overinterpretations of perhaps purely linguistic contingencies. In any case, the shift-indicating markers, which have been discussed so far, do not suffice to exclude perspective ambiguities. But subjects clearly try to avoid ambiguities with respect to the perspectives they use. For this, they follow different strategies:

1. Systematic variation of temporal and spatial deictics.

(a) Spatial deictics used in the deictic perspective are explicitly linked to the primary reference frame (13).

(b) When (a) does not apply, expressions of spatial deixis alone are used, where as a matter of fact no ambiguity between deixis and intrinsics can arise (14).

(c) When neither (a) nor (b) applies, spatial relations are denoted by temporal expressions like *anschließend* (subsequently), *danach* (after this), *dann direkt* (directly then) in various combinations (16).

2. Where 1(a)–(c) don't come into force, Miller and Johnson-Laird's statement, that the intrinsic interpretation will dominate the deictic one, becomes operative.

Examples (to be checked against the drawings):

(14) [...] Dann weiter, auf der rechten Seite, *wenn man reinkommt* [...]. (T1A)

[...] Then further, on the right-hand side *as you enter* [...].

[...] Und dann an der rechten Wand, *wenn man zur Tür reinkommt* steht das Bett [...]. (T2A)

[...] And then on the right wall, *as you enter the door*, there is the bed [...].

[...] Danach ist so eine Couch und gleich auch ein Bett, und man kann das, wo man sich da anlehnt, da kann man nach oben so hinstellen, ne, das is so umklappbar, und hat man son bißchen größeres Bett, *also gleich, wenn man reinkommt hinten links*, ne. [...]. (T12A)

[...] After this, there is a sort of couch, and immediately also a bed, and this you can, where you lean on it, there you can lift up, it is convertible, and one has a slightly bigger bed there, thus *immediately, as you enter in the back on the left*, you know. [...].

(15) Da *vor* diesem Schrank stand dann früher noch dieser kleine Tisch. (T2, D2)

There *in front* of this cabinet there used to be this little table.

Und *vorm* Fenster dann die zwei Schreibtische. (T7A)

And *in front of* the window then the two desks.

Und ich hab dann den Schreibtisch direkt unterm Fenster stehn, und den andern Tisch *rechts* dadran. (T9, D9)

And I have the desk directly under the window, and the other table *to the right* of it.

| Ich hab Stühle keine, nur den einen Schreibtischstuhl und der steht auch *vorm* Schreibtisch. (T9, D9) | I have no chairs, only the one desk chair, and that is of course *in front* of the desk. |

(16) [. . .] Da ist, links hinter der Tür ist das Waschbecken, *dann* kommt dieser große Kleiderschrank direkt anschließend, *dann* is etwas Raum ne, also n Meter fünfzig etwa, *dann* kommt der Schreibtisch, *dann* kommt schon die Ecke zum Fenster [. . .].

[. . .] There is, to the left behind the door, there is the wash basin, *then* comes this big wardrobe immediately alongside, *then* there is some space, about one metre fifty or so, *then* comes the desk, *then* you're already to the corner leading to the window [. . .].

Man kommt also rein, dann ist rechts der Schrank links ist die Küche und *daran anschliessend* links praktisch die Duschzelle. (T9A)

So you come in, then to the right is the cabinet, to the left is the kitchen and then *subsequently to it* on the left the shower cell.

(17) *Neben* dem Kleiderschrank steht der Kühlschrank. (T3A)

Beside the wardrobe is the refrigerator.

Und *direkt neben* muß ich vorher noch sagen, neben eh diesem Küchen geht nun ist dann ne Wand abgeteilt also und man geht dann is so ein kleines Bad rein. (T7A)

An *directly alongside* I have to say this first, next to er this kitchen is now there is a separating wall and you enter then a small bathroom.

The expressions of temporal deixis are of particular relevance for spatial descriptions in the *Round About* format. In this format, the deictic orientation changes two times (from front → back, to left → right, to back → front—see Figure 10). Hence the same item b, which when seen from the front → back orientation can be referred to as being *in front of a* would have to be described as being *behind* in the back → front orientation. But if, *within a tour* b is introduced by use of a temporal expression, as for example in 'Hinten rechts in der Ecke ist a *und dann kommt* b direkt anschließend (Backwards right in the corner there is a, and *then* there is b coming *directly subsequent*)', it becomes clear from the presupposed direction of the tour where in fact b is located. If this statement is correct, the perspective shift in the last line of (7) ('Und hinter dieser verbleibenden Wand ist dann also diese Naßzelle'/And behind this last wall is then this shower-stall) has to be considered to be a

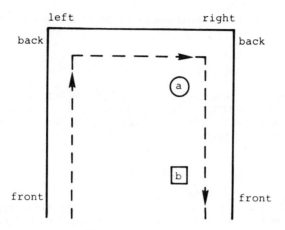

Figure 10   Two changes in deictic orientation occur
following the path drawn

mistake. Of course, even in this case there will perhaps be no doubt as to
where to locate the shower stall (because of the presupposed tour direction),
but locating it by *dann . . . anschließend* seems to be unambiguous in any case,
whereas locating it by *hinter* is ambiguous as long as the deictic perspective is
maintained. In other words, the use of temporal expressions for the linguistic
representation of spatial information is based on the tour format. The tour
being a temporally ordered sequence of events allows reference to its units by
temporal indication. The *Round About* format determines the direction of the
tour. Temporal expressions therefore refer to the respective next spot on the
tour, such that the objects filling these spots can be located unambiguously.

SUMMARY

In this paper the macro- and microstructural organization of some (comparatively simple) discourses as well as their mutual interaction have been investigated. The basic microstructural organization principle found, the *gaze tour*,
has been reconstructed in terms of microstructural features like sentence
subject selection, verb selection, word-order and origo shift. With respect to
linearization characteristics of the discourse two different principles are discussed, *Round About* and *Parallel Line*. The choice between these higher
level linearization principles is determined by lower level principles called
Sequencing and *Grouping*, which in turn are determined by the func-
tionality/dysfunctionality of the arrangement to be described. Furthermore,
problems of perspective shift in the use of secondary spatial deictics are
discussed. It is shown that people avoid ambiguity between deixis and intrinsics by using temporal in place of spatial expressions, which—due to the under-

lying tour format of the descriptions—provide the desired singularity of descriptions.

NOTE

1. I wish to thank Stephanie Kelter, Wolfgang Klein, Willem Levelt, Herbert Tropf, Jürgen Weissenborn, and Dieter Wunderlich for commenting on an earlier draft of this paper, and Charlotte Koster and Robert Jarvella for suggestions for translating some of the protocols given into English.

REFERENCES

Bühler, K. (1934). *Sprachtheorie*. Jena: Fischer.

Canter, D. (1977). *The psychology of place*. London: The Architectural Press.

Clark, E. V. (1977). From gesture to word: on the natural history of deixis in language acquisition. In J. S. Bruner & A. Garton (eds), *Human growth and development*. Oxford: Oxford University Press.

Clark, H. H., & Haviland, S. E. (1977). Comprehension and the given-new contract. In R. O. Freedle (ed.), *Discourse production and comprehension*, Vol. 1. Norwood, N.J.: Ablex.

Dik, S. C. (1978). *Functional grammar*. Amsterdam: North Holland.

Downs, R., & Stea, D. (eds) (1973a). *Image and environment*. London: Arnold.

Downs, R., & Stea, D. (1973b). Cognitive maps and spatial behavior. In R. Downs & D. Stea (eds), *Image and environment*. London: Arnold.

Fillmore, C. (1975). Santa Cruz lectures on deixis, 1971. Bloomington, Ind.: Indiana University Linguistics Club.

Givón, T. (1976). Topic, pronoun, and grammatical agreement. In C. N. Li (ed.), *Subject and topic*. New York: Academic Press.

Klein, W. (1977). Wegauskünfte. *Zeitschrift für Literaturwissenschaft und Linguistik*, **33**, 9–57.

Kosslyn, S. M. (1977). Imagery and internal representation. In E. Rosch & B. Lloyd (eds), *Cognition and categorization*. Hillsdale, N.J.: Erlbaum.

Kuno, S. (1975). Three perspectives in the functional approach to syntax. In R. E. Grossman, L. J. San, & T. J. Vance (eds), *Papers from the parasession on functionalism*. Chicago: Chicago Linguistics Society.

Leech, G. N. (1969). *Towards a semantic description of English*. Bloomington, Ind.: Indiana University Press.

Levelt, W. J. M. (1979). Describing spatial networks. Paper presented at the Symposium on Formal Semantics and Natural Language Processing, Austin, Texas, March 1979.

Linde, C. (1974). The linguistic encoding of spatial information. Unpublished doctoral dissertation, Columbia University.

Linde, C., & Labov, W. (1975). Spatial networks as a site for the study of language and thought. *Language*, **51**, 924–939.

Lynch, K. (1960). *The image of a city*. Cambridge, Mass.: The MIT Press.

Miller, G. A., & Johnson-Laird, P. N. (1976). *Language and perception*. Cambridge, Mass.: Harvard University Press.

Pylyshyn, Z. W. (1973). What the mind's eye tells the mind's brain: a critique of mental imagery. *Psychological Bulletin*, **80**, 1–24.

Saile, G. (1977). *Die Beschreibung räumlicher Operationen*. Unpublished doctoral dissertation, Technical University of Berlin.

Schegloff, E. A. (1972). Notes on a conversational practice: formulating place. In D. N. Sudnow (ed.), *Studies in social interaction*. New York: The Free Press.

Wilton, R. N. (1977). Knowledge of spatial relations: the determination of the relation 'nearest to'. *Quarterly Journal of Experimental Psychology*, **29**, 685–698.

Wilton, R. N., & File, P. A. (1977). The representation of spatial information in memory. *Quarterly Journal of Experimental Psychology*, **29**, 383–388.

Wunderlich, D. (1971). Pragmatik, Sprechsituation, Deixis. *Zeitschrift für Literaturwissenschaft und Linguistik*, **1/2**, 153–190.

Speech, Place, and Action
Edited by R. J. Jarvella and W. Klein
© 1982 John Wiley & Sons Ltd.

Cognitive Styles in the Use of Spatial Direction Terms

WILLEM J. M. LEVELT

Let us, by way of introduction, consider two spatial descriptions obtained in an experiment to be described more fully below. The two descriptions are of the same spatial pattern, namely the one presented in Figure 1, but were given by two different subjects. One subject was a male student, while the other was a female housekeeper. Subsequently, they will be referred to as 'he' and 'she'.

The subjects had been instructed to describe the pattern in such a way that a listener familiar with the type of patterns involved would be able to redraw the pattern accurately from a tape recording made of their speech. The instructions moreover asked the subjects to start the description at the node marked by an arrow.

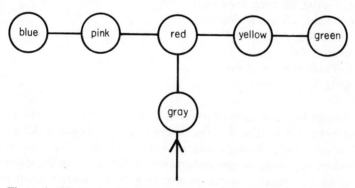

Figure 1 Network of coloured nodes and black arcs, presented to subjects to describe. The arrow indicates where the description should begin

His description:
0. In het middel beginnen, een grijs knooppunt
In the middle to begin, a grey nodal point

251

1. Vandaaruit naar boven, een rood knooppunt
    From there upwards, a red nodal point
2. Dan naar links toe, een roze knooppunt vanuit rood
    Then to the left, a pink nodal point from red
3. Dan vanuit roze weer naar links toe een blauw knooppunt
    Then from pink again to the left a blue nodal point
4. Dan weer terug naar rood
    Then back again to red
5. Dan van rood naar rechts toe een geel knooppunt
    Then from red to the right a yellow nodal point
6. En vanuit geel weer naar rechts toe een groen knooppunt
    And from yellow again to the right a green nodal point

Her description:

0. Ik start bij kruispunt grijs
    I start at crossing point grey
1. Ga rechtdoor naar rood
    Go straight on to red
2. Ga linksaf naar roze
    Go left to pink
3. Ga rechtdoor naar blauw
    Go straight on to blue
4. Draai rond ga terug naar roze
    Turn around go back to pink
5. Ga terug, eh rechtdoor naar rood
    Go back, uh straight on to red
6. Rechtdoor naar geel
    Straight on to yellow
7. Rechtdoor naar groen
    Straight on to green

Both descriptions are *tours* of some sort. Each tour starts at the grey node indicated by the arrow (line 0 in the descriptions), and ends at the green one, meanwhile traversing all the nodes in a more or less connected way. The tours, moreover, consist of elementary *moves* (lines 1–7 in the descriptions) consisting of an optional source phrase (e.g. 'from there'; 'from pink'), a directional phrase ('to the left', 'back again', 'straight on', etc.), and a goal phrase ('a blue nodal point', 'to red', etc.). But within this rather fixed frame, the two descriptions exhibit some striking differences. The maker of the tour is unspecified in his description, but 'I' in hers (although this is deleted in all moves subsequent to the first one, so that the moves also sound like instructions for the addressee). He usually gives the source phrase at each move, but she doesn't. Her description is also more elliptical in that, except for line 0, the nodes are referred to by their colour only (e.g. 'blue'), whereas he often uses a full noun phrase ('a blue nodal point'). In the one case where they both use the colour term adjectivally, namely in line 0, there is still a marked difference: he uses the indefinite article, and normal Dutch word order ('een grijs knooppunt'), whereas she omits the article and uses inverse order ('kruispunt grijs'), as if to accentuate the given/new structure.

In the following we will not deal with all these differences or many others that could be detected. Instead, we will limit ourselves to a discussion of some differences in the use of directional expressions, such as 'left', 'right', and 'straight on', and in the way such expressions are strung together. Our aim is to show that such individual differences are not more or less random fluctuations in idiolect, but are due to systematic variations in the ways people operate on internal representations of space.

In order to focus on the phenomena we have in mind, compare the following differences between the two descriptions:

(i) In his move 1 the directional term is 'upwards' ('naar boven'); the corresponding term in her move 1 is 'straight on' ('rechtdoor').

(ii) Moving from pink to blue is described by him as 'again to the left' ('weer naar links') in move 3, whereas for the same move she uses 'straight on' ('rechtdoor').

(iii) His move 4 brings him back to the red crossing point in one leap, unspecified as to direction ('back again'), whereas she uses two specified moves to accomplish this: her move 4 which describes the turning around and return to pink (this node is not mentioned again by him at all); and her move 5 for reaching the red crossing node, which starts out with 'go back', but then is corrected to the more specific 'straight on'.

(iv) In order to move from red to yellow he uses as directional phrase 'to the right' ('naar rechts toe') in his move 5, whereas she accomplishes this in her move 6 with 'straight on' ('rechtdoor').

(v) Finally, the concluding move to green is specified by him (move 6) as 'again to the right' ('weer naar rechts toe'), whereas she indicates it (move 7) as 'straight on' ('rechtdoor').

One might want to ascribe the differences (i) and (iii) to superficial variation in wording: 'upwards' and 'straight on' in (i) are synonymous in the context of use; each subject could have used the other term without much consequence for the listener. Similarly for (iii), the combination of 'go back' and 'straight on' in her description may just be a bit more specific than his 'back again', but still they would be largely synonymous in the given context. However, such an explanation cannot hold for differences (ii), (iv), and (v), where either 'right' or 'left' in his description corresponds to 'straight on' in her description. These expressions are neither synonymous nor differ in degree of specificity, and one should worry for the subjects who have to draw the pattern on the basis of these descriptions.

There are two different, but related factors which can account for the observed discrepancies. The first factor I will call 'linearization type', and the second factor I will denote by 'orientation type'. These are to be considered as cognitive style factors in dealing with space. Let us consider them in turn.

1   LINEARIZATION TYPES

In order to describe a spatial pattern like that in Figure 1, one needs to map a non-linear spatial configuration onto a linear sequence of verbal expressions, or statements. This should be done in such a way that a listener can draw the pattern given the description and acquaintance with the class of actual patterns. In this particular setting, therefore, the description should, together with the foreknowledge of the listener, uniquely specify the pattern. Let us call this task requirement 'completeness'.

The speaker may approach this requirement of completeness in several ways. One way to form a complete linearization would be to give a global structural description, and then provide the details of increasingly smaller parts. That is, one could start out by saying 'This pattern is T-shaped', and then continue by mentioning the nodes on the vertical bar, and from left to right those on the horizontal bar. Of the 53 adult subjects who participated in our experiment, and described the pattern shown in Figure 1, only one started out like this ('On this figure I see a vertical and a horizontal line. On the vertical line the first one is a grey dot', etc.). In all other cases the linearization strategy was to make a *tour*, as in the two examples given above. The dominance of tour-like linearizations in spatial descriptions has been observed in earlier studies as well: in Linde & Labov's (1975) seminal paper on apartment descriptions, in Klein's (1979, also this volume), Wunderlich & Reinelt's (this volume), and Munro's (1977) studies of route directions, and in Ullmer-Ehrich's (1979 and this volume) study of room descriptions. Although there are marked differences between these studies with respect to the character of such tours (in room descriptions, for instance, only a 'gaze tour' is made, contrary to the other cases), the tour strategy for dealing with linearization of spatial structures seems to be a fairly general one.

What is less apparent, however, is that there are systematic individual differences in the *way* tours are constructed. In an earlier paper (Levelt, 1981) I have shown that the 53 subjects from the present experiment quite neatly divide into two main linearization types, the so-called 'jumpers' and 'movers'. The essential difference between them lies in the way they deal with backtracking to choice points. Jumpers deal with choice points in the pattern in the following way: they first select one branch and describe it entirely;

they then *leap* back to the choice point in order to describe the (or an-) other branch. Movers do not leap back, but *move* step by step back, along the branch already described, until they again reach the choice point. The male subject above is a jumper (see move 4), whereas the female subject is a mover (see moves 4 and 5). These types are quite consistent. The subjects in the present experiment not only described Figure 1, but 53 different patterns in total. Of these patterns, 45 involved choice points, and it almost always turned out that if a subject was a jumper in the description of one pattern, he was a jumper for all the others too, and also once a mover, always a mover. Of our 53 subjects, only four jumped in some patterns and moved in others, but even these had a strong preference for either moving or jumping. Among the 49 'pure' types, there were just about twice as many jumpers (33) as movers (16).

From the findings in that study we have reason to believe that jumpers and movers differ in the way they cope with their own memory requirements in producing a description. Both jumpers and movers keep a record of the nodes and branches they have already mentioned. But it seems that, over and above this, jumpers mark for themselves the choice node(s) they will have to return to after finishing the description of one branch. This is not a wholly trivial matter, since the branch being described may contain a choice point of its own. An example is given in Figure 2. If a jumper starts moving through

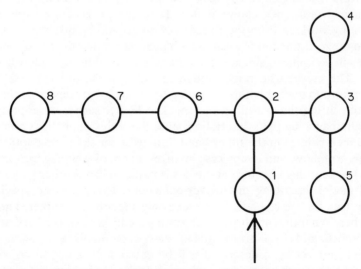

Figure 2   Network of coloured nodes and black arcs with an 'embedded' choice node. (Numbers are presented only for ease of reference in the text)

Figure 2 in the succession $1 \rightarrow 2 \rightarrow 3 \rightarrow 4$, he has not only the first choice node 2 to return to (for finishing $2 \rightarrow 6 \rightarrow 7 \rightarrow 8$), but also the later choice point 3. This return is necessary in order to describe the alternative branch that leads from node 3 to node 5. If a jumper marks for himself the nodes to which he has to return, he must also impose some order on them. After reaching node 4 in Figure 2, which of the two return addresses will get priority? If it is the first choice node encountered (2), the jumper will describe branch $6 \rightarrow 7 \rightarrow 8$ first, but if it is the last choice node (i.e. node 3), then priority will be given to description of the branch to 5. If no specific order is imposed there will be within- and between-subject differences in order of return. What we predicted and found in the earlier study was that jumpers return to choice nodes in reverse order. In Figure 2, for instance, they return to node 3 for completing the description of $3 \rightarrow 5$ before returning to 2 for the description of branch $2 \rightarrow 6 \rightarrow 7 \rightarrow 8$. The prediction was based on an Augmented Transition Network (ATN) model which contains a push-down store for choice node addresses, and thus has the required first-in-last-out characteristic. For a large variety of complex patterns, jumpers almost without exception adhered to this reverse order of return to unfinished choice nodes. This is in agreement with what Linde & Labov (1975) found in their study of apartment descriptions. Still, the situations were quite different: in their study, subjects described from memory, whereas in our study they described a perceptually available pattern.

Movers, we supposed, can make their descriptions without explicit book-keeping of unfinished choice nodes. They can produce a complete linear-ization by working from their record of nodes and branches described. The return move at the end of each branch guarantees that the unfinished choice point will be found again, and even that this will be the *last* unfinished choice node. The mover who runs through Figure 2 in the order $1 \rightarrow 2 \rightarrow 3 \rightarrow 4$ *must* return to node 3 before returning to 2. The mover describes the pattern 'without lifting the pencil', so to speak. Clearly, such a description is less efficient than a jumper's description, since the nodes along the return path are mentioned twice. On the other hand, it may be an easier description for the listener to follow, and in any case involves less book-keeping for the speaker since no recording of return addresses is required. The earlier paper gives an ATN model describing this mover-behaviour. It contains no special push-down stack for choice nodes, but keeps only a record of completed nodes and branches. What the mover does, according to this model, is return at the end of a branch, and check his records for each node on his return path. Any arc that has not yet been described will be entered. It seems to be somewhat expensive to check each node and arc described before, but in a perceptual situation this involves very little effort: the visually present nodes and arcs are, one after another, retrieval cues for the records; there is no special memory load involved. It should be noticed that this would be quite different if a subject has to work from memory as in the apartment descriptions. A mover would then have to retrieve each node's records by means of a retrieval cue which is itself a trace in memory, namely the earlier node or arc. This, of course, is harder than perceptually guided retrieval. It is not surprising that there are no movers in the Linde and Labov study, where subjects have to describe from memory. Almost all subjects there are jumpers.

If these hypothetical differences in cognitive style between jumpers and movers are essentially true, one might predict that jumpers would try to linearize a pattern in such a way as to minimize their memory load, or more precisely the stack of return addresses they have to keep in mind. In describing the pattern in Figure 2, for instance, jumpers should show a preference for going to the left first at choice point 2. In that case, they have to store only one choice point while describing $6 \rightarrow 7 \rightarrow 8$. Jumping back to 2, this can now be removed from their memory stack. Arriving at 3 on the following move, this choice point will now be stored, so that again a memory load of just one element results. If, however, a jumper goes to the *right* first on reaching point 2, he must store that choice point, and later, on top of that, choice point 3. That would result in a memory load of two elements. So, jumpers should prefer to go left first at choice point 2, in order to minimize memory load.

Movers, on the other hand, might try to minimize the amount of backtracking they have to do. If they go right first at choice point 2 they will have to make three return moves, namely $4 \rightarrow 3$, $5 \rightarrow 3$, and $3 \rightarrow 2$. But if they go left first they must make four return moves: $8 \rightarrow 7$, $7 \rightarrow 6$, $6 \rightarrow 2$ and $4 \rightarrow 3$ (or $5 \rightarrow 3$ dependent on the direction they take first at 3). It is thus more efficient for them to turn right first at 2; this is just the opposite of what the jumpers are predicted to do. The experiment gave clear support for these different strategies. Of our 33 jumpers 26 went left first in Figure 2, and only seven went right first. Of the 16 movers, however, only four went left first, the others started going right at choice node 2. Similar results were obtained for other patterns.

So much for linearization types. The distinction between jumpers and movers explains one difference between the two descriptions we started out with. Under (iii) we mentioned his coming back from blue to the red crossing point in one unspecific move ('then back again to red'), whereas she used two more specified moves to accomplish this ('Turn around go back to pink' and 'Go back, uh straight on to red'). This difference is not due to a global tendency on her part to be a bit more specific in her description (in fact, she isn't, leaving out almost all of the source phrases), but to a well-defined difference in linearization strategy. As we will see in Section 3, difference (iv) is probably also due to linearization type. That analysis, however, requires some insight in the other style factor, orientation type.

2   ORIENTATION TYPES

The discussion of orientation types can be best introduced by a quotation from Miller & Johnson-Laird (1976, p. 396):

> 'We will call the linguistic system for talking about space relative to a speaker's egocentric origin and coordinate axes the deictic system. We will contrast the deictic system with the intrinsic system, where spatial terms are interpreted relative to coordinate axes derived from intrinsic parts of the referent itself. Another way to phrase this distinction is to say that in the deictic system spatial terms are interpreted relative to intrinsic parts of ego, whereas in the intrinsic system they are interpreted relative to intrinsic parts of something else.'

This distinction is directly applicable to the present case. The subject in our experiment was always provided with a customary physical position with respect to a pattern. The patterns of Figures 1 and 2 were placed on a table before the subject in the position they would be if the present seated reader put the book down flat in front of him, oriented for easy reading. Now, consider Figure 1, and let us assume that the last move that was made by the subject was from red to pink. There are, basically, two ways of describing the location of blue. If the deictic system is used, the subject will relate blue to pink by (tacit) reference to coordinates of ego, and select an expression such as 'left from pink is blue'. If the intrinsic system is used, reference will be taken from intrinsic parts of the pattern, here presumably the last path moved along in the tour (i.e. the path from red to pink). So, now the expression will be something like 'straight on from pink is blue'. Thus, it turns out that the same pathway can be denoted by 'left' or 'straight' depending on the coordinate system used. Ideally, the speaker should inform the listener which of the two systems he has in mind. Miller & Johnson-Laird suggest that there might be a convention that the intrinsic system is used, unless the deictic system is explicitly introduced ('from my point of view'), or unless the intrinsic system *cannot* be used (if the relatum has no intrinsic orientation). This ideal situation is not approached in the present experiment: we find that in roughly two-thirds of the cases where deictic and intrinsic use can be distinguished, the deictic system is used, and it is almost never the case that this use is explicitly mentioned to the listener.[1] Still, the listener's position is not hopeless. There is a combination of two factors which may help the listener find out which of the systems is in fact used.

The first factor is the use of specific directional terms. If the speaker in the setting of the present experiment uses terms such as 'above', 'up', 'under', 'below', etc., i.e. terms related to a vertical dimension, the listener can safely conclude that the speaker is operating in the deictic system. This is not at all a trivial matter, and we will discuss it at length after some supporting data have been presented. If the orientation system can be discovered, the listener must, moreover, be justified in assuming that it is used *consistently*. If the speaker switches perspective at every move *within* a pattern, the listener will be lost. But it would also be helpful to the listener if he could make the reasonable assumption that in the present task, where the speaker gives a sequence of pattern descriptions, consistency also exists *across* patterns. If the assumption is correct, one could speak of orientation types. Some subjects would be of the *pattern-oriented* type, consistently using the intrinsic system; others would be of the *ego-oriented* type, consistently using the deictic system.

There is evidence that these types exist. Let us first give some indication of within-pattern consistency. There are three moves in the description of the pattern in Figure 1, where an ego-oriented use of terms can differ from a pattern-oriented one. Firstly, going from pink to blue would be 'left' (or some synonym 'left side', 'to the left', etc.) for ego-oriented types and 'straight' (or some synonym) for the pattern-oriented types. Secondly, the move from yellow to green would, similarly, be 'right' for the ego-oriented types, and again 'straight' for the pattern-oriented ones. Finally, the use of 'up' or some synonym would indicate deictic use, as mentioned earlier and to be discussed shortly; this may distinguish the ego-oriented type in describing the very first move, from grey to red.

Let us first compare the subjects' behaviours in the first two cases. We categorized each term used in these two moves as pattern-oriented ('straight on', or its synonyms), or ego-oriented ('left', 'right', or synonyms). This could not always be done, for instance when a subject merely said 'and then' or 'and'. For the fully categorizable cases, Table 1 gives the contingency distribution. It appears that there is only one inconsistent subject. This subject combines 'straight on' ('rechtdoor') with 'keep going left' ('links blijven gaan'), an expression which allows for both a durational and a repetitive interpretation, so that this inconsistency is at best a weak one. If we remove this subject from further consideration, 34 subjects can be categorized as explicitly ego- or pattern-oriented, 22 being ego-oriented, and 12 pattern-oriented. Let us see how these 34 behave at the first move, from grey to red. Will there be more 'ups' and 'aboves' among the ego-oriented subjects? This can be seen in contingency Table 2. The table shows a highly significant interaction: with only two exceptions, the ego-oriented subjects use a vertical-dimension term

Table 1   Ego- and pattern-oriented responses for two moves in Figure 1 (from pink to blue, and from yellow to green)

	Move from pink to blue	
Move from yellow to green	Ego-oriented	Pattern-oriented
Ego-oriented	22	0
Pattern-oriented	1	12

Table 2   Use of vertical dimension terms at first move (grey to red) in Figure 1
('up', etc.) by ego- and pattern-oriented subjects

Subjects	Vertical-dimension term used	Other term used
Ego-oriented	20	2
Pattern-oriented	1	11

to describe the first move from grey to red, whereas only one of the pattern-oriented subjects does.

From all this it can be concluded that three of the differences which we observed at the beginning of this paper between our male and female subjects' descriptions are linked intimately together. Distinction (i) concerned the first move where he said 'up', and she 'straight on'; distinction (ii) concerned move 3 from pink to blue, where he used 'again to the left', and she 'straight on'; and distinction (v) involved the last move, from yellow to green, where he used 'again to the right', and she 'straight on'. All three differences can be explained by orientation type: he being ego-oriented (deictic), and she being pattern-oriented (intrinsic).

Still to be explained is why vertical-dimension terms are consistently used in deictic orientation, and not in intrinsic orientation. There are various possible accounts of this. One could argue that in deictic orientation the subject mentally rotates the page into vertical position (somewhat like holding a newspaper). This explanation would only shift the problem to the question as to why this mental rotation does not take place in intrinsic orientation. Another account could be that in deictic orientation the direction 'away from ego' coincides with what is normally called 'top of page': the top/bottom of page terminology would then be metaphorically extended to the use of 'up' and 'down'; since the orientation of page to ego is irrelevant in the intrinsic system, the vertical metaphors will only appear in the case of deictic orientation. This account is not convincing either, or at least it is not very elegant: why would somebody who prefers to operate in ego-centric (deictic) orientation resort to a metaphor which is intrinsic; the top of a page is an intrinsic property of the page, defined by the conventional shape and way of printing. Moreover, there was no print on our patterns, and the sheets were exactly square.

We prefer a more literal account of the use of vertical-dimension terms in deictic orientation. In the tour strategy the ego-centric orientation is mediated by movement of gaze. The subject's tour is a gaze tour, and the directions of the gaze shifts correspond exactly to the directional terms used: in deictic orientation it is not only the case that 'left' and 'right' agree respectively with leftward and rightward shifts of gaze, but that 'up' and 'down' indeed conform to upward and downward gaze movements. In intrinsic orientation, the rela-tions to 'watching ego' are irrelevant, and direction of gaze is irrelevant for the selection of directional terms. What matters there is the change or con-tinuation of direction in the plane, whatever the gaze and orientation of the speaker—no vertical dimension is involved. This account would predict that for deictic subjects vertical dimension terms will diminish or disappear if the horizontal plane of the pattern is lifted to (almost) eye level: this will almost completely eliminate vertical eye movements.

Let us now consider whether these deictic versus intrinsic characteristics carry over to the descriptions of other patterns. Are orientation types consis-tent *across* patterns? Here we will report some evidence in support of such consistency. Remember that we defined the orientation type of our 34 'clear cases' by the terms they used for the two extreme moves in Figure 1: 'left' and 'right' defined the ego-oriented subject, 'straight on' the pattern-oriented subject. We have claimed above that such differences in use of terms are not superficial variations in idiolect, but are due to underlying cognitive style factors. An idiolect explanation would be that some people just prefer using terms like 'left' and 'right', whereas others have a tendency to say 'straight' wherever they can. In order to exclude the possibility of such an explanation, we have analysed the description of two other patterns where a consistent ego-oriented subject should *not* use 'left' and 'right', and a consistent pattern-oriented subject should *not* use 'straight on', but in fact 'left' and 'right'. These patterns are given in Figures 3 and 4. They are mirror images of one another, and essentially present the same problem. Let us, therefore,

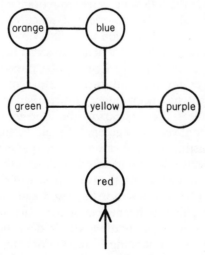

Figure 3   Pattern with a loop. The description begins at the arrow

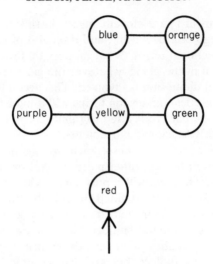

Figure 4   A mirror image of the network shown in Figure 3

discuss the case of Figure 3, the other one being the same, *mutatis mutandis*. The pattern contains a loop, and usually subjects describe a loop by working all the way around it. In this case they either go from yellow to blue to orange to green, and back to yellow, or the other way around. Let us assume a subject starts making the loop via blue. Irrespective of being ego- or pattern-oriented, the next move direction, to orange, will be described by a term like 'left'. But now consider the following move from orange to green. This *cannot* be called 'left' if the subject is ego-oriented, since in that framework it is 'towards ego', and a vertical dimension term, like 'down', is the most appropriate one. If the subject is pattern-oriented, however, he *cannot* use 'straight' here, but must instead use 'left'. So it should be possible to distinguish the same orientation types for this pattern by the use of other terms than in Figure 1. That is what has been done. Notice that the distinction cannot always be made: if the subject linearizes the loop by going the other way round, moving first from yellow to green, it should be the move from blue to yellow that would distinguish ego-oriented and pattern-oriented direction terms. But often subjects use the unmarked 'back to yellow' in that case. So, it is not always possible to distinguish the two types. Tables 3 and 4 present the distribution of our 34 'clear cases', for Figures 3 and 4 respectively.

Both tables show highly significant consistencies among our subjects. Only three subjects have changed orientation type in describing Figure 3, and no more than two out of 34 in describing Figure 4. For completeness it should be remarked that, on the average, 25 other patterns intervened between the descriptions of Figure 1 and either of Figures 3 and 4. Figures 3 and 4 were on

Table 3   Distribution of ego- and pattern-oriented descriptions of Figure 3 for ego-
and pattern-oriented subjects*

Subjects	Description of Figure 3		
	Ego-oriented	Pattern-oriented	Indeterminable
Ego-oriented	21	1	0
Pattern-oriented	2	10	0

*Categorized on the basis of their descriptions of Figure 1.

Table 4   Distribution of ego- and pattern-oriented descriptions of Figure 4 for ego-
and pattern-oriented subjects*

Subjects	Description of Figure 4		
	Ego-oriented	Pattern-oriented	Indeterminable
Ego-oriented	21	0	1
Pattern-oriented	2	9	1

*Categorized on the basis of their descriptions of Figure 1.

the average also 25 patterns apart in the series, and all order permutations
were possible. We also checked separately whether our 53 subjects were
consistent in type between their descriptions of Figures 3 and 4. They were:
only one subject out of 47 clear cases was pattern-oriented for Figure 3 and
ego-oriented for Figure 4, all others being consistent. Finally, we did one
more global analysis over all 53 subjects and 53 patterns. We used an indication for intrinsic orientation which can best be explained from Figure 3. If a
subject uses the term 'left' for the direction from green to yellow, this can only
be due to intrinsic orientation (or to error); in deictic orientation this direction should be 'right'. Let us, just for shorthand purposes, call this 'contradictory left'. Similarly, one can define 'contradictory right' as for instance 'right'
for green to yellow in Figure 4. By means of a computer program we sorted
out all cases of contradictory left and contradictory right in our 53×53
pattern descriptions. We found that 33 subjects did not show a single case of
contradictory left or right. One could argue that these include all ego-oriented
subjects, but they may also include some pattern-oriented (intrinsic) subjects
since there is not a single pattern where it is *necessary* for an intrinsic subject
to use contradictory left or right. (In Figures 3 and 4 such a subject could, for
instance, say 'back to yellow', and in so doing evade the use of 'left' or 'right'.)
But if orientation types are consistent across patterns, a subject who uses
contradictory left or right at least once should be intrinsic as a whole, i.e. all
20 remaining subjects should be of the pattern-oriented type. Counter-
evidence against this would be if any of these subjects occurred among the 22

'clear' ego-oriented cases of Table 1. This turned out to be the case for four of the 20 subjects (as compared to 18 for the 33 'non-contradictory' subjects). It shows that absolute consistency does not occur, but even for this very strong test (the subject has 53 patterns in which to be 'contradictory' at least once) the number and seriousness of the deviations is small. The four deviant subjects gave contradictory left or right in three cases on the average. For all 20 subjects who showed such use of left and right the average was eight cases, the range from 2 to 24. A final statistical datum for the consistency of the orientation types is the correlation between the use of contradictory left and use of contradictory right. If we correlate the number of cases 'left' and 'right' over all subjects, we find $r = 0.88$: a subject who tends to use contradictory right also tends to use contradictory left.

From all this, we may conclude that our subjects have a rather consistent style of orientation in describing spatial patterns, both within and across descriptions. Roughly two-thirds of the subjects are ego-oriented in their descriptions, using their own orientation axes as a basis for selecting directional terms. The other one-third consists of subjects who are pattern-oriented; they use the direction of the last move they have made as an orientation for the direction mentioned in the next one.

The obvious question now is whether orientation type has anything to do with linearization type. This will be the topic of the next section.

3   LINEARIZATION TYPE VERSUS ORIENTATION TYPE

The two subjects used as examples turned out to differ in both linearization type and orientation type: he is an ego-oriented jumper and she a pattern-oriented mover. Is it more generally the case that jumpers tend to be ego-oriented and movers pattern-oriented? Let us consider the evidence. Remember that the descriptions of Figure 1 allowed us to find 34 'clear cases' of orientation type. It was also noticed above that 46 out of 47 cases agreed in orientation type between Figures 3 and 4. So, these 46 subjects can also be considered as 'clear cases', though on a different basis. Tables 5 and 6 show how these clear ego- and pattern-oriented subjects distribute over the three linearization types: jumpers, movers, and mixers. Inspection of these tables shows that no significant differences exist in the distribution of ego- and pattern-oriented subjects over linearization types: we have no basis from these data for claiming that linearization and orientation types are related.

Still, it would be surprising if the linearization strategy would affect orientation at no point in the pattern description. The reason is purely procedural. It was noticed in Section 1 that jumpers presumably store unfinished choice points in working memory, in order to ensure correct backtracking. Movers need not do this, as no such storage is required for producing complete descriptions. But what does it mean to 'store a choice point'? Will it be stored

Table 5   Distribution of ego- and pattern-oriented subjects over linearization types (basis: Figure 1 descriptions, $N = 34$)

Linearization type	Orientation type	
	Ego-oriented	Pattern-oriented
Jumper	11	8
Mover	8	4
Mixer	3	0

with or without the direction that led into it? The simplest hypothesis is that only pattern-oriented subjects will store the direction, whereas ego-oriented ones will not. A pattern-oriented subject must always relate the subsequent direction *from* a node to the antecedent direction *into* that node, which must be specially registered. But what is the direction into a choice node after a jump? Is it the direction from some far-away node, that happened to be the end of one branch from the choice node? That would not be a very valid system, since that direction can be oblique to different degrees, so that terms like 'left', 'right', and 'straight' cannot be used in a determinate way. It is thus simpler to register the original direction into the choice point, and keep it in working memory for later reference.

Ego-oriented subjects, however, will never need such directional information. They base the choice of their directional terms solely on the direction *from* a node plus their personal orientation. The direction *into* the node is simply irrelevant, and hence needs no storage in their linearization procedure.

If this hypothesis is correct, both ego-oriented and pattern-oriented jumpers will use 'left' or 'right' after jumping back to the red choice point in Figure 1, but for different reasons: the ego-oriented jumpers will label the next move out of red by reference to their own body, the pattern-oriented jumpers will do it by reference to the original move into the red point coming from grey. These two referential devices happen to coincide in this case. What about the movers? If movers don't register choice nodes, they also don't store the direction of the original move into the choice node. Ego-oriented movers

Table 6   Distribution of ego- and pattern-oriented subjects over linearization types (basis: Figure 3 and 4 descriptions, $N = 46$)

Linearization type	Orientation type	
	Ego-oriented	Pattern-oriented
Jumper	20	7
Mover	9	6
Mixer	4	0

will simply use their body orientation as the orientation for the next move out of a choice point. They will say 'left' or 'right' when they leave the red choice point of Figure 1 for the second time. Pattern-oriented movers will also have no trace of the earlier move into the choice point, so they will use the last return move as the basis for orientation. They will therefore *not* use terms like 'left' and 'right', but 'straight on' or an unmarked term like 'and then', signalling unchanged continuation of direction. So, in summary: (1) *all* jumpers will use 'left' or 'right' to describe their second move out of the red choice point; (2) *all* ego-oriented movers will do the same; and (3) *none* of the pattern-oriented movers will do so. What we find is that indeed out of our 34 clear cases all of the 11 ego-oriented and eight pattern-oriented jumpers use 'left' or 'right'; all of the eight ego-oriented movers do the same, and none of the four pattern-oriented movers do. (There are further three mixers, all ego-oriented, in the sample; they each use 'left' or 'right', as they should.) These numbers are too small for statistical evaluation, but at least they are in full correspondence with the assumptions. If this result receives further confirmation, one would in general find an interaction between linearization type and orientation type after returns to choice nodes. But this interaction does not signal a correlation between two style factors; it rather is a necessary processing consequence *given* these style factors.

It should have become clear by now that difference (iv) between our example subjects, his saying 'to the right', and her saying 'straight on' after returning to the red choice point, can be explained by such an interaction.

4   SEX AND HANDEDNESS

The use of a male versus a female subject as illustrative cases may have created the impression that females are pattern-oriented movers, and males ego-oriented jumpers. Whether or not this would correspond to any of the pet stereotypes of our culture, the simple fact is that the data show no evidence for this. The 30 female and 23 male subjects of our study distribute about equally over the linearization types, and also over the orientation types.

The situation is somewhat different for handedness, however. After finishing the experiment, and thanks to a suggestion of John Marshall, we were able to recover handedness data for 40 of our 53 subjects. These were categorized as 'pure right-handed' (20 cases) or 'different'; the latter category contained five left-handers, and 15 right-handers who claimed to have left-handers among their own or their parents' siblings.

We found no relation whatsoever between handedness and linearization type, but a noteworthy connection appeared between handedness and orientation type. Tables 7 and 8 show the distribution of the 33 out of 34 clear orientation cases for Figure 1, and the 34 out of 46 clear cases for Figures 3 and 4 for whom we had handedess information.

Table 7   Handedness versus orientation type in Figure 1 descriptions

Handedness	Orientation-type	
	Ego-oriented	Pattern-oriented
Pure right-handers	11	5
Different { Left-handers	2	2
Left-handed siblings	5	8

Table 8   Handedness versus orientation-type in Figure 3 and 4 descriptions

Handedness	Orientation-type	
	Ego-oriented	Pattern-oriented
Pure right-handers	14	4
Different { Left-handers	2	1
Left-handed siblings	6	7

Fischer tests for 'pure right-handed' versus 'different' showed marginal significances: $p = 0.08$ for Table 7, and $p = 0.07$ for Table 8. On the basis of these data we should consider the interesting possibility that pure right-handers take a predominantly deictic perspective, i.e. use their own orientation as a basis for the use of deictical terms, whereas genotypic left-handers (whether phenotypic or not) are less inclined to do so: they easily take an intrinsic perspective, using the pattern's orientation for the selection of their directional terms. This may be an indication of their more general approach to spatial orientations in language use.

In conclusion, then, we have reported strong evidence that systematic individual differences exist in the use of deictical terms, which are not so much due to superficial variations in idiolect, but rather to differences in the ways people operate on spatial information. There is, moreover, some indication that these differences may be in part genetically determined.

NOTE

1. One could argue that what we call intrinsic orientation in the present task is in actuality also deictic: it is ego who makes the tour, and at any moment it is the orientation of ego which determines what is straight, left, and right. If, for Figure 1, ego moves from yellow to red, then grey is left of red. If, however, ego moves from pink to red, then grey is right of red. If both are possible, the direction could hardly be called intrinsic to the pattern. Though we agree that the latter is true, we feel that this is at most a difference in degree with more common examples of intrinsic orientation. If a lampshade is said to be ('intrinsically') to the right side of a chair this is only so

because ego has a preferred orientation with respect to the chair. The ambiguous orientation in the above example of Figure 1 is matched by a 'classical' intrinsic case of a couch. If a flat couch is in the middle of a room, it does have intrinsic orientation, but an ambiguous one: a lampshade is right or left of the couch dependent on how ego 'takes place' on the couch. Intrinsic orientation can be ambiguous in this way because it depends crucially on the *interpretation* of the pattern. Only deictic orientation is always unambiguous because it does not depend on such interpretation.

REFERENCES

Klein, W. (1979). Wegauskünfte. *Zeitschrift für Literaturwissenschaft und Linguistik*, **9**, 9–57.

Levelt, W. J. M. (1981). Linearization in describing spatial networks. In S. Peters & E. Saarinen (eds), *Processes, beliefs, and questions*. Dordrecht: Reidel.

Linde, C., & Labov, W. (1975). Spatial networks as a site for the study of language and thought. *Language*, **51**, 924–939.

Miller, G. A., & Johnson-Laird, P. N. (1976). *Language and perception*. Cambridge, Mass.: Harvard University Press.

Munro, A. (1977). *Speech act understanding*. Unpublished doctoral dissertation, University of California, San Diego.

Ullmer-Ehrich, V. (1979). Wohnraumbeschreibungen. *Zeitschrift für Literaturwissenschaft und Linguistik*, **9**, 58–83.

Part 3

GESTURE, DEIXIS, AND ANAPHORA

Speech, Place, and Action
Edited by R. J. Jarvella and W. Klein
©1982 John Wiley & Sons Ltd.

Conceptual Representations in Language Activity and Gesture [1]

DAVID MCNEILL and ELENA LEVY

INTRODUCTION

Conceptual basis of language activity

We use the expression 'conceptual basis' to mean that language is generated directly from patterns of meaning, not passing through a level of grammatical representation. Grammar (in the technical linguistic sense) refers to the object produced as a result of language activity, not the action itself of producing it. In this conceptual approach to language, sentences emerge from conceptual patterns that are adjusted by the speaker to play roles in higher level activities defined by the context of speaking, including the rest of the discourse in which the sentence is embedded. For example, an activity may be to add to the store of information accumulated about some particular thematic referent. The speaker adjusts the meaning pattern so that the new information comes into focus and the presupposed referent is lowered in degree of focus. At the sentence level, the conceptual representations the speaker manipulates in these ways often seem to consist of concrete models of reality. It is as if the speaker were observing or manipulating concrete objects, events, locations, motions, etc. Even when the meaning intended by the speaker is abstract the representation seems to consist of concrete models. For example, the abstract idea of a meaning is represented as an object at a location in 'you're wrong there, at any rate'; and the idea of a narration is represented as an object in motion in 'the story came to a halt'. Such examples are extremely common, but their significance for the psychology of language activity has not been widely appreciated. We propose that concrete models of reality occupy favoured positions in the mental processes of language users. Even when it is possible to describe the meaning of sentences in formulae using smaller units, e.g. semantic primitives (cf. Schank, 1972), this level of description may not provide the correct psychological 'packaging', and may miss important aspects of the speaker's language activity.

271

On the discourse level there appear to be conceptual representations also. For example, the speaker must keep track of the main story line and what is supplemental to the main story line (Hopper, 1979). This discourse property can be represented as a distinction between the centre and the periphery of a space (the centre of a stage versus the side of a stage), and a spatial model can be used for the demaracation of the different functional parts of the discourse. Such a concrete representation may also occupy a favoured position in the speaker's language activity.

The two levels of language activity, sentence and discourse, interact on a moment-by-moment basis. Every sentence must be shaped by the speaker to reflect the sentence's discourse level functioning. In the representation of discourse where there are two spatially separate parts, part of the speaker's meaning will be that the narrative event line is central and the extra-narrative supplemental commentary is peripheral, and this may have an effect on how sentences are shaped (for example, sentences felt to be peripheral will be shaped so as not to connect to the event line).

Our interest in this paper lies in the representations used by speakers at both the sentence and discourse levels of organization and in their interactions.

Gestures as evidence for concrete models

Some gestures seem to reveal concrete models to direct observation. The form of the gesture conveys information that suggests the existence and character of the concrete model with which the speaker is representing the information he conveys in speech. We have found evidence for the organization of language at two levels concurrently. Each level is associated with an apparently different gesture system. Rather than mere ornamentation, these gestures seem to be part of the language generation process itself. The systematic differentiation of gesture systems according to the level of language organization has been cited as evidence for the integration of gestures into language generation as a whole (Kendon, 1972). We agree with the proposal and add to it the idea that what is integrated into language generation are concrete models with which the speaker represents meaning. Gestures are then the signs of these concrete models.

Our evidence shows three types of gesture system: iconix, beats, and metaphorix. These are associated during language generation with two main levels of organization: iconix with narrated events (the main story line), and beats with the extra-narrative commentary that surrounds the main story line. Metaphorix may appear with either narrative or extra-narrative discourse functions.

METHOD

This section presents the method we have evolved for eliciting, identifying, and coding gestures and speech.

Stimulus materials

Gestures were transcribed from six videotaped narrations. In each case, one subject viewed an animated cartoon containing three principal cartoon characters, and consisting essentially of a sequence of independent episodes. Viewing time was approximately seven minutes. The subject was then re-seated in the viewing room, facing a second subject who was unfamiliar with the cartoon, and was asked to narrate the plot. The average length of these narrations was just under five minutes. This task generated a large number of iconic gestures.

Subjects

The six narrators comprised five young adult females and one young adult male. The six listeners were all young adult females.

Coding procedure

Each narration was orthographically transcribed, and then divided into 'episodes'. Narrated episodes were defined as references to objectively delineated scenes in the cartoon itself. Each clause in each subject's narration was then categorized as 'narrative' or 'extra-narrative'. Narrative clauses referred to events actually seen in the cartoon and appeared in a sequential order (relative to surrounding clauses) that was the same as the ordering of the indexed events in the cartoon itself. Extra-narrative clauses were those which did not bear this iconic relationship to the event sequence of the cartoon.

A gesture was defined as any visible movement of the hand (s), excluding 'self-adaptors' (scratching the head, fixing the hair). Each gesture in each narration was classified as either iconic, or as a 'beat'. Gestures were classified as iconic if in their form or manner of execution they seemed to bear a formal similarity to some aspect of the situation described by the accompanying speech; that is, if some observable aspect of the gesture appeared similar in form to some aspect of the event as described by the speaker. Beats are small formless gestures, often quickly made, but the essential characteristic is that they do not appear to be iconic. Although all gestures were categorized, only those accompanying verbs have been used in the analyses.

Iconic gestures and beats were further coded according to physical properties ('gesture features') such as hand configuration, orientation of palm, and direction of movement (see Figure 1). Iconic gestures typically have a 'preparatory phase' preceding the start of the iconic part of the gesture; that is, preceding the 'stroke' (Kendon, 1979). During the preparatory phase, the hand positions itself for the stroke. Following the end of the iconic segment is often a period of 'retraction' during which the hand(s) return to rest, or position themselves for another gesture.

LH:
1. Phase (preparatory, iconic, or retraction)
2. Spatial location (centre or periphery)

AT START –
3. Hand configuration (fingers curled, fingers extended, fist, . . .)
4. Tension (tense, relaxed, . . .)
5. Orientation of palm (palm up, palm down, to left, to right, . . .)
6. Position relative to other hand (tips of fingers touching, palms together, . . .)

AT END –
7. Change in configuration (fingers extended, fingers spread, . . .)
8. Change in orientation of palm (palm rotates clockwise, counterclockwise, . . .)
9. Absolute direction of movement (up, down, to left, to right, . . .)
10. Relative movement (toward other hand, toward self, . . .)
11. Path of movement (straight line, arc, . . .)
12. Quality of movement:
    (a) Rate (fast, slow)
    (b) Evenness (continuous, jerky)
    (c) Cyclicity (reduplicated)
    (d) Length (elongated, abbreviated)
    (e) End marking (+/– end marked)

RH:
Same as LH

Figure 1   *Gesture features*. This is an outline. In the complete list 44 gesture features appear

Data for analyses have been taken from different episodes for iconix and beats. The episodes used in the analysis of iconix were chosen because they evoked the largest number of iconix, and similarly, the data-base for the analysis of beats were those which contained a large number of beats.

In addition to beats and inconix, we noted occurrences of metaphorix. The existence of metaphoric gestures was suggested to us originally by G. Lakoff (personal communication). Like an iconic gesture, a metaphoric gesture is formed but this form does not depict aspects of the situation being described. Rather, the form depicts the vehicle of a metaphor. The gesture is iconically related to this vehicle, not to the meaning, or tenor, of the metaphor (Richards, 1936). Like a verbal metaphor, a gestural metaphor conveys meaning indirectly. An example of a metaphoric gesture is alternately lifting the two hands with the palms cupped upward, in a situation where the verb 'decide' or 'choose' would be appropriate. The metaphoric vehicle in this case for choosing is comparing weights, and the gesture iconically depicts this vehicle.

All transcriptions and codings were carried out by at least two independent observers, and the results reported reflect the consensus of the judgements of these individuals.

FINDINGS

Contrary to an assumption which seems widespread, that gestures are part of a separate system of 'non-verbal communication', only incidentally connected to speech, we find that gestures correlate closely with meaning on several levels of language organization. We present empirical data on these correlations in the first section below for iconix and in a second for beats.

Iconic gestures

According to our definition, an iconic gesture is a formed gesture which depicts in its form or manner of execution aspects of the event or situation being described verbally. This definition applies to gestures that accompany several grammatical categories (at least contentives: nouns, adjectives, adverbs, and verbs). We confine our attention in this paper to the iconic gestures that accompany verbs. In correlating gestures with verb meanings, we consider only the specific senses of verbs which apply to the situation being described; for example, if a speaker used 'fly' to describe an airplane, we would disregard the sense of 'fly' in which movement is by wings flapping (even if this sense is more prominent when the word is considered in isolation). The motivation for this selection of the appropriate senses of verbs should be transparent. We wish to correlate gesture features with mental representations; not with verb meanings as such, but with the representations the verb meanings suggest.

We find that in iconic gestures speakers tend to depict whole scenes. The scenes are reproduced in the gesture in several of their aspects. This contrasts with the verbal (linguistic) descriptions, where speakers characteristically present a more restricted aspect of the scene related (this aspect is also depicted in the gesture). The speaker's choice of words, verbs for example, is constrained by the system of English grammar and its historically in-built manner of dividing and grouping experience with the world. The choice of gestures, in contrast, is much freer and is able to reflect the complexity of the representation of experience.

Correlation of iconic gestures with meaning

We present here an analysis of the features of gesture form and movement that appear to be identified with aspects of the meaning of accompanying verbs. Every iconic gesture which accompanied a verb ($N = 74$) produced by the six narrators in the three scenes was coded for form and movement features according to the coding scheme in Figure 1. We also classified the verbs according to their meanings as used in the narratives. We then correlated the verb meanings with the gesture features. By looking at these correlations we can study systematically the choices of particular verb features the subjects made for iconic depiction and of the particular gesture features they used for these depictions. Included among the iconic gestures were index finger points, which carried 'locational' meaning (presumably location within some conceptual space created by the speaker).

For the verb classification, we adopted 38 meaning features (which we will refer to as 'verb features'). Where possible we made use of previous analyses of verb meanings (Miller & Johnson-Laird, 1976), though often the verbs our subjects produced were not to be found in these earlier analyses. We have added features where necessary. We also tailored our verb features to fit the narrative situations our subjects were describing and eliminated irrelevant senses of verbs.

The result of the comparison of verb features to gesture features is a large table, 38 verb features by 44 gesture features, which shows the number of times gestures with a given gesture feature and verbs with a given verb feature co-occurred. Extracted from this table, Table 1 presents the 14 gesture features and eight verb features which met the criterion of having at least 10 instances occurring in the data.

Though distinctive patterns of iconic gestures appear with different verb features in Table 1, looking first at the number of gestures showing different gesture features (shown at the bottom of the columns in Table 1), we can draw a kind of profile of the typical iconic gesture of our subjects. Many gestures were made with curled fingers, both hands, or the right hand, and left-to-right movements; fewer but still substantial numbers were made with downward movements, reduplication, and the palm facing down; various more specialized gestures were made with movements along straight lines, the two hands moving in the same direction together or alternatingly, the palm facing the self, the index finger extended (pointing), all fingers extended or the hand in a fist, and upward movements.

Gestures and verb features can be correlated either positively or negatively or both. In the positive direction, we observe that a gesture feature tends to appear when a verb has a certain verb feature. In the negative direction, we observe that a gesture feature tends not to appear whenever a verb has a certain verb feature. In such cases, there may be an incompatibility of the

Table 1 Correlation of gesture features with verb features for iconix (shows percentage of gestures in each row that have given gesture feature)

| | Gesture features | | | | | | | | | | | | | | Number of gestures |
Verb features	RH	BH	Fist	Fs curled	Fs extended	IF extended	Palm down	Palm self	BH same	Up	Down	L–R	St line	Redup	
Entrance/exit	0	90	0	70	10	20	10	40	30	0	50	60	20	10	10
Downward	62	31	8	62	8	15	31	15	0	0	54	23	31	0	13
Horizontal	30	57	8	43	24	5	30	19	35	8	16	73	13	35	37
Rotation	58	42	8	50	17	8	17	17	17	17	8	67	25	25	12
Longitudinal	52	35	4	48	17	22	22	22	9	4	22	61	30	30	23
End state	29	67	17	50	25	21	17	17	17	0	46	42	0	21	24
Closure/contact	54	45	27	36	36	18	18	18	0	9	36	9	18	18	11
Use feet	14	57	21	29	21	0	7	7	29	21	21	64	29	43	14
Number of gestures successively	30	37	10	38	12	13	18	13	14	11	21	36	15	21	—

Key: RH means right hand alone; BH means both hands; F means finger; IF means index finger; Palm self means palm facing self; BH same means both hands moving in the same direction or alternating; L–R means movement left to right; St line means movement in a straight line; Redup means reduplication of movement.

gesture and verb feature or some other reason why the gesture feature does not occur.

The names of the verb features in Table 1 are generally self-explanatory. A longitudinal verb implies movement along the longitudinal axis of some track; for example, 'barrel up (the pipe)', 'come along (the wire)', etc. An end state verb describes an action that includes as an integral part reaching some end state. Vendler (1967) called these verbs achievement verbs. For example, the action of catching up to somebody can be said to occur only if one actually catches up to the person. If one doesn't, the action has to be called something else—chasing, for example. 'Catch up to' is an end state verb, whereas 'chase' is not.

The entries in Table 1 show the percentage of the gestures accompanying a given verb feature that had a given gesture feature (percentages of the number of gestures shown at the end of each row). For example, 54% of all gestures that accompanied verbs with a downward meaning included a downward movement, but none included an upward movement.

The following remarks refer to some of the more notable empirical correlations of gestures and meaning found in Table 1.

Downward goes with curled fingers in more than 60% of the gestures and with downward motions in more than 50%. We have observed the former feature in gestures produced by other speakers to depict changes of state that are beyond the control of the participants in the scene (such as falling due to gravity). Rhetoric manuals used to recommend curved fingers when the speaker wanted to emphasize passivity (Austin, 1806).

The downward verb feature does not go with gestures whose meanings are the opposite of downward: upward and the fingers extended (this has the meaning of active participation according to Austin). Downward also does not appear with gestures in which both hands go in the same direction. This gesture seems to have the meaning of parallel motion by two objects, which is not opposed to the downward meaning but happens not to be combined with downward actions in the narrative materials. Finally, downward does not go with reduplicated gestures, and this also seems to be because the meaning of rapid locomotion (with which reduplication co-occurs) does not appear in the narrative materials with downward.

The model suggested by this pattern of correlations contains downward motion, passivity, single objects or participants, and a form of movement not due to locomotion. This model reflects quite accurately the information in the episodes being described.

Horizontal goes with left-to-right movements in more than 70% of the gestures (in contrast to the downward verb feature) and with two-handed movements in nearly 60% of the gestures. Two-handed gestures have various meanings (end state, exit/entrance, etc.), and its correlation with the horizontal meaning reflects the occurrence of these other meanings with horizontal in the narrative materials.

The horizontal verb feature does not go with upward gestures, due to meaning incompatibility. It also does not go with two other gesture features associated with closure and contact (fist and pointing). These features are not opposed to the horizontal meaning but, as before, correspond to meanings that do not appear in the situations containing horizontal movements.

The model suggested by this pattern of correlations contains lateral movements involving two elements of some kind (see discussion below), but not closure or contact; and this model also fits the episodes being described.

End state goes with two-handed gestures. The iconic appropriateness of these gestures is that the concept of an end state involves two phases of an action—the action itself and the new state that it reaches. In some cases the hands are used in a differentiated way to depict the moment of reaching the end state. For example, the left hand moved to the right and touched the right-hand index finger as the speaker said 'is connecting', reproducing the achievement of the end state. This two-handed gesture reproduces (in Vendler's sense) achievements of new world states, and is a microcosm of this form of reality.

Entrance/exit goes with two-handed gestures very strongly. As with end state, the iconic appropriateness of this gesture feature is that the entrance and exit meanings involve two elements—an object or person in motion and an entrance or exit. Sometimes the hands also were used in a differentiated way to show the two elements of the action separately. For example, 'go into Sylvester' was accompanied by this gesture, which shows the position and size of the entrance and the relative direction of the movement:

LH encircles RH space, then RH moves downward along LH palm

Such a gesture suggests a detailed concrete model in which different parts are related to each other as described by the verb feature.

In general, verbs that describe actions where two elements necessarily appear seem to go with two handed gestures. With the end state feature there are two phases; in the closure/contact and use-the-feet-successively features there are two participants; in the entrance/exit feature there is a participant and a reference point. In all of these cases the roles assigned to the two hands can be differentiated and show the two elements of the action separately, and we sometimes observe this.

To summarize Table 1, there is evidence in iconic gestures for various concrete models of the narrative materials. It appears that speakers are able to capture in gestures aspects of whole scenes. That is, the speakers include in the iconic depiction multiple features present in the scene, and exclude features not observed in the scene. This complexity of the representation was evident in the patterns of positive and negative gesture features for the horizontal and downward verb meanings, and in the differentiated gestures for the end state and entrance/exit meanings. In performing these gestures the speakers reproduced the situations they were describing. Such iconic gestures are microcosms set up by the speaker. In this way, they reflect the speaker's concrete representational models of reality.

The following are examples of iconic gestures which depict several aspects of whole scenes:

>she chases him out again
>LH in fist moves down and to the right.

Here the gesture shows the hand of the protagonist grasping an umbrella (the weapon of choice in the narrative materials) and simultaneously the pursuit of the target and/or the swinging of the umbrella. The verb 'chase' underdescribes this scene (omitting the role of the umbrella), although the speaker evidently represented this information in the gesture.

>he makes a very careful blueprint
>BH enact drawing movements in the air

The movements and the position of the gesture in space reproduce the actions of the protagonist as seen in the cartoon. In this example, also, the verb 'make' underdescribes the scene, and the gesture shows considerably more detail.

Discourse function

Correlation of gestures with discourse function   According to our definition, a narrative statement describes an event actually seen in the cartoon and the succession of narrative statements reproduces the chronology of events. All other statements in the discourse are considered to be extra-narrative. We find that narrative statements tend to be accompanied by iconic gestures, while extra-narrative statements lacking the sequentiality constraint tend to be accompanied by more formless gestures, or beats. (We discuss beats in detail in a later section.) Here we only contrast beats and iconix with respect to discourse function. To construct Table 2, each clause in each subject's

Table 2   Relationship of gesture type to narrative function

	Frequency of gesture type			
Narrative function	Iconix	Beats	No gesture	Total
Narrative	62	38	86	186
Extra-narrative	1	30	26	57
Extra-narrative–narrative	11	3	8	22
Total	74	71	120	265

narrative was classified as narrative or extra-narrative in function (or both). Gestures accompanying the verbs in these clauses were then noted as iconix or beats or neither (the latter being clauses where no gesture appeared).

Table 2 shows that beats and iconix are approximately equally frequent in our data, and that narrative statements are three times more frequent than extra-narrative. Iconix are virtually restricted to narrative contexts. Beats occur about equally often in narrative and extra-narrative contexts. When the difference in number of narrative and extra-narrative statements is taken into account, iconix are still much overrepresented in narrative contexts, and beats, we can now see, also are strongly overrepresented in extra-narrative contexts. Narrative–extra-narrative statements are sentences in which both functions are combined. Their gestures seem to distribute as with pure narrative statements.

We explain the abundance of iconic gestures in the narrative event line by reference to the concrete models with which subjects mentally represent the events of the story. The strong association of the extra-narrative surround with beats may also reflect a model of the discourse, in which there are two parts and formed iconic gestures accompany the event sequence and formless beats accompany information supplementary to this sequence.

Correlation of linguistic form with discourse function In our data, extra-narrative statements are likely to include co-referential clauses in which there is a form of 'be' ('it was a cartoon'), 'try' as a complementizing verb ('the whole cartoon is Sylvester of course trying to get Tweety Bird'), and a type of indefinite lexical aspect marker ('whenever', 'anytime') in which no particular occurrence of specific events is implied. These linguistic properties are proportionately overrepresented in extra-narrative sentences and underrepresented in narrative ones ('be' is proportionately seven times more frequent, 'try' 15 times more frequent, and the indefinite types of lexical aspect marker nine times more frequent in extra-narrative sentences). These are syntactic forms whose specific use is to introduce and explain events and characters, and to mark information (as with 'try' and the indefinite aspect markers) which is not part of the narrative event line. Narrative sentences in our data, on the other hand, are likely to include action verbs ('and the granny comes and throws him off the window sill down back to the ground') and a definite type of lexical aspect marker that implies the occurrence of specific events ('everytime', 'A starts to do X'). Action verbs are proportionately more than twice as frequent in the narrative event line, and the definite type of lexical aspect marker appears only in narrative sentences.

From the point of view of shaping sentences for discourse function, narrative sentences are geared to describe sequences of events in the correct chronological order, and we see that their linguistic properties are adjusted to perform this function. Extra-narrative sentences, on the other hand, are geared to present supplemental information of various kinds not part of the narrative sequences—scene introductions and descriptions, summaries, explanations, etc.—and their linguistic properties also are adjusted to perform these functions. This distinction between sentences that preserve and those that do not preserve sequentiality is equivalent to Hopper's between foregrounded and backgrounded information in narratives (Hopper, 1979).

Point of view with iconic gestures

The expression 'point of view' means emphasizing some parts of an episode over others (cf. Kuno, 1976). Within an episode details are equal in the sense that one can attend to any of them. By taking a particular point of view some details will be emphasized over others. It may be inherently part of forming a concrete model of reality that one adopts a specific point of view.

In the iconic gestures of the speaker to be described in this section, different points of view were expressed systematically. We describe the performance of this single speaker, because it shows remarkable features.

The subject, J, was fulfilling the task of re-telling to another person a comic book story which he (J) had just previously read.[2] An example of a gesture that reflects the agent's point of view is the arm extended upward and forward, the hand forming a grip, then the arm moving downward and toward the self; this appeared with the narrative statement, 'and then he bends it way back' (in which 'it' refers to a tree). The gesture iconically depicts the movement of the agent. For the same event a gesture reflecting the point of view of the patient (the tree) would have been different; for example, the arm and hand extended upward and moving downward together, re-enacting the movement of the tree (omitting the agent's grip). An example of such a patient point of view gesture is the right hand extended laterally to the left and rotating around the axis of the arm in a series of circles; this appeared with the statement, 'he finished powering the dynamo', and the gesture represents the movement of the armature of the dynamo.

The difference between the agent and patient point of view gestures illustrated in these examples is systematic with J. When the point of view adopted was that of the agent of a transitive verb, the gesture depicted the agent's hand performing the transitive verb action; when it was that of the patient of a transitive verb, the gesture depicted the entire patient undergoing the transitive verb action. The agent point of view (for the actions that figured in the comic book story) typically involved grip hand postures. The patient point of view always involved a schematic depiction of the entire patient with an extended or curved hand and no other features of the patient shown.

One of the remarkable features of J's iconic gestures appears when we turn to intransitive verbs. For example, the hand with fingers extended moves upward and away from the self in a single thrust as J said 'she dashes out of the house'. Gestures of this type regularly appeared with intransitive verbs, and depict the action from the agent's point of view by showing the change of state undergone by the agent. Notice that the intransitive verb gesture is like the patient gesture with transitive verbs; that is, it is a schematic depiction of the entire intransitive verb agent undergoing the action. Within J's iconic gesture system, the agents of intransitive verbs and the patients of transitive verbs are treated in the same way; the gesture depicts the entire person or thing undergoing the action. Treated uniquely are the agents of transitive verbs, which are only partially depicted through their hands performing the action.

Language systems in which the patients of transitive verbs and the agents of intransitive verbs are treated alike and both treated differently from the agents of transitive verbs, are called ergative (the agent of the transitive verb is said to be in the ergative case; cf. Silverstein, 1976). An ergative structure manifests itself in J's expression of point of view through iconic gestures. This means of organization, of course, existed side by side with his speech, which followed the accusative pattern of English (i.e. the agents of transitive and intransitive verbs are treated alike and the patients of transitive verbs are in the unique accusative case). Evidently the gap between the ergative and accusative modes of organization for expressing meaning is not as wide as is usually believed, psychologically speaking, for here is one speaker who spontaneously adopted both modes at once.

Psychologically, the accusative mode of organization emphasizes the point of view of the performer of the action, while the ergative mode emphasizes the receiver. Seen as the result of adopting different points of view toward events, either point of view seems fully available to English speakers.

Once one is alerted to the ergative point of view, one can find other instances of it within English grammar itself. Some events can be described either by using a transitive verb or an intransitive verb; the speaker, choosing one, expresses a point of view. For example, 'spins' can be used transitively as in 'he spins it', to emphasize the role of the performer of the action; or it can be used intransitively as in 'it spins', to emphasize the role of the receiver. For the function of expressing the point of view of the speaker, transitive and intransitive agents are therefore not necessarily the same within the accusative speech system itself. In fact, it is the transitive patient and intransitive agent that are the same in this example. This analysis again shows that ergative and accusative modes of organization may reflect the same underlying psychological phenomena.

Timing of iconic gestures

The claim has been made that gestures precede and forecast speech to come (Butterworth & Beattie, 1976). Though the questions we put forth in this paper do not depend on the timing of gestures, we can look at our data with this question in mind.

Immediately we must consider how gestures and speech *can* be compared temporally. It might appear that if a gesture depicts an action it should be compared to the verb. However, this decision is arbitrary and we think fundamentally misconceived. A gesture that depicts the point of view of the agent may begin well before the verb and should not be called an 'anticipation'. Such a gesture is not related only to the verb but to the entire clause. Trying to refer gestures to specific points in sentences (such as their verbs) imposes an artificial speech-like segmentation. While the information in sentences is distributed over several words, in a gesture this information can be concentrated at a single point.

Table 3 Temporal distribution of onset of iconic portion of gesture relative to verb onset

	Gesture before verb (ms)							Gesture after verb (ms)				
	600– 501	500– 401	400– 301	300– 201	200– 101	100– 1	0	1– 100	101– 200	201– 300	301– 400	401– 500
Number of gestures	2	0	3	2	3	8	1	6	5	2	3	1

Nonetheless, even when we arbitrarily time gestures in relation to specific linguistic segments (verbs), the claim of Butterworth & Beattie is not supported. In our data from J, it is true that half the gestures precede verbs; but the other half follow by the same distance; and the mean of the entire distribution is only 3 milliseconds in the gesture-precedes-verb direction. Table 3 gives the distribution of the onsets of the iconic segment of all gestures depicting actions which J produced, in relation to the onset of the corresponding verbs. Only present tense verbs are included. We felt that the best test of the temporal relation between gesture and speech could be made by eliminating past and future tense verbs, since it is possible that, due to the meaning of these two tenses, gestures might tend to precede past tense and follow future tense forms. (In fact, non-present tense verbs were few in number in J's narrative.) The data-base, then, was composed of an exhaustive sample of all iconic gestures accompanying present tense verbs. The measurements were made by means of a frame counter recorded on the video image. An oscilloscope trace of J's speech also was recorded on the video image. Thus it was possible to compare frame counter numbers at the onsets of the gesture and verb. The average error of measurement with this method is one-half the duration of a video frame, or $8\frac{1}{3}$ milliseconds.

Beats

According to our definition, beats are small rapidly made gestures with indefinite form that do not depict any aspect of the verbally described situation. We present in this section an analysis of beats; their gesture features and the verb features with which they appear.

Table 2, earlier, showed that beats are strongly associated with extra-narrative statements lacking the sequentiality constraint of the narrative. Beats thus demarcate discourse into functionally different parts, but do not clearly reflect the speaker's models for representing the sequence of events in the narrative.

We present here an analysis of every beat which accompanied a verb ($N = 76$) produced by the six narrators in the three scenes selected as strongly evoking this type of gesture. As in the analysis of iconix, we coded the gestures for form and movement features using the scheme in Figure 1. We also classified the verb meanings with the verb features used previously in the analysis of iconic gestures plus several additional features.

The result of the comparison is again a large (in fact, larger) table, 53 verb features by 44 gesture features. Table 4 is extracted from this table and shows the co-occurrence of the 15 gesture features and five verb features that had 10 or more instances in the data.

One notices immediately the absence of most verb features appearing in Table 1. Only one of the verb features that appear in the iconic analysis (end state) was used often enough to meet the frequency threshold for verbs accompanying beats. The other verb features used frequently (not surprisingly) are those likely to be involved in extra-narrative statements. Verbs with the activity feature (Vendler, 1967) are continuous in time but not tied to any definite time and do not include an end state. Examples are 'act like', 'make like', and 'include'. Verbs with the goal-directed feature relate to achieving goals (not to be confused with end states). Example are 'act like', 'climb', and 'steal'. Most verbs that apply to human or human-like subjects have this feature (though not 'end up' or 'overhear'), but not so many that including it in Table 4 is trivial; and it is relevant, since extra-narrative statements often explicitly describe goals. Verbs with the complex action feature describe actions that are carried out with complex, not well-defined movements, such as 'act like', 'foil', and 'mug'.

The number of instances of each gesture feature (the bottom of each column) provides a profile of the typical beat, and this profile can be compared to the profile of iconic gestures given previously. The largest number of beats were made with the palm facing down and the left hand; a smaller number were made with the fingers curled or extended and separated, rotation of the palm, and movements of slight extent, some upward.

The typical beat thus looks different from the typical iconic gesture.

Table 4 Correlation of gesture features with verb features for beats (shows percentage of gestures in each row that have given gesture feature)

Verb features					Gesture features											
	RH	LH	BH	Fs curled	Fs extended and separated	Palm down	Palm self	Palm rotates	Up	Down	L–R	Redup	Slight	Fs extend	Fs spread	Number of gestures
End state	33	56	11	44	41	67	4	33	37	52	30	15	15	26	19	27
Activity	14	71	14	52	38	86	10	38	52	24	48	14	38	19	10	21
Goal directed	30	50	21	42	34	50	3	39	39	39	34	18	37	16	13	38
Complex action	27	47	27	33	27	40	0	13	40	13	20	20	20	13	0	15
Cognitive state/ process	46	54	0	54	38	77	0	31	31	38	46	15	15	15	15	13
Stative	14	79	7	0	36	93	0	43	64	29	50	7	14	21	7	14
Number of gestures	20	44	12	34	27	47	10	28	28	26	22	14	27	14	10	—

Key: RH means right hand; LH means left hand; BH means both hands; F means finger; Palm self means palm facing self; Palm down means palm facing down; L–R means left to right; Redup means reduplicated movement; Slight means a movement of small extent.

Whereas iconix are structured and graphic, beats are simple movements in which the hand briefly springs to life (extending, spreading, rotating to the side, or simply rising) and then subsides. Typical iconic gestures are performed with greater expenditure of energy than beats. If we examine the separate verb features of Table 4, we find generally the same patterns of high and low frequency of gesture features appearing with each verb feature, and this curve generally follows the pattern of the frequency of beats overall shown at the bottom of the table. In other words, with different verb meanings there is little systematic variation from the standard form of a beat. In contrast is Table 1, for iconix, in which the different verb features often have quite distinctive patterns of frequency. Iconix, in other words, have different gestural forms depending on the verb meaning.

Parallel to Table 1, the entries in Table 4 give the percentage of gestures accompanying each verb feature that had a given gesture feature. As expected, beats show no correlations with verb meanings that can be recognized as iconic. This absence of correlation is most apparent with the end state feature, which in iconix was positively correlated with use of both hands and in beats is negatively correlated with the same gesture feature. Rather than control by the structure of the event being described, beats are controlled by other properties related to discourse structure (as shown in Table 2). The strongest positive gesture feature is the palm facing down, but its overall frequency in beats is so high that its co-occurrence with any particular verb feature is hard to interpret. We are unable to see any pattern in the set of negative gesture features.

Lateralization of gesture types

Table 1 shows that iconix were performed either with two hands (37 instances) or the right hand (30 instances). The left hand was rarely used, only seven times. Table 4 shows a quite unexpected reversal of this tendency for beats; they are largely performed with the left hand (44 instances).[3] The right hand was used for beats half as often (20 instances) and two hands only a quarter as often (12 instances). One can speculate that beats, accompanying extra-narrative non-sequential statements, are performed with the left hand to emphasize the distance of the extra-narrative from the narrative. In any case, this result implies some restriction on the generality of Kimura's (1973) finding that right-handed speakers perform gestures largely with the right hand; this apparently is true only if the gestures are iconix accompanying narrative statements.

To study this phenomenon in more detail, we examined the entire narration produced by each subject (not only the episodes selected previously). As it happens, two of the subjects are left-handed, and we present their data separately. As shown in Table 5, right-handed subjects used the right hand

Table 5   Lateralization of gesture types

Handedness of subject	Total number of gestures							
	Iconix				Beats			
	Right	Left	Both	Total	Right	Left	Both	Total
Right handed	92	19	81	192	28	53	47	128
Left handed	24	27	42	93	9	49	24	82

for iconix nearly five times more frequently than the left hand. For beats they shifted to the left hand, which they used twice as frequently as the right hand. Use of both hands together was proportionately the same for iconix and beats. Left-handed subjects used the left and right hands equally often for iconix, and shifted for beats to the left hand, which they used five times as frequently as the right hand. Left-handed subjects used both hands together proportionately somewhat more often for iconix than for beats.

Thus right-handed subjects seem to be lateralized to the right for iconix and to the left for beats, and left-handed subjects are not lateralized for iconix and are strongly lateralized to the left for beats. This overall result suggests some interesting lateralization phenomena, but the situation is seen to be complex when we look at individual subjects' performances. We find, among right-handed subjects, two who show extreme shifts from nearly exclusive use of the right hand for iconix to nearly exclusive use of the left hand for beats (Table 6). The other right-handed subjects show a right-handed preference for both beats as well as iconix (though stronger for iconix). Thus, not all right-handed subjects shift to the left hand for beats; but of those who do, in our sample, the shift is almost complete.

The left-handed subjects also show different individual patterns. One subject writes with an uninverted hand, thought to be an indication of stronger lateralization towards the right (Levy & Reid, 1978), and had a consistent

Table 6   Lateralization of gesture types in two right-handed subjects

Subject	Total number of gestures							
	Iconix				Beats			
	Right	Left	Both	Total	Right	Left	Both	Total
Subject 1 (male)	14	4	6	24	2	21	5	28
Subject 2 (female)	21	4	24	49	1	22	17	40

preference for use of the left hand for both iconix and beats (though stronger for beats: the left hand was used 13 times as frequently as the right for beats, compared to twice as frequently for iconix). The other left-handed subject writes with an inverted hand, thought to be an indication of partial lateralization to the left, and shows a preference for the *right* hand for iconix (used twice as often as the left hand) and equal use of right and left hands for beats.

From our present results it is not possible to tell whether it is the form or the function of gestures that determines when they are made with the left hand by right-handed subjects. For example, beats may be made with the left hand because they characteristically involve less energy. Alternatively, background statements may be accompanied by left hand gestures because they are distant from the main line of the discourse. These factors can be disentangled if the discourse is one of discussion or exposition. In such a discourse, explanations, summarizations, etc., become the foreground, and narrative descriptions which may be used for illustrative purposes become part of the background. Are iconix still made with the right hand and both hands, and beats with the left hand in this genre, or do the types of gesture exchange places?

Metaphoric gestures

A metaphoric gesture according to our definition iconically depicts the vehicle of a metaphor. Unlike a true iconic gesture, a metaphoric gesture does not directly reproduce its meaning (its tenor, which may be in any case unreproducible), but conveys this meaning indirectly, as in a verbal metaphor, through the vehicle. We give here several examples of metaphoric gestures. Possibly because the narrative materials are so concrete and action dominated, relatively few metaphoric gestures appear in the narrations of the six subjects who have provided most of the previous data. We have supplemented their material with examples from other sources. One of these is J, whose iconic gestures were described earlier. The other is a videotaped technical discussion between two professional mathematicians (McNeill, 1979).

An important metaphor or rather family of metaphors of English is the 'conduit metaphor' (Reddy, 1979), a metaphor about language, meaning, and communication. It is very widespread in daily speech. In the conduit metaphor, language is regarded as a container, meaning as a substance placed into or removed from the container, and communication is the sending of language containers (full or not!) over a conduit to a destination. This metaphor is the source of a number of gestures.

Within the conduit metaphor are several sub-metaphors. The following show gestures which iconically depict the vehicles of some of these sub-metaphors.

(1) *Concepts are palpable substances* (cf. 'lay it out on the table', 'where did you get that idea?', etc.):

you just get one thing that way?

right hand curved, up high in front of the face, fingers and thumb forward and apart (looks like holding onto something)

The 'thing' referred to is an abstract mathematical object. The gesture, however, depicts a concrete object of some sort which is shown to exist but is not in motion or altering from. This statement was followed immediately by the statement 'in order to get the finite group scheme' from the other speaker (facing the first) in which the same gesture was made with the *left* hand, as if the same object were being grasped first by one speaker, then the other.

(2) *Concepts can be transmitted along a conduit* (cf. 'I gave him that idea', 'it's hard to get that idea across', etc.):

you take the full linear dual

both hands extended, move downward (looks as if presenting an object to the other person)

In this case the gesture depicts an object in motion, as if along the conduit.

(3) *Speech is a container* (cf. 'words full/empty of meaning', 'I can't get these ideas into words', etc.):

as I say

both hands form cups, fingers curled and palms up

The gesture depicts two containers.

(4) *Concepts are brought out of containers* (cf. 'this idea comes out of an old tradition', 'this idea arises in the second paragraph,' etc.):

the co-multiplication that arises

right hand forms cup at face level

The gesture seems to show the object rising.

Besides the conduit metaphor are other metaphors such as the following:

Understanding is seeing (cf. 'I see your point', etc.; from Lakoff & Johnson, 1980):

I see another proof in it

right hand index finger points forward and down

The gesture appears to point to an object in space (or possibly represents the process of looking).

Choosing is weighing (cf. 'on the other hand', 'weigh the alternatives', etc.):

> trying to figure out what to do

> both hands form cups, alternating up and down

The gesture seems to involve the hands hefting two objects.

An argument, proof, experiment, book, etc., is a journey (cf. 'our findings', 'we began with the following problem'):

> start with an affine group scheme

> both hands, fingers extended, push forward (looks like either pushing on an object or simulating forward motion)

In addition to the journey metaphor, there is a metaphor according to which an argument, proof, experiment, book, etc., is a machine. We have no examples in our materials of this metaphor, though they are easy to construct; for example, 'the results of the experiment' (thus in our own paper we have chosen the journey metaphor over the machine metaphor; the present section is called 'findings', not 'results'; one can speculate on the passion of experimental psychology for 'results').

Temptation is a tractional force (cf. 'in the grip of a vice', 'I was drawn to the theatre', etc.):

> so he lures the guy's monkey away

> left hand in grip moves toward self

In the cartoon, there was no direct contact between the two characters; the gesture appears to depict the metaphoric vehicle.

Many verbal metaphors represent abstract ideas with concrete vehicles. Though the exact mechanism by which metaphors convey meaning is in dispute (see the discussions in Sacks, 1978; Ortony, 1979), there is no doubt that the meaning of a metaphor goes beyond the direct literal meaning of the vehicle. Nonetheless, the appearance of metaphors in gestures seems to establish that metaphoric vehicles are part of the speaker's representations. In this respect they support the arguments of Lakoff and Johnson.

In terms of discourse function, metaphoric gestures appear both with narrative and expository speech. Examples of the first function are the metaphor of temptation as a tractional force and of choosing as weighing; examples of the second function are the conduit metaphors in the mathematics discussion.

THEORY

Our evidence shows a close connection between the form of gestures and the organization of speech. We interpret this to mean that concrete conceptual representations (or models) are involved at different levels of speech organization. What can we say about these models?

A theory of the conceptual basis of language shows how language can be generated directly from patterns of meaning. The generation process is not routed through grammar at some stage. Conceptually based theories and iconic gestures have a close almost symbiotic relationship. The theories can explain the iconic gestures and the gestures can provide evidence for the theories.

The notion of the conceptual basis of language activity contrasts with other theories of language production such as Garrett's (1975), Fromkin's (1971), or MacNeilage's (1970). To take Garrett's theory as the most complete, according to it the expression of meaning in speech involves passing through a series of steps. Each step corresponds to a different level of linguistic representation, and all the steps together correspond to the full grammatical representation of the sentence (underlying structure, surface structure, phonetic spelling). To produce a sentence means finding successive mappings of one level onto the next until, finally, a representation is reached that can be input for control over the speech musculature. The data this theory was designed to explain are various kinds of speech errors.

In contrast, a theory of the conceptual basis of language attempts to explain how speech can be generated directly from meaning patterns in the absence of grammatical structure. In the conceptually based theory described in McNeill (1979), the basic representations out of which speech emerges are concrete images co-ordinated with actions; these images are called sensory-motor. A sensory-motor image is a concrete model of reality. According to this theory, iconic gestures provide information concerning what is in sensory-motor images, or concrete models. As we have seen in our data, there are concrete models for specific situations. There was a model, for example, of passive downward motion of a single object in which movement is not due to locomotion. Such a conceptual model can be the basis of a syntagma, or single integrated output of speech. In the repertoire of speakers, a very large number of specific concrete models is assumed.

The theory traces the sensory-motor images of speakers back to ontogenetically primitive stages of early childhood and shows how they continue to play a role in generating language for adult speakers. Sensory-motor images are extended to abstract meanings and are present in the mental representations involved in adult language activity. This process is called semiotic extension. Through semiotic extension, abstract meanings are treated by the language system as if they were events or objects able to change state, move, be at a location, have a size and weight, etc. In the examples mentioned previously, 'you're wrong there, at any rate' and 'the story came to a halt', the models of an object at a location and object in motion are used for the abstract ideas of meaning and narrative. Metaphors and metaphoric gestures are a type of semiotic extension in which the vehicle of the metaphor is a sign for a more abstract meaning. But the process of semiotic extension is regarded as more general and involves higher level (sentential) structures as well. For details, see the discussion in McNeill (1979).

The advantage to the speaker of sensory-motor models for representing meaning is that they are also part of motor action. They are simultaneously part of the representation of meaning and the co-ordination of action, and in this respect the sensory-motor level is unique. What is necessary for the smooth well-ordered flow of speech is that the speaker be able to use cognitive schemas to organize the processes of speech articulation. Together with the concept of semiotic extension the duality of sensory-motor models provides a route from meaning at all levels to the realm of motor control, as required for an explanation of speech output. It is for this reason, we suppose, that concrete models play a major role in language generation.

At the level of sensory-motor representations, gestures and language generation are not really distinguishable. Iconic gestures, in this theory, are windows onto the process by which meaning joins speech motor action control. Iconic gestures show a crucial element of speech itself. We see (through these windows) that concrete models are specific and detailed, and embody a particular point of view. The corresponding motor programmes (syntagmas) must be equally specific where they meet these models.

What factors influence the speaker's choice and manipulation of concrete models? One factor which filters down to the level of motor control comes from the contextual surround of language activity. The previous discourse context, which 'sets the stage' from the vantage point of the thematic or main characters of the discourse, influences the speaker's point of view at the level of the individual utterance. At the foundation of the utterance, this induces conceptual reorganizations. However, the speaker is always free, at any moment of speaking, to adopt any point of view on the information being presented. While the discourse influences sentence generation, it does not absolutely control it; we view the process of choosing and manipulating language generation as a constant interplay between preceding contextual influences (for example, on choice of point of view) and on-going, immediate actions at the local, utterance level.

DISCUSSION

The research described in this paper is merely a start. We wish to describe in this section some of the directions we foresee the research taking in the future.

We plan to try materials that are less graphic; for example, route instructions, directions for assembling or using equipment, reasoning, etc. The narrative materials in the present study are extremely simple and graphic, characteristics chosen in order to have iconic gestures that are identifiable, but this also has the effect of reducing the disparity between the gestures and the corresponding verbal descriptions. Even so, we found examples of gestures that more richly depicted scenes than the accompanying clauses did, and we assume that greater disparities are possible.

Also, we plan to try stories without the utterly linear plot structure of cartoons; more hierarchical stories with more intricate chronology and thematic organization.

We intend to carry out experiments on the communicative effect of gestures (cf. Duncan & Fiske, 1977). For example, are observers able to distinguish the functional significance of beats and iconix? Can they identify on the basis of iconic gestures alone the sentences that originally accompanied the gestures (given alternative sentences that contrast on verb meaning features)?

A goal of our future research is further investigation of the influence of discourse context on the formation of conceptual representations; the interplay between the global, discourse-generated point of view (the overall point of view of the discourse), and the local point of view taken by individual utterances.

Finally, we intend to initiate studies of the genesis of the different types of gesture—iconix, beats, metaphorix, and other modes such as deixis—in children. Preliminary observations suggest that at age 9 or 10 years deixis and iconix are well developed but beats are still quite rare.

NOTES

1. We wish to thank Laura Pedelty and Debra Stephens for assisting in the transcription, coding, and analysis of the data; Nobuko B. McNeill for reading and commenting on the manuscript; and NIMH and The Spencer Foundation for financial support.

2. We are grateful to William Marslen-Wilson for permission to analyse this narration. The same narration is analysed from another point of view in the paper by Marslen-Wilson, Levy and Tyler in this volume.

3. This shift was first noted by Laura Pedelty.

REFERENCES

Austin, G. (1806). *Chironomia, or a treatise on rhetorical delivery*. London.

Butterworth, B., & Beattie, G. (1976). Gesture and silence as indicators in speech. Unpublished paper, University of Cambridge.

Duncan, S., & Fiske, D. W. (1977). *Face-to-face interaction: research, methods, and theory*. Hillsdale, N. J.: Lawrence Erlbaum Associates.

Fromkin, V. (1971). The non-anomalous nature of anomalous utterances. *Lanugage*, **47**, 27–52.

Garrett, M. (1975). The analysis of sentence production. In G. Bower (ed.), *Psychology of learning and motivation*, Vol. 9. New York: Academic Press.

Hopper, P. (1979). Aspect and foregrounding in discourse. In *Syntax and semantics*, Vol. 12. New York: Academic Press.

Kendon, A. (1972). Some relationships between body motion and speech. In A. Siegman & B. Pope (eds.), *Studies in dyadic communication*. New York: Pergamon.

Kendon, A. (1979). Gesticulation and speech: two aspects of the process of utterance. In M. R. Key (ed.), *Relationship between verbal and nonverbal communication*. The Hague: Mouton.

Kimura, D. (1973). Manual activity speaking—I. Right-handers. *Neuropsychologia*, 11, 45–50.

Kuno, S. (1976). Subject, theme, and the speaker's empathy—a re-examination of relativization phenomena. In C. N. Li (ed.), *Subject and topic*. New York: Academic Press.

Lakoff, G., & Johnson, M. (1980). *Metaphors we live by*. Chicago: University of Chicago Press.

Levy, J., & Reid, M. (1978). Variations in cerebral organization as a function of handedness, hand posture in writing, and sex. *Journal of Experimental Psychology: General*, 2, 119–144.

MacNeilage, P. F. (1970). Motor control of serial ordering of speech. *Psychological Review*, 77, 182–196.

McNeill, D. (1979). *The conceptual basis of language*. Hillsdale, N. J.: Lawrence Erlbaum Associates.

Miller, G. A., & Johnson-Laird, P. N. (1976). *Language and perception*. Cambridge, Mass.: Harvard University Press.

Ortony, A. (ed.), (1979). *Metaphor and thought*. London: Cambridge University Press.

Reddy, M. J. (1979). The conduit metaphor—a case of frame conflict in our language about language. In A. Ortony (ed.), *Metaphor and thought*. London: Cambridge University Press.

Richards, I. A. (1936). *Philosophy of rhetoric*. New York: Oxford University Press.

Sacks, S. (ed.) (1978). *On metaphor*. Chicago: University of Chicago Press.

Schank, R. C. (1972). Conceptual dependency: a theory of natural language understanding. *Cognitive Psychology*, 3, 552–631.

Silverstein, M. (1976). Hierarchy of features and ergativity. In R. M. W. Dixon (ed.), *Grammatical categories in Australian languages*. New York: Humanities Press.

Vendler, Z. (1967). *Linguistics in philosophy*. Ithaca, N.Y.: Cornell University Press.

Speech, Place, and Action
Edited by R. J. Jarvella and W. Klein
© 1982 John Wiley & Sons Ltd.

From Gesture to Sign: Deixis in a Visual-gestural Language[1]

URSULA BELLUGI and EDWARD S. KLIMA

The primary focus of this book is on space, time, and person in the speech setting, how these concepts make their way into language, and how their linguistic expression interacts with a speaker's gestures and other actions. In languages studied to date, speech and gestures can be clearly distinguished: words and gestures are expressed in different modalities and thus are naturally separable. In the research we report here, we take a rather different point of departure. We examine manual gestures which have become forged into linguistic systems: languages which have arisen in the visual-manual (rather than vocal-auditory) modalities.

In the past decade, it has become clear that there are primary gestural systems, passed down from one generation of deaf people to the next, that have taken their own course of development as autonomous languages. Our research focuses primarily on one such system, American Sign Language (ASL), the language learned by deaf children of deaf parents, which is the common form of communication used by deaf native signers among themselves across the United States. We have found that American Sign Language is a primary visual-manual linguistic system, not based on, nor derivative from, any form of English. Signed languages vary from one country to another: the signed language used by deaf people of deaf parents in Great Britain, for example, is mutually incomprehensible with that used in the United States, even though the written language of the two countries is the same. Signed languages, just as spoken languages, have their own internal mechanisms for relating visual form with meaning. (See Stokoe, 1972, 1980; Liddell, 1977; Siple, 1978; Klima & Bellugi, 1979; Wilbur, 1979; Lane & Grosjean, 1980; Bellugi & Studdert-Kennedy, 1980; Ahlgren & Bergman, 1980.)

American Sign Language, for example, has the same expressive power as English and is fully translatable with spoken English, yet it is an autonomous language. There are classes of signs which have no counterpart in English (size-and-shape specifiers, classifiers); there is a rich system of morphological

processes—compounding processes, derivational and inflectional processes—which are inherent to ASL and bear no relationship to morphological
processes in English. In overall typology, ASL (unlike English) is a heavily
inflective language: there are inflectional distinctions for marking person on
verbs, for number, for temporal aspect, temporal focus, and distributional
aspect which are unrelated to any distinctions made in English morphology.
At all levels there are grammatical devices in ASL that are analogous in
function to those of spoken languages.

But many of the formal devices that ASL has developed make use of
possibilities either not available or not so used in the vocal-auditory modality
of spoken languages. For example, conforming with the unique spatial characteristics of this visual-gestural language, its morphological and syntactic
devices make structured use of space and movement, nesting basic sign forms
in spatial patterns or within complex contours of movement. ASL exhibits
underlying principles of formal organization that are strikingly similar to
those found in spoken languages despite the difference in transmission modalities.

Aspects of this visual-gestural linguistic system appear radically different
(at least at first glance) from comparable aspects of spoken languages. Unlike
spoken languages, for example, many symbols and symbolic processes in ASL
have their source in an attempt to represent experience (shapes, objects,
actions) directly in the hands. This is perhaps most evident in the way deictic
terms are expressed; several distinctions are made by pointing to what is in
the immediate context of a situation. However, the grammatical mechanisms
developed within the language for expressing anaphoric reference are opaque,
and rely on a variety of spatial devices, involving systematic manipulation
of space.

Signed languages, then, pose rather different questions and raise different
issues from those addressed generally throughout this book. In a language
system based on gesture, how do language and context interact? And what
are the mechanisms by which utterances are abstracted from, separated from,
the discourse situation? What are some of the mechanisms used for talking
about what is *not* present in the immediate context?

Before the recent decade of research on signed languages, the answers to
such questions were by no means obvious. The available literature on signed
languages generally stressed only the icons and images behind the global
forms of signs. We read that sign language is 'a collection of vague and loosely
defined pictorial gestures'; that it is pantomime; that 'sign language deals
mainly with material objects, dreads and avoids the abstract'. As recently as
1975, in a book called *Thinking and language*, Greene remarks on

'the crudity of sign language for expressing abstract relationships. Even deaf and
dumb humans who rely entirely on sign languages find it cumbersome to make

complicated abstract statements because of the lack of subtle grammatical inflections . . . it is easier to stick to obvious remarks which are clear in the immediate
context' (Greene, 1975, p. 78).

These views, as we shall indicate, are quite inappropriate with respect to ASL,
but they do suggest that interesting issues with respect to signed languages
have to do not only with how the speech setting is co-ordinated with language,
but also the more traditional issues of how language has become abstracted
from the speech setting.

The system of person deixis in ASL gives us a particularly striking entry into
this question. The word *deixis* itself derives from the Greek word for 'indicating', and deixis in spoken languages is considered a verbal surrogate for
pointing; in ASL, instead, it *is* pointing. The grammatical category of person
is defined with respect to participant roles in discourse; first person is used by
speaker to refer to himself, and in ASL, the signer points to his own torso;
second person refers to addressee, and in ASL it is realized by pointing
toward the torso of the addressee. These pronominal signs in ASL are, in fact,
the same as the pointing gestures that hearing people sometimes use to supplement their words non-verbally. We may say, 'I mean *you*' while pointing at
a specific person to single him out. What is paralinguistic with respect to a
spoken language, then, is a lexical item within the context of a fully developed
gestural language.

Such deictic terms form the underpinnings of a variety of linguistic differentiations involving person reference, definiteness, verb agreement, grammatical relations, and the complex system of aspectual and numerosity inflections
of ASL. We will describe the formal devices that ASL has developed to
express such distinctions. In this context, we will also consider aspects of the
acquisition of this system by young deaf children of deaf parents, searching
for clues to the nature of the underlying system from the way in which children acquire it.

DEICTIC TERMS IN ASL

Pointing in ASL performs several syntactic and semantic functions. The
major syntactic function is as part of the pronominal reference system of
ASL, serving the same functions as personal pronouns, definite articles,
demonstratives, and locative proforms in English and other spoken languages. For deictic pronouns, pointing serves to index the referent; that is, to
point out the referent in the real world context of the discourse. Indices for
non-present referents are established at specific loci in the signing space, as
we shall describe.

The basic deictic contrasts for the grammatical category of person involve
pointing to self, to addressee, to non-addressed third person—(ME),[2]

(YOU), (IT). Different handshapes specify distinctions such as personal pronoun (YOU), possessive (YOUR), emphatic forms (SELF), and honourific forms. Number differentiations are made with other changes in handshape and/or movement to indicate distinctions such as 'two of us', 'two of them', 'three of us', 'three of them', 'to them', 'to each of them', 'to certain ones', 'to members of a group including a signer', 'to members of a group not including signer', and so forth.

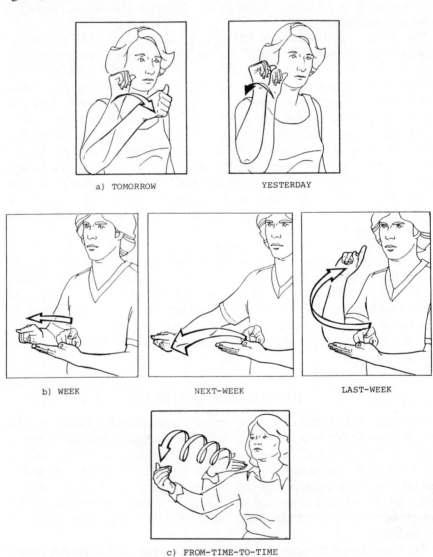

Figure 1   Some ASL expressions for time reference

Aspects of the system for referring to place and time are described in Frishberg (1973), Friedman (1975), and Klima & Bellugi (1979). Past and future reference is made, for example, along a line that moves forward or backward from anchored points with respect to the signer: TOMORROW moves forward from the cheek; YESTERDAY moves backward from the same place (see Figure 1(a)). Signs for calendric time are made with the hands in the neutral space in front of the torso (MINUTE, HOUR, DAY, WEEK, YEAR). Time relative to some signs (e.g. WEEK) moves forward and backward from the spatial locus of the sign; Figure 1(b) shows the basic sign WEEK and the sign forms meaning 'next week' and 'last week'. There are other ways in which the expression of temporal contrasts is spatialized in ASL: in describing an event prior to the time of reference in an utterance, a signer may move the locus of the signs to a space closer to his body. To indicate the temporal contour of events, the bent hand moves in distinctive spatial contours along a specific line in front of the signer: Figure 1(c) shows the form meaning 'from time to time'.

NON-PRESENT REFERENCE

If a referent (third person) is actually present in the discourse context between signer and addressee, specific indexical reference is made by pointing to that referent. But for non-present referents that are introduced by the speaker into the discourse context only 'verbally', there is another system of indexing. This consists of introducing a nominal and setting up a point in space associated with it; pointing to that specific locus later in the discourse clearly 'refers back' to that nominal, even after many intervening signs (see Lacy, 1974; Kegl, 1976*a,b*; Hoffmeister, 1978; Wilbur, 1979; Padden, 1979, 1980).

Such spatial indexing allows explicit co-reference and reduces the possibility of ambiguity. The English sentence 'He said he hit him and then he fell down' doesn't specify which, if any, of the pronoun instances are co-referential. In ASL, such distinctions are obligatory and are made by indexing to different points in space.

The space used by the signer is partitioned in very special ways. Indexing to loci in space occurs with respect to a specific horizontal plane in front of the signer's torso. This plane is the locus for indices of specific reference; that is, when the speaker has a referent in mind which he introduces into the discourse. If the speaker is making indeterminate reference, indices are established at a different (higher) level. Generic references are also indexed with respect to higher planes. Different spaces can be used for contrasting events, for indicating reference to a time prior to the time of the utterance, and for hypothetical and counterfactual situations. Points in such spaces are associated not just with nominals referring to concrete persons, places, things, but

with any nominal with determinant reference: GOVERNMENT, GRAM-
MAR, DERIVATIONAL PROCESS, IDEA.

The structured use of space in ASL is nowhere more evident than in the
means by which verbs reflect their arguments. Discourse roles are indicated
not just by pointing, but also by changes in their movement as part of the verb
inflectional system in ASL (see Klima & Bellugi, 1979, Chapter 12).

INDEXIC REFERENCE ON VERBS

The system of verb agreement in ASL, like the pronominal system, is essentially spatialized: verb signs move between loci in signing space. Verbs like
ASK, INFORM, TELL, GIVE are obligatorily marked for person (and
number) when spatial indices have been established for the nominals identified with the verb's arguments. The indices dictate the verb's path (the
starting and ending points) from one indexic locus to the other. Figure 2
shows the uninflected form of INFORM (without any spatial indexing) and its
path of movement when indexed for first-, second-, and third-person reference.

Verb signs also inflect for loci in the indexic plane that have been associated
with non-present references. Figure 3 shows the uninflected sign ASK (Figure 3(a)) and its form when indexed from one third-person locus to another,
as in 'the boy asks the girl' (Figure 3(b)):

$$\text{BOY (INDEX:}i\text{) GIRL (INDEX:}j\text{) ASK}^{[i \text{ to } j]}$$

Note that the same signs in the same order, but with a change in the direction
of movement of the verb (from j to i) would indicate 'the girl asks the boy'
(Figure 3(c)):

$$\text{BOY (INDEX:}i\text{) GIRL (INDEX:}j\text{) ASK}^{[j \text{ to } i]}$$

Furthermore, meaning can be preserved under a different temporal order of
signs, since relationships are specified by direction of movement of verbs
between spatial indices.[3] Several utterances later in this discourse, a pointing
sign, or another verb form could be directed toward locus (i) and still
unambiguously reference the boy.

Thus the system of indexing permits relative freedom of word order and yet
provides clear specification of grammatical relations by spatial means. Note
that several different third-person references may be included in one sentence
(assuming nominals have been associated with the indices), as in

$$\text{(SHE) FORCE}^{[i \text{ to } j]} \text{ INFORM }^{[j \text{ to } k; \text{ multiple}]}$$

meaning 'she forced him to inform them'. (See Padden, 1979, 1980 for
further discussion.)

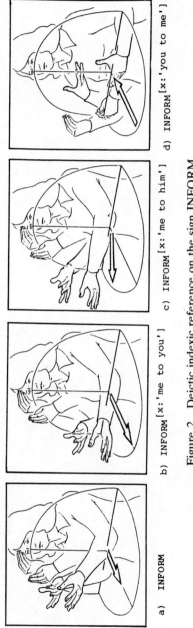

a) INFORM

b) INFORM[x:'me to you']

c) INFORM[x:'me to him']

d) INFORM[x:'you to me']

Figure 2   Deictic indexic reference on the sign INFORM

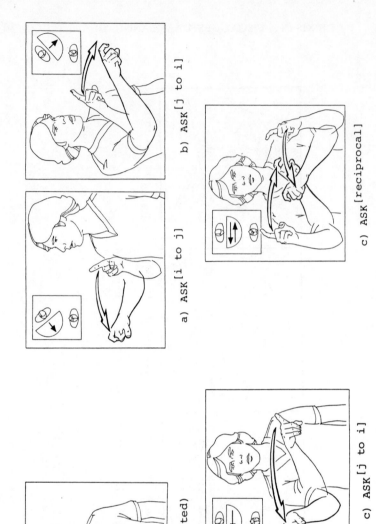

b) ASK[j to i]

a) ASK[i to j]

c) ASK[reciprocal]

Figure 4   Third-person indexic reference with body shift ((a) and (b)) and as reciprocal (c)

a) ASK(uninflected)

c) ASK[j to i]

b) ASK[i to j]

Figure 3   Third-person indexic reference on ASK

The simple assignment of role in discourse as signer and addressee can acquire an added layer of complexity in the indexic reference system. Third-person non-present referents can be assigned to what is normally a first-person locus through body and head shifts. Figure 4 shows an alternative way of indicating, for example, 'he asks her'; 'she asks him' (Figure 4(a) and (b)). Figure 4(c) shows the reciprocal form of ASK, meaning 'the two of them ask each other'.

DIFFERENTIATION FOR NUMEROSITY AND TEMPORAL ASPECT

On the basis of the mutability of verbs with respect to space—movement of verbs between indexic loci—a complex system of inflections has evolved in ASL. Grammatical number, for example, is obligatorily marked on classes of ASL verbs. The distinctions that are inflectionally coded in ASL, aside from person marking, include reciprocal inflections indicating mutual relation or action; number inflections that include dual, trial, multiple with respect to arguments of the verb ('verb to both', 'verb to three', 'verb to them', e.g. more than three); inflections for distributional aspect, which indicate how the action is distributed ('to each', 'to any', 'to certain ones', 'among members of a group'); and inflections for temporal aspect and focus ('regularly', 'over time', 'again and again', 'for a long time', 'incessantly').

Let us consider a few of the ways lexical stems are built up in inflectional patterning to create complex single unit forms into which considerable information has been simultaneously compacted. Figure 5 presents the uninflected sign GIVE and six different inflectional forms that show a systematic relationship in form and meaning.

The uninflected form of GIVE, shown in Figure 5(a), has a single movement away from the signer. Under the inflection in Figure 5(b), meaning 'give to them', the root form is embedded along an arc of the indexic plane. Under the inflection in Figure 5(c), meaning 'give to each', the root form is embedded in multiple iterations along the same arc, replacing the single movement with ordered iterated movements. Under the inflection in Figure 5(d), meaning 'give to certain ones', the hands are doubled in alternating movements and the serially ordered iterations are replaced with non-seriated iterations. These are all inflections for numerosity, specifying number with respect to the object of the verb.

The remaining drawings in Figure 5 show the same sign GIVE built up with inflections for temporal aspect. Under the inflection in Figure 5(e), meaning 'give continuously', the root form is embedded in circling contours of repeated movement. The form in Figure 5(f) is like that of Figure 5(e) but is made with two hands alternating, meaning 'give different things continuously'. Finally, under the inflection in Figure 5(g), meaning 'give to any over time', the two hands alternate with enlarged circling contours of repeated move-

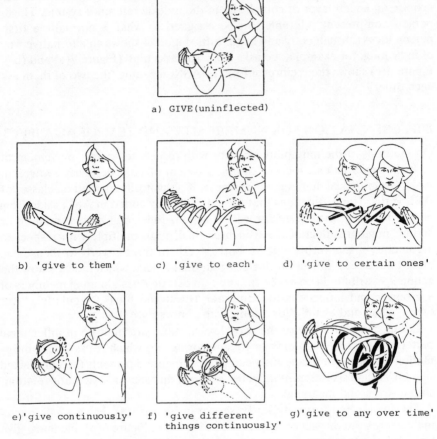

a) GIVE(uninflected)

b) 'give to them'   c) 'give to each'   d) 'give to certain ones'

e)'give continuously'   f) 'give different things continuously'   g)'give to any over time'

Figure 5   The parallel build-up of form and meaning in inflectional processes in ASL

ment toward non-seriated targets. The form in Figure 5(g) differs from that in Figure 5(f) in that height and non-seriated targets are added. It differs from that in Figure 5(d) in that height and rounded contouring are added. The complex parallel build-up in these inflectional patterns indicates the extent to which such processes constitute a coherent system of form and meaning. (Klima & Bellugi, 1979, Chap. 12, describe these and other ASL inflections in greater detail.)

Each of these inflectional operations marks regular changes in form across classes of ASL verbs resulting in systematic changes in meaning. And each of the modulated forms for person, number, and distributional aspect has associated pronominal-indexic forms to match. Thus, starting from the simple action of pointing, of indexing points in space, and incorporating spatial loci in verbs, a more elaborate system of differentiation of meanings has evolved in the language.

Deictic and anaphoric reference in ASL make use of some of the same formal mechanisms: establishment of loci within signing space, association of referents with these loci, and movement of verbs and pronouns with respect to these loci in space. This system clearly makes structured use of manipulations of space and movement. A natural question arises. How is this system of deictic and anaphoric reference acquired by young deaf children of deaf parents?

ACQUISITION OF DEICTIC PERSON REFERENCE

What might make terms like *I* and *you* in spoken languages like English difficult for children to learn? Such deictic terms all involve shifting reference, as we have noted, which is very different from names or nouns. Having agreed to call one person *Jane* or *Mother*, each speaker uses the same name. But with terms like *I* and *you*, the term does not go with the person, but rather with a person's turn as speaker or as addressee. There have been some indications that these *shifters*, as Jakobson (1957) calls them, present problems for young children learning spoken languages. Clark (1977) points out that children begin by using first-person forms, and do so only sporadically at first, often in alternation with the child's own name. The first uses generally seem to be correct; however, they may be part of set phrases or frozen forms, such as 'Me too'. The problem arises when children begin to use the contrasting form *you*. Clark posits that some children form the hypothesis that the *I* used by an adult speaker is an alternative to that person's name; and that the use of *you* is in reference to themselves. According to Clark, around the age of two, a child might produce *I carry you* with the clearly intended meaning 'you carry me'. Clark cites examples of such observations from a number of different studies and in a variety of languages. The child's 'incorrect hypothesis' is generally corrected within a few months. By the age of three, most normal children have stable self–other reference through the use of shifting pronominal terms.

Studies by Fraiberg & Adelson (1975) on language development in blind children, however, suggest another dimension to the question. These researchers longitudinally followed a group of children were blind from birth. They report that in all the children there was a distinct delay in the acquisition of pronouns of self-reference, although the children were otherwise normal linguistically. It is noted that there were very definite 'delays in the achievement of *I* as a stable pronoun, and a concomitant delay in the representation of the self in imaginative play' (Fraiberg & Adelson, 1975, p. 178). The authors suggest that in the absence of vision, blind children are late in symbolically representing themselves as apart from their environment. Mulford (1980) reviews the evidence that blind children are late in aspects of deictic pronoun acquisition.

In our own research, we have had the opportunity to examine the acquisition of language in a different group of children: those who are deaf from birth, and born to deaf parents. The children in our study are exposed from birth to a visual-manual language and to that only. How do they learn those aspects of the language we have described here? Some results are reported in Meier (1980a,b), Meier et al. (1980), and Loew (in press).

Given the apparent directness of the ASL first- and second-person pronominal signs, we expected that they might be learned early by young deaf children and that there would be no evidence of the problems caused by spoken language shifting terms. In our acquisition study, we were very surprised to find that with two year old deaf children, mothers often use name signs in addition to or instead of pronominal forms, and that the deaf children do likewise. This parallels the finding with hearing mothers and children.

Deaf mothers on our videotapes frequently signed sentences like WANT MOMMY HELP JANE? rather than using pronominal forms. Children also used their own name signs as in JANE WANT PLAY, or referred to their mothers as MOMMY in sentences, instead of using the appropriate deictic pointing signs. We asked the deaf parents in our acquisition study why they sometimes used names rather then pronoun forms with their young deaf children, and each family reported that there had been actual instances of misunderstandings on the part of the child that motivated the switch. The mother signed, for example, '(I) WASH (YOU)', and the child attempted to wash the mother as if misunderstanding the mother's pronoun references.

Testing of comprehension of pronominal forms in a task modelled after Charney (1978) confirmed that the two year old deaf child makes errors in understanding pronominal forms, but that these distinctions are mastered by about three years of age (Pizzuto & Williams, 1980). An instance on one of our videotapes lends indirect support to this developmental progression. In a deaf family, the mother was showing photographs to her two children, aged two and three years old. She brought out a picture of herself, and signed to the older child: '(THIS) (ME)', meaning 'This is a picture of me'. Then she turned to the two year old child and signed: '(THIS) *MOMMY* PICTURE', meaning 'This is a picture of Mommy', switching from the pronominal form to the name form for the younger child.

What might lead the deaf child to overlook the simplicity of reference of the pointing gesture? One aspect may be that pointing signs in ASL share formal properties with other ASL signs: there is nothing in their form that singles them out as different. The sign glossed as (ME) is made with the index finger extended from a closed fist (configuration) with a contact (movement) on the torso (location). There are many ASL signs that share in just those properties: the same configuration occurs in the signs HOUR, CANDY, GO; the same location in FEEL, DRESS, ANIMAL; the same movement in FINE, VACATION, MOTHER. Thus no aspect of their formational proper-

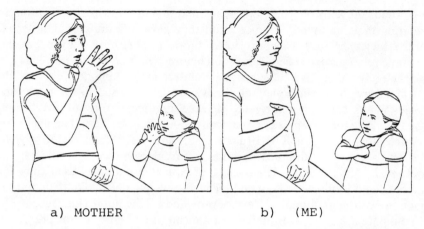

a) MOTHER   b)   (ME)

Figure 6   Deaf child and mother signing MOTHER and (ME)

ties would indicate their special status as deictic pointing signs. Figure 6, for example, shows a deaf child imitating the signs MOTHER and (ME). It might well be that the child in the early stages of acquiring signs assumes that the pointing sign (ME) is a formal name—perhaps an alternate name—just as is the sign MOTHER, and he might temporarily assume that they refer to the same person. Deaf children, just as do hearing children, appear to have problems acquiring signs that mark shifting reference and require adopting shifting perspectives.

For young deaf children, then, there is suggestive evidence that the acquisition of deictic terms parallels that in hearing children. Unlike blind children, deaf children are not late in acquiring mastery of such forms; however, the apparent directness of reference does not seem to lead them more quickly into mastery of such forms. Indeed, compatible with our observations is the view that deaf children learn pronominal forms in much the same way as they learn non-shifting names, and thus appear to ignore the apparent iconicity that is available to them.

ACQUISITION OF NON-DEICTIC REFERENCE

As we have pointed out, ASL provides a mechanism for establishing abstract loci for persons, objects, and events not present in the speech situation. Later reference is by indicating the established locus, by a pointing sign, or by verb agreement. The use of space is a grammaticalized part of the system of ASL signing, and is far from obvious to the language learner. It is common for children acquiring ASL to fail to use (or misuse) indexic loci for non-present referents, despite the fact that they use other means to discuss what is not in the speech situation.

Around two years of age, young deaf children tend to strip off inflections in imitating their mothers' sentences, and they generally produce uninflected forms (Meier, 1980a). Newport & Ashbrook (1977) have shown that the semantic relations expressed in deaf and hearing children's early language are the same; and that (like their hearing counterparts) young deaf children do not make use of the morphological devices that are used in the adult language. Young deaf children tend to sign the uninflected form of a verb even when marking for person is grammatically required in the adult language. For example, the child signs 'GIVE(uninflected) (ME)' for the meaning 'give to me' which would require incorporation of first-person locus into the verb in adult ASL. (In the adult language, the explicit pronoun is used only for emphasis and is otherwise dropped.) The very young deaf child, then, fails to make use of the grammatical devices provided by the adult language.

Young deaf children certainly communicate about what is not present in the immediate context of the discourse, before the age of three; however, they do so with nominal signs and without the establishment of abstract loci in signing space. They generally fail to index verbs, producing the uninflected verb. Often their communications are simply referentially unclear; that is, not explicitly marked (as in signing LOOK-AT, without indicating who is looking, and at whom). By the age of three, deaf children begin to learn the system of person reference for non-present referents, but still with many mistakes. Sometimes they index incorrectly; for example, using a possessive form directed toward the object possessed, rather than (as required) to the possessor, or indexing a single referent at two distinct loci.

From three years of age on, deaf children master much of the system of indexing in space and indexic inflection on verbs (Meier, 1980b; Meier et al., 1980). They first mark only one argument on verbs (even in those cases where agreement with two arguments is required). Young deaf children sometimes index verb signs to abstract loci, but often do not establish the referential identities of the loci, thus not specifying who is doing what to whom; nor do they always maintain a one-to-one referent-to-locus mapping. In telling the story of Rapunzel, a three-and-a-half year old child indexed three verbs in space—TAKE(from father); PUSH(to witch); LOOK(at Rapunzel)—yet all were indexed at the same locus. In effect, all three referents (father, witch, Rapunzel) were 'stacked up' at a single abstract locus (Loew, in press). For another deaf child, one of the first occurrences of abstract loci established in space involved a story with 10 characters, all indexed to one locus (Petitto, personal communication). In ASL, non-present referents are assigned unique spatial loci, used for anaphoric reference. It is these kinds of distinctions that young deaf children often fail to make.

In one particularly complex example, a four year old child tried various ways of making her intended reference clear. Jane was recounting an imaginary situation in which she (Jane) had 10 children, and another woman arrived to claim them as her own. Jane (in the role of the other woman) signed:

'(I) WANT (MY) . . . (YOUR) . . . JANE'S CHILDREN'.

One can understand why she finally resorted to use of her own name sign to clear up reference in this situation!

By the age of five, almost every nominal is appropriately indexed in space when required, and almost every verb appropriately uses indexic incorporation. By that time, verbs are indexed for the appropriate marking; although there are still occasional discourse problems in establishing and maintaining a one-to-one mapping between abstract loci and anaphoric reference (Loew, in press). Also by that age, deaf children are well on their way to mastering inflections for number, distributional aspect, and temporal aspect.

It appears that despite the radical difference in modality of language, deaf and hearing children show a similar course of development, given a natural language input at the critical time. The deaf child, as does his hearing counterpart, analyses out discrete components of the system presented to him. Furthermore, the evidence suggests that even when the modality and the language offer possibilities that seem intuitively obvious (pointing for deictic pronominal reference), he appears to ignore their putative iconicity. The deaf child treats the input—even when it includes deictic pointing signs—as part of a formal linguistic system.

We have examined some of the ways in which American Sign Language expresses deictic and anaphoric reference—how the language interacts with context and what mechanisms it has evolved to free itself from context. While these formal devices may well derive historically from simple pointing, in their contemporary guise they involve a complex system of space and movement contrasts—contrasts specially available for structured use in a visual-gestural language.

NOTES

1. This work was supported in part by National Science Foundation Grant #BNS79-16423 and National Institutes of Health Grant #NS15175 and HD13249 to The Salk Institute for Biological Studies. Illustrations were drawn by Frank A. Paul, copyright Ursula Bellugi.

2. Words in capital letters represent English glosses for ASL signs. The gloss represents the meaning of the unmarked, unmodulated form of a sign. Glosses within parentheses, as in (IT) and (THIS) indicate that the sign is a pointing sign. A bracketed symbol following a sign gloss indicates that the sign is made with some regular change in form associated with a systematic change in meaning, and thus indicates grammatical changes on signs. A bracketed [+] indicates some inflectional change but does not specify which. Points in space associated with indexing are marked by location indices

(*i, j*). Inflectional forms embedded within other inflections are indicated by nested brackets.

3. There are phrasal and intonational accompaniments to differential orderings; see Liddell (1977).

REFERENCES

Ahlgren, I., & Bergman, B. (eds) (1980). *Papers from the first international symposium on sign language research*. Leksand, Sweden: Sveriges Dovas Riksforbund.

Bellugi, U., & Studdert-Kennedy, M. (eds) (1980). *Signed and spoken language: biological constraints on linguistic form*. Dahlem Konferenzen. Weinheim/Deerfield Beach, Fl./Basel: Verlag Chemie.

Charney, R. (1978). *The development of personal pronouns*. Unpublished doctoral dissertation, University of Chicago.

Clark, E. (1977). From gesture to word: on the natural history of deixis in language acquisition. In J. S. Bruner & A. Garton (eds), *Human growth and development*. Oxford: Oxford University Press.

Fraiberg, S., & Adelson, E. (1975). Self-representation in language and play: observations of blind children. In E. Lenneberg & E. Lenneberg (eds), *The foundations of language development: a multidisciplinary approach*, Vol. 2. New York: Academic Press.

Friedman, L. (1975). Space, time and person reference in American Sign Language. *Language*, **51**, 940–961.

Frishberg, N. (1973). Time on our hands. Unpublished manuscript, The Salk Institute for Biological Studies, La Jolla, Calif.

Greene, J. (1975). *Thinking and language*. New York: Methuen.

Hoffmeister, R. J. (1978). *The development of demonstrative pronouns, locatives, and personal pronouns in the acquisition of American Sign Language*. Unpublished doctoral dissertation, University of Minnesota.

Jakobson, R. (1957). Shifters, verbal categories and the Russian verb. Russian Language Project, Department of Slavic Languages and Literature, Harvard University.

Klima, E. S., & Bellugi, U. (1979). *The signs of language*. Cambridge, Mass.: Harvard University Press.

Kegl, J. A. (1977). Pronominalization in American Sign Language. Unpublished manuscript, M.I.T.

Lacy, R. (1974). Putting some of the syntax back into semantics. Paper presented at the 49th Annual Meeting, Linguistic Society of America.

Lane, H., & Grosjean, F. (eds) (1980). *Recent perspectives on American Sign Language*. Hillsdale, N.J.: Erlbaum.

Liddell, S. K. (1977). *An investigation into the syntactic structure of American Sign Language*. Unpublished doctoral dissertation, University of California, San Diego.

Loew, R. C. (in press). Learning America Sign Language as a first language: roles and reference. In F. Caccamise, M. Garretson, & U. Bellugi (eds), *Proceedings of the third national symposium on sign language research and teaching, 1980*. Silver Spring, Md.: National Association of the Deaf.

Meier, R. (1980*a*). Acquisition of inflections in American Sign Language. Working paper, The Salk Institute for Biological Studies, La Jolla, Calif.

Meier, R. (1980*b*). A cross-linguistic perspective on the acquisition of inflectional morphology in American Sign Language. Working paper, The Salk Institute for Biological Studies, La Jolla, Calif.

Meier, R., Loew, R., Bahan, B., Fields, J., Launer, P., & Supalla, S. (1980). An overview of one child's acquisition of American Sign Language. Working paper, The Salk Institute for Biological Studies, La Jolla, Calif.

Mulford, R. (1980). *Talking without seeing: some problems of semantic development in blind children*. Unpublished doctoral dissertation, Stanford University.

Newport, E., & Ashbrook, E. (1977). The emergence of semantic relations in American Sign Language. *Papers and reports on child language development*, **13**, 16–21.

Padden, C. (1979). Verbs in American Sign Language. Working paper, University of California, San Diego.

Padden, C. (1980). Complement structures in American Sign Language. Working paper, University of California, San Diego.

Pizzuto, E. (1980). The acquisition of indexic reference in American Sign Language. Working paper, The Salk Institute for Biological Studies, La Jolla, Calif.

Pizzuto, E., & Williams, M. (1980). The acquisition of possessive forms in American Sign Language. In B. Frokjaer-Jensen (ed.), *Recent development in language and cognition*. Copenhagen: University of Denmark.

Siple, P. (ed.) (1978). *Understanding language through sign language research*. New York: Academic Press.

Stokoe, W. C. (1972). *Semiotics and human sign language*. New York: Humanities Press.

Stokoe, W. C. (ed.) (1980). *Sign and culture*. Silver Spring, Md.: Linstok Press.

Wilbur, R. (1979). *American Sign Language and sign systems: research and applications*. Baltimore: University Park Press.

Speech, Place, and Action
Edited by R. J. Jarvella and W. Klein
© 1982 John Wiley & Sons Ltd.

Anaphora and Deixis: Same, Similar, or Different?[1]

KONRAD EHLICH

1 DEIXIS AND ANAPHORA

In *Sprachtheorie* (1934), Karl Bühler introduced a new frame of reference for the analysis of the so-called 'demonstrative pronouns'. He showed that demonstrative pronouns, as well as 'demonstrative adverbs', are categorically distinct from other words, and belong to a '*Zeigfeld der Sprache*' (deictic field of language) which is bound to the actual speech situation. And *speech activity* provides the theoretical framework within which the analysis, description, and explanation of such demonstratives can be handled. Bühler used the terms 'deixis' and 'deictic' to denote the linguistic characteristics of demonstrative pronouns and adverbs. (He made *analytic* use of these two terms—see below.) Bühler's analysis is part of the psychology of language, since, according to it, the activities involved in using deictic expressions are, or at least include, mental activities. While Bühler's concept of deixis is commonly acknowledged nowadays, and has been insightfully developed and refined in, for example, the work of Fillmore and Wunderlich, its theoretical implications and consequences demand further reflection and discussion. Bühler did not elaborate his concept in a systematic way, and he did not cover the full field of deixis.

In the analysis of deixis, a promising beginning has at least been made. The analysis of *anaphora* is in a sadder state. The terms 'deixis' and 'deictic' developed the idea of '*demonstratio*' contained in the categories of the ancients. And they present a psycholinguistic interpretation of speech activity as part of the '*Verständigungshandeln*' (the activities of making oneself understood) between a speaker and a hearer. The term 'anaphora' is derived from the Greek 'anapherein'. The term 'anapherin' translates as 'to re-fer', 'to re-late', in the literal sense of the Latinate forms. In *linguistic* terminology, the word has two different analytic meanings: (a) it denotes a certain function, namely the activity of 're-ferring' which is performed by means of a variety of word classes such as the 'article', the 'correlative pronoun', or the 'relative pronoun' (see as examples Apollonios Dyskolos, peri synt. 26; Dionysios Thrax; Bühler, 1934, Chap. 26); (b) it denotes a certain class of expressions, the so-called 'third-person pronouns'. The word 'refer' has a meaning in modern logical-philosophical contexts besides its literal one of 'backward relation'. It denotes the relationship between a word on the one hand, and an entity in the real world and/or its mental representation on the other. Employing this latter sense of 'refer', anaphora can be and usually is described as 'cross-referring': an anaphor is related to a word in what was previously said which, in turn, refers to an entity of the real world and/or its mental representation. The function of anaphora is described in reference to another linguistic activity, namely the activity of referring itself. Anaphors in this sense are seen as words which 'refer' only *indirectly*, by means of other words. This description of the function of anaphora is compatible with the classical definition of the pronoun 'standing for a noun'. The noun 'refers' to an entity, while the anaphor 'stands for' the noun and 'cross-refers' to the entity.

This analysis, however, describes only part of what the linguistic entities under consideration do (of their Leistung). (There is a third use of the terms 'anaphora', 'anaphoric' as a purely conventional term for 'third-person pronoun' (untreated here).)

An explicative hypothesis for the analysis of anaphoric expressions, similar in nature to Bühler's '*Zeigfeld*'-interpretation of deictic expressions, is still lacking. Bühler's view has had one important consequence, however, for the analysis of the 'third person pronoun' concept, making obvious the lack of analytic clarity in the field as a whole. The traditional analysis yielded the three paradigms 'personal pronouns' (A1), 'demonstrative pronouns' (A2), and 'demonstrative adverbs' (A3). That classification has been shaken to the extent that a new paradigm of deictic expressions (B1) was established, whereas the 'third-person pronouns' were set apart (B2).[2] In linguistic discussions, paradigms (A) and (B) are commonly used in combination though their analytic claims are not compatible.

(A1)   Personal pronouns

First person	ich
Second person	du
Third person	m. er
	f. sie
	n. es

(A3)   Demonstrative adverbs

	Near	Far
Temporal	jetzt	dann
Local	hier	da

(A2)   Demonstrative pronouns

		Near		Far	
Substantive	m.	der (hier)	dieser	der da	jener
	f.	die (hier)	diese	die da	jene
	n.	das (hier)	dieses	das da	jenes
Adjective	m.	dieser ...	der ... hier	der ... da	jener ...
	f.	diese ...	die ... hier	die ... da	jene ...
	n.	dieses ...	das ... hier	das ... da	jenes ...
		I	II	III	IV

(B1)

Referring to items within the domain of the speech act				Personal	Impersonal	Temporal	Local
Involved in the speech activity	Speaker			ich			
	Hearer (addressee)			du			
Not involved in the speech activity	Near	Substantive		der (hier) dieser		jetzt	hier
		Adjective		dieser . . . der . . . (hier)			
	Far	Substantive		der da jener		dann	da
		Adjective		der . . . da . . . jener . . .			

(B2)

Anaphora		
m.	er
f.	sie
n.	es

In fact, within linguistic theory, no clear-cut distinction between deixis and anaphora has to date been proposed. The terms are used not only conventionally as mere labels and analytically (i.e., they are meant to give an analysis of the linguistic entities to which they are attached), but also to refer to partially overlapping sets of linguistic entities. And though these entities are in general classified by means of the parts-of-speech classification handed down from Greek and Roman linguistics, this classification, though still of paradigmatic use, is itself neither adequate nor sufficient (see Ehlich, 1979, especially Sections 3.6 and 9.2). The confusion becomes especially clear in the case of deictic expressions used in texts: these are often said to be used 'anaphorically'. The idea of an 'anaphoric use of deixis' shows that the terms need clarification. In the present paper, I analyse and try to re-define the concepts of 'deixis' and 'anaphora' in order to re-organize the linguistic entities of the above paradigms. I start off with the problem just mentioned, by asking whether text deixis and anaphora can be used for one another.

2   TEXT DEIXIS AND ANAPHORA

A problem arises out of Bühler's definition of deictic expressions. Bühler's idea of *'Zeigfeld der Sprache'* is bound to the *performance* of speech acts. *Texts*, however, are characterized by the fact that they are removed from the speech situation in which they are first produced. A text is an undertaking of a kind such that a *transfer* between situations is made possible (Ehlich, 1979, Section 6.2). Thus, the existence of deictic phenomena within texts (except for their use in quotations) confronts the analyst with a problem as to the definition of deixis itself. If categories taken from the speech situation are used, text deixis is a contradiction in terms.

There are at least three ways of handling this problem:

(1) The subclass of so-called text deixis and the class of anaphora are understood as being *identical* (position (C)).

(2) The feature 'anaphoric' is *added to* or imposed upon the deictic nature of words like 'this' and 'that', due to specific conditions of context or the like (position (D)).

(3) The whole of deixis is interpreted from the point of view of anaphoric function; that is, a *'phoric' interpretation* is given to all deictic phenomena. This begins with the anaphoric (and a parallel cataphoric) function of the deictic expressions in question which is found in intra-textual uses; other uses of deixis are then seen as 're-ferring (back)' to non-textual phenomena. These functions are described as exophoric, taking us, so to speak, 'out of' the text (or discourse) (position (E)).

Position (E) obviously ignores the very discovery of a specific function of deictic expressions, the *Zeigfeld–Symbolfeld* distinction, and the connection between speech act situation and the use of deixis. The three positions (C)–(E) have one thing in common: they ultimately lead to an *identical* functional concept for the two classes of expressions. This, of course, might be a plausible solution provided that text deixis and anaphora are only occasionally interchangeable within texts and provided that they do not show differences in use.

At first glance, there seem to be at least some occurrences of deixis which support such a view. Consider, for example, German (1) as compared with (2) or English (3) with (4):

(1) Das ist schön.
(2) Es ist schön.
(3) That's fine.
(4) It's fine.

The *prima facie* identity of 'das'–'es'/'that'–'it' can be upheld, however, only if we use this kind of isolated sentence comparison, instead of construing actual situations of language *use* or, even better, taking into account actual speech data.

In texts (5)/(6) and (7)/(8) respectively (with (9)/(10) and (11)/(12) as English equivalents) the seeming identity of use of 'das' and 'es' (or 'that' and 'it') does not work as well as in (1)–(4):

(5) A: Ich komme morgen pünktlich.
     B: Das ist schön.
(6) A: Ich komme morgen pünktlich.
     ?B: Es ist schön.
       ((6a) A: Ich komme morgen pünktlich.
              B: Is schön.)
(7) A: Was halten Sie von dem Bild?
     ?B: Das ist schön.
(8) A: Was halten Sie von dem Bild?
     B: Es ist schön.
       ((8a) A: Was hältst Du von dem Bild?
              ?B: Is schön.)
(9) A: I'll be on time tomorrow.
     B: That's fine.
(10) A: I'll be on time tomorrow.
      ?B: It's fine.
        ((10a) A: I'll be on time tomorrow.
                B: Fine.)
(11) A: What do you think of the drawing?
      ?B: That's fine.

(12)   A: What do you think of the drawing?
        B: It's fine.
        ((12a) A: What do you think of the drawing?
               B: Fine.)

(6) and (10) do not seem to be quite 'okay' (I use the expression 'okay' in order to avoid the current disputes on acceptability and the like).

(5) and (9) on the one hand, and (6) and (10) on the other, show that there are differences between deixis and anaphora. They also show that analysing these differences is not a task easily fulfilled by following some rough criterion. The two kinds of phenomena seem to be closely related, and a subtle procedure will be needed to clarify them. This consequence is also seen in examples (7) and (11). The close interrelation between these phenomena suggests why linguists might easily content themselves with analytic procedures of the kind characterized above. And it might be taken as a reason for continuing to be satisfied with interchanging use of the categories (text-) deixis and anaphora.

There are, however, examples in which, even by means of standard procedures of linguistic analysis, the interchangeability of text deixis and anaphora does not work. This is the case when we apply the commutation test to the following example (taken from a text on the theory of literature):

(13)   Anpassung seiner Leser an ihre soziale Situation, *das/es** leistet der Roman, indem er ein entsprechendes Wertsystem bestätigt und dessen Vertreter belohnt.

(14)   Adaptation of its reader to their social situation, that/it* ('s what) the novel does in that it confirms an appropriate value system and rewards its representatives.

There are examples of a similar type, as (15) and (17). (All examples are taken from newspaper articles.)

(15)   'Kein Hahn würde nach dem Gezänk unter dem Kirchturm von Oberammergau krähen, wenn die volkstümliche Darstellung der Passion Jesu Christi nichts weiter wäre als naives Dorftheater. *Dies/es** ist sie aber längst nicht mehr . . . ' (*Süddeutsche Zeitung*, 14 May 1978).

(16)   Nobody would give a hoot about the squabbling under the church-tower of Oberammergau, if the folk representation of Jesus Christ's passion were nothing more than naive village theatre. *This/it**, however, it hasn't been for a long time.

(17)   'Wer das Pech hat, beruflich in der Stadt herumkurven zu müssen, *der/er** merkt: Die Autos werden zu viel und zu vieler' (*Süddeutsche Zeitung*, 14 April 1978).

(18) Whoever is unlucky enough to have to drive in the city on business, (he*) will notice: . . .

In German *der* here is used as a 'substantive' deictic which points back to the initial clause which begins with '*wer*'; it is not possible to use '*er*' (the 'third-person pronoun') instead.

A similar proximate relationship and a similar difference can be seen between 'da' and 'es' in at least some examples. Consider (19) and (20):

(19) 'Da könnte ja jeder kommen!'
(20) ?'Es könnte ja jeder kommen!'
(21) ('Then everybody could come')

Sentence (20) can't be made into English at all, while (19) means 'All and sundry would come.' Moreover, (20) generally demands a continuation, e.g. with 'und'. In (22), a replacement of 'da' by 'es' is impossible. This, however, might be due to a categorial difference of the 'da' in this case as compared with (19).

(22) 'Wo kommen wir denn da hin?'
(23) *'Wo kommen wir denn es hin?'
(24) Where would that lead (us to) then?

(22) has no exact translation, since 'that' is not identical with 'da'. (23) is untransferable.

Having shown that there does not seem to be a functional identity of text deixis and anaphora, I come back to the question of their frequency of use. Without giving any statistics for the moment, it can be seen from texts such as, for example, newspaper articles, that *both* text deixis *and* anaphora are in common use. Further, the dichotomy between 'demonstrative pronoun' and 'third-person pronoun' seems to have developed in many languages. Both facts make it highly improbable that the existence and common use of the two classes of expressions can be explained by mere redundancy requirements. On the contrary, I think that these facts demand a functional explanation which clarifies the reasons for their coexistence and their differences in use, and thus, the functional (meaning) difference of the two types of linguistic items. I want to discuss this proposal in more detail. Before doing so, however, let me state hypothesis (F):

(F) The classes of 'third-person pronoun' and 'demonstrative pronoun' are functionally different in speech activity.

The elaboration of hypothesis (F) will also have to address the question of the specific nature of text deixis.

3   FROM 'PARTS OF SPEECH' TOWARDS LINGUISTIC PROCEDURES

3.1   Introducing Hebrew as another reference language

The examples discussed so far have been taken from English and German. In paradigm (B), I have distinguished the substantive use of the 'demonstrative pronoun' from its adjectival use. There seems to be a certain difference between German and English here. In English the adjective forms seem to be pre-dominant. This may be due to general restrictions in English on the nominalization of adjectives. German use of the 'demonstrative pronouns' thus covers a larger domain of phenomena than, perhaps, English can. That is why I have used mainly German examples up to now.

In order to discuss hypothesis (F), I will introduce another language which is still more illustrative of the problem at hand: (ancient) Hebrew. Both English and German have only substantive uses of the 'third-person pronouns'. In Hebrew, the situation is different. Thus, this language provides a case which makes the discussion of hypothesis (F) still more germane. In Hebrew, we find the following paradigm (G) (I only incorporate the masculine singular form):

(G)

I	Deixis				Anaphora
	II Local	III Temporal	IV Personal	V Impersonal	VI Personal/impersonal
Substantive	zä	zä	zä	zä	hu
Adjective			hazzä	hazzä	hahu

The '*ha*' shown with the adjective form is a determiner which is prefixed to the adjective in cases where the adjective belongs to a determined phrase. There are almost no occurrences of *ZÄ* and *HU* in adjective position without this determiner.

The situation which is described in (G) means we can find the following four varieties:

(25a)	*zä' iš*	der hier (ist) ein Mann	this (person is) a man
(25b)	*hu' iš*	er (ist) ein Mann	he (is) a man
(25c)	*hā'iš hazzä*	dieser Mann	this man
(25d)	*hā'iš hahu*	——	——

(25d) does not yield an adequate translation. If we try to simulate the facts of Hebrew exactly in German and English, we need to form real adjectives from the stem of *dieser* or *this* etc. and then append the article, as

> *hazzä*   'der diese'   'the this-ish'
> *hahu*   'der er-ige'   'the he-ish'

The whole phrases (25c) and (25d) thus would have as translation (26) and (27). (I use the postpositional adjective as in Hebrew)

(26)   *hā'iš hazzä*   der Mann, der diese   the man, the this-ish

(27)   *hā'iš hahu*   der Mann, der er-ige   the man, the he-ish

I hope to have given an impression of the situation in Hebrew and to have shown its relevance in general to the problem I am discussing. Detailed examples from the corpus will follow.

The following table is a comparison of the distribution of the substantive and adjectival use of deixis and anaphora in the three languages:[3]

(G')

	English	German	Hebrew
Anaphora, substantive	×	×	×
Deixis, adjective	×	×	×
Deixis, substantive	(×)	×	×
Anaphora, adjective			×

The Hebrew system of deixis and anaphora as shown in paradigm (G) reveals a complete complement of deixis and anaphora for personal and impersonal objects (see columns IV, V, and VI). In order to discuss hypothesis (F), an extensive analysis of data is necessary, which will provide insights into the functions of both classes. I have undertaken such an investigation elsewhere (see Ehlich, 1979, Sections 6 and 9). This paper will be restricted to some examples and a summary of results.

3.2   The deictic procedure

Firstly, I should like to come back to the analysis of the deictic procedure. What it accomplishes has already been discussed in Section 1: Deixis is a linguistic means for specific uses in direct reference to elements of the speech situation. Its various forms apply to the primary dimensions of this situation. With forms like 'this' and 'that' speech-act-based reference is possible to entities other than speaker and hearer, but still belonging to the speech situation. Deictic expressions are related to a specific type of domain, the *Zeigfeld* (deictic field); in this regard they differ from all other words, which are related to the *Symbolfeld* (symbolic field).

The explanation that deictic expressions are used in direct connection to the speech situation in which they are uttered is highly plausible. This very plausibility has perhaps led to its theoretical standpoint having never been questioned. But in fact the explanation falls within a theoretical framework not very different from the one we discussed in considering the concept of 'anaphora' in its usual sense. Its theoretical interest and context are determined by the *act of reference*, which in turn is analyzed within a theory of the properties of signs. This point is very clear in Bühler's treatment, in which the discussion of deixis follows his theoretical analyses of the sign in the beginning (the 'axiomatics') of his book. On the one hand, Bühler developed his insights into the speech act dependency of deictic expressions as part of a theory of signs, a *semiotic model*. In doing so, he adhered to a principal tendency in linguistic thought: to identify, describe, and explain *inherent qualities of (isolated) linguistic entities*, such as signs, words, or sentences.

On the other hand, Bühler did not incorporate his findings into a general theory of signs, but a *psychology* of language. I think it is necessary to follow this second train of thought to further elaborate the analysis of deixis. In his search for the '*Zeigfeld*', Bühler arrived at the concept of speech situations as fundamental for the analysis of deixis. But the above-mentioned restriction to a semiotic model of language is not in accord with psychological interests, and in fact conflicts with them. This contradiction has continued into the present, though its effects sometimes remain unperceived.

There are other linguists and psychologists who demand theoretical reflection of speech activity in its full complexity as a basic concept for linguistic analysis, such as, for example, Hörmann (1976). Besides the speaker and his activities, the speech act as a whole includes the hearer or addressee. This statement is a truism. Not at all trivial, however, are its analytic implications.[4] Many linguists who dismiss the restrictions of a purely semiotic model of linguistics nevertheless neglect the hearer's activities in the communication process. They see him as a relatively passive 'receiver' of the speaker's speech act. This concept does not do justice to the complexity of the hearer's activities as an integrated part of the *Verständigungsprozeß as a whole*.

A speech act is realized by a speaker, by executing a series of activities. These are largely determined by his *anticipation of the hearer's capacities* in the '*Verständigungshandlung*'. The hearer in turn needs to execute a series of reconstructive procedures which serve to determine what the speaker has meant. Thus, the speech or communication act is composed of meaning and understanding (as in the title of Hörmann's book). It is within this context that the deictic procedure is to be understood. To communicate effectively, the hearer's attentiveness needs to be brought into concord with that of the speaker. I wish to use the term '*to focus*' to denote this job of communication. One of the main means of focusing the attentiveness of the hearer is the *deictic procedure*. It works on the basis of a previous common orientation (*Orientiertheit*) of speaker and hearer. By means of deictic expressions, the speaker brings the hearer to focus on some specific, directly accessible element, making use of the speech act space. (I leave aside the more complicated forms of deixis for the moment.)

This analysis is generalized in the form of definition (H):

> (H)   The deictic procedure is a linguistic instrument for achieving focusing of the hearer's attention towards a specific item which is part of the respective deictic space (*deiktischer Raum*). The deictic procedure is performed by means of deictic expressions.

Thus, the use of a deictic expression can be understood by the hearer as an instrument (cf. Weinrich, 1976) to execute a series of orientation processes which the speaker believes to be necessary for achieving the goal of the communication.

3.3   The anaphoric procedure

The analysis of the deictic procedure as a whole in terms of activities in the *Verständigungshandlung* raises the question whether a parallel analysis of the *anaphoric procedure* can be made. I hope to show in the following that it can. First, I give two illustrations for the standard use of anaphoric expressions. One example (30) makes use of the adjective form of Hebrew anaphora. I will then discuss some examples containing both deictic and anaphoric expressions, and analyse the function of anaphoric procedure which leads to a definition of the anaphoric process.

The standard use of anaphors in simple cases is quite clear. Consider (28), the beginning of a children's story by Peter Bichsel, and a fit illustration:

> (28)   '(a) Ich will von *einem alten Mann* erzählen, von einem Mann, der kein Wort mehr sagt, ein müdes Gesicht hat, zu müd zum Lächeln und zu müd, um böse zu sein. (b) *Er* wohnt in einer kleinen Stadt, am Ende der Straße oder nahe der Kreuzung. (c) Es lohnt sich fast nicht, *ihn* zu beschreiben, (d) kaum etwas unterscheidet *ihn* von andern. (e) *Er* trägt einen grauen Hut, graue Hosen, einen grauen Rock und im Winter den langen grauen Mantel, (f) und *er* hat einen dünnen Hals, dessen Haut trocken und runzelig ist, (g) die weißen Hemdkragen sind *ihm* viel zu weit. (h) Im obersten Stock des Hauses hat *er* sein Zimmer, (i) vielleicht war *er* verheiratet und hatte Kinder, (j) vielleicht wohnte *er* in einer anderen Stadt. . . .'

(29) (a) I want to tell a story about *an old man*, about a man, who doesn't say a word any more, who has a tired face, too tired to smile, too tired to be mean. (b) *He* lives in a little town, at the end of the street or near the corner. (c) It's almost not worth it to describe *him*, (d) hardly anything distinguishes *him* from others. (e) *He* wears a grey hat, grey trousers, a grey jacket, and in the winter the long grey overcoat, (f) and *he* has a skinny neck, the skin of which is dry and wrinkled, (g) white shirt collars are for *him* much too big. (h) On the top floor of the house, he has *his* room, (i) perhaps *he* was married and had children, (j) perhaps *he* lived in another town. . . .

The story starts by introducing 'an old man' (a). Nine anaphors take up this phrase in the following text (parts (b)–(j)).

Text (30) is taken from the beginning of the book of Job. It reads[5]

(30)	' 'iš hāyā b.'äräṣ ʿuṣ	(a)	A man existed (was) in the land of Uz.
	'iyyob ṣ.mo	(b)	Job (was) his name.
	w.hāyā hā'iš hahu	(c)	And was the man, the he-ish,
	tām w.yāšār wire 'ᵃlohim		whole and even and fearing God
	w.sār merāᶜ		and turning away from evil.
	wayyiwāl.du lo	(d)	And were born for him
	šibᶜā bānim w.šāloš bānot		seven sons and seven daughters.
	wayhi miqnehu	(e)	And was his possession
	šibᶜat 'alpe – ṣon		seven thousand (head of) small cattle
	uš.lošät 'alpe g.mallim		and three thousand camels
	waḥᵃmeš me'ot ṣämäd – bāqār		and five hundred yoke of oxen
	waḥᵃmeš me'ot 'ᵃtonot		and five hundred she-asses
	waᶜ ᵃbuddā rabbā m.'od		and a very great household.
	wayhi hā'iš hahu	(f)	And was the man, the he-ish,
	gādol mikkol – b.ne – qādäm		bigger than all people of the east.

(30) displays a use of anaphoric elements parallel to that of (28). The story starts by introducing *a man* (a). By two adjective anaphors, the phrase is taken up in the following text, namely in (c) and in (f). In addition, there are several 'possessive' anaphoric expressions, as in (b), (d), (e). The introduction uses an undetermined noun ('iš, 'man') which is syntactically a part of a compound nominal sentence. The man is located within a geographic

framework which is part of the hearer/reader's common knowledge. Thus, he is connected to their knowledge and is integrated into it. After having achieved a minimum of familiarity on the hearer/reader's side with the agent in the story, the speaker can continue by introducing a proper name under which the knowledge which is now common to himself and the hearer/reader is made accessible (b). Thus, the frame of the narrative is established by making use of, and expanding, the hearer/reader's knowledge.

Before the narrative is developed, in a series of scenes, this knowledge is elaborated by a further characterization. To establish a relation to the agent in the following sentences the speaker makes use of three procedures:

(α) He uses the adjective anaphora in (c) and (f).
(β) He uses the 'possessive' anaphora in (b), (d), (e).
(γ) He uses the so-called 'third person' of the verb-inflection in (c) and (f).

Next, I will discuss two examples which contain both deictic and anaphoric expressions to illustrate what marks the difference between them.

(31) (a) 'And Jacob went his way,
 and the angels of God encountered him.
 And Jacob said when he saw them:
 (b) maḥ^{a}ne '^{a}lohim zä
 The camps of God (are) this/here
 (c) wayyiqrā šem – hammāqom hahu maḥ^{a}nāyim
 and he called the name of the place, the it-ish, camps.'
 (*Genesis 32, 2 f.*)

The deictic expression '*zä*' refers to the place at which the speaker of sentence (b) utters (b), and is in concordance with the usual explanation of deixis.[6] As the narrator continues, he needs to change the means for referring to the place at which the story happens. He no longer uses the deictic expression '*hammāqom hazzä*' (which would be a perfectly well-formed Hebrew phrase), but changes the deictic procedure (which he has only quoted from the protagonist's (Jacob's) mouth) into an anaphoric procedure. The 'place' has been previously introduced in the course of the narration by three different means: (α) the description of Jacob's journey,

'w.yac ^{a}qob hālak l.darko
and Jacob went his way';

(β) a standard inference from the act of encounter needing no explicit mention since encounters necessarily happen at a certain *place*, as speaker and hearer know from their encyclopedic knowledge; (γ) the information passed on within the quote. By all three means, the hearer/reader is oriented to

certain domains of his knowledge. In going on, the speaker can make use of
these orienting results of his previous speech activity. This he does by means
of the anaphoric procedure. That a change of deixis to anaphora coincides
with change of quoted to unquoted text is distributionally frequent in the
corpus I have analysed.[7]

There are also joint uses of deictic and anaphoric expressions within larger
units of quoted speech (both speech act sequels with one and two speakers).
This is shown in (32).

> (32) 'And the vision of (that) all was for you like the words of the
> sealed book that is given to him who knows to read, with the
> words:
>
> (a) q.rā' nā'–zä
> read this!
>
> and he says:
>
> (b) lo 'ukal ki ḥātum hu
> not can I for sealed (is) it.
> (= I cannot for it is sealed.)'

$$(Isiah\ 29,\ 11)$$

The first speaker in (a) uses the deictic procedure to refer to the book
which is part of the speech act situation. After he has done so, the second
speaker (the addressee of the first quote) answers with (b). He uses not the
deictic procedure but an anaphoric one, involving 'hu', which relates back to
the deictic expression in (a).

This sort of conjuncture of deictic and anaphoric expression is standard.
The majority of occurrences follow the next rule:

> (I) If deictic and anaphoric expressions refer to the same entity in the
> speech act space, the deictic expression is used in the first instance
> whereas the anaphoric expression(s) is/are used in the following
> instance(s).

The usual postposition of an anaphoric expression after a deictic one is a
special case of the general use of anaphoric expressions which 're-fer' (in the
etymological sense of the word) or are *related back* to another element of
discourse which has been focused on previously. Cases which seem to violate
this particular tendency arise for special reasons, as I have shown in detail
elsewhere (Ehlich, 1979, Section 9.1.4).

Next consider this characteristic in view of the activities of speaker and
hearer in the *Verständigungshandlung*. To what purpose does the speaker put
the anaphoric procedure in the activities he undertakes in communicating
with the hearer? Just what instructions does the speaker in using an anaphoric

expression give to the hearer? I believe the answer is to be found by regarding the nature of the deictic as being like that of a foil. In using an anaphor, the speaker's instruction to the hearer is somehow the exact opposite to the instruction he gives by using a deictic element. He instructs the hearer to treat a previously verbalized element as remaining in focus. Instead of instructing the hearer to orient his attention towards a new item, he asks him to *sustain the previously obtained orientation of attention*. The anaphoric expression is used to perform this retrograde instruction.

The contrasting character of anaphora and deixis can be seen if we change personal anaphora in text (28) into personal deixis, as in (33).

(33)　(a) Ich will von einem alten Mann erzählen, von einem Mann, der kein Wort mehr sagt, ein müdes Gesicht hat, zu müd zum Lächeln und zu müd, um böse zu sein. (b) *Dieser* wohnt in einer kleinen Stadt, am Ende der Straße oder nahe der Kreuzung. (c) Es lohnt sich fast nicht, *diesen* zu beschreiben, (d) Kaum etwas unterscheidet *diesen* von andern. (e) *Dieser* trägt einen Hut, graue Hosen, einen grauen Rock und im Winter den langen grauen Mantel, (f) und *dieser* hat einen dünnen Hals, dessen Haut trocken und runzelig ist, (g) die weißen Hemdkragen sind *diesem* viel zu weit. (h) Im obersten Stock des Hauses hat *dieser* sein Zimmer, (i) vielleicht war *dieser* verheiratet und hatte Kinder, (j) vielleicht wohnte *dieser* in einer anderen Stadt. . . .

(34)　(a) I want to tell a story about an old man, about a man who doesn't say a word any more, who has a tired face, is too tired to smile, too tired to be mean. (b) *This (one)* lives in a little town, at the end of the street or near the corner. (c) It's almost not worth it to describe *this (one)*, (d) hardly anything distinguishes *this (one)* from others. (e) *This (one)* wears a grey hat, grey trousers, a grey jacket and in the winter the long grey overcoat, (f) and *this (one)* has a skinny neck, the skin of which is dry and wrinkled, (g) white shirt collars are for *this (one)* much too big. (h) On the top floor of the house, *this (one)* has his room, (i) perhaps *this (one)* was married and had children, (j) perhaps *this (one)* lived in another town. . . .

This text is not 'okay' in the sense of Section 2, but rather sounds strange. What, then, has happened by the substitution of deictic for anaphoric elements? In brief, we have changed the instructions we give to the hearer: we no longer ask him to continue the focus upon that old man who is introduced in sentence (a); instead, we continually demand a new orientation on his side. As soon as he heeds our request, however, and tries to orient his attention towards the elements in the domain of speech we identify by use of the deictic expression, he comes upon an item he has in focus already. Thus, he is *over-oriented*—which instead of leading to a sharpening of his attentional focus actually has the effect of *disorienting* him. In so far as the hearer becomes aware of what is happening, he knows that the speaker is violating a principle of co-operation for communication between them. The result for actual communication is confusion; empirical investigation into the consequences the hearer draws from this kind of violation is merited.

In the following, I want to discuss another example important to refining the interpretation of the anaphoric procedure.

> (35)   It is 5.20. A and B are sitting in a room. They are expecting C, who had promised to come at five o'clock. They have been waiting since five o'clock in silence. Suddenly A hears footsteps from the staircase. He says to B:
> (a) 'He's coming.'

In this example, (a) is the first and only speech act. There has been no discourse prior to it; or therefore no verbalization of any element linguistically.

In the previous discussion, I suggested that the anaphoric expression establishes a relation to a previously *verbalized* element; the hearer is instructed to keep this element as an object of his attention in the on-going linguistic activity. Though this is true for many occurrences, in (35) there is no such element. This explication of anaphora thus proves to be too narrow and must consequently be enlarged. Consider example (35) from the point of view of the *psycholinguistic activities* involved in use of the anaphor: the use of the anaphoric expression is in full agreement with the psycholinguistic interpretation we have given to the function of the anaphoric procedure. It appeals for attention to some item that previously has been in the hearer's focus. This is the case with (35): the attention of both the speaker and hearer is focused upon a third person C whom they *expect*. This is a sort of paraphrase, though not, however, an exact equivalent, of the psycholinguistic activities described above. The orientation towards C has not been brought about by previous parts of any *actual discourse* (though it was effected by C's promise to come at five).

In order to include cases like (35), then, I give the following definition (J) of the anaphoric procedure:

> (J)   The anaphoric procedure is a linguistic instrument for having the hearer continue (sustain) a previously established focus towards a specific item on which he had oriented his attention earlier. The anaphoric procedure is performed by means of anaphoric expressions.

3.4 Difference and affinity between deixis and anaphora

Definition (H) and definition (J), the results of functional analyses of deictic and anaphoric expressions, give an answer to the question raised in the first two sections of this paper: there *is* a *functional difference* between the two classes of expressions and the respective procedures they are used to perform in the *Verständigungshandlung* between a speaker and a hearer. This functional difference reflects the psycholinguistic activities the hearer has to perform in order to understand a speaker. He is, in effect, instructed to alter *or* to sustain his focus of attention in the on-going process of communication. The two procedures, and the classes of linguistic expressions used to execute them, form a contrasting pair or, to use the classical structuralist terminology, an *opposition*. The opposition is *an opposition of functions*. These functions belong to the communicative activities performed in the everyday process of language use. Their scientific treatment is part of the psychology of language, in the broad sense that Bühler used this term.

The concept of 'opposition' does not, however, contain *only* a notion of difference. Rather, it also implies a certain *affinity* of the two members standing in contrast to each other. This also seems to be the case with deixis and anaphora. In being in contrast with each other, the two also belong together. Their characteristic in common is their linguistic function: directing a hearer's attention in the on-going process of communication. The affinity of such opposites usually implied by this concept is of importance for the analysis of cross-linguistic data in general, and in understanding the varied history of linguistic analysis of deixis and anaphora in particular.

4 TEXT DEIXIS RECONSIDERED

We have found a difference between deixis and anaphora. What consequences does this have for understanding text deixis?

The answer is easy: the text-deictic use of deictic expressions is to be seen as a subtype of the use of *deixis* in general. The deictic procedure in this case shares the properties of deictic procedures elsewhere. The difference between text deixis and other forms of deixis is not categorical, implying a need to transform deictic expressions into anaphoric ones. Rather, the difference is constituted by different *Zeigfelder* (to use Bühler's term) or by different *deictic spaces* (*Verweisräume*), to which the deictic procedure is related (definition (H)). With text deixis, the procedure is bound not to the speech act situation as a whole, but to the *text* itself. Thus, elements in the text are its potential objects. The communicative function of the procedure within the *Verständigungshandlung* is the same as in other cases, namely to make the reader focus his attention within the deictic space (the text).

Since texts are organized in a specific way, we find text-specific characteristics of this space. Texts are linguistic macro-entities which, when produced, are serially ordered in time and which form 'a whole' in the sense of Gestalt psychology. Their serial order is transposed into a linear sequel of graphic forms when they are written down. Temporal or spatial organization marks the main lines along which the deictic procedures within texts are organized. They constitute the coordinates along which the hearer can direct his attention. Taking the temporal extension of texts, we arrive at the notions of 'pointing back' or 'forward' within a text. Taking the spatial one, we get those of 'pointing up' or 'down'. To cover this range in text, we can differentiate an *anadeictic* from a *catadeictic procedure*.

(36)

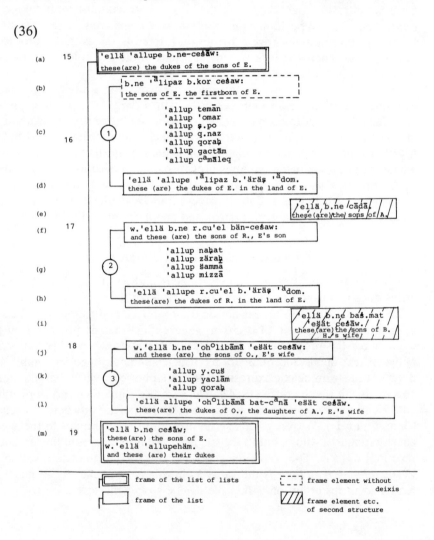

Let us reconsider what was probably meant by 'anaphoric' use of deictic expressions. It is the phenomenon of *pointing back* within texts. The activity is a kind of *pointing*, a real deictic procedure, and not an anaphoric one. It has specific properties according to its specific deictic space.[8] Accordingly, the use of text deixis is bound to specific linguistic situations. An interesting case is their use in connection with *lists of proper names* in Hebrew texts which I have analysed elsewhere (Ehlich, 1979, Sections 6.4–6.5).

These lists are of great importance for our understanding of the ancient world. They constitute one of the oldest forms of literature. The lists are forms for the organization of collective knowledge on history, ethnography, politics, geography, and so on. Their genealogical organization is imprinted on family and tribal life. Perhaps the most impressive (and strangest) document of this text-type can be found in *Genesis 36*, which is almost completely made up of such lists, standing in complex relation to one another. It is in these texts that we find much anadeixis and catadeixis, located at the *border-lines* of the lists.

Text (36) is part of *Genesis 36*.[9] In it, we find three lists (verses 16, 17, 18). At the beginning (the first list excepted) and at the end of each is a text deixis (*'ellä*, plural of *zä*) pointing forward or backward. Most of the deixeis are used in nominal sentences consisting of two determined noun phrases (and sometimes of a non-obligatory prepositional phrase):

(37)

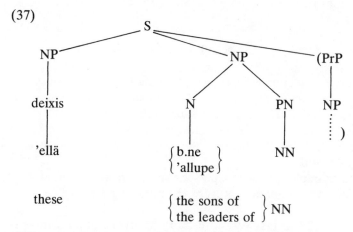

where PN = personal name and PrP = prepositional phrase.

Two other occurrences of text deixis, in (a) and (m), are located at the beginning and at the end of the conjunction of lists as a whole. Their position and their structure is the same as those in (f) and (h) or (j) and (l).

Now, what are the specific functions of these occurrences of ana- and catadeixis? Each pair hold between them a list and form a frame for this list.

The catadeixis (a) and the anadeixis (m) themselves form a frame for a *conjunction of three lists*. Thus these text-deictic expressions establish frames for and mark the boundaries of other units of text.

Consider the functions of anadeixis and catadeixis for the speech act activities performed by means of this text. Following definition (H), we can say: by using text-deictic expressions, the writer orients the focus of attention of the reader to specific parts of the text. The re-application of the deictic procedure within the text implies that the reader has to perform a shift of focus at various points along the continuum of linguistic entities he is reading. The function of the deictic procedure is to bring this shift of focus about. The shift is called for at each border-position of the smaller units in the text, the single lists. The nominal sentences incorporating these deictic elements inform the reader as to how he can digest and store the information presented. To do this, the reader must know where one list ends and the next begins, and the context into which he has to put the information they contain. The deictic procedures making use of ana- and catadeixis help him do this. The same holds for occurrences (a) and (m), with the only difference that they orient the reader to a *list of lists*. Thus, these text deixeis are used to structure the text and present the identification of its parts and subparts. Another significant use of text deixis occurs in the marking of *comments* on preceding or succeeding parts of the text, and in orienting the hearer's attention to the specific sections being taken up (cf. Posner, 1972).

5 'CATAPHORA'

Though there is directional difference (pointing backwards versus forwards) in the use of anadeictic and catadeictic expressions, it does not make either of them any less deictic. However, the situation is quite different with phoric expressions. In definition (J), the direction of the procedure is essential, namely a *retrograde* relation between the anaphoric expression and a previous element of attention.

There are examples in which a phoric expression is used without any such previous element of attention. Regard the following three cases:

(a) Example (38) is taken from the very beginning of a scientific report:

(38) 'Ursprünglich war *sie*, dem bisherigen zweijährigen Turnus entsprechend, für 1976 angesetzt, wurde dann aus verschiedenen Gründen verschoben (unter anderem, um ein zeitliches Zusammentreffen mit der International Conference on Computational Linguistics in Montreal zu vermeiden), und fand nunmehr—vom 8. bis 26. August 1977—statt: die IV. International Summer School on Computational and Mathematical Linguistics in Pisa.'

(39) 'Originally *it* was, in accordance with usual two-year cycle, scheduled for 1976, then postponed for various reasons (among others, to avoid a time conflict with the International Conference on Computational Linguistics in Montreal), and finally took place—from 8 to 26 August 1977—: the Fourth International Summer School on Computational and Mathematical Linguistics in Pisa.'

The example is a well-formed and acceptable sentence of German. Nevertheless, it is not formulated in the usual way. The phoric element 'sie' at the beginning of the sentence lacks a reference which is only supplied later.

(b) We find similar uses of phoric elements in literature, when an author begins with an isolated use of 'he' and supplies the reader with the information as to who 'he' is only gradually.

(c) A third type is found in complex sentences such as (40):

(40) Indem er die Tür öffnete, verlor Fritz Müller den Halt.
(41) As he opened the door, Fritz Müller lost (his) balance.

In all these cases, one might be tempted to speak of a 'cataphor', or, perhaps more appropriately, the cataphoric use of an anaphor, since the phoric expression is related to items which follow. We cannot simply take over the definition of anaphora for 'cataphors'. Rather, 'cataphors' constitute *derived* uses of anaphoric expressions. They are complex cases which activate a hearer's linguistic knowledge of the functions of anaphors. The cataphoric use of an anaphor demands an inference by the hearer which can be understood as follows.

The hearer recognizes the occurrence of an anaphora in the speaker's utterance. If the structure of the speech situation does not permit him to understand the anaphor as an instruction to maintain continuity of focus, the hearer concedes that the speaker probably has an item in mind which he will communicate only *afterwards* to the hearer. Thus, the hearer does not take the anaphor to be an anaphor in its standard use (dependent on a previous interactional common focus), but as a *second level anaphor* and *indication that* the speaker has such a focus. To the extent that the hearer can expect the co-operation principle to be followed, he can expect that the information as to *what* item is being focused upon will follow the announcement that there is such an item. The hearer will grant the speaker a certain amount of time to fulfil his expectation. The extension of this period probably differs with various kinds of texts and communication situations. If the speaker does not supply the item in question after that time, the hearer may reinterpret the speaker's use of the anaphoric expression as misuse of an anaphor of the first level and ask for an explanation. The derived status of cataphoric expressions makes using anaphora like this a rather risky sort of communicative procedure. It occurs mainly in certain standard contexts, especially in fixed syntactic constructions such as cleft sentences, the stereotyped uses of 'es' in German, etc.

6 LANGUAGE-SPECIFIC CHOICES FOR THE USE OF DEICTIC AND ANAPHORIC EXPRESSIONS

I finally want to return to the affinity between deixis and anaphora. This affinity finds its expression in the fact that there are language-specific choices as to whether the one or the other will be standardly used. This fact is obvious from table (G') showing the different deictic and anaphoric structures present in Hebrew, English, and German. It is also obvious if one compares different languages by translating phrases which contain a deictic or an anaphoric expression from one language into another. Compare the following excerpts from dictionary entries:

> (42) 'Iß nur *da*von   please, eat off *it (scil. the plate)'*
> (43) 'er ist nur 2 Jahre   he is only 2 years short of *it (scil. sixty)'*
>   *da*von entfernt
> (44) 'sprich nicht *da*von   don't talk of *it'*
> (45) 'er eilte *da*zu   he hastened to *the spot'*
>   (Wildhagen & Héraucourt, 1972, see entries under 'davon', 'dazu').

I think it is possible to generalize examples (42)–(45) to the hypothesis (K).

> (K)   German prefers a combination of prepositions plus deictic expressions; English does not.

Comparing German and French, the situation seems different. French seems to employ the deictic procedure still more extensively than German. Compare the following example from a French lesson of a TV course.

> (46)   French: *C'*est pour moi? Oui, *c'*est pour toi.
>   German: Ist *das* für mich? Ja, *es* ist für dich.
>   (*Les Gammas 10*, Westdeutscher Rundfunk III, 27 May 1978)

Apart from the interchange of deictic and anaphoric procedures in idiomatized settings, we also find an interchange between deictic expressions and expressions belonging to the *Symbolfeld*, as is shown in (47), an entry in a French Grammar:

> (47)   'Merke: *ceci* folgendes' (Klein & Strohmeyer, 1974, p. 158).

All these differences need special contrastive analysis. I hope that the differentiation between deictic and anaphoric procedures proposed in this paper will provide the means which permit this analysis to be done efficiently.

NOTES

1. I thank Florian Coulmas, Carol Wallace, Jullie Bradshaw, Constance Guhl and Robert Jarvella for many improvements to the English text. Constance Guhl kindly translated the German examples into English.

2. I use German examples for reasons given in Section 3.1, and only give the singular forms.

3. I do not include the so-called 'possessive pronoun' in this paper for reasons of place. This part of the 'pronominal' system does not exhibit any new aspects for the issue under discussion. The formal structure of the 'possessive pronouns' is different in Hebrew, as compared with English and German, since Hebrew uses suffixes on the noun instead of adjective-like forms.

4. Cf. Coulmas (1977).

5. The translation is 'literal' or interlinear; for example, I do not introduce 'there' in (a), which is obligatory in English, because in doing so I would introduce a deictic element which is not in the original text.

6. In so-called 'dead' languages, the quotations of direct language enable us to identify uses of deixis in the standard way (cf. Ehlich, 1979, Section 4).

7. For further examples, see, among other texts, *2 Kings 8*, 5, *Genesis 21*, 30 f., or *Judges 7*, 4, and cf. Ehlich (1979, Section 9.1.2).

8. For ana- and catadeixis in German cf. Ullmer-Ehrich (1979).

9. For technical reasons the transliteration given differs from that in examples (25)–(27) and (30)–(32).

REFERENCES

Apollonios Dyskolos. Apollonii Dyscoli de constructione libri quattuor. In G. Uhlig (ed.), *Grammatici Graeci II: II*. Leipzig: Teubner, 191£. Reprint Hildesheim: Olms, 1965.

Bühler, K. (1934). *Sprachtheorie*. Jena: Fischer.

Coulmas, F. (1977). *Rezeptives Sprachverhalten*. Hamburg: Buske.

Dionysios Thrax. Dionysii Thracis Ars Grammatica. In G. Uhlig, (ed.), *Grammatici Graeci I: I*. Leipzig: Teubner, 1883. Reprint Hildesheim: Olms, 1965.

Ehlich, K. (1979). *Verwendungen der Deixis beim sprachlichen Handeln*. Frankfurt, Bern, Las Vegas: Peter Lang Verlag.

Fillmore, C. (1972). Ansätze zu einer Theorie der Deixis. In F. Kiefer (ed.), *Semantik und generative Grammatik I*. Frankfurt: Athenäum.

Halliday, M. A. K. and Hasan, R. (1976). *Cohesion in English*. London: Longman.

Hörmann, H. (1976). *Meinen und Verstehen*. Frankfurt: Suhrkamp.

Klein, H.-W., & Strohmeyer, F. (1974). *Französische Sprachlehre*. Stuttgart: Klett.

Posner, R. (1972). *Theorie des Kommentierens*. Frankfurt: Athenäum.

Ullmer-Ehrich, V. (1979). *Da* im System der lokalen Demonstrativadverbien des Deutschen. Nijmegen: mimeo.

Weinrich, H. (1976). *Sprache in Texten*. Stuttgart: Klett.

Wildhagen, K., & Héraucourt, W. (1972). *Deutsch–Englisches Wörterbuch*. Wiesbaden: Brandstetter.

Wunderlich, D. (1970*a*). *Tempus und Zeitreferenz im Deutschen*. München: Hueber.

Wunderlich, D. (1970*b*). Die Rolle der Pragmatik in der Linguistik. *Der Deutschunterricht*, **22**, 5–41.

Wunderlich, D. (1971). Pragmatik, Sprechsituation und Deixis. *Zeitschrift für Literaturwissenschaft und Linguistik*, **1/2**, 153–190.

Speech, Place, and Action
Edited by R. J. Jarvella and W. Klein
© 1982 John Wiley & Sons Ltd.

Producing Interpretable Discourse: The Establishment and Maintenance of Reference

WILLIAM MARSLEN-WILSON, ELENA LEVY, and
LORRAINE KOMISARJEVSKY TYLER

> . . . To see a world in a grain of sand
> (William Blake)

INTRODUCTION

Successful participation in a spoken discourse places stringent demands on both the speaker and the listener. The speaker must produce utterances that cohere with what has been said earlier, while the listener must discover how what the speaker is saying can be related to what has just been said. The listener maintains a constantly developing mental representation of the current discourse, and the communicative success of a subsequent utterance largely depends on the extent to which the appropriate linkages can be established between the utterance and this discourse representation.

Given this perspective on language in context, a fundamental issue concerns the cognitive conditions under which the speaker and the listener jointly handle the complex processing dependencies between them. In this preliminary study, we approach this issue from the perspective of a theory of the listener, by confronting a naturally produced discourse with a set of analytic questions that derive from a theory of speech comprehension. In doing this, we make the basic, and plausible assumption that the ways humans produce speech are necessarily closely adapted to the ways that humans can comprehend speech. Thus, by examining speech production from the perspective of speech comprehension, we should be able to add to our overall understanding of both aspects of language use.

To make this general enterprise at all manageable, we will restrict it here in two ways. First, by using a relatively constrained form of discourse—the telling of a story, and, second, by focusing on a single, though central, aspect of the production and comprehension of a text—namely the establishment and maintenance of reference to the principal actors in the story. The dependent variable in this study will be the ways in which a speaker introduces and subsequently refers to the actors in the story.

More specifically, the way a speaker chooses between different forms of referential device, under different informational conditions during the course of a narrative, should reflect his presuppositions about the recoverability, by the listener, of the intended referents. The actual recoverability of such referents will depend, in practice, upon the ways in which listeners can link the information carried by the speech signal to their mental representation of the discourse. These mapping processes are, in turn, ultimately dependent upon, and constrained by, the basic properties of the speech comprehension system. Thus, if language production is indeed tuned to the properties of the comprehension system, and given a theory of the properties of this system, then this theory should be consistent with the patterning of different referential devices across the narrative.

The background for the present study is the set of claims we are making about speech comprehension. The theory we will assume here is one that has been developed on the basis of several processing experiments with adults and children (cf. Marslen-Wilson, 1980; Marslen-Wilson & Tyler, 1980a; Marslen-Wilson & Welsh, 1978; Tyler, 1981). There are two salient features of this model which are relevant to the present study. First, it proposes a comprehension system capable of the immediate interpretation of the speech input, word-by-word as it is heard. What is meant here by 'interpretation' is not simply the putative development of a sentence-internal syntactic or semantic analysis, but also, and critically, the mapping of the utterance onto its discourse and world context. There is good evidence that this integration process is in progress right from the beginning of an utterance heard in a discourse context (cf. Marslen-Wilson & Tyler, 1980a,b; Tyler & Marslen-Wilson, 1977; Tyler & Marslen-Wilson, 1980).

The second important feature of the model is its claims about the internal organization of the processing system, which make immediate interpretation possible in principle. The model allows for the co-operative interaction of different sources of processing information with respect to the primary perceptual goal of interpreting the incoming utterance in its discourse context. Thus, the system operates on-line by continuously generating multiple partial lexical and structural readings of the input, and simultaneously assessing these in terms of their compatibility with, and implications for, a discourse-level interpretation.

This implies that the appropriate analysis of the input need not be fully specified with respect to each and every processing source—in contrast to a more strictly bottom-up system of analysis (cf. Marslen-Wilson & Tyler,

1980*a*). To the extent that the context for interpretation is more richly specified, then a less fully specified speech input can be tolerated. For example, relative to the process of word-recognition, less acoustic-phonetic information needs to be provided by the speaker for the unique identification of the intended word when an appropriately constraining context is available (cf. Marslen-Wilson & Tyler, 1980*a*). Similarly, in the case of anaphor resolution, the anaphoric device can vary in the specificity with which it itself indexes its antecedent, as a function of the availability of other cues to the correct analysis of the anaphor (Marslen-Wilson & Tyler, 1980*b*; Tyler & Marslen-Wilson, 1980). In other words, this is a processing system that can directly exploit any potential 'redundancy' in the relationship between a message and its context, by allowing, on-line, for this compensatory balancing between knowledge sources.

The significance for the present study of these features of the comprehension system—on-line interpretation and the co-operation of knowledge sources—is first of all the general analytic attitude they lead us to adopt. To relate this view of speech comprehension to properties of speech production, we need to pay close attention to the word-by-word informational properties of a discourse; we need to determine *what* information the speaker gives to the listener *when*, and *how* he delivers it. Given this overall approach, then various more concrete issues arise.

The major set of questions involve the specific manner in which reference is established and maintained. First, if the interactive properties of the listener's comprehension system allow for a compensatory balancing between different sources of processing information—relative, here, to the perceptual goal of determining the intended referent—then does the speaker regularly exploit this? That is, does he systematically adjust the nature of the referential devices he is using to the informational conditions under which they occur? Since the context for speaking, in a face-to-face interaction, has both intra- and extra-linguistic aspects, the answer to this question will involve an analysis not only of the speech channel, but also of non-verbal channels—in particular, of the use of gestures in relation to verbal referential devices.

A second, and closely related, question concerns the actual processing information on which the successful resolution of a given referential device will depend. What is the nature of the information that one can reasonably assume that the speaker is providing for the listener, such that a given referential device can be unambiguously interpreted? The comprehension system allows for a relatively free flow of interaction between the lexical, structural, and interpretative aspects of the analysis process. The question here is whether this is reflected, in the speaker's output, in the types of information which the resolution of referential devices in fact requires, and in the ordering of the availability of this information over time. Does one find a genuine on-line co-ordination of different information sources, or, instead, the sort of serial sequencing of information input that would be predicted by other types of comprehension model (cf. Marslen-Wilson & Tyler, 1980a).

Given an analysis of a discourse from the perspective of the above two questions, we can then determine whether, and in what sense, the speaker does normally produce an input for the listener which is fully interpretable as it is heard. For the present study this translates into the question of how far the referential devices used in a narrative can be unambiguously resolved by the listener at the point at which they occur in the speech stream.

We now turn to a description of the quasi-experimental situation we used to obtain the appropriate corpus of referential devices. It should be stressed that this is an exploratory study, using a single speaker telling a single story. Its purpose is to investigate the feasability and validity of the sort of discourse analysis that our questions about the informational properties of natural speech production seem to require; to find out how far a perspective based on a theory of the listener can illuminate the behaviour of the speaker.

METHOD

The story

Given the decision to focus on referential devices, the first priority was to set up a discourse situation in which there would not only be a large number of such devices produced, but also a large number of references to the same individuals, so that we would have an adequate basis for a distributional analysis. We therefore decided to choose a suitable story in advance, which the speaker would read beforehand, and which he would then be required to re-tell from memory in the experimental situation.

The story chosen was a 20-page Marvel comic-book, from the 'Fantastic Four' series. These stories are vividly illustrated, have a clearly segmented narrative structure, and are easily read and remembered. In the particular story we chose—'Hulk vs. Thing', or 'The Battle of the Behemoths'—the two main actors occupy most of the story, and are presented in a range of situations, violently interacting with each other in various ways.

Recording situation and procedure

The test dialogue and the recording situation were set up as follows. The speaker was a male graduate student in psychology, who did not know the true purpose of the project. He was told that he should first read the comic-book until he was confident that he knew the story thoroughly. He would then be required to tell the story to a second person, who had not read the comic-book, and who, in turn, would be required to re-tell the story after the first speaker had finished.

After the speaker had read the comic-book, he was seated in a chair facing the listener, such that they were about one metre apart. There was no table or other obstruction between them, so that each was completely visible to the other. Throughout the dialogue, the speaker had on his lap a copy of the comic-book. This proved important, since the cover of the comic-book included pictures of both The Hulk and The Thing (the two heroes of the story), and these pictures could be seen by both the speaker and the listener. The speaker made frequent use of these pictures while telling the story.

The speaker told the story straight through, in a single session lasting 10 minutes. He paused only to answer occasional requests for clarification from the listener. The entire production was videotaped, with the camera's angle giving a complete view of both participants. A separate audio recording was also made, to simplify later analysis of the participants' speech output.

The analyses

For the purposes of the present study, the main analysis of the speech output was a transcription of the entire session, using standard English orthography, and noting false starts, hesitations, and filled and unfilled pauses. Secondarily, a prosodic analysis was carried out, segmenting the speech into breath groups, and indicating the intonation contour, as judged by an experienced phonetician. Up to three levels of accent (or stress) were then assigned within each prosodic unit.

The transcript was then scanned to pick out all occurrences of reference-establishing and reference-maintaining devices involving the two protagonists—The Hulk and The Thing. A total of 122 of these were found. Ten of these (chiefly possessive pronouns) were not included in the present analysis. Of the remainder, 88 occurred in the main body of the narrative, while 24 others occurred during answers to questions asked by the listener at different points. We will concentrate here on the 88 devices used during the main narrative.[1]

The videotape of the session was also examined, to determine whether any gestures occurred in conjunction with the verbal references to The Thing or The Hulk. The only gestures that both co-occurred with the verbal references, and that could be interpreted as having a referential function, were a total of 20 deictic points to the cover of the comic-book. As we mentioned above the cover of the comic-book, which had on it a large colour picture of both The Hulk and The Thing, remained on the speaker's lap throughout the session.

Of these 20 deictic gestures, 12 involved index or mid-finger points towards the comic-book (often including tapping movements on the surface of the comic-book). The remaining eight gestures involved either one or both hands, with all fingers extended, used in points (and/or taps) in the direction of the comic-book. Some of the sequences of gestures, coded here as a single deictic, in fact involved complex sequences of movements that appeared to be closely co-ordinated with the linear organization of certain complex referential devices. These will be briefly discussed later on. A final observation was that in 17 out of the 20 cases the deictic point towards the comic-book was preceded and accompanied by a shift in the speaker's gaze direction, in which he looked away from the listener's face and down towards the comic-book in his lap.[2]

DISCUSSION

We will begin by presenting a general distributional analysis, based on the main set of 88 verbal references to The Hulk and The Thing, and including the 20 deictic gestures to the comic-book. This analysis, developed to answer our questions about the relationship between types of referential device and their informational context, provides the necessary framework for the discussion of our further questions about the on-line interpretability of the speech output, and about the detailed characteristics of the referential devices used.

The analysis is summarized in Figure 1, which shows the patterning of

DEGREE OF EMBEDDING				DEGREE OF SPECIFICITY OF FORM OF REFERENCE									
	STORY	EPISODE	EVENT	NAME + DEFINITE DESCRIPTION		NAME ALONE		NONSPECIFIC NP OR PRO-FORM		PERSONAL PRONOUN		ZERO ANAPHOR	
				+ G	- G	+ G	- G	+ G	- G	+ G	- G	+ G	- G
1	x	-	-	3			2*				1*		
2_a	✓	x_F	-			5	1				2*		
2_b	✓	x_{NF}	-				1	6					
3_a	✓	$✓_F$	x_F	1		2	7				2		
3_b	✓	$✓_F$	x_{NF}			2	3	1					
4_a	✓	$✓_F$	$✓_F$				4				28		13
4_b	✓	$✓_F$	$✓_{NF}$								2		2
				4	0	10	17	6	1	0	35	0	15

Figure 1   The distribution of references to the main actors as a function of type of referential device and of narrative and discourse context

referential devices across a two-dimensional matrix. These two dimensions—the degree of lexical specificity of the referential device, and the depth of embedding in the narrative at which a given device occurs—need to be discussed in detail. The amount of detail we go into here, and the number of classificatory distinctions we will make, are the minimum that we found necessary to capture the major dependencies between the types of referential device and their context of occurrence.

Degree of lexical specificity

This dimension, the horizontal axis on the figure, orders the different referential devices according to what we will label here as their 'lexical specificity'. This term is used as a shorthand for the degree to which, from the listener's perspective, the discourse interpretability of a given referential device depends, on the one hand, on the lexical (semantic) information carried by the lexical item(s) constituting the surface structure referential device, and, on the other hand, on information that must be recovered from the prior or posterior discourse context. The less lexically specific a device is, in these terms, then the more strongly it can be seen to presuppose, for its interpretation, information that has to be supplied by the listener (cf. Silverstein, 1976a,b). This gradient of specificity, which also roughly coincides with the usability of a device for establishing as opposed to maintaining discourse reference, runs here from what we call 'names + definite descriptions' to 'zero anaphors'.[3]

The first two categories both involve the use of the names of the two main actors. As such, they are in principle sufficient, as referential devices, to designate uniquely who is being referred to at that point in the discourse. Within the set of devices using names, we separate out, and place in the leftmost category, the cases in which the names are accompanied by additional information about the individual being referred to. Examples of these are sequences like 'The Hulk, the green guy, . . .' or 'The Thing, the orange guy with the scales . . .'. This class of sequences, which has distinct distributional properties, regularly adds to the names of the actors the only further feature that distinguishes them from each other—namely, their colour. In all other respects The Hulk and The Thing have more or less identical properties (that is, as large, male, belligerent, superhuman monsters).

Moving further to the right on the scale, the third category (labelled 'non-specific noun-phrases or pro-forms') is the first point on the scale at which the referential devices necessarily require integration with other sources of information in order to be interpreted by the listener. This category covers cases like 'one or the other of the two', 'one of these guys', etc. The items in this category are distributed quite differently both from the preceding two categories and from the two rightmost categories in the scale.

These last two categories—'personal pronouns' and 'zero anaphors'—are the least lexically specific, and presuppose to the greatest degree the recoverability of the information necessary for their interpretation from the discourse context. The personal pronouns here include forms such as 'he', 'him', 'they', etc. The rightmost category, of zero anaphors, are cases in which the specification of the referential device becomes lexically empty. In the present sample, the zero anaphors occur either in co-ordinate constructions (such as 'he takes the merry-go-round and ∅ whips it around at supersonic speed'), or in participial constructions (such as 'so he's sitting there ∅ waiting . . . '). The co-referents of these types of zero anaphor are completely structurally determined; the missing agent in subject position in the second clause must be interpreted as co-referential with the subject of the first preceding clause.

Finally, this five-category dimension is cross-classified, at each level, according to the presence ('+G') or the absence ('−G') of a deictic gesture (to the comic-book) accompanying the referential device in question. These deictic points to the pictures of The Hulk and The Thing are clearly a potential source of information for the listener about the identity of the individual(s) being verbally referred to. The distributional analysis should therefore also include the use of information that derives from the extra-linguistic context of speaking. This allows us, in particular, to ask how the gradient of verbally defined specificity interacts with the use and the function of extra-linguistic information in the establishment and maintenance of reference.

Degree of embedding

This second dimension, degree of embedding in the narrative, emerged from our preliminary analyses as the most revealing general classification of the informational contexts in which different referential devices occurred. Given that the speaker is telling a story, this fact will determine the large-scale informational structure of his output. In examining the transcript, we could usefully distinguish three major levels in the organization of the narrative, labelled here as the 'story', 'episode', and 'event' levels.[4]

The highest, least 'embedded' level, is the story itself, considered as a separate domain within the discourse. This level is necessary to capture the fact that the protagonists in the story cannot be talked about until they have been introduced into the story in the first place. This process of introduction requires the use of referential devices that are appropriate to these minimal informational conditions.

The second level we distinguish is the 'episode' level. The comic-book itself is segmented into a cinematic series of distinct scenes. This segmentation was faithfully reproduced by the speaker, who explicitly signalled each change with remarks like 'so the scene cuts back to . . .', 'so then it cuts back to . . .', etc.

Each such episode constitutes a distinct subdomain in the speaker's narrative. Within an episode, the speaker is again faced with the problem of introducing the central actors, and then continuing to talk about them appropriately. Since The Hulk and The Thing were the central actors in the story as a whole, they were introduced at the beginning of the narrative, so that for all later episodes the problem was to re-establish reference to them.

The deepest level of embedding we distinguish here is called the 'event' level. Each episode in the story typically contained a number of distinct sequences of actions, with each sequence marked by a change of actor(s), and/or a change of location within the overall location of the episode. These sequences, verbally signalled by the use of connectives like 'so then . . .', etc., form further subdomains in the narrative, within which the actors need to be established and subsequently referred to.

These three levels of embedding are cross-classified by two further categories. The first of these codes whether a referential device is being used to establish or to maintain reference at a given level. In the figure, an '×' indicates that the device in question is being used to establish (or embed) an actor at a given level; a '√' indicates that he has already been embedded at a given level. Since the three levels of embedding can apply simultaneously, it is possible for a referential device to be coded as maintaining reference with respect to one level while establishing reference at a deeper level.

The relationship of this category to the levels of embedding can be illustrated in the following sequence, produced at the beginning of an episode:

> 'so then it cuts back . . . to *The Hulk* and *The Thing* and *they're* still battling and $\emptyset$ knocking down chimneys . . .' (references to the main actors italicized).

The devices 'The Hulk' and 'The Thing' are coded here as occurring at the episode level, and as functioning to establish their referents at this level of the narrative (cf. level 2a in the figure). Simultaneously, they are also coded as maintaining reference at the story level. The next device, 'they're', is coded as establishing reference at the event level, while maintaining reference at the episode and story levels (cf. level 3a in the figure). The final device in this sequence, the zero, is coded at the event level also, but as maintaining reference at this and at all higher levels (cf. level 4a in the figure).

The second extra category codes whether or not the actor being referred to by a given device is 'in focus' at a particular level. This reflects an intuitive notion of who the central actor or actors are in an episode or an event (since the story as a whole is about The Hulk and The Thing, they are always in focus, or central, at the story level). This distinction is necessary here to capture the quite different forms of referential device used when The Hulk or The Thing are referred to in episodes where they are the central actors, as opposed to episodes where they are not. The distinction turns out to be less useful at the event level, presumably because neither main actor can slip very far out of focus, once they have been introduced as central in an episode. The code 'F' is used for references to central actors, and 'NF' for non-central.

The vertical axis of the matrix represents, in summary, the general informational context in which a referential device occurs, as well as coding the function of that device in establishing or maintaining reference, and the centrality or salience of the referent at that point. Only the seven combinations of these three orthogonal variables that actually occurred in the narrative are given in the figure.

Movement down this vertical scale should be read simultaneously as increasing the richness of the informational context for reference, and as gradually shifting from the reference-establishing to the reference-maintaining function. Thus, at level 1 on the scale, the actors are being initially embedded in the story. This is the minimal informational condition for using a referential device, where the speaker should use the least presupposing—and most lexically specific—types of device. In contrast, at levels 4a and 4b at the bottom of the scale, the referents are most deeply embedded in the narrative (either as central or non-central actors), so that the speaker can in principle use maximally presupposing, and least lexically specific referential devices.

Referential devices and their contexts of occurrence

A general question we asked in the Introduction was whether there would be a regular correspondence between informational contexts and types of referential device. The distribution across the diagonal of the matrix shows this to be the case. The most lexically specific devices cluster in the upper left quadrant, while the least specific devices cluster in the lower right quadrant. This general sensitivity of the speaker's use of referential devices to their informational contexts becomes the more impressive the more closely we examine it. But first we should dispose of some anomalous points occurring at levels 1 and 2a in the figure (marked with an asterisk).

These devices were produced in the introductory sequence of the narrative, as the speaker switched back and forth between establishing the main actors in the general background to the story, and setting them up in a preliminary episode. Naturally, as he continues to talk about them here, he can use less specific devices to refer to them. This is not captured in the coding scheme, which is only able to code these devices as establishing their referents at the story or episode levels. While being, strictly speaking, correct, this fails to reflect the fact that a given discourse function can have an extensive internal structure of its own. To have represented this here would have meant adding a third axis to the matrix; since this coding problem did not arise anywhere else, we chose to leave these inadequately coded devices where they were.

We now turn to the distribution of each category of referential device. The discussion of each of these will also cover their associated deictic gestures.

Names and names + definite descriptions

The distribution of these two categories, and the co-occurrence patterns of the associated deictic gestures, reveal great systematicity and delicacy in the speaker's use of personal names. To appreciate this, we have to separate two distinct aspects of successful discourse reference. For an expression to be able to refer, the speaker has to ensure both that the referential device is sufficient to index some unique location in the listener's mental representation of the discourse, and that there in fact exists (or can be constructed) some such unique location in the representation. In other words, we need to distinguish between how a device can map onto a representation and what there is for it to map onto. Thus while a personal name is a paradigmatically adequate specifier of a unique location, it does not function referentially for the listener unless there is a unique location onto which it can map. In highly Kripkean fashion,[5] then, the present speaker initially fixes and differentiates the reference of the two main actors' names both by ostension (deictic points to the pictures) and by associating them with a definite description ('the green guy', 'the orange fellow').

Thus the four uses of names + definite description occur early in the narrative, when the difference in colour (marked by the descriptions) is essentially all that can be given to the listener to differentiate the two protagonists. In the introductory sequence (level 1) these forms are used three times, while the fourth use occurs when The Hulk is being established in the first major event in which he is the central actor. And on each occasion the verbal reference is accompanied by a clear deictic point to the appropriate picture on the comicbook.

The speaker's command of the pragmatic conditions governing the adequate discourse functioning of names is further reflected in the patterning of deictic gestures when the names are used alone. The actors' names alone are used seven times to establish initial reference to them in an episode (levels 2a and 2b). Six of these uses are accompanied by a deictic gesture to the comicbook.[6] But when names are used to maintain reference within an episode, then deictic gestures accompany the names much less frequently: four times out of 18. Two of these four apparent exceptions bear closer analysis, since they turn out to confirm the general pattern.[7]

These two uses of names alone + gestures occur early in the narrative, in the first major episode involving The Hulk and The Thing. What we see displayed across this episode is a precise gradient in the use of ostension and definite description in the process of establishing and maintaining the actor's names as referential devices. As the two actors become more differentiated from each other in the discourse model, then the more adequate names alone become as a means of reference.

The episode begins with a scene-setting statement which re-establishes The Hulk and The Thing together in the narrative, using names + gestures. This is directly followed by the establishment of The Hulk as the sole actor in the first action-sequence of the episode. This means that he has to be clearly differentiated from The Thing, and to do this the speaker uses a name + definite description + gesture. Towards the end of this action-sequence The Thing is brought into the narrative at the event level, first as a non-central actor (3b), and then as the sole actor in the following action-sequence. These two references to The Thing are subserved by a name + deictic gesture. Finally, in the last action-sequence of the episode, The Hulk is brought back on stage, this time using a name alone. Thus as the two actors accrue distinctive properties in the discourse, as a result of their different actions within the episode, then this reduces the need to accompany their names with additional supporting devices.

This general gradient can be traced across the narrative to the next major episode in which The Hulk and The Thing are the main actors. Here no definite descriptions are used, and deictic gestures only accompany the names once, when the actors are being established at the beginning of the episode. For the rest of this long episode names are only used alone. In fact, as the later analysis of pronouns will show, names are only used at all within this episode when a less specific device, such as a pronoun, would have failed.

Non-specific NPs or pro-forms

This category only fulfils one major discourse function here—to establish reference to the main actors in episodes in which they do not otherwise occur. Six of the seven tokens in this category occur at this level, and in each case what the speaker is doing is to mention the main actors and their actions in order to establish their relationships to the subsidiary actors in the various sub-plots. As we noted earlier, the referential devices in this category are not lexically adequate in themselves to successfully make reference. Their use therefore presupposes the availability to the listener of additional disambiguating information. But their contexts of occurrence are such that this information is not extractable from the immediate intra-linguistic context. The speaker is clearly sensitive to this, since all six of these devices are accompanied by a highly specific deictic point to the comic-book—that is, to an extra-linguistic source of information. This can be contrasted with the one other use of this type of device, in a context where The Hulk and The Thing are both already established in the immediate discourse (level 3b), and where *no* deictic gesture accompanies the device.

Note that the role of deictic gestures in supporting reference for this category is not completely analogous to the role of deictics in relation to names and names + definite descriptions. When used with the non-specific NPs, the deictic gestures support the actual process of mapping onto a specific location in the listener's mental representation of the discourse, by compensating for insufficient intra-linguistic information. But when they are used with personal names, the function of the deictics (as we argue above) is to help construct the mental location itself.[8] The names of the actors are entirely adequate to index a unique location in the mental model, but they cannot successfully refer unless there are differentiated locations onto which they can map in the first place.

For both non-specific NPs and names, the general function of the deictics can be described in terms of some form of informational balancing, where information is drawn in from the extra-linguistic context to compensate for information that is not available intra-linguistically. But the cognitive role of this compensatory information, with respect to different aspects of the reference process, seems quite distinct for the two classes of referential device.

Pronouns and zero anaphors

These two categories are the least lexically specific, and this is strongly reflected in their distribution. Of the 48 tokens of these categories (we exclude the inadequately coded items in levels 1 and 2a), 46 of them occur at the most embedded levels of the narrative, functioning to maintain reference within an action sequence. The two partial exceptions, at level 3a, both occur in grammatically highly constrained co-ordinate constructions, in the first half of which The Hulk and The Thing are being initially established (by name and gesture) in the episode.

The use of these lexically minimal devices strongly presupposes a context from within which their referents can be recovered. For the 48 tokens here, this context is always provided intra-linguistically. This is reflected both by the level of narrative embedding at which they occur, and by the complete absence of any co-occurring deictic gestures. The distributional facts are striking here. Of the 36 referential devices in the three leftmost categories, 20 co-occur with deictic gestures, and 16 do not. Whereas no deictics at all co-occur with the 48 pronouns and zeros.

This patterning of the deictic gestures confirms that their use is not determined by the lexical specificity *per se* of the co-occurring verbal device. Their use here is governed, instead, by the complex properties of the entire referential process, assessed relative to the intra- and extra-linguistic context of occurrence of a given verbal device. We have already seen how these criteria subtly control the use of deictics to support personal names and non-specific NPs. In the case of pronouns and zeros, where both the initial mapping onto the appropriate location in the discourse model and the existence of the mental location itself are adequately supported intra-linguistically, then the extra-linguistic support provided by the deictic gestures is not necessary, and they never occur.

The intra-linguistic contexts in which pronouns and zeros occur are not, however, themselves differentiated by the analytic categories we have used so far. Except for the two pronouns at level 3a, all tokens of each category fall at the same levels of embedding (4a and 4b). Furthermore, when we analyse each token according to the embeddedness of its discourse antecedent—the preceding surface device with which it is co-referential—then we again find relatively little difference between the two types. For the pronouns, 66% of their surface antecedents are already established at the event level (4a and 4b), while this holds for 80% of the antecedents of the zeros. This tendency is clearly not enough by itself to account for the use of one device or the other. The patterning of zeros and pronouns appears to involve additional types of regularity, to the analysis of which we now turn.

Contrasting environments for pronominal and zero reference

The question here is to determine the discourse conditions under which the speaker uses a zero rather than a pronoun—and, indeed, a pronoun rather than a name. To do this, we first need to isolate those cases in which the choice between these devices is simply a function of the local informational context; that is, the cases in which the use of a more lexically specific referring device is forced by the fact that a less specific device would either fail to refer or would misrefer. We therefore re-analysed all the occurrences of names, pronouns, and zeros from this perspective.[9]

The way we did this was to take each occurrence of a more specific device, and judge whether the substitution of a less specific device would cause either reference failure or misreference.[10] Take, for example, the following short episode (unfilled pauses indicated by '. . .'):

> 'so then it cuts back . . . to The Hulk and The Thing and *they're* still battling and knocking down chimneys . . . and nothing . . . no- nobody's really getting any . . . temporary advantage . . . and *The Hulk* is getting stronger . . . but *The Thing* keeps catching him off guard and tripping him up . . . so then they cut back to the laboratory . . .'.

Consider first the two italicized uses of the actors' names (which did not have co-occurring deictic gestures). In the first case, substituting 'he' for 'The Hulk' simply fails to refer, while zero disastrously misrefers (it has to be taken as co-referential with 'nobody'). In the second case, the substitution of either a pronoun or zero for 'The Thing' would clearly misrefer. Finally, if zero is substituted for the italicized 'they're' early in the episode, it also misrefers, with the deleted agent being taken as co-referential with the 'it' of 'it cuts back'. As these examples illustrate, the proper use of zero requires a strict parallelism between successive clauses, since the zero element in one clause is necessarily taken as co-referential with the structurally parallel element in the immediately adjacent clause.

The alternation between pronouns and names turns out to be completely straightforward. Names are used six times as patients (surface objects) and 25 times as agents (surface subjects). For 17 of these 31 cases a pronoun would have failed to refer, while for the other 14 it would have misreferred. In each case a zero would have been even worse. Thus an informational analysis accounts perfectly for the use of names instead of pronouns; this speaker *only* uses names when a lexically less specific device would fail to establish or maintain reference. This result is not surprising for the cases where the initial reference of names is being fixed, or where actors are being established at the beginning of a new episode. But it is striking that it also holds for every use of a name within an episode and within an event sequence.

The local informational context only partially accounts, however, for the choice between pronouns and zeros. For all 11 occurrences of pronouns in object position, zero would have been impossible. But for the 24 occurrences of pronouns as agents (subjects), in only 15 of these would zero have either misreferred or otherwise failed. This leaves nine uses of pronouns for which zero could have been successfully substituted. In addition there were 13 uses of zero for which a pronoun could have been substituted.[11]

An examination of the detailed properties of these remaining 22 cases revealed two main distributional classes, correlated with differences in verb aspect. These aspectual differences reflect contrasts in the types of actions and events being reported, and in their relationships to the main narrative sequence (cf. Hopper, 1979). The first class, signalled by V-ING verb forms ('fighting away', 'waiting', etc.), covers six of the uses of zero anaphors. The actions described here by these verbs are always continuing, incomplete actions, that run simultaneous with other actions in the narrative—either within an episode or relative to other episodes.

There were no cases, among the nine uses of pronouns for which zero could have been substituted, of clauses with V-ING verbs and imperfective aspect. Looking further afield, at all of the references to the main actors in the narrative in which V-ING forms occurred, we find that names and pronouns only co-occur with these forms when the local conditions make it impossible for zero to be used—that is, when the appropriate parallelism between successive clauses does not hold.

The other class, covering six of the remaining uses of zero and seven of the remaining pronouns, is signalled by the use of the narrative present tense ('he bends it', 'knocks out', etc.).[12] The properties of the clausal environments in which these tokens of zero and pronoun occur are listed in Table 1. All 13 cases occur in identical environments as far as clausal parallelism, verb aspect, and relationship to the narrative are concerned. In each case the verb has perfective aspect, indicating a completed action, and describes an action that carries forward the main sequence of the narrative. Where we do find differences, however, is in whether or not the clause describes the beginning of a new action-sequence.

This is an aspect of narrative organization which is not captured in Figure 1, since it does not take place at an additional level, deeper than 4a, but is rather a continuation at the same level (i.e. 4a). There are a few occasions in the narrative where the speaker describes a chain of action-sequences performed by the same actor throughout, and we can now see that the shift from one sequence in the chain to the next is marked by the use of a pronoun. None of the uses of zero occur at the beginning of an action-sequence, whereas five of the seven uses of pronouns do so. There is a tendency here for this shift to be also marked by the use of the connective 'so', which never occurs with zero (all of the zeros are preceded by 'and').

Table 1   Properties of clausal environments for use of zero and pronoun reference (narrative present only)

Case no.	Relationship to narrative	Verb aspect	Clausal parallelism	New action sequence	Type of connective	Referential device
1.	Sequential	Perfective	Yes	No	and	Zero
2.	Sequential	Perfective	Yes	No	and	Zero
3.	Sequential	Perfective	Yes	No	and	Zero
4.	Sequential	Perfective	Yes	No	and	Zero
5.	Sequential	Perfective	Yes	No	and	Zero
6.	Sequential	Perfective	Yes	No	and	Zero
7.	Sequential	Perfective	Yes	Yes	so	Pronoun
8.	Sequential	Perfective	Yes	Yes	. . .	Pronoun
9.	Sequential	Perfective	Yes	Yes	so	Pronoun
10.	Sequential	Perfective	Yes	No	and	Pronoun
11.	Sequential	Perfective	Yes	No	and	Pronoun
12.	Sequential	Perfective	Yes	Yes	and	Pronoun
13.	Sequential	Perfective	Yes	Yes	so	Pronoun

There remain, finally, two uses of pronouns (cases 10 and 11 in Table 1) which do not mark new action sequences but where zero is not used. These may represent a stylistic variation on the part of the speaker, and have the effect of increasing narrative vividness. They appear, however, to be the only clear cases where the alternation between pronouns and zeros cannot be straightforwardly accounted for by the informational and narrative contexts in which they occur.

Interim summary and conclusions

The detailed analysis of pronouns and zeros, reported above, shows that the patterning of these types of devices is sensitive to essentially the same types of regularity as we observed in the earlier analyses of other types of device. The speaker's use of referential devices, throughout the discourse, is governed by the intersection between two major aspects of the process of telling a story—on the one hand, the properties of the narrative itself, and, on the other, the local context of speaking. The narrative has an overall organization, into sequences of episodes and events, and this determines at which points the speaker needs to make reference to which actors. Given these requirements, the actual deployment of referential devices turns out to be precisely constrained by the local environment in which the devices will have to function, and by the extent to which the available intra- and extra-linguistic context can support the requirements of different types of device.

The central status of The Hulk and The Thing in the narrative means that they have to be established in the story both at the beginning of the narrative and then later as central actors in several subsequent episodes. These narrative functions are subserved by the use of the actors' names, accompanied by deictic gestures, and, for the earliest occurrences of the names, by definite descriptions as well.

This use of names is required, first of all, by the basic narrative function of naming the characters. The co-occurrence of deictic gestures and definite descriptions is explained by the fact that assigning a name requires the fixing of its reference relative to some distinctive set of properties, and that the gestures and descriptions indicate what these properties are. This reference-fixing function of the deictic gestures carries through the narrative, reappearing whenever the actors have to be re-established as central actors in a new episode.

Once the Hulk and The Thing have been established in the story and in an episode, then the speaker has to fulfil the further narrative function of describing the events that take place within each episode. Where the main sequence of the narrative is concerned, the speaker's alternation between names, pronouns, and zero is determined by the segmentation of the episodes into sequences of distinct actions, and by the local context in which a device is to be used. The use of names seems to be completely determined by this second variable, since names, as lexically fully specific devices, are only used when a less specific device would fail. This occurs most often at event boundaries, in those cases where the narrative is shifting focus among the main actors (cf. levels 3a and 3b in Figure 1). Within an event, names only occur when both actors are simultaneously involved in the narrative, and a name is the only way of keeping them referentially distinct.

Pronominal reference within the major narrative sequence is used to mark event boundaries, even when zero could be used instead. Within action-sequences, pronouns are normally (but not always) used whenever zero would fail. For all other references within episodes, zero anaphors are used. The other domain in which zero occurs is when this speaker is describing actions with imperfective aspect (most often as background or scene-setting information), and here zero is used unless the local context does not provide the necessary clausal parallelism.

A final narrative function involves establishing the relationship of the various subplots to the main action of the story. This requires the speaker to mention the main action and the main actors during episodes which are otherwise only concerned with the subplots. He normally does this by using non-specific noun-phrases and pro-forms.[13] These devices require contextual support to function referentially, and, in the absence of any possibility of support from their linguistic contexts, they are always accompanied by deictic gestures to the comic-book.

This summary of the distributional analysis shows that this speaker's deployment of different types of referential device is very closely tied to the narrative and informational contexts in which they occur. This clearly answers the first major question we asked in the Introduction. However, to be able to evaluate this result from the perspective of speech comprehension, we also need an answer to our further questions about the types of information on which the resolution of each class of device depends, and about the organization of this information in time. This requires additional analysis of the corpus, to which we now turn.

On-line resolvability of referential devices

The questions here involve determining, first, what information would be sufficient for the resolution of a given device, and, second, how this information is co-ordinated in time with the actual occurrence in the speech stream of the device in question. These analyses need to be applied to three distinct classes of device. In the first two cases, this involves the co-ordination of gestural information with names (± definite descriptions) and with non-specific noun-phrases. The third, much more complex case, involves the types of intra-linguistic information that could be available to the listener when she hears a pronoun. The zero anaphors used in this discourse need little discussion, since they could all, in principle, be resolved as soon as the gap at the beginning of the clause containing the zero could be detected.

The co-ordination of gestures and speech

For the first case, names and names + definite descriptions, we have verbal devices which are in principle capable of immediate resolution as soon as the names are recognized. As we have argued, however, the proper functioning of these names requires additional support in order to fix the names' reference. This support is in part provided by deictic gestures, whose temporal co-ordination with the speech stream can therefore be evaluated.

These gestures are always closely locked in time onto the verbal devices they support. For example, in the initial naming of the main actors we find the pattern shown below (where the underlining represents the duration of the gesture and the asterisk represents the peak(s) of the gesture):[14]

'. . . The Hulk is this green fellow and The Thing is this orange fellow
who's somehow been damaged by . . .'

The gesture is already in progress at the beginning of this excerpt, and at the first peak the speaker's index finger is resting on the picture of The Hulk on the comic book. The finger then starts to move across the comic-book so that at the next peak, concurrent with the word 'Thing', it is resting on the picture of The Thing, where it stays until the end of the gesture. A second example occurs slightly later in the discourse:

'and uh . . . The Hulk . . . the green guy . . . finally takes off . . .'

The gesture begins during the word 'Hulk', with the speaker starting to bring his middle-right finger down towards the comic-book, where it peaks in two tapping movements, once on 'green' and once on 'guy'.

The gestures associated with names alone are much less complex, usually taking the form of a brief pointing movement down towards the comic-book. These gestures average 800 milliseconds in duration, and are tightly linked to the verbal devices they support. The next example is typical of the entire sample:

'. . . and then the uh . . . The Thing . . . uhm . . .'

The gesture begins at the onset of the referential noun-phrase, reaches its peak 400 milliseconds later during the word 'Thing', and returns to rest about 350 milliseconds afterwards.

The second set of devices, non-specific noun-phrases and pro-forms, also require support from extra-linguistic sources, although for different reasons. These verbal devices are generally quite complex, and the accompanying gestures are noteworthy not only for their temporal co-ordination with the speech stream, but also for the way in which their internal structure matches the content of the concurrent verbal device. The most striking example is as follows:

'. . . the young woman I think is married to one of these guys and has one
of their kids . . . but I'm not really sure . . .'

At the onset of this gesture the speaker's right hand starts to come down to the comic-book, with the index-finger extended and the other fingers curled up into the palm. The index-finger touches down on the comic-book at the first peak (on 'one'); the little finger of the same hand then starts to come down as well, reaching its full extension on the word 'these'. Both fingers then stay down until, about 150 milliseconds before the third peak, the little finger starts to retract again, so that on the 'one' of 'one of their' there is again only one finger pointing at the comic-book. It looks very much as if the structure of the gesture is exactly mimicking the changing quantificational structure of the verbal device.

It is evident, then, from these analyses of the deictic gestures, that they are indeed exactly co-ordinated with their associated verbal devices. Thus, given that the information carried by a gesture is necessary for the resolution of a verbal device, then this information is made available as the verbal device is being produced and heard.

A final point that needs to be commented on is how far these gestures were actually used by the listener, or, indeed, were produced by the speaker because of their communicative value. As, for example, McNeill (McNeill, 1979; McNeill & Levy, this volume) has argued, gestures may in large part accompany speech as a sort of reflex of the sensory-motor conceptual structures that underlie speech itself. Some such hypothesis of common origin would certainly be a parsimonious way of explaining the close temporal and structural co-ordination of gestures with speech in this sample. But this would not exclude the possibility that these deictic gestures also have a genuine function for the listener.[15] There are two points here that are consistent with this.

First, the way that the deictic gestures were distributed in the present discourse seems difficult to explain unless one takes into account their role in supporting different aspects of the referential process. A second, more indirect point, is that 85% of the deictic gestures used here were preceded and accompanied by a shift in the speaker's gaze direction, in which he looked away from the listener's face and down towards his hands and the comic-book. While the speaker may have needed to do this to visually guide his gestures, this would also have been a clear cue to the listener to look down at the speaker's hands as well.

The resolution of pronominal reference

The use of anaphoric pronouns presupposes that contextual information will be available to support the recovery of the correct antecedent. Since the pronouns in this discourse were never accompanied by deictic gestures, the necessary support has to be found in the intra-linguistic context. We therefore analysed each occurrence of an anaphoric pronoun to determine what types of information could have been available to the listener to help locate its referent in her mental representation of the discourse.

The informational constraints on the resolution of a pronoun derive, first of all, from the lexical properties of the pronoun itself; these constrain, for example, the number and gender of the antecedent. A second class of constraints derive from the relationship of the pronoun to its immediate syntactic and prosodic environment. The syntactic configuration in which a pronoun occurs can constrain its possible co-reference relations to NPs in the same configuration. Thus, in the sentence 'John saved him', 'John' and 'him' cannot be co-referential, since this relationship would have required the use of a reflexive pronoun.[16] The prosodic environment of a pronoun determines whether it carries a pitch accent or not. The presence or absence of such accents on an anaphoric element can affect the assignment of reference (e.g. Nooteboom, Kruyt, & Terken, 1980).[17]

Many approaches to pronoun resolution in the artificial intelligence (AI) and psychological literature emphasize the importance of these three types of constraint in determining the early stages of the resolution process. These approaches postulate an initial search process which evaluates the set of possible antecedents provided by the current discourse, to determine which member of this set best matches the lexical properties of the pronoun, subject to the available syntactic and prosodic constraints. Although these types of preliminary search strategies reflect, as we will shortly argue, a basic misconception of the nature of the pronoun resolution process, they do provide a method for assessing the referential implications of the lexical, syntactic, and prosodic properties of the pronouns in the present sample. We therefore evaluated these pronouns according to the main types of search strategy in the current literature, determining for each strategy how far it could have been sufficient to identify the correct antecedent of each pronoun.

Two classes of strategy turned out to work rather well. One type of strategy is based on the concept of 'recency', where the correct antecedent is the entity most recently referred to in the discourse that matches the various properties of the pronoun (cf. Clark & Sengul, 1979; Hobbs, 1976; Winograd, 1972). When only the lexical properties of the pronoun were considered, this strategy chose the correct antecedent in 23 out of the 35 cases (66%), with the proportion correct rising to 87% when syntactic non-coreference constraints were included, and to 94% with prosodic cues as well. A second type of strategy, based on the more complex notion of a 'focus' set or space (cf. Grosz, 1979; Reichman, 1978; Sidner, 1979), worked nearly as well. It selected the correct antecedent from among the elements in the focus set in 89% of the cases, when lexical, syntactic, and prosodic constraints were all taken into account.[18, 19]

The implication of these analyses is that when this speaker uses a pronoun, then the lexical properties of the pronoun, together with constraints derived from its syntactic and prosodic environment, would for the most part be sufficient to disambiguate its reference, relative to the available discourse antecedents. These results do not mean, however, that these types of information are in fact the only types of information on which pronoun resolution in this discourse is based. Nor, furthermore, can the apparent success of these recency- and focus-based strategies be straightforwardly interpreted as meaning that a search process mediates the first stages of pronoun resolution.

First, it is not clear that the success of these two strategies here is really telling us anything more than that pronouns are normally used to refer to discourse entities that are already being talked about. We know this from the distributional analysis, which shows that pronouns are typically used when their antecedents have already been embedded in an action sequence. These restrictions on pronoun use mean that the discourse conditions under which a focus- or recency-based search strategy could work will hold whether or not a search process is actually being used by the listener. Thus, while the analyses here are certain compatible with the use of such search strategies, they do not by themselves compel us to conclude that pronoun resolution actually functions in this way; that this is the correct type of account of the nature and the ordering of the cognitive operations involved.

A second issue is that some recent experimental research (cf. Marslen-Wilson & Tyler, 1980b) seems inconsistent with the central assumption on which the functioning of these search processes is based. If such a process is to be primarily responsible for pronoun resolution, then it must assign a decisive role to the lexical properties of the pronoun itself. It has to assume that the search through the set of possible antecedents is mediated by an all-or-none selection process which accepts or rejects possible antecedents solely on the basis of lexical matching criteria (plus whatever syntactic and prosodic constraints might be available). The antecedent selected on this basis, and this antecedent alone, is then made available for the further analysis of the utterance. The results of some recent experiments on the on-line resolution of anaphora suggest, however, that the lexical properties of the pronoun operate in a less decisive way. Instead of functioning in a separate stage of the process, to decide uniquely between potential antecedents, lexical constraints seem to be used concurrently with other, more central types of selection processes. Lexical constraints provide an important input to these processes, but they are not normally the sole determinant of their outcome.

This leads us to a third, and fundamental problem with lexically based initial search strategies; that they misconstrue the role of inferentially based constraints on pronoun resolution. This type of constraint derives from the role of inference in determining whether the further properties predicated of the pronoun in the utterance are pragmatically consistent with the properties assigned to potential antecedents in the discourse model. Thus, in the utterance 'When John came into the room, he switched on the light', the resolution of the anaphor involves not only checking the number and gender of the potential antecedent, but also whether the property predicated of the anaphor (i.e. switching on the light) is consistent with what is already known about the potential antecedent (i.e. that he has just entered a room).

In many cases, this type of inferentially based 'pragmatic checking' will appear to be the only way of discriminating among antecedents—as, for example, in the following utterance-pair: 'Bill took his dog to the vet this morning. He injected him in the shoulder and he should be all right now'. The resolution of the various pronouns in the second sentence primarily depends on an inferential assessment of the three possible antecedents in the light of pragmatic assumptions about the likely agents and patients of the action of injecting, taking into account the relationships between the antecedents that the first sentence suggested. Our claim here is that this is not a special case, that places unusual or undesirable demands on the listener. We claim instead (cf., Marslen-Wilson & Tyler, 1980b; Tyler & Marslen-Wilson, 1980), that these processes of inferential assessment, made phenomenologically more apparent in this type of example, in fact reflect the basic and normal processes of pragmatically interpreting an utterance in its discourse context. So that what we are really dealing with is a general process of *utterance* resolution, rather than a series of separate processes, one of which is pronoun resolution (for some related arguments, see Hobbs, 1976, 1979; Karmiloff-Smith, 1980).

This is clearly a quite different picture of the properties and role of pronoun resolution from what is assumed in a system based on an initial search strategy. 'Pragmatic checking' may indeed have a function in these systems, but can only apply after the initial lexically based search (e.g. Sidner, 1979). This type of organization of the system may well be necessary for AI applications, in which unrestricted inference is computationally very difficult to manage. But the evidence suggests that, for human listeners, inference-based matching processes are not necessarily more costly, even when no pronominal lexical constraints at all are placed on the possible antecedents of an anaphor (cf. Tyler & Marslen-Wilson, 1980).

Thus, with these considerations in mind, we can examine our sample discourse from this inference-based perspective, emphasizing the relationships between the entire utterance in which a pronoun occurs and the discourse context. Two main observations can be made. The first is that all of the 35 pronouns in the sample are disambiguated by the pragmatic properties of the utterances in which they occur, when interpreted relative to the discourse properties of the potential antecedents. This means that the particular actions, intentions, locations, etc., that were predicated of the pronouns in each utterance could only plausibly be assigned to one of the possible antecedents. Like the initial search strategies, an inference-based 'strategy' also assumes that the current discourse makes available some set of possible antecedents. Where it differs, of course, is in the nature of the process that operates upon this set.

A second point is that there are a number of cases in the discourse where inference-based processes are clearly essential for successful resolution, and where a strict lexically based selection strategy would run into problems. The clearest examples are cases in which the lexical properties of the pronoun, as evaluated by such a search strategy, would lead to the selection of one antecedent but where the subsequent properties predicated of the pronoun are pragmatically incompatible with this antecedent and point to a quite different one. Take the following two examples:

> '. . . and $they_1$ go at it again . . . and the woman comes up . . . and the guys with the laser cannon or whatever it is come up . . . and . . . somewhere in there . . . $they_2$ sort of left out a frame where The Thing has turned his eyes to the side for a second . . .'

> 'and $they_1$ wrestle and fall off the edge of the building . . . as $they_2$ do in all good comic strips and cartoons . . . and when $they_1$ fall off the edge of the building . . .'

In each case $they_1$ refers to The Hulk and The Thing, while $they_2$ refers in the first example to the authors of the comic-book, and in the second to comic-book characters in general.[20]

It is clear in both cases that $they_2$ occurs in a context where the immediate discourse provides lexically appropriate antecedents for the pronoun (by both focus and recency criteria), but that what determines its actual reference is the pragmatic implications of the further properties predicated of the pronoun in the clause in which it occurs. In another striking case, we find four successive alternations between $they_1$ and $they_2$. This occurs at the end of the narrative, and involves an interchange with the listener (so that the pronouns in the answer were not included in the earlier analyses here):

> '. . . and The Hulk is turned back into a normal guy and The Thing is lying there on the pavement . . . and it closes out . . . be sure to tune in next week for the concluding . . . blah blah blah . . . so I think that's more or less the story . . .'
> 'Did $they_2$ ever tell you why $they_1$'re fighting in the first place?'
> 'Uhmmm . . . no other than that $they_1$'re the two biggest things around so . . . why not . . . uhmm . . . $they_2$ never really say . . . I suppose $they_1$ have some sort of personal . . . $they_1$ do have some sort of personal vendetta because $they_1$ talk about . . . having fought before . . .'

Again, $they_1$ indexes The Hulk and The Thing, while $they_2$ refers to the people who wrote the comic-book, and again the choice between the two possibilities can only be based on an evaluation of the sometimes rather subtle pragmatic differences between the predicates assigned to the pronouns in the various clauses in which they occur.

We can also see evidence for the importance of inference in cases like the following, of which there are a number in the sample. This excerpt occurs in a scene where The Hulk and The Thing were fighting on top of a skyscraper, and The Hulk has just fallen 60 storeys to the ground below:

> '. . . so The Thing has to get down to . . . to the ground level . . . before
> The Hulk recovers enough . . . while he_1's still stunned . . . so he_2 rips
> open the elevator doors and just sort of slides down the cable . . .'

Note, first, that while a recency strategy would assign the correct antecedent to he_1, it would fail for he_2. A focus strategy could not determine the correct antecedent in either case, since it would be possible to pronominalize both The Hulk and The Thing on each occasion.

For the utterance containing he_1, the critical information is clearly carried by the verb 'stunned'. This pragmatically implicates The Hulk, whom we know to be recovering from the effects of a 60-storey fall, which would be likely to stun even The Hulk. The importance of the verb is shown by the fact that we could just as well make the utterance refer to The Thing, by changing it to something like '. . . while he's still got the advantage . . .' . Similarly, for the utterance containing he_2, the critical information is the pragmatic implications of ripping open the elevator doors; this action is inconsistent with being stunned, and consistent with The Thing's already established desire to get down to ground level in a hurry. Again, reference could be switched by changing the predicates appropriately.

A final and crucial point that this last excerpt brings out is the dynamic nature of the relationship that must be presupposed between the inferences drawn from the utterance and the relevant properties of the discourse antecedents. In discriminating between possible readings of the utterances containing he_1 or he_2, it is necessary to know not just about the properties of The Hulk and The Thing in general, but also about their properties at that particular instant of the discourse. The necessary inferences can only be made on the basis of a constantly up-dated knowledge of their local situations—whether they're located at the top of a building or the bottom, what actions they might be in the middle of, what their current state of consciousness might be, and so on.

The consequences of the two actors' accumulation of distinctive local properties within the discourse can be related back to the gradient in the use of names, gestures, and definite descriptions that we brought out in the distributional analysis. As the narrative moves through an episode, the speaker becomes able to keep the two actors referentially separate by relying on differential pragmatic inferences, without having to use referential devices that themselves differentiate lexically between the actors. In other words, he can move from names to pronouns even when both actors are involved in an action-sequence.

Implications for a processing analysis

To complete the analysis of the pronoun sample, we need to find a more direct processing interpretation of the phenomena that these examples suggest. The analyses so far clearly exclude the type of serial processing model which can only deal with one candidate analysis at a time, and which therefore requires a pre-selection process to pick out a single candidate for each attempt at a pragmatic interpretation. A more distributed processing model, which allows for the *simultaneous* analysis of different interpretative possibilities, has already proved necessary to account for the real-time properties of spoken-word recognition in discourse contexts (cf. Marslen-Wilson, 1980; Marslen-Wilson & Tyler, 1980*a*; Marslen-Wilson & Welsh, 1978). A natural extension of this approach leads to the following general view of the pronoun and utterance resolution process.

We need to assume, as do all procedures for establishing discourse reference, that the listener's mental representation of the discourse is organized in such a way that certain mental knowledge structures—corresponding to potential discourse antecedents—will be preferentially accessible for the processing of a subsequent utterance. When a new utterance begins, the different types of information provided by the incoming utterance will be projected onto every potential antecedent provided by the discourse representation. The relative acceptability of different antecedents will thus be assessed in parallel, and these multiple analysis processes will continue until a coherent discourse relationship can be established between the utterance and its context.

Given this distributed processing framework, the lexical information carried by pronouns no longer functions in an all-or-none fashion to pre-select candidate antecedents. Rather, the pronoun contributes just one of several inputs to a distributed utterance resolution procedure, whose outcome depends on decision criteria that cannot be satisfied just by the information carried by the pronoun alone. What the system is doing when it resolves discourse reference is to establish a pragmatically coherent relationship between some discourse antecedent and the incoming utterance. But anaphoric pronouns, considered as lexical items, are so semantically attenuated (cf. Bolinger, 1977) that they cannot by themselves provide the framework for establishing this type of relationship.

This means that the immediate effect of an anaphoric pronoun will depend on whether the necessary framework has already been established, at the moment when the pronoun is heard, within which pragmatic assessment decisions can be made. This will depend on where the pronoun comes in a given utterance, and on the nature of the preceding discourse environment.

Consider first the case where the pronoun occurs in subject position in an utterance. There seem to be three main conditions under which the discourse implications of a subject pronoun can be immediately and fully assessed. The first is when the pronoun is directly connected to a referent extra-linguistically, through the use of a deictic gesture. A second is when the pronoun occurs in a highly determined discourse frame, such as a question–answer pair.

The third, and most relevant condition, is when the pronoun is co-referential with a discourse entity that has already been established as the main actor and agent in some continuing discourse sequence. Karmiloff-Smith (1980) identifies this use of pronouns as reflecting what she calls the 'thematic subject strategy'. When a narrative contains a single central actor, then speakers typically follow a pronominalization strategy in which the use of personal pronouns in utterance-initial position is exclusively reserved for this main actor, or 'thematic subject'.

The discourse we analysed here had two main actors, so that this strategy could not be used everywhere in the narrative. But there were some events which did involve only The Hulk or The Thing, and where they remained the sole actor for several utterances. There was, for example, a sequence of nine successive utterances in which The Thing, after being established by name, always occurred in subject position, and where only pronouns or zeros were used.[21]

Under such conditions, as Karmiloff-Smith suggests, the pronoun is not functioning computationally as an anaphoric referential device. As far as reference is concerned, it is functioning more like a zero—and, indeed, it is being used here in precisely the discourse conditions under which zero can be used, since there is the appropriate parallelism between successive clauses. Zeros certainly maintain discourse reference, but they clearly do not do so on the basis of some process which takes the information carried by zero and assesses the set of possible antecedents to find one that matches. There is no need for an assessment process because the use of zero means that there is no choice to be made. The same would apply, then, to the reference-maintaining function of an utterance-initial pronoun once a thematic subject is established in a stretch of discourse.

It is important to remember here that what is *not* said can be just as significant for the listener as what *is* said. In fact, saying nothing at all—using a zero—can establish the strongest discourse linkages of all. Equally, there is a significance to saying *more* than needs to be said. When the speaker here uses a pronoun when he could have used a zero, then the pronoun is certainly doing work for the listener, but not primarily as a referential device. It is, as we saw from the distributional analysis (see Table 1), serving other discourse functions; most usually to mark the beginning of a new action sequence within the narrative.[22]

In any case, it is clear that the discourse implications of a pronoun in subject position can, under these conditions, be immediately and fully assessed. But under other discourse conditions, where the pronoun does have a genuine informational function as a referential device, then an utterance-initial pronoun cannot be fully evaluated when it is heard. This can only be done when the appropriate information has accumulated in the utterance to support the establishment of the type of pragmatic relationship between the utterance and the discourse in terms of which discourse reference is defined and resolved. This information is not carried by pronouns, but by lexical items like verbs and nouns ('content' words) which have sufficiently rich semantic intensions that they can provide an adequate basis for inferences in the pragmatic domain.

This is clear enough for cases where the pronoun is lexically ambiguous between two antecedents—as, for example, in the utterance 'while he's still stunned' that was discussed at the end of the previous section. The pronoun 'he' here is certainly analysed when it is heard, and presumably functions to increase the potential acceptability of the two matching antecedents relative to whatever else might have been referred to (such as the distance The Hulk had just fallen). But it is only during the analysis of the word 'stunned' that semantic intensions become available which can be pragmatically assessed relative to what is known about the antecedents.[23] Until this point is reached, none of the potential antecedents can be finally excluded and they all remain available for parallel assessment against the information carried by the utterance.

We also assume that the same holds true when the pronoun is lexically unambiguous, and matches only one of the potential antecedents. The pronoun may well have the effect of increasing the acceptability of this antecedent relative to the others, but the actual resolution of discourse reference still depends on the establishment of pragmatic coherence between the antecedent and the utterance. Thus all potential antecedents continue to be assessed against the incoming utterance until this relationship is established. This claim for lexically unambiguous pronouns is supported both by preliminary experimental evidence (cf. Marslen-Wilson & Tyler, 1980b), and by anecdotal evidence. In particular, the use of lexically incorrect pronouns, which is especially common in children, does not have as disruptive an effect as one would expect if this lexical information immediately committed the listener to one antecedent rather than any other, such that only this antecedent could continue to be analysed.[24]

The final case we need to discuss is when a pronoun occurs later in an utterance—for example, as object or indirect object of the verb. Here the lexical properties of the pronoun can be immediately evaluated, as long as the appropriate pragmatic domain has already been created earlier in the utterance. Pronouns in object position are usually constrained by syntactic noncoreference restrictions as well, which helps to exclude potential antecedents.

Thus, in the following example from the discourse, '. . . and The Hulk is getting stronger . . . but The Thing keeps catching him off guard', the pronoun 'him' can have immediate consequences for discourse reference. Lexically, it implicates both The Hulk and The Thing, syntactic restrictions rule out The Thing, while the pragmatic implications of the verb, relative to the preceding discourse (and the use of the connective 'but'), make it plausible for The Hulk to be the patient of the action involved.

We can conclude this analysis of pronoun resolution—or, rather, of how pronouns contribute to utterance resolution—by placing it in the general functional context of the discourse here. Given the communicative task he has been set, the speaker's primary concern is to tell the listener about what happens in the story; about the particular actions that are carried out and their effects. In doing this, he has to keep straight who is doing what to whom, and, depending on the local context, he will often use pronouns to do this. Their primary function, then, is to act as tags or markers that signal agent and patient relations with respect to some action or state, which itself carries the major communicative and informational weight. Thus, it is only with respect to the discourse interpretation of these actions and states that the pronouns themselves can be fully interpreted. In effect, therefore, in utterances containing anaphoric pronouns, the entire utterance is functioning as the referential device.

General implications

The processing analysis that we have developed here can be generalized to provide a unified account of all of the referential devices in the sample discourse. This more general perspective derives from a processing interpretation of the cognitive functions that an utterance has to subserve for the listener. We distinguish two basic functions here, which we will label, respectively, as the *location* and the *predication* functions. These reflect two aspects of the fundamental process of mapping an utterance onto a representation of the current intra- and extra-linguistic context of speaking.

By the location function, we mean the requirement that the utterance be in some way mappable, by the listener, onto some location, or region, in her mental representation.[25] There must be some property of the utterance that enables the listener either to connect it directly to some discourse structure already present in the representation, or else to construct a new mental location for it, using her knowledge of the context of speaking and her general knowledge of the world. Unless such a connection can be made, the listener will literally not know what the speaker is talking about.

By the predication function, we mean the requirement that the utterance should in some way succeed in *telling* the listener something, relative to the varieties of types of knowledge (about states of affairs, intentions, attitudes, etc.) that are already associated with the mental location onto which the utterance maps (or which it causes to be constructed). The utterance should have the property of in some way changing or adding to what the listener already knows. To assume this is to assume no more than that every utterance has some communicative purpose.

These two functional properties, of location and predication, are what constitute the discourse coherence of an utterance. Unless it satisfies both functions in some way, it will not succeed communicatively (unless, of course, its failure is intentional). In the paradigmatic realization of these functions in an utterance, we could suppose that each function is subserved by separate parts of the surface structure string. Thus the subject noun-phrase—say, an anaphoric repeated noun-phrase—could fulfil the location function, while the rest of the utterance could fulfil the predication function—that is, by predicating something of the subject NP.

When realized in this way, then the distinction between location and predication seems very similar to many other such distinctions in linguistics and psychology—between theme and rheme, topic and comment, given and new, etc. But it differs from the linguistically motivated distinctions by being motivated and stated in terms of a real-time processing approach, and it differs from other psychological distinctions of this type (e.g. Clark & Haviland, 1977) by assuming a different type of processing theory. Furthermore, as we will now show, utterances by no means always separate predication and location in the binary fashion that the other types of distinction are best able to cope with.

We begin with the use of personal names, with and without accompanying gestures and definite descriptions. As we noted in the earlier discussion of these devices, a name can in principle uniquely specify a location in a mental representation. But it cannot properly do so unless there is some distinctive body of mental knowledge that the speaker can presuppose to be already associated with the name. Thus, in introducing the names of the actors into the narrative, the speaker fixes their reference by associating them with definite descriptions and deictic gestures.

These definite descriptions, in utterances like 'The Hulk is this green fellow', are evidently predicating something of the subject NP. But, to rephrase our earlier analysis, these predications are not subserving just the predication function. They are indeed telling the listener something new about the individual named in the subject NP, but this new information, at this stage in the narrative, has a primarily locative function. It is providing the listener with the basis for constructing a differentiated location for each name. The deictic gestures are reinforcing this function, by associating differently coloured pictures with each of the names and each of the definite descriptions.

As the actors become established in the narrative, and acquire distinctive properties as they move through each episode, then names alone become able to function as effective locative devices. Thus, in a later utterance like '. . . and The Hulk is turned back into a normal guy and The Thing is lying there on the pavement', we have the paradigmatic split between location and predication. The function of the two names is solely to locate the utterances with respect to the mental representation, while the rest of each utterance serves only to add new information to the discourse structures indexed by the names.

But despite the analytic appeal of this split between location and predication, the speaker only uses names when he has to. Otherwise he uses pronouns or zeros. In utterances containing anaphoric pronouns, as the analysis in the previous section implies, the locative and predicative functions once more thoroughly overlap. The pronoun, as subject NP, is indeed locative in function, but it is not adequate to serve that function by itself, and only does so in the context of the locative consequences of what is predicated of the pronoun. The manner in which such predicates fulfil these dual functions is quite different, however, from the mode of dual functioning of the definite descriptions associated with names.

In the latter case, we have a potentially full referring expression (a name), but, because the speaker cannot presuppose any knowledge attached to that name in the mental representation, he explicitly attaches new information to the name in the surface string. In the former case we have a much weaker referring expression (a pronoun), but, because the speaker *can* presuppose a distinct body of knowledge already present in the representation, he uses a predicate which can be directly attached, through the use of differential pragmatic inference, to this knowledge structure, and which thereby carries the pronoun with it. This means that the identical piece of speech (the predicate) is simultaneously fulfilling both the location and the predication functions, and that its ability to fulfil either function is inseparably linked to its ability to fulfil the other.[26]

This communicatively economical combination of functions is only feasible in the context of particular computational assumptions about the processing system. Predication and location can only be directly combined in this way within a processing system in which the set of properties defined by the intensional semantics of the verb-phrase can be simultaneously evaluated against all of the different sets of properties that characterize the different potential antecedents in the discourse representation. This requires a genuinely parallel system, and is simply not computationally feasible (in anything approaching real time) for a serial processing system (cf. Fahlman, 1979). Such a system must instead select a candidate antecedent on some other basis (such as a preliminary search), and only then check the pragmatic plausibility of this candidate. Thus, in an approach to discourse reference conditioned by serial computational assumptions, the location and predication functions must be strictly separated, even in utterances containing pronouns. In effect, such an approach must treat pronouns as if they were a kind of name.

Another type of referential device used by the speaker shares some properties with pronouns. These were the non-specific NPs and pro-forms (such as 'one of these guys'), which, like pronouns, are semantically too attenuated to be able to fulfil the locative function by themselves. But, unlike pronouns, these devices (with one exception) did not occur in discourse or utterance contexts where pragmatic inference could play the locative role it plays with respect to pronouns. This is because the devices occurred in episodes where the speaker was establishing the sub-actors in the sub-plots, and where the non-specific NPs were being used as the predicates which located the sub-actors relative to the main action of the narrative—as, for example, in the following sequence: 'this is . . . uh . . . Alicia Masters or someone . . . and she's obviously involved with some other guy . . . of these two' (where 'these two' refers to The Hulk and The Thing).

This created a problem for the speaker, since he was using as a locative predicate a device which, because it was itself not adequately located, could not adequately fulfil its ultimate discourse function. He solved this problem by using deictic gestures, which extra-linguistically located the reference of the non-specific NPs. This analysis of the non-specific NPs and their associated gestures reveals, then, a complex interweaving of predication and location. At one level, the deictic gestures provide the locative support for the functioning of the non-specific NPs as predicates, but, at another level, these predicates are themselves functioning as locative devices.

Finally, in the one case where a non-specific NP is not accompanied by a deictic gesture, it is subserving quite different discourse functions. Instead of being used to predicate new information of some entity, it is being used more like a pronoun, to keep agent–patient relations straight in an environment where its antecedent was already established in the immediate discourse. A pronoun would in fact have misreferred here, and have indexed a third potential antecedent. The device actually used ('this other guy') is sufficiently more lexically selective to do the necessary extra locative work.

The last major class of referential devices is the zeros, which are the maximally economical devices for fulfilling the locative function. In utterances containing zeros, the locative function completely disappears from the surface string, and the entire clause is predicative in function (in relation, at least, to the 'antecedent' of the zero). There are no lexical items marking location, nor is pragmatic inference necessary to connect the predicates to some discourse structure. The absence of any signalling of the location function requires instead that a location which has already been established will continue to hold across the current utterance. Just which location is involved is determined by the manner in which the structure of the clause containing the zero parallels, or overlays, the structure of the representation of the immediately adjacent clause.

CONCLUSIONS

The various analyses we have carried out here, in examining the behaviour of the speaker from the perspective of a theory of the listener, lead to a reasonably coherent—though by no means complete—picture of the use of different referential devices. The possibility of constructing such an account clearly requires both of the general types of analysis we undertook; the distributional analyses and the analyses of the processing conditions underlying these distributional facts.

The distributional analysis had two main aspects, which together define the context of occurrence of each device. The first is the analysis of the narrative conditions under which entities were being referred to. This tells us why the speaker is referring to a given entity at a given point in the discourse. The narrative function that a referential device is serving turns out to be of critical importance—whether reference is being established or being maintained, and whether this is occurring at the story, episode, or event levels. Given that we know the narrative function of a device, then the second aspect of the distributional analysis—of the informational properties of the local context of speaking—enables us to understand why a given function is being served by one type of device rather than another.

These analyses of contexts of occurrence, taken together, give us the local and the general history of the entity to which a given device is referring. Unless one is aware of this, of the *entire* history of a discourse entity, then the proper analysis of any given discourse reference to this entity is simply not possible.

In choosing a referential device, the speaker takes into account not only what might just have been said about a potential antecedent, but also the status of the antecedent in the listener's mental representation as a result of much earlier references to the individual concerned. Reference is established in one way, for example, at the beginning of the story, and in the first major episode, but then in different, less specific ways at the beginnings of later episodes. This gradient across the narrative, in the use of names, definite descriptions, and deictic gestures, is only explicable given that the speaker is aware of the past history of a discourse entity in the narrative, and that this knowledge controls his deployment of more or less specific referential devices.

By the same token, the organization of referential devices within an episode reflects a complex adjustment to the history of each potential antecedent within that episode. Establishment of reference at the start of the episode reinstates the actors in the situation in which they were last seen; building upon this, the speaker goes on to lay out the interlocking patterns of activity of the protagonists. In maintaining and establishing reference as he does this, the speaker is precisely constrained by what the immediate informational context permits. His alternation between names, pronouns, and zeros is only fully explicable if this informational factor is taken into account.

The point is not that his choice of devices is deterministically forced by the local environment, since he can always choose to use a more specific device than is necessary (as in his use of pronouns when a zero was possible). But without this precise command over what needs to be said for discourse reference to be successful, the speaker could not be confident that he was in fact using an adequate device. This also provides, furthermore, the necessary basis for exploiting the communicative implications of saying *more* than needs to be said.

These remarks make it clear that the study of referential devices using only isolated sentences is of very limited value. Given an isolated sentence containing, for example, an anaphoric pronoun, we can perhaps construct some surrogate discourse history to give the device a semblance of a referential function. But given that different referential devices are chosen by a speaker in natural discourse under quite specific and highly constrained referential conditions, it is only when these conditions actually hold that the linguistic and cognitive functions of such devices can be properly elucidated.

The distributional facts we uncovered remain, however, rather opaque without some attempt to relate them to the cognitive conditions under which they actually function. What we have tried to do here, in the further analyses and discussion of the processing properties of different devices, is to provide a cognitive rationale for the general informational patterns revealed by the distributional analyses.

As it is developed in this paper, this cognitive rationale has two main aspects. The first involves the general cognitive distinction, made most explicit in the previous section, between the two basic functions that an utterance must serve—namely, of predication and location. The value of these concepts is that they make explicit the fact that successful language production must be evaluated in terms of its effectiveness (in location and predication) relative to a listener's mental representation. Unless the use of referential devices is seen in this light, then many aspects of the speaker's performance would be quite mysterious.

A case in point is the contrasting use of deictic gestures in association with different types of referential device. Unless one takes into account the cognitive functions that a device has to fulfil, it is difficult to explain either why deictic gestures occur with some devices but not with others, or how the function of these gestures differs when used with non-specific NPs, for example, as opposed to definite descriptions and names.

The second aspect of the cognitive analysis tried to bring out the properties of the on-line processes underlying the realization of predication and location by different referential devices. These analyses not only make clear the precision of the real-time co-ordination of different inputs (as, for example, in the temporal integration of gestures and speech), but also the complexity of the processing interactions involved. We saw, for example, in the use of pronouns, how their successful functioning reflects a close functional interdependence between the lexical properties of the pronoun, its grammatical function in some structure, and the pragmatic consequences of the intensional semantics of the utterance.

These analyses make clear, above all, how central a role pragmatic inference is playing in the discourse referential process. For pronouns in particular, but also for the other devices, the cognitive analysis shows how the real-time pragmatic analysis of the semantics of the incoming utterance can form the basis for successful location and predication. Silverstein (1976b, 1980b) has stressed, on the basis of cross-linguistic analyses of form-function universals, the interplay between the two fundamental referential systems of language—of extensional, pragmatic reference and of intensional, semantic reference. We can now begin to see, from the perspective developed here, how these two analytically distinct systems are functionally woven together in the cognitive processes underlying the establishment and maintenance of discourse reference.

Two final points remain to be made. The first concerns the methodological implications of having used only one speaker and one story. Obviously, the various arguments we have made here need to be tested against a wider data-base. However, the particular aspects of this speaker's performance that were the most theoretically important are precisely those that are least likely to be peculiar to him as an individual, or to the specific communicative situation in which he was placed. What has been significant here is the general sensitivity of the speaker's use of referential devices to the environment in which they occurred, where this environment is a function of narrative and local informational context interacting with the speaker's implicit assumptions about the manner in which different clusters of referential devices can subserve the location and predication functions. It is difficult to believe that the performance of any other normal speaker would not be determined by the same basic categories; by the same range of sensitivities to the conditions under which a given device can successfully map onto a listener's mental representation.

A second, more programmatic issue, brings us back to one of the original motivations for the research here. This involves the relationship between laboratory studies of language and the study of language in more natural communicative contexts. Part of what we have tried to do here has been to show that a genuine connection can exist between the two approaches.

The reason we need to mention this is because of the widespread assumption that laboratory studies of language—especially those using reaction-time tasks—necessarily operate on some mutilated residue of language function, and thus can have little to say about the properties of language use in general. Our assumption, instead, was that the central properties of real-time language processing can, to begin with, only be properly identified under the special conditions of controlled and timed processing experiments. If our assumptions here were correct, and this type of research does tap the basic properties of the speech understanding system, then these properties should underlie language use in general, and should be demonstrably at work in normal production and comprehension.

To the extent that the present research has managed to integrate the analysis of a natural discourse with the claims of a speech processing theory, then these assumptions have been validated. But what we also see here is the interdependence of the two types of approach. Language cannot be understood as cognitive process without an understanding of the communicative functions that these processes underpin in natural interaction. But without some understanding of the cognitive substrate for language use, then the particular ways in which languages do subserve their communicative functions will also ultimately remain arbitrary and mysterious.

ACKNOWLEDGEMENTS

The research was started when all three authors were attached to the Committee on Cognition and Communication at the University of Chicago, and was then supported by a grant from the University of Chicago Social Sciences Research Committee. We thank David McNeill, Starkey Duncan, and Victor Yngve for advice and for the loan of equipment, and Bob Jarvella for his comments on the manuscript. We are indebted to Michael Silverstein for his help and inspiration throughout the project, and especially in advising us on the distributional analysis. Franci Deutsch collaborated on the early stages of the project, and was primarily responsible for the analysis of the deictic gestures. Finally we thank Marion Klaver, for cheerfully typing the endless versions of the manuscript.

NOTES

1. These 88 narrative tokens were syntactically and pragmatically quite independent of the 24 tokens that occurred in the question–answer sequences.

2. A detailed analysis of another type of gesture made by this speaker, classified as 'iconic', is reported elsewhere (McNeill & Levy, this volume).

3. These particular category labels were chosen because they straightforwardly describe the natural clustering of referential devices in this discourse. They are not intended to have any special further implications.

4. Since the comic-book is explicitly structured at each of these levels, their appearance in the speaker's narrative, and in the coding scheme, should not be taken to have any bearing on the psychological relevance of such concepts as 'story grammars'.

5. Kripke argues that the successful use of a name requires an initial fixing of its reference: 'An initial baptism takes place. Here the object may be named by ostension, or the reference of the same may be fixed by a description' (Kripke, 1972, p. 302).

6. The seventh case occurs in a compound ('The Hulk and The Thing'), where the deictic gesture only comes in halfway through, after The Hulk has already been named.

7. The other two exceptions occur in the final scene of the narrative, when all the actors from all the four sub-plots are brought on stage. This part of the narrative is rather confused, which is why the speaker might have felt it necessary to re-differentiate deictically the two main actors.

8. The use of deictic gestures in association with personal names later in the narrative may have an increasingly 'metapragmatic' content, in the sense defined by Silverstein (1980a), for a quite different context, as 'shorthand devices not of some definite description of the referent, but of some baptismal event in which reference to the individual referent was fixed' (cf. Note 5).

9. We included here the five starred items in levels 1 and 2a, since they are not miscoded relative to this more local analysis.

10. The following procedures were used here. First, in substituting a pronoun for a name, we directly replaced the name in the utterance with a pronoun agreeing in gender, number, and case. In substituting a zero, we permitted some syntactic reorganization within a clause (e.g. the deletion of an auxiliary verb), but we did not change the original organization into separate clauses (e.g. the deletion of a connective was not permitted). Second, 'failure to refer' is defined here either as the absence of any appropriate antecedent for the substituted device or as the failure of the device to select between more than one potential antecedent. 'Misreference' is defined as the indexing, by the substituted device, of some antecedent other than the one originally referred to in the utterance.

11. The remaining two cases of zero were syntactically conditioned by the use of the verb *to stop from*. Since a pronoun could not have alternated here, we do not include these two cases.

12. Of the three remaining cases, one occurred in an utterance that was repaired halfway through the verb-phrase, and so could not be evaluated here. A second use of a pronoun involved the past tense, and occurred in a concluding comment on an action-sequence ('. . . so he's taken care of that . . .'). The third, involving zero, was also in the past tense, and occurred when the speaker essentially repeated the same utterance word-for-word twice, omitting the subject and verb auxiliary the second time around.

13. The speaker might, of course, have used the actors' names in these situations. There seem to be good pragmatic reasons why he did not. First, in some of the cases, he was clearly not so much referring to The Hulk and The Thing as individuals, but rather to the whole situation in which they were involved, using phrases like 'the battle between these two guys'. Second, in at least two cases the speaker was evidently not certain as to which of the main actors was involved in a particular relationship to an

actor in a sub-plot. Thus he says of one such actor: 'she's obviously involved with some other guy . . . of these two'.

14. The 'peak' of a gesture was defined here in two ways. First, for a continuous movement, the peak was defined as the apex of the movement—usually the point of furthest extension of the hand or finger. Second, for gestures where the speaker paused during the gesture—for example, maintaining a finger-point on the comic-book—then the peak was defined as the point where this stable position was first reached.

15. We should also point out that McNeill (1979, p. 256) distinguishes between internally and externally focused gestures, and suggests that internally focused gestures are the most plausibly generated from a sensory-motor scheme held in common with speech. He classes deictic gestures as externally focused gestures, and leaves open the possibility of whether or not they are also generated from the sensory-motor base.

16. When a pronoun is functioning as a bound variable, its syntactic configuration can determine 'co-reference' as well as non-coreference. However none of the pronouns here were of this type.

17. Nooteboom et al. (1980) informally define the effect of a pitch accent as a sort of warning that the accented element may not be referring to the single most probable choice from among its potential referents.

18. For the purposes of these analyses, we defined the focus set operationally, as the set of items that could be successfully pronominalized at the point at which the anaphor occurred. Thus a focus-based search strategy would be successful when there was only one element in the focus set that matched the various properties of the pronoun. Note that the use of the term 'focus' here is much more restrictive than in our use of it in the distributional analysis earlier in the paper.

19. Since it is frequently studied in the psychological literature on pronoun anaphora, we also evaluated the 'parallel function' strategy (cf. Caramazza & Gupta, 1979; Cowan, 1980; Sheldon, 1974), which predicts that a pronoun will be co-referential with the noun-phrase in the immediately preceding clause which has the same grammatical function. This prediction was successful here only 40% of the time. This lack of success is not surprising, since this speaker normally used zero anaphora when this type of clausal parallelism obtained.

20. There were not, as far as we could determine, any prosodic cues that might have differentiated the two uses of 'they' (either in these two excerpts or in the following one). The pitch contour seems quite flat across all the occurrences, and certainly none of them are accented.

21. There were also some apparent repairs here, in discourse situations where one main actor was established, which support Karmiloff-Smith's analysis. The speaker started to pronominalize some other antecedent in subject position, but then immediately repaired the utterance so that the pronominalized 'thematic subject' of the sequence was moved into initial position—for example, by changing from an active to a passive construction (cf. Silverstein, 1976b).

22. Similar phenomena occur in the use of prosodic accent by this speaker. Eight of the 35 pronouns are accented, but in only four of these does accent seem to have a referential function of the type mentioned earlier (see Note 17). In the other four, the antecedent of the pronoun is so unambiguous that the potential referential function of accent is clearly superfluous—the speaker is saying more than needs to be said. The

discourse function that accent is serving in these cases is to emphasize some pragmatic contrast, and has nothing to do with the determination of discourse reference.

23. We should stress that it is indeed *during* the analysis of the word 'stunned' that these interactions between semantic intensions and pragmatic interpretation would take place. Evidence from word-recognition studies show that within 150–200 milliseconds after word-onset the pragmatic plausibility of possible word-candidates is being assessed against the available context, so that the primary process of word-recognition is directly affected by the pragmatic acceptability of the correct word-candidate (cf. Marslen-Wilson, 1980; Marslen-Wilson & Tyler, 1980*a*).

24. This approach to pronoun resolution is clearly inconsistent with the approach recently taken by Mackay & Fulkerson (1979), who argue for a 'pronominal dominance' theory of pronoun comprehension, in which the lexical properties of the pronoun 'determine the interpretation of its antecedent'. They find support for this in the special situation of a generic 'he' or 'she', used in isolated utterances such as 'A student usually sees his counsellor during office hours'. However, it is doubtful whether their analysis has any application outside this special situation.

25. Throughout this section we use the term 'mental representation' as a shorthand for the listener's mental representation of the previous and current intra- and extra-linguistic discourse context.

26. Another type of device with related properties, which this speaker happened not to use, is an anaphoric definite noun-phrase that picks out the appropriate referent by an equivalent process of pragmatic matching—for example, the referential device 'the animal' in the sequence 'John will have to get rid of his dog. The animal has started to terrorize the neighbourhood children'. The semantics of the referring expression are what enable it to locate successfully; but at the same time as locating, it is also predicating, since the choice of term will be informative (e.g. using 'the crazy beast' instead of 'the animal' in the above example).

REFERENCES

Bolinger, D. (1977). *Pronouns and repeated nouns*. Bloomington: Indiana University Linguistics Club.

Caramazza, A., & Gupta, S. (1979). The roles of topicalisation, parallel function and verb semantics in the interpretation of pronouns. *Linguistics*, **17**, 497–518.

Clark, H. H., & Haviland, S. E. (1977). Comprehension and the given-new contract. In R. O. Freedle (ed.), *Discourse comprehension and production*. Norwood, N.J.: Ablex.

Clark, H. H., & Sengul, C. L. (1979). In search of referents for nouns and pronouns. *Memory and Cognition*, **7**, 35–41.

Cowan, J. R. (1980). The significance of parallel function in the assignment of intrasentential anaphora. In J. Kreiman & A. E. Ojeda (eds), *Papers from the parasession on pronouns and anaphora*. Chicago: Chicago Linguistic Society.

Fahlman, S. E. (1979). *NETL: a system for representing and using real-world knowledge*. Cambridge, Mass.: MIT Press.

Grosz, B. J. (1979). Focusing and description in natural language dialogues. Technical Note 185. Menlo Park, Calif.: SRI International.

Hobbs, J. R. (1976). Pronoun resolution. Research Report 76–1, Department of Computer Sciences, City College, City University of New York.

Hobbs, J. R. (1979). Coherence and coreference. *Cognitive Science*, 3, 67–90.

Hopper, P. (1979). Aspect and foregrounding in discourse. In T. Givon (ed.), *Syntax and semantics*, Vol. 12, *Discourse and syntax*. New York: Academic Press.

Karmiloff-Smith, A. (1980). Psychological processes underlying pronominalisation and non-pronominalisation in children's connected discourse. In J. Kreiman & A. E. Ojeda (eds), *Papers from the parasession on pronouns and anaphora*. Chicago: Chicago Linguistic Society.

Kripke, S. A. (1972). Naming and necessity. In D. Davidson & G. Harman (eds), *Semantics of natural language*. Dordrecht: Reidel.

Mackay, D. G., & Fulkerson, D. C. (1979). On the comprehension and production of pronouns. *Journal of Verbal Learning and Verbal Behaviour*, 18, 661–673.

Marslen-Wilson, W. D. (1980). Speech understanding as a psychological process. In J. C. Simon (ed.), *Spoken language generation and recognition*. Dordrecht: Reidel.

Marslen-Wilson, W. D., & Tyler, L. K. (1980a). The temporal structure of spoken language understanding. *Cognition*, 8, 1–71.

Marslen-Wilson, W. D., & Tyler, L. K. (1980b). Towards a psychological basis for a theory of anaphora. In J. Kreiman & A. E. Ojeda (eds), *Papers from the parasession on pronouns and anaphora*. Chicago: Chicago Linguistic Society.

Marslen-Wilson, W. D., & Welsh, A. (1978). Processing interactions and lexical access during word-recognition in continuous speech. *Cognitive Psychology*, 10, 29–63.

McNeill, D. (1979). *The conceptual basis of language*. Hillsdale, N.J.: Lawrence Erlbaum Associates.

Nooteboom, S., Kruyt, T., & Terken, J. (1980). What speakers and listeners do with pitch accents: Some explorations. Manuscript no. 397, Instituut voor Perceptie Onderzoek, Eindhoven.

Reichman, R. (1978). Conversational coherency. *Cognitive Science*, 2, 283–327.

Sheldon, A. (1974). The role of parallel function in the acquisition of relative clauses in English. *Journal of Verbal Learning and Verbal Behavior*, 13, 272–281.

Sidner, C. L. (1979). Towards a computational theory of definite anaphora comprehension in English. TR-537, AI Laboratory, MIT.

Silverstein, M. (1976a). Hierarchy of features and ergativity. In R. M. W. Dixon (ed.), *Grammatical categories in Australian Languages*. New Jersey: Humanities Press.

Silverstein, M. (1976b). Cognitive implications of a referential hierarchy. Manuscript, Department of Anthropology, University of Chicago.

Silverstein, M. (1980a). Naming sets among the Worora (Northern Kimberley, Australia). In H. C. Conklin (ed.), *Proceedings of the American Ethnological Society, Symposium on Naming Systems*.

Silverstein, M. (1980b). Of nominatives and datives: Universal Grammar from the bottom up. Manuscript, Department of Anthropology, University of Chicago.

Tyler, L. K. (1981). Syntactic and interpretative factors in the development of language comprehension. In W. Deutsch (ed.), *The child's construction of language*. London: Academic Press.

Tyler, L. K., & Marslen-Wilson, W. D. (1977). The on-line effects of semantic context on syntactic processing. *Journal of Verbal Learning and Verbal Behavior*, 16, 645–659.

Tyler, L. K. & Marslen-Wilson, W. D. (1980). Processing utterances in discourse contexts: On-line resolution of anaphors. Manuscript, MPI für Psycholinguistik, Nijmegen.

Winograd, T. (1972). *Understanding natural language*. London: Academic Press.

List of Contributors

Ursula Bellugi, *The Salk Institute for Biological Studies, La Jolla, California, USA*

Michael Brambring, *Fachbereich Psychologie, Phillips Universität, Marburg, Federal Republic of Germany*

Konrad Ehlich, *Subfaculteit Letteren, Katholieke Hogeschool, Tilburg, The Netherlands*

Charles J. Fillmore, *Department of Linguistics, University of California at Berkeley, Berkeley, California, USA*

Robert J. Jarvella, *Max-Planck-Institut für Psycholinguistik, Nijmegen, The Netherlands*

Wolfgang Klein, *Max-Planck-Institut für Psycholinguistik, Nijmegen, The Netherlands*

Edward S. Klima, *Department of Linguistics, University of California at San Diego, La Jolla, California, USA*

Willem J. M. Levelt, *Max-Planck-Institut für Psycholinguistik, Nijmegen, The Netherlands*

Elena Levy, *Committee on Cognition and Communication, University of Chicago, Chicago, Illinois, USA*

John Lyons, *School of Social Science, University of Sussex, Brighton, England*

William Marslen-Wilson, *Max-Planck-Institut für Psycholinguistik, Nijmegen, The Netherlands*

David McNeill, *Committee on Cognition and Communication, University of Chicago, Chicago, Illinois, USA*

George A. Miller, *Department of Psychology, Princeton University, Princeton, New Jersey, USA*

Rudolf Reinelt, *Institut für Allgemeine Sprachwissenschaft, Universität Düsseldorf, Düsseldorf, Federal Republic of Germany*

Arnim von Stechow, *Fachbereich Sprachwissenschaft, Universität Konstanz, Konstanz, Federal Republic of Germany*

Mark J. Steedman, *Department of Psychology, University of Warwick, Coventry, England*

Lorraine Komisarjevsky Tyler, *Max-Planck-Institut für Psycholinguistik, Nijmegen, The Netherlands*

Veronika Ullmer-Ehrich, *Max-Planck-Institut für Psycholinguistik, Nijmegen, The Netherlands*

Dieter Wunderlich, *Institut für Allgemeine Sprachwissenschaft, Universität Düsseldorf, Düsseldorf, Federal Republic of Germany*

The postal address for the Max Planck Institute is Berg en Dalseweg 79, NL-6522 BC Nijmegen

Author Index

381

Subject Index